A NATION IN MAKING

A NATION IN MAKING

SURENDRANATH BANERJEA

GYAN

Published by

GYAN

Gyan Publishing House
5, Ansari Road
Daryaganj, New Delhi-110002
Phone: 011-47034999, 9811692060
E-mail: books@gyanbooks.com

Distribution Network
gyanbooks.com
India, USA, Canada, UK, Australia

ISBN: 978-93-7316-736-7 (PB)

First Published, 1925

2nd Impression 2025

Printed at: Gyan Press, Delhi.

A NATION IN MAKING
Author: SURENDRANATH BANERJEA

A NATION IN MAKING

Sir Surendranath Banerjea
as editor of 'The Bengalee'

ILLUSTRATION BY COURTESY OF SURENDRANATH COLLEGE, CALCUTTA

A NATION IN MAKING

being the
REMINISCENCES OF
FIFTY YEARS OF PUBLIC LIFE

SIR SURENDRANATH BANERJEA

Oxford University Press
BOMBAY CALCUTTA MADRAS

TO THE MEMORY OF

the founders and early builders of the

INDIAN NATIONAL CONGRESS

whose achievements the present generation
is apt to forget, but who have placed
India firmly on the road to
constitutional freedom to be attained
by constitutional means this book
is dedicated by an old colleague
who has lived to witness the partial
fruition of their labours,
destined to culminate in
full dominion government for India.

Preface

I HAVE for some time been thinking of writing the Reminiscences of my life. I have been encouraged in the idea by some of my friends, who think (and I share their view) that they may throw light on some of the most interesting chapters in our current history and help to elucidate them from the Indian standpoint. I belong to a generation that is fast passing away; and I have been in close touch, and I may add in active association, with some of its most illustrious men, devoted workers in the public cause, who by their labours have largely contributed to our own Province and to foster the beginnings of a real national life throughout the country. Their work lies buried in the forgotten columns of contemporary newspapers. Perhaps a generation hence it will all be forgotten. I hope in these pages to do some justice to their honoured memories; and these Reminiscences will not have been written in vain if I am able even in part to accomplish this object.

The need for Reminiscences such as these has become all the more pressing in view of recent developments in our public life, when unfortunately there is a marked, and perhaps a growing, tendency among a certain section of our people to forget the services of our early nation-builders – of those who have placed India on the road to constitutional freedom to be achieved by constitutional means.

S. N. Banerjea

Contents

1

My Boyhood and Early Days

My parentage – early influences – school and college life – evils of child-marriage – the Brahmo-Samaj movement; Keshub Chunder Sen – the temperance movement; Peary Churn Sircar – re-marriage of Hindu widows; Pundit Iswar Chunder Vidyasagar.

I BELONG TO A *Kulin* Brahmin family which, since the creation of Kulinism by King Ballal Sen, had maintained their purity with proud and inflexible consistency. Neither the allurements of wealth nor the prospects of an easy and comfortable living diverted them from their firm and traditional resolve to uphold the integrity of their status. The rich Brahminical possession of plain living and high thinking gave them a dignity that no wealth could confer.

My grandfather was a Brahmin of the old school, rigid in his orthodoxy. His regular and methodical life, with its old-world sense of ease and contentment, the round of his daily duties, chiefly religious, performed with an exactitude not always associated with the life of the East, gave one a vivid and fascinating picture of what an orthodox home was in the early sixties of the last century. He had, however, given his eldest son, my father, the best kind of English education available at that time.

My father was brought up in the Hindu College, where he greatly distinguished himself, and was a favourite pupil of David Hare, one of the pioneers of English education in Bengal. The memory of David Hare is still adored, though more than two generations have elapsed since his death; and on the first of June every year, the anniversary of his death, the unpretentious monument standing on unconsecrated ground (for orthodox Christianity in those days would not permit his burial within consecrated precincts) is covered with flowers and wreaths by those who never saw him in the flesh, but who enshrine his memory in their grateful hearts. He came out to India as a watch-maker and died as a prince among philanthropists, loved in Hindu homes by their inmates, with whom his relations were friendly, and even cordial. The story is told (and it is a tradition in our family) that he came to see my grandmother, to comfort her in her sorrow, when my father ran away from home to avoid the displeasure of my grandfather for an outrage upon Hindu orthodoxy.

My father subsequently joined the Medical College, and became the most distinguished Indian medical practitioner of his time. His culture had dispelled from his mind the orthodox ideas fostered by his domestic environment. He belonged to a generation, some of whom had sat at the feet of Derozio, and, like the first converts to a new cult, their alienation from the faith of their fathers was complete and even militant. Peary Chand Mitter, in his life of David Hare, has told us how this group of young *alumni* of the Hindu College, fresh from their contact with the learning and literature of the West, rejoiced in an open and ostentatious parade of defiance, how they ate forbidden food, and threw the remnants into the houses of their orthodox neighbours. It was with this new spirit that my father was saturated. Thus, in our home, the two conflicting forces of those times met, but in no spirit of antagonism. The predominant influence, however, was that of orthodoxy, represented by my grandfather, for the authority of the head of the family, even in matters of belief, was still paramount.

Nevertheless, an atmosphere of controversy was generated, which stimulated a spirit of research and enquiry. It was amid this conflict of opposing forces that my earliest years were spent, and what was happening in my family was symbolical of the strife and contention between Eastern orthodoxy and Western culture that was going on in every educated home in Bengal. It must not be imagined for one moment that it disturbed our peace, except on rare occasions, for tolerance is ingrained in the Hindu nature; and in those days, so long as we were not interfered with in our religious beliefs or practices, we did not mind what others around us, it might be our own kith and kin, said or did. The present spirit of opposition and intolerance observable among some of our people was unknown; and reverence for the head and the elders of the family was the resounding note of the Hindu household.

My earliest recollections go back to the days when, as a boy of five years, I was sent to a *pathsala* (indigenous school) to learn Bengalee. The *guru mohashoy* (teacher) treated me with the consideration due to my Brahminical rank and the fame of my father. But he was a strict disciplinarian and on one occasion he called me *mara Brahmin* (a sheepish Brahmin), and I refused to go back to the *pathsala*. I was obdurate and my parents had to yield. I was then sent to a Bengalee school to complete the study of my mother tongue. Here I stayed for a couple of years, and was later admitted into the Parental Academic Institution to learn English. My real work as a student now began. This was a school founded mainly with the aid of the benefactions of Captain Doveton of the Nizam's service, and it was attended chiefly by Anglo-Indian boys. When I joined the school I did not know a word of English. I had just finished the alphabet and was crawling through a spelling-book in which I had made very little progress. Thus equipped, I was thrown among boys who spoke nothing but English. My difficulties were great and my position most uncomfortable. But I muddled through somehow; and in a short time managed to speak the language, I presume not very correctly, and without knowing a word of the grammar.

The fact illustrates the truth, which is now recognized, that a language is best learnt through the ear and not with the aid of the grammar and the dictionary. As a matter of fact, I never studied English grammar as thoroughly as is now done by our boys; and when I went up for the Matriculation Examination my grammatical knowledge was confined to Lennie's little book. In these days, and perhaps rightly, a great deal of importance is attached to tutorial instruction and to the personal attention bestowed upon boys by the teachers. Throughout my career in school and college I never had a tutor, and had to depend entirely upon myself in learning two such difficult languages as English and Latin. Occasionally, when the situation seemed hopeless, I had to appeal to my father, who had himself been a teacher. It was hard and uphill work, but it afforded me a lesson in self-help that has been of infinite value to me through life. My career in school and college and in the University was fairly distinguished. I was a prizeman every year. I cannot say that I occupied the highest place, though I was always very near the top ; but in the course of a few years, and in the long run, I left behind those boys who had beaten me at the start; and in life I think I have out-distanced every one of my school or college rivals. I presume it is tenacity of purpose that is the crowning quality of life.

My Anglo-Indian and European teachers and professors were throughout very kind to me, and they did not show a particle of racial feeling in their treatment of me. In that temple of learning, in which I passed some of my happiest years, I was never allowed to hear the faintest echo of those racial and sectarian controversies that sometimes distracted the country. From those early days the levelling influence of knowledge was presented to me in a concrete form, which in itself was a part of my education; and when, after having taken my B.A. degree, I was about to leave the college, my Principal, Mr. John Sime of the University of St. Andrew's, who afterwards became Director of Public Instruction in the Punjab, strongly urged my father to send me to England to compete for the Indian Civil Service. My father readily assented; and it is due to his honoured memory to state that throughout he was an ever-living source of encouragement and inspiration to me. Great physician that he was, he was an even shrewder judge of men; and in 1853, when I was barely five years old, he drew up a will, a copy of which subsequently fell into my hands, in which he directed that I should be sent to England to complete my education. From the days of my infancy he had formed the idea that education in England would be helpful to me in life. On March 3, 1868, I sailed for England along with my friends, Romesh Chunder Dutt and Behari Lal Gupta.

Before I leave this part of my Reminiscences, relating to my school and college life, it may not perhaps be out of place to refer to a lesson which I learnt then and which I have practised through life with great advantage to myself. I was taught when still quite a boy the need of taking regular and daily exercise. My father took a personal interest in this part of my education, for, being a doctor, he realized that health is the basis of all success in life. We had an *akra* (Indian gymnasium) in our own house with a *palwan* (trained Indian gymnast) to teach us the various forms of Indian athletic exercises. We attended the gymnasium daily with the regularity with which we attended our schools; and one of my brothers, Captain Jitendranath Banerjea, who took to his exercises with great ardour, was able to hold his own against almost any athlete, and had the reputation of being the strongest man among the Bengalees. I have often thought of his wonderful physical strength, and it has always struck me that, however much he might have been indebted to the training he had given himself, there must have been a basis, an original fund of physical stamina, to account for it.

For more than three generations early marriage was unknown in our family. My ancestors were not reformers, but rigid orthodox Brahmins; and, strangely enough, it was this orthodoxy which re-acted upon their domestic institutions and prevented early marriage in the family. Coming from one of the highest *Kulin* families, it was difficult for them to secure suitable husbands for their marriageable daughters from amongst men of the same social status, whose number was necessarily limited. They had to wait till the girls grew in years and then they were married. My mother and my grandmother were quite grown-up young ladies when they were married, and, I believe, the same was the case with my great grandmother, whom I saw in my early years when she was over a hundred years of age. In the life history of my family I found the strongest argument against child-marriage, and I was never tired of repeating it when I had an opportunity in my public and private utterances. The members of my family have always enjoyed exceptional health, and I ascribe the fact largely to the absence of child-marriage for generations among them. This was the explanation I gave to Lord Hardinge, at one of the earliest interviews I had with him. He expressed his surprise at my physical alertness, which he thought was quite extraordinary for an Indian of my years. An ounce of fact is worth a ton of theory. I have placed these facts on record in the hope that they may influence the judgment of my countrymen in a matter of vital importance to their well-being. For, after all, the health and physique of a nation is the first condition of national progress.

I have as yet said nothing of the public movements of my youthful days. They did not, indeed, acquire the volume and intensity of those that followed them, for they did not appeal to as wide a public and had not behind them the same measure of public support or approval. The newspaper Press had not then become a power; public speaking on the platform had not come into vogue. The speeches of the great Ram Gopal Ghose were made at public meetings not very largely attended, or at the meetings of the Justices, who then, like the Corporation of to-day, were entrusted with the municipal administration of Calcutta.

It was Keshub Chunder Sen who first made use of the platform for public addresses and revealed the power of oratory over the Indian mind. In the early sixties and seventies of the last century the Brahmo-Samaj movement was a potent and living force, which exercised a profound, though possibly an indirect, influence even over orthodox Hindu society. Its immediate effect was to check the conversions to Christianity that were then taking place. Those who were dissatisfied with the old faith and felt the stirrings of the new spirit created by the eloquence of the great Brahmo leader, found comfort and consolation in the teachings of the new religion. Keshub Chunder Sen, originally a follower of Debendra Nath Tagore, had seceded from the Brahmoism as taught by the

Maharshi. His was an open breach with the Hindu social system, which Debendra Nath Tagore, following the lead of the great Raja Ram Mohun Roy, sought to reform and adapt to the spirit of the Vedic teachings. Keshub Chunder Sen's addresses created a deep and abiding impression on young minds. They drew large audiences. There was a visible religious awakening. His marvellous oratory, set forth with all the accessories of a sonorous voice, a noble diction and a commanding presence, and inspired by the fervour of a deep and burning conviction, fascinated his hearers. I was often at his meetings and listened with breathless attention and ever-increasing admiration.

Keshub Chunder Sen had an eloquent coadjutor in Protap Chunder Mazumdar. The latter's oratory was of a different type. It was imaginative, picturesque, brimful of wit, but was wanting, compared with that of his great chief, in those resources which appeal to the heart and stir the feelings.

Keshub Chunder Sen was a great organizer, a born leader of men with a penetrating insight into human nature. He was a religious teacher with all the asceticism of the Hindu Vaishnav ingrained in him by his family associations; but he was also a man of affairs, understood the world and knew how to deal with the world. If he had not chosen to be a religious leader, he might, if he had had the opportunities, have been a statesman, occupying a front rank among statesmen. His personality was charming, and in his society his followers found a pleasing companion and a great leader. The indirect effect of Keshub Chunder Sen's teaching was great. It not only broadened and liberalized educated thought in matters social and religious, but it also produced an opposite effect, namely, it strengthened the orthodoxy of the extreme reactionaries. They were alarmed; they retired within their shell and surrounded themselves with a hard incrustation of the most narrow and obsolete prejudices. Hinduism under modern influences has slowly developed a tendency towards liberalism, but any attempt to run it precipitately in the same path creates suspicion and fear, and is apt to check the forward movement.

Associated with the Brahmo movement of the early sixties and seventies of the last century was the temperance movement under the leadership of Peary Churn Sircar. I never had the honour of sitting at the feet of Peary Churn Sircar, but he was one of the greatest teachers of youth that Bengal has produced. A temperance movement for the protection of the young was a real necessity at that time. Some of our best men had fallen victims to the curse of drink. It was considered to be an inseparable part of English culture. A man who did not drink was hardly entitled to be called educated. The saintly Raj Narayan Bose tells us in his autobiography (and I have heard the story from his own lips) how one afternoon he went to Ram Gopal Ghose's house, and, meeting other friends there, called for a drink from the servant, the master being away; and how, when Ram Gopal came back from office, he found them all lying on the floor in a state of more or less hopeless inebriety. The youth of Bengal had to be rescued from this terrible vice, and a complete transformation of the opinion of the educated community was an urgent necessity.

No man was better qualified to lead the movement than a teacher of youth so universally respected as Peary Churn Sircar. The outward look and demeanour of the man would, however, produce the impression that he was far more fit to follow than to lead. One so gentle, so quiet, so amiable, seemed to be hopelessly wanting in the sterner qualities of the leader of a great public movement. The result, however, showed that there was the mailed fist concealed under the velvet glove, and that the gentle head master of the Colootola Branch School had been gifted by nature with what are believed to be incompatible qualities, a child-like simplicity and a fascinating amiability, combined with the firmness and strength of a leader of men.

The temperance movement was a great success. We all joined it. We were enthusiastic about it, held meetings and made speeches. Keshub Chunder Sen, Iswar Chunder Vidyasagar and the Reverend C. H. A. Dall, a highly esteemed American missionary of the Unitarian Church, were active promoters of the movement. It made an abiding impression on the young generation, and helped to stem the tide of intemperance, which had assumed ominous proportions.

There was one other public movement that marked the period of my student life and which deserves a passing reference. It was the movement for the re-marriage of Hindu widows, inaugurated by the great Pundit Iswar Chunder Vidyasagar. His is an honoured name in Bengal and will, I think, occupy, next to Raja Ram Mohun Roy, the proudest place in our history. I knew him well and admired his great personality, his wonderful strength of purpose, the breadth and liberality of his views, and his deep and burning sympathy for the helpless and the poor. It was this last trait of his character that made him the champion of the Hindu widow. At the time he happened to possess great influence with the Government, and succeeded in passing a law legalizing the re-marriage of Hindu widows.

I well remember the stir and agitation which the movement produced and how orthodox Hindus were up in arms against it. Young as I was, I felt an interest in what was going on; and one of the earliest recollections of my boyhood is the sense of grief that I felt at the lot of a Brahmin girl, a neighbour of mine who had just lost her husband, and how strongly I wished her to be re-married. I never could pass her house as a boy without the liveliest emotions. The movement, however, made no impression upon the community at the time. My grandfather was violently opposed to it; my father was as eager in its support. For the time being orthodoxy prevailed; and the champion of the Hindu widows died a disappointed man, like so many of those who were in advance of their age, leaving his message, unfulfilled, to a posterity that may yet do justice to his patriotic endeavours. The progress which the movement has made since his death in 1891 has been slow. A new generation has sprung up, but he has found no successor. The mantle of Elijah has not fallen upon Elisha. The lot of the Hindu widow to-day remains very much the same as it was fifty years ago. There are few to wipe her tears and to remove the enforced widowhood that is her lot. The group of sentimental sympathisers have perhaps increased – shouting at public meetings on the Vidyasagar anniversary day, but leaving unredeemed the message of the great champion of the Hindu widow. 'When will that message be fulfilled?', cried I in the days of my youth. Let me repeat it in the evening of my life.

2

My First Visit to England

The voyage; obstacles and prejudices – successful in the Civil Service Examination, 1869 – disqualified; the Commissioners' mistake – public resentment in India – lawsuit and my re-instatement – my father's death, 1870 – Sripad Babaji Thakur, Romesh Chunder Dutt, and Behari Lal Gupta – my English tutors.

AS I HAVE OBSERVED, I started for England on March 3, 1868, with Romesh Chunder Dutt and Behari Lal Gupta. We were all young, in our teens, and a visit to England in those days was a more serious affair than it is now. It not only meant absence from home and those near and dear to one for a number of years, but there was the grim prospect of social ostracism, which for all practical purposes has now happily passed away. We all three had to make our arrangements in secret, as if we were engaged in some nefarious plot of which the world should know nothing. My father was helping me in every way, but the fact had to be carefully concealed from my mother, and when at last on the eve of my departure the news had to be broken to her, she fainted away under the shock of what to her was terrible news.

We received the most substantial help from the late Mr. Monomohan Ghose, who had just returned from England and had joined the Bar of the Calcutta High Court. A finer and a nobler man I have hardly ever set eyes upon. A warm patriot, he heartily desired that his countrymen should visit England in large numbers, and he was always ready with his advice and with such practical encouragement as lay in his power. So great was the interest he felt in this matter that Michael Madhu Shudan Dutt, our great national poet, nicknamed him 'Protector of Indian Emigrants Proceeding to Europe'. We passed the night preceding our departure at his house at Cossipur, where he was then staying, and before daybreak we started for the steamer at Chandpal Ghat.

Early on the morning of the third of March my father came to wish me good-bye. It was the last sight I was destined to have of him in this world; for he died while I was away in England. I went down with him to his carriage. He was dressed in simple *dhoti* and *chudder,* and, as he walked down the steps looking at me he uttered the word, 'Farewell', and turned his back, though his eyes were still fixed on me, the tears trickling down his cheeks.

It was the last word that I heard him say. Was it uttered with a prophet's prevision, in unconscious response to a voice sounding in the depths of his soul, that he and I were to meet no more on this side of the grave? It is now over fifty years since then, but the incident remains graven on my memory as a precious treasure. Father and son, we parted for ever – I on my long journey onwards in that strenuous life beset with the strangest vicissitudes, and he back to the old home and to my sorrowing mother, to console her as best he could. We parted, never again to meet, myself retaining through life a more than filial affection and reverence for a father who more than any human being had contributed to my up-building. His disinterestedness, his sympathy for the poor, his abhorrence of sordid means, have left an abiding impression on me, and have strengthened the roots of that filial piety which is one of the cardinal virtues of the Hindu. All this may seem to be high-strung sentiment to the European reader, but to the Hindu it is natural and represents the spontaneous outflow of the soul.

In those days a trip to England seemed to our people to be even more perilous than a voyage to the North Pole. Things were much worse still in the days of Ram Mohun Roy, and his biographer tells us that Dwarakanath Tagore's house, from which the Raja started for his ship, was filled with an eager crowd of visitors who had thronged to have their last look at one whom they believed they were never again to see alive. Our attitude has now greatly changed; and it is one of many signs of the transformation that has taken place within the last fifty years.

The sea-voyage was thoroughly enjoyed by us. None of us was sea-sick, and we had a good deal to see in the various ports where the vessel touched. We arrived at Southampton after a voyage of nearly five weeks. Mr. W. C. Bonnerjea, who had been written to by Mr. Monomohan Ghose, met us at Southampton and took us to London. He put us up at a boarding-house in Barnard Street, near University College, London. After a short stay there, we settled down in our respective quarters and applied ourselves in right earnest to the work that lay before us. I lived near Hampstead Heath, as a pupil in the family of Mr. Talfourd Ely, a teacher of Latin in University Collegiate School, London. I greatly benefited by my stay in his family. It was a happy English middle-class home, and it impressed me with the clean, orderly, methodical lives of the English middle-class. There was an all-pervading air of discipline in the family. I was treated as one of its members, and when, eighteen months after, I left Mr. Ely's house to live in lodgings, we parted with mutual regret. I worked hard and passed the Open Competitive Examination for the Indian Civil Service in 1869.

Within a few weeks after the publication of my name in the list of successful candidates my troubles began. In filling up the form required by the Calcutta University (of which I was a graduate) I had put down sixteen years as my age when I appeared for the Matriculation Examination of that University in December, 1863. The regulations for the Open Competitive Examination for the Civil Service of India then in force required that a candidate should be above nineteen, and below twenty-one, years of age. If I were sixteen in 1863, I would be above the required limit of age in 1869 and would be disqualified on that ground. The difference, however, was easily explained. Born in November, 1848, I was fifteen and not sixteen years of age when I went up for my Matriculation Examination, and if I were fifteen years at the time, I was within the limit of age prescribed by the regulations. How, then, came I to state in my Matriculation form that I was sixteen years? The truth is, that the Indian method of reckoning the age of a man is different from that followed among Englishmen. We reckon the age not from the time of one's birth, but from the time of the conception of the child in the mother's womb, and, accordingly, when the boy has completed his fifteenth year, he would be known as sixteen years old and would describe himself as such. Among Englishmen his age would be only fifteen.

It may here be mentioned that the school records fully bore out that I was only fifteen years old, according to the English method of calculation, at the time I appeared for the Matriculation Examination. These records were based upon information obtained from home. The entry in the Matriculation form was made by me and I naturally put the age down as I knew it according to our way of reckoning.

However that may be, this apparent discrepancy between my age as given in my Matriculation form and as stated in the certificate submitted to the Civil Service Commissioners was well known to my Indian friends in London (for we were a handful at the time) and nobody thought that there was anything in it or that it was likely to be used for the purpose of removing my name from the list of selected candidates. But a few weeks after the declaration of the result of the examination, an advertisement (supposed to be the work of an Indian) appeared in the newspapers to the effect that if the fifty-first candidate (he was the first among the unsuccessful candidates) would communicate with a person whose address was given, he would hear something to his advantage. Among the Indian colony in London at that time there was no doubt as to who had published that advertisement.

The discrepancy was brought to the notice of the Civil Service Commissioners; and it so happened that there was this difference between the University record of age and that before the Civil Service Commissioners in the case of two other successful Indian candidates, namely, Behari Lal Gupta, who rose to high office in the Indian Civil Service, and Sripad Babaji Thakur, who became a District Judge in the Bombay Presidency. We were requested to furnish explanations. Our explanations were practically the same and we reconciled the discrepancy by pointing out the difference between the English and the Indian methods of reckoning age. Our explanations were deemed unsatisfactory. My name and Thakur's were removed from the list of successful candidates. Mr. Gupta escaped the same fate, because, even if he had been sixteen according to the English method of reckoning when he went up for the Matriculation, he was still within the prescribed limit.

I was not prepared to take this decision lying down; and, what is more, the removal of our names from the list of successful candidates evoked a universal outburst of indignation throughout India, especially in Bengal. The great leaders of the Indian community, among whom I may mention Maharaja Romanath Tagore, Maharaja Jotindra Mohon Tagore, Pundit Iswar Chunder Vidyasagar, Raja Rajendra Lal Mitter and Rai Kristo Das Pal Bahadur, joined in an affidavit testifying to the Indian method of reckoning age to which I have already referred.

The Indian newspapers of the time were full of articles condemning the decision of the Civil Service Commissioners. At the head of the Commission was Sir Edward Ryan, who for many years had been Chief Justice of the High Court of Bengal; and it is curious that he should have been ignorant of the method of reckoning age usual amongst us, or, knowing it, failed to have recognized its obvious application to our case.

We decided to move the Queen's Bench for a writ of mandamus upon the Civil Service Commissioners. Our friends in England were unanimously of opinion that the only remedy lay in an appeal to the Law Courts. Two names occur to me in this connexion, to which I cannot refer without emotions of the deepest gratitude – those of Mr. John D. Bell, and Sir Taraknath Palit, who was then in England, having been recently called to the Bar. They took the matter up with earnestness and enthusiasm. Mr. Bell was for many years a leading barrister of the Calcutta High Court, and was now in retirement in England, practising before the Privy Council. He declined to take any fee, for, he said, it was a just cause, and he had eaten the salt of India. It is no exaggeration to say that the success of our application was largely due to his earnest and disinterested advocacy. Those who knew Sir Taraknath Palit in his later life knew the ardour of his soul, the warmth of his friendship, and his invincible tenacity of purpose in any cause that he made his own; and these qualities, which made him the distinguished citizen and the eminent advocate that he became in after life, were already conspicuously in evidence.

Sripad Babaji Thakur did not move in the matter. Wise man that he was, he rightly concluded that if I won he would win too; for the two cases stood exactly on the same footing. I engaged Mr. Mellish, who afterwards became Lord Justice of Appeal, as the leading counsel, and Mr. John D. Bell as his junior. On June 11, 1869, Mr. Mellish applied before the Queen's Bench Division for a mandamus upon the Civil Service Commissioners to show cause why my name should not be restored to the list of probationers for the Indian Civil Service.

The Bench that heard the application consisted of some of the greatest English judges, and was presided over by the Lord Chief Justice of England, Sir Alexander Cockburn. Mr. Mellish had no difficulty in obtaining a favourable hearing, and the following résumé of the proceedings in Court will explain the attitude of the judges in regard to the merits of the case :

Mr. Mellish said that this was the first instance in which a native of India – necessarily at very great disadvantage – had succeeded in this examination; and it would be most unfortunate if he should be unfairly defeated on such a ground as this. After a successful career at the University of Calcutta, this gentleman, in the face of immense difficulties, had come over to this country to compete with Englishmen in examinations upon English subjects conducted in the English language, and he had succeeded. It would be lamentable that it should go forth to India that he had been, after all, defeated upon such a point as this, and without the least foundation for it. The Commissioners, in answer to his statement clearly showing that he was within the prescribed age, had written back that he had 'admitted' that he was beyond it (*a laugh*), and they had declined to hear evidence upon the point.

The Lord Chief Justice: They say, in effect, 'Any evidence you may adduce we shall set at nought'.

Mr. Justice Mellor: They say, 'You are estopped by your statement at Calcutta', though it plainly appears that it is quite consistent with his present statement.

Mr. Justice Blackburn: They totally misapprehend his statement, and then they tell the applicant that upon their (mistaken) construction of it they consider it conclusive against him, whereas in reality it is not so.

Mr. Justice Hannen: They appear to represent it as imperative upon them to take the eastern mode of computation.

The Lord Chief Justice: Show us that we have jurisdiction, and I think there is no doubt we shall exercise it.

Mr. Mellish submitted that the jurisdiction was clear. The statute gave every native Indian subject a legal right to admission upon certain conditions prescribed by the Queen, all of which he contended that he had satisfied. The Commissioners proposed to deprive the applicant of this legal right upon grounds clearly untenable, and this without hearing his evidence. This was clearly contrary to those obligations of natural justice which were incumbent upon all tribunals, or upon all bodies which had legal duties to perform, however domestic the tribunal might be. Therefore the applicant was entitled to a mandamus to compel the Commissioners to hear and consider his evidence, and adjudicate or determine upon it, as to the actual truth of the matter of fact in dispute.

The rule was granted, but the Civil Service Commissioners did not wait to contest it. Their position was indefensible and their decision perhaps hasty; and before the case came on for hearing they wrote to Sripad Babaji Thakur and myself, re-instating us in our positions as selected candidates for the Indian Civil Service.

I won my case, but my father died before the news could reach him.

My father died on February 20, 1870. I was then living with my friend, Mr. K. M. Chatterjee (who afterwards became a Judge of the Calcutta Court of Small Causes) in lodgings in Gaisford Street, Kentish Town. The circumstances in which I received the news of my father's death were so peculiar and even extraordinary that they may perhaps be mentioned here. To the spiritualist, and the believer in the relations between the visible and the invisible world, they may perhaps lend countenance to their theories.

It was about the middle of March that I first received the news of my father's death. The night before I was restive, excited and unhappy, I knew not why. But my thoughts were turned homewards. I thought of those whom I had left behind. I thought most of my father. It was a bad night for a heavy sleeper like myself. I rose early, dressed and went down to the parlour where Mr. Chatterjee and myself used to have our meals. He soon joined me, and we had our breakfast. Later on the postman's knock was heard. It was mail day. Chatterjee got his Indian letter, but there was none for me. It added to my uneasiness. My friend read my thoughts in my face; and, with the quick and responsive sensibility of his nature, he opened his letter in my presence and began to read it aloud. I followed him with the closest attention. He was seated in an easy-chair at one end of the room; I was reclining on a sofa at the other end. All of a sudden, he stopped reading, and, with a sad face and swollen eyes, struggling to conceal his emotion, he gazed affectionately at me. Years have rolled by. I am in the evening of my life, soon perhaps to join him for whom I grieved. But I have a vivid recollection of the emotions that overwhelmed me. I said to my friend, 'Why do you stop? Go on.' He would not answer, nor read, but grew sadder as he looked at me. The dark event which was soon to overwhelm me had already cast its shadows ahead. With a trembling voice, but with unfaltering directness of purpose, as if some voice from within was moving my heart and inspiring my tongue, I said to my friend, 'Why don't you read? Is anybody ill at home?' Still no answer. Chatterjee, so frank and communicative, was mute. But I pressed on. The voice within would give me no peace or rest. I repeated, 'Is my father ill?' Still no response. Chatterjee sat like a statue. Finally came the explosion. I asked, amid a flood of tears, 'Is my father living or dead?' Chatterjee immediately dropped the letter and ran to the sofa where I was sitting, and grasped me in his embraces, his tears commingling with mine.

I was dazed, overpowered and lay half stunned. Lalmohan Ghose, Taraknath Palit (afterwards Sir Taraknath Palit), Woomesh Chunder Mazumdar, who died three years later as the result of a riding accident, Keshub Chunder Sen, who was then in England, and other friends saw me soon after. Mazumdar stayed with me the night, as my friends would not allow me to be alone in my room. The incidents of that day I can never forget, and associated with them now are the hallowed memories of departed friends who grieved with me and consoled me in one of the saddest moments of my life.

We had lost nearly a year in fighting the case, and we were given the option of going up for the final examination with the men of our year (1869) or with the candidates who would be selected in 1870. I decided in favour of the former course; Sripad Babaji Thakur preferred to join the batch for 1870.

Of Sripad Babaji it may not be out of place to say a word or two. In every way he was a remarkable man. His genius for the mastery of languages was phenomenal. Constitutionally he was averse to hard work; but he found ample compensation in the bountiful gifts of a beneficent nature, which made good his lack of steady industry.

A little story occurs to my mind in connexion with him, which shows the man and the large part which the chapter of accidents sometimes plays in human life. On the eve of our examination we were of course all very busy, but not so Sripad Babaji Thakur. Chess was his favourite diversion and he was an expert chess player, able to direct the moves from a different room from where the game was being played. As usual he had finished a game; and then perhaps a qualm of conscience seized him and he felt that he must do something for the examination at which he was to appear on the following morning. He took up Webster's Dictionary, which happened to be near him, and read the chapter on the requisites of a good dictionary. His memory was marvellous, and every idea that was in the chapter was imprinted on his mind. As luck would have it, we were asked in the paper on English Composition to write an essay on the requisites of a good dictionary, and, as might have been expected, Thakur, who had read the subject up the previous night, acquitted himself well.

With his great intellectual gifts Thakur was one of the most amiable of men. Sir Taraknath Palit was his guide, philosopher and friend. When he arrived in London Thakur was a vegetarian and used to wear his hair like the rest of his orthodox countrymen. Sir Taraknath soon made him a meat-eater and induced him to dress and wear his hair like an Englishman; and Thakur was never happier than with his new habits and in his new habiliments. We used to chaff him about them, and his loud laughter 'that spoke the vacant mind', the echoes of which I still remember, added to our hilarity and enjoyment.

Among the Indian candidates who competed with us for the Indian Civil Service in 1869 was another remarkable man whose early death deprived the world of a Sanskrit scholar of great promise – I mean Anandaram Barua. In regard to him also there was the difficulty about the age to which I have referred; but, the point having been settled in my case, it was no longer raised in his. He came from Assam and distinguished himself at the examinations of the Calcutta University. Having obtained a State scholarship, he went to England to compete for the Indian Civil Service. He secured a place for himself among the successful candidates in 1870. As a member of the Indian Civil Service he combined the duties of an administrator with extraordinary devotion to literature, and at the time of his death, I understand, he was engaged in preparing a dictionary of the Sanskrit language which, alas, never saw the light. His was a case of blighted promise which in its fruition would have enriched the world of letters.

Of my two friends, Romesh Chunder Dutt and Behari Lal Gupta, what shall I say? They were to me more than brothers. Throughout life, though our activities lay in different spheres, we were linked by the closest ties of friendship and affection, the memory of which death has only served to sanctify. They were pioneers in the hitherto untrodden path of Indians entering the Bengal Civil Service. Their position was difficult; and their anxieties great. But they excelled in those high qualities which should distinguish all pioneers; and when, as in their careers it sometimes happened, there was a conflict between the claims of the Service and those of the nation, they preferred the latter and exalted the interests of the motherland above the sectional concerns of the class to which they belonged. An illustration of this was found in the Ilbert Bill controversy, of which Behari Lal Gupta, in his capacity of Presidency Magistrate of Calcutta, might be said to have been the originator. As for Romesh Chunder Dutt, he was a man amongst men, a prince among his peers (*primus inter pares*). His superiority was observable in every gathering that he adorned with his presence. Yet this distinguished Civil Servant, such was the reactionary tendency in those days, never rose beyond the position of an officiating Commissioner of a Division, though an Indian Prince, one of the greatest in the Empire, the Maharaja of Baroda, subsequently, when Dutt was no longer in the Indian Civil Service, appointed him his Prime Minister. When he was appointed a member of the Bengal Legislative Council, his presence was immediately felt. I was a member, and we all noticed it. He would not move in the usual official groove. There was a flutter in the official benches; and Sir

Charles Elliot, who, as Lieutenant-Governor, was President of the Council, put the best appearance he could upon this somewhat novel feature in the Council atmosphere by declaring that he welcomed an independent outlook, such as Mr. Dutt had shown, amongst official members.

Before I leave this part of my Reminiscences I should like to say a word or two about our English professors and tutors. Soon after our arrival we joined some of the classes in University College, London, and we took private lessons from some of them. We were treated by them all with the utmost kindness, and by some of them, Professors Goldstucker and Henry Morley in particular, with what I may call an affectionate solicitude. They perhaps realized that we were strangers in a strange land, far away from those near and dear to us. Mr. Morley treated us more or less as members of his household, and Dr. Goldstucker, who was a bachelor, with no household except a dog that barked whenever we came, and an old maid-servant with one tooth in her head, greeted us with the affectionate but stern authority of a Hindu *guru*. On one occasion I was late in arriving, and the first thing he said to me after the dog had done its barking was, 'Well, Banerjea, your ancestors lived without time, and you are keeping up their traditions. That will not do in London. Here time means money.' I put in the best excuse I could, but definitely made up my mind to sin no more, and ever since I have tried to practise the precept that punctuality is the virtue of princes and even of men who are not, and never can be, princes.

Dr. Goldstucker was Professor of Sanskrit in University College, and he was my Sanskrit tutor. He was a veritable pundit of the old type, straight, stern, irritable, but with a large fund of the milk of human kindness. He was lame and had a wooden leg. In the course of a conversation I mentioned that one wasted time in coming up by tram. He said, 'Oh, yes. I walk all the way and I don't stop to take people in as the tram does.' He had many fine qualities; but his weak point, as it seemed to me, was his uneasy feeling about the fame of Max Müller, a brother German.

Bred in the atmosphere of Sanskrit learning, he was, like our own pundits, apt to be irritable. On one occasion we were all walking along Charing Cross when Professor Goldstucker flew into a temper about some trifling matter. Professor Morley, who was one of our party, whispered into my ear, 'Banerjea, don't you mind it. The heel of one of his boots is off, and he has become fidgetty.' We all laughed.

In striking contrast with the irritability of the Sanskrit professor was the sweet serenity, the real love of life and the work of life which Professor Henry Morley displayed in all his dealings with us. Life was to him a pleasant sunshine, brightened by the cheeriness of his own home. He was always working and always smiling. In my troubles with the Civil Service Commissioners he gave me all the help that he could, and enlisted the sympathies of Charles Dickens, the great novelist, who wrote a strong article in *Good Words,* a journal that he edited. From him there was always a cheery look and an encouraging word to hearten me in the hour of my troubles. Once he said to me, 'Banerjea, they will yet raise a statue for you for the fight you are putting up.' An Englishman, no matter what his station or calling may be, has a soft corner in his heart for a good fighter; and this quality does not leave him even when he is abroad, separated from those influences which largely determine his character and conduct.

We have heard complaints in these days about the treatment of Indian students in England and the prejudice that is supposed to exist against them. In our time there was no such feeling and no such complaint. We were welcomed wherever we went, and everywhere there was a disposition to treat us with the kindness due to strangers. We were of course few in number and thrown largely in the company of Englishmen. We thus had an opportunity of studying English life and English institutions at close quarters, to the mutual advantage of both Englishmen and ourselves. For, I fear, ignorance is too often the mother of prejudice, and closer knowledge hardly ever fails to dissipate misunderstanding and establish good relations. An Englishman once publicly declared that I was more English than most Englishmen. I freely confess that I have a genuine admiration for those great institutions which have helped to build up English life and the fabric of British constitutional freedom.

3

My Home-coming and Official Career, 1871-1874

London to Brindisi – taken for German spies at Versailles – Calcutta again: socially ostracized by orthodox Brahmins – work as Assistant Magistrate at Sylhet – racial prejudices – the circumstances of my dismissal from the Service.

AS I HAD MADE UP MY MIND to appear at the Final examination of 1871, I had to do two years' work in one year's time. For in those days it was a two years' course for the probationers for the Indian Civil Service, and the subjects of examination, which comprised Indian and English Law and Jurisprudence, Political Economy, and Indian Languages, were arranged with special reference to the time allotted. It was hard work, but I did not grudge it. Having won my point in the controversy with the Civil Service Commissioners, I was in high spirits, and, now that my father was dead, I was anxious to return home as quickly as my business permitted. Fifty-five years have now rolled away, and many things of surpassing interest have happened within that time in my country and to myself. But I still retain a vivid recollection of those laborious days when I could think and dream of nothing else, except of my books and the examinations, and there were occasions when the night passed into the day, and the faint, grey streaks of the dawn were visible, and I was still poring over my books, hardly conscious of Nature's change. Without sleep I appeared at the examination and felt none the worse for it. It was the spirit that overmastered the flesh.

I passed the Final examination of 1871 along with my friends, Romesh Chunder Dutt and Behari Lal Gupta, and together we started for home in August, 1871. Previous to our starting we had sketched out a scheme of a tour through some of the European countries, and we carried it out with almost military precision. We visited Paris, went up the Rhine, ascended the heights of St. Gothard, saw the beautiful mountains and lakes of Switzerland, passed through Italy, staying for a few days at Venice, and went on board the P. & O. steamer at Brindisi.

An incident happened at Versailles which is worth recording and which shows that the police can be foolish not only in Calcutta but also elsewhere, and in many places far more enlightened than Calcutta. From Paris we had gone on a day's visit to Versailles, the old capital of the Bourbons. We were returning in the evening, and had come to the railway station to take the train to Paris. We were waiting, three of us, for the train. Paris, which is the resort of the world, is more cosmopolitan than many European towns, but the Versailles police had probably never before seen Indians, especially in the Indian garb in which we were all dressed. Their fears and suspicions were roused at the sight of strangers attired in a strange costume and speaking a strange language. They took us to be Prussian spies! Frenchmen at the time were in a state of unusual excitement. The Franco-Prussian War had ended disastrously only a year before. Paris had just passed through the revolt of the Communists, many of whom were then on their trial. As we were walking up and down the platform, a French policeman approached us and asked us to follow him to the police-station. We protested, but we thought that discretion was the better part of valour, and we followed him to where he led us. We were taken to a room where a police officer was asleep. He got up, rubbed his eyes, looked at us (I think he was not quite sober) and asked us to produce our passports. We did so, but the man was not satisfied. How was he to know that we were the identical persons named in the passports? I produced a letter addressed to me, which I had in my pocket, and it tallied with my name in the passport. But even then his suspicions were not removed. He had a talk in French, which we did not understand, with the man who had arrested us, and he was evidently satisfied that we were after all Prussian spies.

The trouble was largely due to misunderstanding, as it is all the world over. We did not understand French and the policemen did not know English. My friends had taken some lessons in French, and they essayed to speak a few words in that language. The effort only served to deepen the suspicion of the police commissaire. He thought we were shamming, and that we knew a great deal more of the language than we pretended.

The discussion lasted nearly half an hour and at the end of it we were ordered to walk across the road to what apparently was the police lock-up. A door which opened into a room was unlocked and we were ushered inside. There was a drunken man confined in the room. He was taken elsewhere and accommodation was made for us. The policeman left us, having locked the door.

It was a small room with a wooden bed, and we lay shut up in it from ten o'clock at night till nine o'clock the following morning. The plank bed was hardly sufficient for three of us to lie down upon. My friends talked away the whole night. There were insects in the plank bed which tormented them, as they afterwards told me. But as for me, wrapped in the gentle embraces of sleep, I was insensible to their attentions. They assailed me, I imagine, the whole night, but they failed to disturb my slumbers.

On the following morning a policeman unlocked the door and took us to the office where we had been examined the previous night. The first thing that we insisted on was that we must have some one who understood and could speak English. An English-speaking police officer was accordingly brought in. He grasped the whole situation in a minute and apologized to us for the trouble and insult to which we had been subjected. He took us to the police prefect, a cultured Frenchman who spoke English well, and *he* was even more profuse in his apologies. The trial of the Communist prisoners was then going on and was exciting European interest. People from different countries had come to witness the proceedings. Our prefect politely offered us tickets of admission to the court. We thanked him, but declined the tickets. We thought we had had enough of France. We straightway hurried to the station and before nightfall we were leaving French territory for a more hospitable country. The incident shows the dark and often unfounded suspicions which pervade the police mind even in the great centres of European civilization.

Our tour through Europe was necessarily a hurried one. Having been away from home so long, we wanted to be in Calcutta during the Durga Pujas, our great national festival, which usually takes place about the end of September or early in October. Venice impressed me as a unique city, both in its physical and historic aspects. Its streets are the inlets of the sea; and its palaces frown upon them. Historic memories crowded upon me as I gazed upon the palace of the Doges, the Prison and the Bridge of Sighs. The Prison which Napoleon wanted to burn down was reminiscent of the dark ages and of the cruel treatment accorded to prisoners in those days. From Venice we proceeded to Brindisi, where we went on board an Italian steamer and arrived at Bombay. We came straight to Calcutta, breaking journey at Allahabad, where Babu Nilcomol Mitter, then the leader of the Indian community, gave us a reception, at which, on behalf of my friends and myself, I made a speech, the first I believe that I ever made in my life. At the railway station at Howrah, Keshub Chunder Sen and other friends met us.

I went straight home and met my widowed mother, how changed from what she was when I saw her last on the day preceding my visit to England! The sorrows and privations of Hindu widowhood had evidently told upon her body and mind.

All three of us (Romesh Chunder Dutt, Behari Lal Gupta and myself) stayed in our homes, and the *Hindoo Patriot,* the leading Hindu journal of the time, edited by Kristo Das Pal, announced that we had been received back into the bosom of our homes and Hindu society. It was a bold step for my mother and my brothers to have given me a place in a Brahmin family, and to have eaten and drunk and lived with me. My father was by no means orthodox in his ways, and his transgressions against strict orthodoxy were numerous and grave; but a visit to England was not one of them. Forbidden food and drink he used to take with an ostentation that shocked my grandfather. But Hindu society said nothing, winked at it, forgot and forgave.

A visit to England, however, was a new form of heterodoxy to which our society had not yet become accustomed. The Anglicized habits of some of those who had come back from England added to the general alarm. The leaders indeed applauded the courage of the members of my family in taking me back into the old home, but the whole attitude of Hindu society, of the rank and file, was one of unqualified disapproval. My family was practically outcasted. We were among the highest of Brahmins; but those who used to eat and drink with us on ceremonial occasions stopped all intercourse and refused to invite us. There were some who, jealous of my father's fame and of my recent success, took advantage of this opportunity to settle old scores. These party and caste squabbles often afforded an admirable opportunity for the satisfaction of private grudges, and I have known of some cases within the last year or two where personal spite stimulated a sense of outraged religion.

I am now talking of a state of things which prevailed little less than half a century ago. But in the meantime a silent and stupendous change has taken place. A sea-voyage or a visit to Europe no longer involves the loss of caste. Among the Brahmins, especially in the mofussil, there may be some squeamishness in the matter; but among other castes, a man may visit any part of the world he likes, cross the seas as often as he pleases, and yet retain his social status as a member of the caste. That the Brahmins will soon be on a line with the other castes does not admit of a doubt; it is only a question of time. There are those who are never tired of telling us that East is East, that it is unchanged and unchanging, and that Hindu society is immobile. It is nothing of the sort. It is moving, slowly it may be, but steadily, and is responsive to the world-forces. The Hindu of to-day is very different from the Hindu as I saw him fifty years ago, and fifty years hence the difference between the old and the new will be even more marked. The car of progress, as it moves forward, gathers forces which impart to it an impetus all their own. There comes a time when with the added momentum it rolls forward in its triumphant career in geometrical progression. Our political activities are reacting upon our social system, and the upward movement, with occasional aberrations, is visible along the entire line.

I arrived in Calcutta about the end of September, 1871. We had a reception given to us at the Seven Tanks Garden by the public of Calcutta. It was organized by Keshub Chunder Sen, Iswar Chunder Vidyasagar and Kissory Chand Mitter. Satyendra Nath Tagore was the first Indian Civilian. We were the second batch. Satyendra Nath Tagore was a Bombay Civilian. We had been appointed to the Bengal Presidency, and the success of three of us in one and the same year had created a profound impression upon Indian public opinion. The whole of Indian Calcutta was present at the function, and we were the cynosure of all eyes. The Seven Tanks and Belgachia Gardens were in those days the favourite centres of public functions organized by the Bengalee community. The *Malliks* and the Paikpara Rajas, who were the proprietors of these villas, were among the wealthiest and most trusted leaders of the community. Others have now come forward, and the representatives of the middle class have taken their legitimate place in guiding the public thought and activities of Bengal.

I stayed in Calcutta after my return from England for about a month. I was posted to Sylhet as Assistant Magistrate and joined my appointment on November 22, 1871. Sylhet was in those days a part of Bengal. In 1874 it was separated from Bengal and included in the new province of Assam, and ever since it has remained a part of Assam, although it is a Bengalee-speaking district. It took me fully a week to reach Sylhet from Calcutta. It is now only a day's journey. Mr. H. C. Sutherland was Magistrate of Sylhet and was my immediate superior. I was supposed to be a sort of apprentice to him, and learn my work from him. He was an Anglo-Indian and not very popular, as I soon discovered. He gave me as much work as I could manage to get through, and he treated me at first with cordiality and with a sense of lofty patronage, of which he liked to make a display.

I rapidly passed the departmental examinations and obtained the powers of a first-class Magistrate. My success was the cause of my official ruin. At any rate I thought it largely contributed to it. Mr. Posford, who was my senior as Assistant Magistrate, and myself appeared together at the departmental examination. I passed; he failed. He was my senior by two years. He was a European and I was an Indian. My success and his failure were necessarily, in a small place like Sylhet, the subject of local gossip and comment. Mr. Sutherland, although an Anglo-Indian, was imbued with a strong racial feeling, which was accentuated by his position as a member of the Indian Civil Service. He did not like it that I should have passed and that Mr. Posford should have failed. The contrast seemed in his eyes to be derogatory to the prestige of the ruling race. I do not know what the practice is to-day; but in 1873, the passing of the departmental examinations was followed by promotion and increase of pay. I was invested with first-class powers, and got the usual increment to my salary. Mr. Sutherland wrote to the Government and had Mr. Posford exempted from further departmental examinations.

At this time, Mr. Anderson was appointed Joint Magistrate of Sylhet. He and I became great friends. He and Mr. Sutherland did not get on at all well. I was new to these little local jealousies and strifes, and in my simplicity I continued to be very friendly with the Andersons. All this led to an alienation between the Magistrate and myself and the suspension of all friendly and personal relations. My troubles now began. Hardly a day passed in which I was not called upon to give an explanation about some case or other. A superior officer can always make things very hot for a subordinate if he wants to; and from the time that these unpleasant relations commenced, my position became extremely uncomfortable, if not absolutely intolerable.

At last the climax was reached in connexion with a theft case in which one Judisthir was the accused. The man was charged with the theft of a boat. The case was originally on the file of Mr. Posford, but was transferred to me. Owing to my heavy work it had to be postponed from time to time. On December 31, 1872, an order was passed (and it bore my initials) that the accused should be entered in the *Ferari* list, the list of absconding prisoners. As a matter of fact the man had not absconded, and the object of the order was to avoid giving an explanation for the long pendency of the case. It was an artifice that was sometimes resorted to by the ministerial officers to save themselves from censure. In the case of a very young and inexperienced officer like myself, delay in the disposal of cases would be regarded by the superior authorities as a fault of the *Peshkar* (or ministerial servant) rather than of the officer, whom he is expected to guide and lead in matters of office procedure. I signed the order along with a heap of other papers. My attention was not drawn to it; nor did I know it or understand the significance of the order. When called upon to give an explanation about another case I inadvertently offered an explanation about this. If I had knowingly signed the order and knew its significance, such a mistake would have been impossible; for then I would have at once remembered that, the man's name being in the *Ferari* list, no explanation could possibly be required. The Magistrate called for the records, and asked me for a full explanation, which I gave. He wrote to the District Judge, who addressed the High Court, and the Government was moved. A Commission was appointed under Act xxxix of 1850 to enquire into the whole matter.

The Commission consisted of three European officers, Mr. H. T. Prinsep, who afterwards rose to be a Judge of the High Court, Mr. H. J. Reynolds, who subsequently became a member of the Board of Revenue, and Major Holroyd of the Assam Commission. There were fourteen charges, but substantially they resolved themselves into two, namely, that I had dishonestly entered Judisthir's name in the *Ferari* list, knowing that he was not an absconding prisoner, and, secondly, that, when called for an explanation, I had falsely pleaded ignorance and said that I knew nothing at all about it. There was a further charge, that I had dishonestly disposed of the case about Judisthir and acquitted him to avoid an explanation.

I prayed for the hearing of the case in Calcutta, and, further, that I should be provided by Government with counsel for my defence. Both the prayers were rejected. I was defended by Mr. Montriou, and the Commission permitted me personally to put in a few arguments at the end of the trial. Some of my friends had suggested that Mr. W. C. Bonnerjea, who was then rising to the position which he subsequently occupied at the Bar, should be engaged as my counsel. But it was thought advisable, in view of the feeling which had been evoked among the officials, that an England-returned Bengalee barrister should not defend an England-returned Bengalee Civilian.

The Commissioners found me guilty of the charges, but they made no recommendation. I returned to Calcutta from Sylhet and obtained a copy of the report, without, however, the recommendations of the Government of India, which, as I subsequently found, were for my dismissal from the Service with a compassionate allowance of Rs. 50 a month.

My case excited very strong feeling in the Indian community, and the general belief amongst my countrymen was that, if I were not an Indian, I would not have been put to all this trouble, and that the head and front of my offence was that I had entered the sacred preserves of the Indian Civil Service, which so far had been jealously guarded against invasion by the children of the soil. Many years afterwards a Lieutenant-Governor told me that it was a wicked proceeding. Sir Edward Baker, another Lieutenant-Governor of Bengal, who knew me well, said in a conversation with Mr. Gokhale, which was repeated to me by the latter: 'I have a soft corner in my heart for Surendranath. We have done him a grievous wrong; but he bears no malice.' Mr. Hume, the father of the Indian National Congress, writing in *India* in 1893, uses language which reflects the feeling of educated India.[1]

It is worthy of notice that in 1882, eight years after my dismissal, I was appointed an Honorary Presidency Magistrate of Calcutta and a Justice of the Peace invested with power of imprisonment extending to two years, and of inflicting fines which might amount to one thousand rupees. Evidently those who trusted me with these plenary powers (and they are the highest which a magistrate under the Indian Law can exercise) thought that either I was innocent of the charges upon which I had been removed from the Indian Civil Service, or that I had outgrown my former self and changed my character within the brief period of eight years. I leave it to the reader to judge which of the two inferences is the more rational.

I may here add (though I am anticipating events by several years) that under the rules for the election of members to the

1. His letter is printed in an Appendix.

Legislative Councils, framed under the Parliamentary Statute of 1910, I was disqualified for election by reason of my dismissal. The disqualification was removed by the Government of Bengal, and subsequently by the Government of India, when I stood as a candidate for election to the Imperial Legislative Council.

4

1875-1882

My second visit to England – exclusion from the English Bar – return to India, 1875 – educational work; my joy in it – Mr. A. M. Bose.

As I HAVE ALREADY OBSERVED, I was furnished with a copy of the report of the Commission by the Government of India, and I was informed that they had recommended my dismissal. I made up my mind to proceed to England and to lay my case before the authorities of the India Office. I left Calcutta about the end of March, 1874, and arrived in London about the middle of April. I at once placed myself in communication with the India Office. The attitude of some of the officials on whom I called was distinctly cold and unsympathetic. It seemed to me that they were unwilling to go behind the report of the Commission or give me a further hearing, and within a few weeks of my arrival I was officially informed that I had been dismissed from the Indian Civil Service.

One chapter of my life was now closed. I had fought a hard battle and lost it. The whole of my official prospects were blasted. The recollection of the emotions then roused is still vivid in my mind. I felt that my dismissal was a relief. It was indeed a crushing, staggering blow, but it meant absolution from a strain upon body and mind which had wellnigh become intolerable. I was indeed prepared for my fate; I might almost be said to have been expecting it; and when, on returning home to my lodgings in Kentish Town, from a dinner-party at Mr. B. Mookerjee's house, I read the official letter, lying on my table, under the gas-lamp dimly burning, informing me of my dismissal, I spontaneously exclaimed, 'The bitterness of death is past and gone'. From April, 1873, to April, 1874, this fight had been going on, first with Mr. Sutherland, and then between the Government and myself; and to me it was a real relief when it was all over and I knew where I stood.

Not for a moment did I lose heart in this supreme crisis. Now and then, indeed, I thought of her who in a distant land would share the blow, but who, I knew, would not bend or reel under it. I closed my eyes upon the past and resolutely set them upon the future, which I painted with a hue as radiant as circumstances permitted. I was already a student of the Middle Temple and had kept eight terms. There were four more terms to keep before I could be called to the Bar. I made up my mind to stay on in England and finish my terms and be called to the Bar. Little did I then dream that even here my hopes were doomed to be frustrated.

I continued eating my dinners, and the time came when I was to be called. That was some time in April or May, 1875. My name was duly put up. An objection was, however, raised, from what quarter or by whom I knew not, nor did I care to enquire then nor do I even now. My dismissal from the Civil Service was considered to be a fatal objection, and the Benchers of the Middle Temple declined to call me to the Bar. An old English barrister, Mr. Cochrane, who for many years was an eminent leader of the Calcutta Bar, warmly interested himself in my case. Old as he was and almost tottering with the weight of years, he did all that was humanly possible. It was a pleasure to see the old man, fired with the enthusiasm of youth on my behalf. He was a grand specimen of a type which I fear is rapidly passing away. But all his efforts were made in vain. From the Civil Service I had been dismissed. From the Bar I was shut out. Thus were closed to me all avenues to the realization of an honourable ambition.

The outlook was truly dark. My friends declared that I was a ruined man, and that there was no hope for me on this side of the grave. Even the great Kristo Das Pal, editor of the *Hindoo Patriot,* took the same view. A friend, now dead, who achieved considerable distinction as a member of the Calcutta Bar, advised me in a sympathetic vein that I should change my name, go to Australia and seek out a career there for myself. I listened to these friendly counsels with all the equanimity I could muster, but I never despaired, nor even was the exuberant joyousness of my youthful nature darkened by the heavy clouds that lay thick around me. In the iron grip of ruin I had already formed some forecast of the work that was awaiting me in life. I felt that I had suffered because I was an Indian, a member of a community that lay disorganized, had no public opinion, and no voice in the counsels of their Government. I felt with all the passionate warmth of youth that we were helots, hewers of wood and drawers of water in the land of our birth. The personal wrong done to me was an illustration of the helpless impotency of our people. Were others to suffer in the future as I had suffered in the past? They *must,* I thought to myself; unless we were capable as a community of redressing our wrongs and protecting our rights, personal and collective. In the midst of impending ruin and dark, frowning misfortune, I formed the determination of addressing myself to the task of helping our helpless people in this direction.

I was in England from April, 1874, to May, 1875; and during these thirteen months I shut myself up in my lodgings, in the village of East Molesey near Hampton Court, devoting myself to such studies as I thought would qualify me for this work. From ten o'clock in the morning after breakfast till dinner time at eight o'clock in the evening, I was incessantly at work, reading books that I thought would inspire me with the fervour and equip me with the capacity for that which was to be my life-work. I used to make copious notes with indices, and these are even now in my possession. Occasionally I used to run up to London, and see friends, and consult as to what should be done in order to be called to the Bar; but it would be no exaggeration to say that I was immersed in my books and felt no higher pleasure than in the companionship of the great masters, with whom I was then in daily communion.

It was a year of preparation, of laborious apprenticeship (from April, 1874, to April, 1875) that was most valuable in my life, and upon which I look back with infinite pleasure. The gloom that surrounded me was dispelled in the new vision that opened out to me in the prospective glories of a dedicated life of unselfish devotion in the service of my fallen country. It was a period of incessant work led by an invisible inspiration. I recovered my buoyancy in the new hope that was awakened in me, and the joy that thrilled me, that all was not lost, but that there was still work to be done by me, perhaps even in a higher sphere than before. Out of death cometh life, a higher life and a nobler resurrection. So it was in my case.

I returned home in June, 1875, a ruined man in the estimation of all, save and except my wife and myself. She received me, when we first met on my return, with a bright and cheery countenance – and here let me for a moment pause to pay a tribute of loving and admiring respect to the memory of my dear lamented wife. She did not indeed receive the education which fortunately is now common among Indian ladies of her class and position. But she possessed extraordinary gifts of commonsense, sympathy and courage. She firmly stood by me in this dark crisis, and never thought that ruin and confusion had seized us. Not one regretful glance did she ever cast upon the past, but bravely looked upon the future, and her courage and confidence were justified.

I came back to Calcutta in June, 1875. What was I to do – how obtain a living and yet do some useful work for the country? The outlook was as gloomy as it could be. On all sides the door was barred. I could not join the Bar, whether as a vakil or a barrister – the professions were closed to me, there was no industry to which I could turn. But I began at once to take a part in public affairs. Soon after my return to Calcutta, a meeting was held in the theatre of the Medical College, to promote the Temperance movement. It was a crowded meeting. The Temperance cause excited much interest in those days. The labours of Peary Churn Sircar, the apostle of the Temperance movement in Bengal, were bearing fruit. It was a living movement; for the dangers of intemperance spreading among the rising generation were real and ominous. They had to be protected against the seductive influence of drink, to which some of the most illustrious men of the last generation had fallen victims. The interest in the question was great and the meeting was largely attended. I was asked to speak. It was practically my first public utterance at a great Calcutta meeting. I made a favourable impression and on the following morning was told by a friend that I had taken my place among our recognized public speakers.

Soon after, Pundit Iswar Chunder Vidyasagar offered me an appointment as Professor of English in the Metropolitan Institution, which I accepted. My speech had already made me popular with the students, and helped me, I think, to get the appointment. The salary was small, Rs. 200 a month, less than half of what I had been getting as Assistant Magistrate, but I was glad that I had something to do and that it afforded me an opportunity, of which I took the fullest advantage. I sought by every possible means in my power to kindle in the young the beginnings of public spirit, and to inspire them with a patriotic ardour, fruitful of good to them and to the motherland. In the lecture-room I attended to my immediate duties as Professor, but I felt that I had a higher call. The Students' Association had already been organized. I became its most active member, and urged the establishment of branch Associations in the different colleges as feeder-institutions.

I soon helped to make student life instinct with a new spirit in Calcutta. I delivered lectures in Calcutta, Utterpara, Kidderpore and other places, upon such subjects as Indian Unity, the Study of History, the Life of Mazzini, the Life of Chaitanya, High English Education, etc. I was in great demand as a speaker and never spared myself. Between the students and myself there grew up an attachment which I regarded as one of my most valued possessions. Amongst those who regularly attended the meetings in those days were Mr. B. Charkravarti, Swami Vivekananda, Mr. Nanda Kishore Bose, Mr. S. K. Agasti and others.

The City College was founded in 1879. The schism in the Brahmo-Samaj, owing to the marriage of Keshub Chunder Sen's daughter with the Maharaja of Cooch-Behar, had important results. It led to the establishment of the Sadharan Brahmo-Samaj, the City College, and other kindred institutions. The leading spirits in that dissentient movement were Ananda Mohan Bose, Shivanath Sastri, Durga Mohan Das, and other Brahmo leaders. I was invited to join the tutorial staff of the City School (for it had not then become a college). I gladly accepted the offer, as it added to my income and extended the sphere of my contact with the student community.

It was hard work for me – to teach four hours daily, and this in addition to my propaganda work among the students and my political work in connexion with the Indian Association, in which I felt the keenest interest. But I never grudged the toil or the strain. The excitement of work has been the pleasure of my life and has kept my spirits up amid disappointment, defeat and disaster. Even now, when I have passed my seventy-fifth year, its fascination is so overpowering that I have to restrain myself from considerations of health.

It may not, perhaps, be out of place to mention here an offer of an appointment made to me about this time, which, if I had accepted it, would have changed the whole tenor of my life. I was offered a post under the Tippera Raj, I think it was the English Secretaryship, on a salary of Rs. 700 a month. I was getting at this time only three hundred rupees a month, and there was no prospect, near or remote, of any substantial increase. I had, however, no difficulty in making up my mind and in refusing the offer. I said to myself that for good or for evil my career in life was definitely fixed, that I had set my hand to the plough and could not look back.

I left the Metropolitan Institution in March, 1880. Pundit Vidyasagar wanted me to give up my connexion with the City College, offering to make good the pecuniary loss that I would thereby sustain. I could not see my way to complying with this request, though I was prepared to give him an additional hour for teaching in the Metropolitan Institution. I tendered my resignation, which he accepted.

A month later, in April, Principal Robertson of the Free Church College invited me to join that institution as Professor of English Literature. I accepted the offer and continued to be Professor in the Free Church College till 1885, when I resigned owing to the growing demands, on my time and attention, of the educational institution that I had founded.

In 1882, I took over charge of a school, teaching up to the Matriculation standard, known as the Presidency Institution. It became the nucleus of the Ripon College, but at the time when I took it over it had only two hundred students on its rolls. I thoroughly reorganized the school. It was affiliated to the Intermediate standard, and eventually to the B.A. and B.Sc. and the B.L. standards, of the Calcutta University. With Lord Ripon's permission, obtained on the eve of his departure, I named the institution after him, and it is now known as the Ripon College. It is a fully-equipped, first-grade college, with a high school attached to it with nearly 2,500 students all told. It has been provided with a building of its own, at a cost of nearly Rs. 1,50,000. I have divested myself of all proprietary rights over this institution and have made it over to the public under a body of trustees created for the purpose.

I was engaged in the active work of teaching from 1875 to 1912, that is, for a period of nearly thirty-seven years. On being elected to the Imperial Legislative Council, in February, 1913, it became necessary for me to travel frequently between Delhi and Calcutta, and I had to withdraw from my professorial duties. Great as is the importance I attach to my political work, to which I shall refer fully later on, far more interesting to me personally were my duties as a teacher.

It was with the greatest reluctance that I ceased to be a teacher, for I loved the students and I rejoiced in their company. I said on one occasion during the Swadeshi agitation, 'If I have contributed to the up-building of student life, the students in their turn have made me what I am. If I have inspired them with the spirit of service, they in their turn have rejuvenated me and filled me with the ardour of youth.' I have grown young in their company and by daily contact with them I have retained even amid advancing years some of the qualities of youth. The late Mr. Philip Smith of the Oxford Mission asked me, when he went to see me in jail in 1883, whether I could explain to him the secret of my great influence over the student community. My reply was prompt and decisive, I said, 'I love the students. I rejoice with them in their joys, I grieve with them in their sorrows, and they reciprocate the sentiment with the generous enthusiasm of youth.'

I regarded my vocation as a sacred calling. My duties were indeed multitudinous, but to those of the class-room I accorded a special preference. I never came to the lecture-room without being thoroughly prepared for my work. Sometimes such was the inspiration of the lecture-room that a difficult point that had evaded my efforts in my own private study became luminously clear under the influence of my environment. Thus there is the play of a living magnetism between the teacher and the taught, and all teachers who have taken a real interest in their work must have felt it. I always set a high value upon my educational work and put it in the forefront of my activities. It may not be out of place to reproduce some remarks that I made in this connexion in one of my speeches:

> 'Political work is more or less ephemeral, though none the less highly useful. Educational work has in it the elements of permanent utility. The empire of the teacher is an ever-enduring empire, which extends over the future. The teachers are the masters of future. I cannot think of a nobler calling than theirs. Theirs is a heaven-appointed task, a sacred vocation. But how few realize their responsibilities or rise to the height of their mission! If the work of the present is to be perpetuated, it must be through those who are to be the citizens of the future. "Suffer little children to come unto me", said the great Founder of Christianity. Jesus Christ appealed not to the callous and the hard-hearted, but to the soft, the gentle, the impressionable, whose souls had not been hardened by the rough buffetings of life.'

In my mind my educational and my political work were indeed interlinked. I felt that the political advancement of the country must depend upon the creation among our young men of a genuine, sober and rational interest in public affairs. The beginnings of public life must be implanted in them. They must have their period of apprenticeship and qualify themselves for their civic duties. They must, on the one hand, be stirred out of their indifference to politics, which was the prevailing attitude of the student-mind in Bengal in 1875, and on the other, protected against extreme fanatical views, which, as all history shows, are fraught with peril in their pursuit. I was resolved, so far as it lay in me, to foster a new spirit and to produce a new atmosphere. This was the underlying idea that prompted me to help in the organization of the Students' Association.

Associated with me in the work of organization was the late Mr. Ananda Mohan Bose. Mr. Bose had come back from England a few months before me, and had founded the Students' Association of Calcutta, of which he was the President. Mr. Ananda Mohan Bose was one of the most brilliant students of the Calcutta University. Born in the district of Mymensingh (he was one year senior to me), he passed the Matriculation Examination from the Mymensingh Zilla School with great distinction, standing sixth in the University list in order of merit. He stood first at the Intermediate, B.A. and M.A. Examinations, and crowned an almost unique career by carrying off the blue ribbon of the University, the Prem Chand Roy Chand Scholarship. He went up to Cambridge, and was the first Indian Wrangler, occupying the eighteenth placc in the list. He was a vigorous and eloquent speaker, and, at a meeting of the East Indian Association held in London, he spoke with a force and eloquence that extorted the admiration of Mr. Fawcett, who was present, and who said that there were not half a dozen speakers like him in the House of Commons. From a man so well equipped, great things were expected by his countrymen, and Mr. Ananda Mohan Bose threw himself into his public work with an earnestness not common among the members of the great profession to which he belonged. He was rising into a good practice at the Bar, but his heart was in the work of the country; and I have no doubt in my mind that his divided attention between the Bar and his public duties interfered with his professional success.

5

The Indian Association

Need for a political Association to represent educated middle classes – inaugurated, July 1875 – Mazzini's influence – the Civil Service agitation, 1877 – my tour in North India – Sirdar Dayal Singh Majeetia and the *Tribune* – tour in Western India, 1878-79; meeting with Mr. Ranade – the first Indian Deputation to England; Mr. Lalmohan Ghose – the Maharani Swarnamoyee, 'Lady Bountiful of Cossimbazar' – success of the Deputation.

AFTER MY RETURN from England in June, 1875, and along with the work of organizing the students and infusing into them a new life and spirit, I began seriously to consider the advisability of forming an Association to represent the views of the educated middle-class community and inspire them with a living interest in public affairs. There was indeed the British Indian Association, which, under the guidance of the great Kristo Das Pal, who was then secretary, valiantly upheld the popular interests when necessary; but it was essentially and by its creed an Association of land-holders. Nor did an active political agitation, or the creation of public opinion by direct appeals to the people, form a part of its recognized programme. There was thus the clear need for another political Association on a more democratic basis, and the fact was indeed recognized by the leaders of the British Indian Association. For some of its most distinguished members, such as the Maharaja Narendra Krishna, Babu Kristo Das Pal, and others, attended the inaugural meeting of the new Association, and encouraged its formation by their presence. And let me gratefully add here that, throughout, the relations between the new Association and the British Indian were of the most cordial character, and this was due largely to the influence and example of Kristo Das Pal, one of the greatest political leaders that Bengal, or India, has ever produced. Mr. Ananda Mohan Bose and myself joined hands in this matter. I had more leisure than he, but we were in frequent consultation.

Associated with us in our efforts to organize a new Association upon popular lines was a devoted worker, comparatively unknown then, and, I fear, even now, whose memory deserves to be rescued from oblivion. Dwarakanath Ganguli began life as a teacher, and while yet young embraced Brahmoism. In the schism that took place between the two wings of the Brahmo-Samaj he sided with the dissentients and actively promoted the establishment of the Sadharan Brahmo-Samaj. An ardent lover of what he believed to be the truth, when he took up a cause he threw his whole soul into it. His co-operation in the organization of the new Association was of great value to us; and so long as health and strength were spared to him he worked in the cause of the Association with an energy and devotion, the memory of which, now that he is dead, his friends cherish with affectionate gratitude.

After a year's preparation, the Indian Association was established on July 26, 1876. The name was the subject of anxious consideration among our friends. Pundit Iswar Chunder Vidyasagar and Mr. Justice Dwarakanath Mitter, while still a member of the Bar, had formed the idea of organizing a similar Association which was to be the voice and the organ of the middle classes. The idea had to be given up as it did not at the time meet with much support; but the name they had chosen for their proposed organization was the Bengal Association. We thought that such a name, or anything like it, would restrict the scope of our work. For the idea that was working in our minds was that the Association was to be the centre of an all-India movement. For even then, the conception of a united India, derived from the inspiration of Mazzini, or, at any rate, of bringing all India upon the same common political platform, had taken firm possession of the minds of the Indian leaders in Bengal. We accordingly resolved to call the new political body the Indian Association.

The inaugural meeting was marked by an incident that deserves a passing notice. Babu Kali Churn Banerjee, who, next to the Rev. K. M. Banerjee, was the foremost Indian Christian leader of his generation, and who subsequently became President of the Indian Association, opposed its formation, chiefly on the ground that a similar Association, under the name of the Indian League, had been established a few months before. I replied to his arguments, and the public meeting ratified the resolution creating the Association.

The Indian League did useful work. Babu Sisir Kumar Ghose of the *Amrita Bazar Patrika,* Dr. Sambhoo Chunder Mookerjee of the *Rais and Rayyet,* and Babu Motilal Ghose, were its moving spirits. It has ceased to exist and some of its leading members have joined the Indian Association.

I attended the inaugural meeting of the Indian Association under the shadow of a great domestic bereavement. At eleven o'clock on the morning of July 26, my son died. I had some idea that the meeting would not pass off quietly and that there would be opposition offered to the establishment of the Association. I made up my mind, despite my personal sorrow and with the full concurrence of my wife, that I should attend the inaugural meeting. No one at the meeting knew anything at all about my bereavement, though it became widely known on the following day. This is not the only time that I have had to perform a public duty under the weight of a great personal bereavement. My dearly beloved wife died on December 23, 1911; on the 26th I attended the meeting of the Indian National Congress of that year, and, in the absence of the gentleman entrusted with the duty, I had to propose the election of the President, Pundit Bishen Narayan Dhur, about whose public career I had only a very general idea.

The Indian Association supplied a real need. It soon focused the public spirit of the middle class, and became the centre of the leading representatives of the educated community of Bengal. Mr. Ananda Mohan Bose was elected Secretary, Babu Akshay Kumar Sirker, who has since made a name for himself as a Bengalee writer, was appointed Assistant Secretary. I held no office, but I was one of the most active members of the Association. In view of my removal from Government service, I kept myself in the background, but I worked zealously for the Association, knowing no higher pleasure or duty, and bent upon realizing through this institution the great ideals which even at that early period had taken definite possession of my mind. They may be set forth as follows: (1) The creation of a strong body of public opinion in the country; (2) the unification of the Indian races and peoples upon the basis of common political interests and aspirations; (3) the promotion of friendly feeling between Hindus and Mohamedans; and, lastly, the inclusion of the masses in the great public movements of the day. I worked for these ideals; others have worked for them too, for they were in the air, and the possession and property of every thoughtful and patriotic Indian; and now, after nearly fifty years of public life, I have the gratification of feeling that, if they have not been wholly realized, they are within a measurable distance of accomplishment. The Indian Association materially helped to promote these ideals. They were the natural and normal development of the efforts of the great men of the past, under the new conditions created by the closer touch of our best minds with the political thought and activities of the West.

Upon my mind the writings to Mazzini had created a profound impression. The purity of his patriotism, the loftiness of his ideals, and his all-embracing love for humanity, expressed with the true eloquence of the heart, moved me as I had never before been moved. I discarded his revolutionary teachings as unsuited to the circumstances of India and as fatal to its normal development, along the lines of peaceful and orderly progress; but I inculcated, with all the emphasis that I could command, the enduring lessons of his noble life, lived for the sake of others, his lofty patriotism, his self-abnegation, and his heroic devotion to the interests of humanity. It was Mazzini, the incarnation of the highest moral forces in the political arena – Mazzini, the apostle of Italian unity, the friend of the human race, that I presented to the youth of Bengal. Mazzini had taught Italian unity. We wanted Indian unity. Mazzini had worked through the young. I wanted the young men of Bengal to realize their potentialities and to qualify themselves to work for the salvation of their country, but upon lines instinct with the spirit of constitutionalism. I lectured upon Mazzini, but took care to tell the young men to abjure his revolutionary ideals, and to adopt his spirit of self-sacrifice and devotion in the paths of constitutional development. I persuaded Babu Jagendranath Vidyabhuson and Babu Rajani Kanto Gupta, both distinguished Bengalee writers, to translate into our language the life and work of Mazzini in the spirit of my addresses, so as to place them within the reach of those who did not understand English. I soon popularized Mazzini among the young men of Bengal. No dire consequences followed, for the conditions that create the revolutionary spirit were wanting. They are the work of Governments that misread the signs of the times, and not of the so-called agitator, or of the ardent patriot who works for the amelioration of the lot of his people.

Within a year of the foundation of the Indian Association, the first great opportunity presented itself for realizing some of those great ideals that had given birth to the Association. Reactionary rulers are often the creators of great public movements. They will no doubt deny the charge or repudiate the credit; but they certainly sow the seeds which, in the fullness of time, ensure the enthronement of popular opinion and the triumph of popular causes. The reduction of the maximum limit of age, for the open competitive examination for the Indian Civil Service, from twenty-one to nineteen years, by the orders of the Marquis of Salisbury, then Secretary of State for India, created a painful impression throughout India. It was regarded as a deliberate attempt to blast the prospects of Indian candidates for the Indian Civil Service. The Indian Association resolved upon organizing a national movement. A great public meeting was held at the Town Hall on March 24, 1877. It was presided over by Maharaja Sir Narendra Krishna Bahadur, and was representative of the whole of Bengal. Not only were the leading men of Calcutta present, but also delegates from the interior of the province. Keshub Chunder Sen, who had never in his life taken part in any political meeting, was persuaded to move the election of the President.

This meeting was one of the biggest public demonstrations held in Calcutta; it was destined to be the forerunner of similar and even more crowded meetings held all over India. The agitation was the means; the raising of the maximum limit of age for the open competitive examination and the holding of simultaneous examinations were among the ends; but the underlying conception, and the true aim and purpose, of the Civil Service agitation was the awakening of a spirit of unity and solidarity among the people of India. It was accordingly resolved to appeal to the whole of India and bring the various Indian provinces upon the same common platform (a thing that had never been attempted before), and to unite them through a sense of a common grievance and the inspiration of a common resolve. It was an inspiring ideal, and to me it appealed with overwhelming effect.

I was appointed Special Delegate to visit the different provinces. This was of my own seeking; the conception was mine, and the agent for carrying it out was myself. I went about collecting subscriptions, and entered upon the task with alacrity and enthusiasm. Taking advantage of the summer vacation of the Metropolitan Institution, where I was then employed as Professor, I started for Upper India on May 26, 1877, accompanied by Babu Nagendra Nath Chatterjee, a member of our Committee, who was well known at the time as a most eloquent speaker in the Bengalee language. We started about the hottest time of the year, and Babu Nilcomol Mitter of Allahabad, with whom I was in correspondence regarding this tour, warned me that I was incurring a grave risk. Risk or no risk, I had made up my mind and there was no going back. We went straight to Agra, where my friend, the late Babu Abinash Chunder Banerjee, was stationed as Subordinate Judge.

Abinash Chunder Banerjee and myself had been playmates. He passed the examinations of the Calcutta University with great credit.

After obtaining the B.L. degree, he established himself in the United Provinces, with a view to practising as a lawyer; but he soon exchanged the Bar for the Bench and joined the Judicial Service. In early life he had been a staunch adherent of the Brahmo-Samaj, when Calcutta was seething with excitement under the eloquence of Keshub Chunder Sen; but when I saw him at Agra in 1877 he had gone back to the old faith. But whether as a Brahmo, or as a Hindu, he was one of the finest of men and one of the most agreeable of companions. His brilliant career on the Bench was prematurely cut short but his memory is still cherished with affection by those who knew him, and he will be remembered as the worthy father of a still more famous son, the late Dr. Satis Chandra Banerjee, whose early death Bengal and the United Provinces mourn. We met after a long time, and revived the memories of olden days. The whole plan of campaign we settled there.

It is worthy of attention that in those days Government servants were permitted to attend political meetings and to take an interest in political affairs. At the Bankipore meeting held in connexion with this question, the young Maharaja of Cooch-Behar, then a ward of the Government, attended, and Major Hidyat Khan Bahadur, C.S.I., a military officer, seconded one of the resolutions. But with the development of public life and the growth of public spirit in the country, the attitude of the Government has changed. Under recent orders public servants may attend political meetings, but they are not to take part in them. As a matter of fact, they usually do not even attend; for, whatever the published orders may be, the settled official attitude towards all public efforts is one of suspicion, if not of mistrust, and the subordinate officers take their cue from those in authority over them. I use the expression 'all public efforts' advisedly, for even the Ramkrishna Mission, a mission of benevolence and philanthropy without a tinge of politics in its aims or aspirations, was the subject of jealous watchfulness by the Criminal Investigation Department. Under the Reforms, however, the authorities are beginning to have a more rational outlook upon political and public demonstrations.

At Agra the Civil Service Memorial, which I had taken with me (it was the Calcutta Memorial) was translated into Urdu and lithographed. It was decided that I should proceed at once to Lahore and hold the first public meeting in the capital of the Punjab. It was felt that a demonstration there would be far more impressive and telling than one held in any other place in Upper India. At Lahore I was received with the utmost kindness by my countrymen of all denominations, Hindus, Mohamedans and Sikhs. It was an exhibition of friendliness that was a revelation to me. It showed that a common system of administration and education had prepared the ground for the realization of one of our most cherished ideals, namely, united action by the different Indian provinces for the fulfilment of our common national aims and aspirations. At a crowded public meeting of all sections of the Indian community held at Lahore, the Calcutta Resolutions and Memorial on the Civil Service question were adopted. At another public meeting I spoke on the question of Indian Unity, and a political Association under the name of the Lahore Indian Association was formed. Its constitution was modelled on that of the Indian Association of Calcutta. It was affiliated to that body. It was, I believe, the first political organization in the Punjab that provided a common platform for all sections of the Indian community. It has done valuable public work for the province.

In the Punjab I formed friendships, the memory of which, though the friends, alas, are now dead, is a grateful treasure of my life. There for the first time I met Sirdar Dayal Singh Majeetia. Our acquaintance soon ripened into warm personal friendship. He was one of the truest and noblest men whom I have ever come across. It was perhaps difficult to know him and to get to the bottom of his heart, for there was a certain air of aristocratic reserve about him, which hid from public view the pure gold that formed the stuff of his nature. He threw himself actively into the work for which I had been deputed. I persuaded him to start a newspaper at Lahore. I purchased for him at Calcutta the first press for the *Tribune* newspaper and to me he entrusted the duty of selecting the first editor. I recommended the late Sitala Kanta Chatterjee of Dacca for the post, and his successful career as the first editor amply justified my choice. His fearless courage, his penetrating insight into the heart of things, and above all his supreme honesty of purpose, the first and last qualification of an Indian journalist, soon placed him in the front rank of those who wielded their pen in the defence of their country's interests.

The *Tribune* rapidly became a powerful organ of public opinion; it is now perhaps the most influential Indian journal in the Punjab, and is edited by a gentleman who in his early career was associated with me as a member of the staff of the *Bengalee*. But it is not the only gift that the Sirdar gave to the Punjab. He gave away all he had for the benefit of his country; and the Dayal Singh College is an enduring monument of one of the worthiest sons of the Punjab, whose early death all India mourns in common with the province of his birth.

Prominently associated with Sirdar Dayal Singh Majeetia in the public work to which I have referred, were Dr. Surajball, Pundit Ramnarain, and last but not least, Babu Kali Prosanna Roy. Dr. Surajball was a graduate of Oxford and rose to a high position in the service of the Kashmir State; Pundit Ramnarain was an able lawyer. He was the first Indian who officiated as a judge of the Punjab Chief Court, and if he had been spared he would have been confirmed in that appointment. Kali Prosanna Roy was a brilliant lawyer who, after qualifying himself for the Bar, had taken up his residence in Lahore to practise his profession. As an advocate he hardly had an equal at the Lahore Bar. But he was not a mere lawyer; he was an agreeable companion, and an earnest Indian patriot. He took a prominent part in all public movements; and, when failing health compelled him to retire to his native village in Bengal, he endowed it with works of public utility. The name of such a man should be rescued from oblivion. But I am afraid, in this country, public services are often readily forgotten; for the prevailing temper is one of criticism and not of service, or of *admiration* for service.

Leaving Lahore, I visited Amritsar, Meerut, Allahabad, Delhi, Cawnpore, Lucknow, Aligarh, and Benares. At all these places crowded public meetings were held, at which the Calcutta Resolutions and the Civil Service Memorial were adopted, and, wherever practicable, political organizations were formed to act in concert with the Indian Association of Calcutta. Such Associations were formed at Lahore, Meerut, Allahabad, Cawnpore and Lucknow. Thus a network of organizations was started, and the foundations were well and truly laid, as subsequent events fully proved, for united and concerted action among our representative men, over an area extending from Calcutta to Lahore. The movement with all its potentialities was to receive a still further expansion when, in the following year, upon the selfsame errand, I visited Madras and Bombay and some of the towns in the western presidency.

My tour through Northern India, great as was its political potentialities, was to me a source of unmixed personal pleasure and instruction. I came in contact with all the leaders of thought in Northern India, belonging to a generation that has now passed away. Sir Syed Ahmed, Pundit Ajodhyanath, Pundit Bishambar Nath, Raja Ameer Hossain of Mahmudabad, Babu Aiswarya Narayan Singh, Babu Hurrish Chunder, and Babu Ramkali Chowdhury of Benares, were men of whom any community might well be proud. They differed in their temperaments, in their intellectual capacity, and even in the quality of their civic spirit, but they all loved the motherland and were eager to serve her.

The most famous of those whom I met was undoubtedly Sir Syed Ahmed, the founder of the Aligarh College and one of the greatest leaders of the Moslem community under British rule. He did not know a word of English, but, more than any other Mohamedan leader of his generation, he realized how necessary English education was for the advancement of his community, and he had the will to resolve, and genius to organize, a movement for imparting it upon a scale of far-reaching comprehensiveness, and under conditions of permanence and utility that have immortalized his name. He received me with the utmost kindness, and our friendly relations continued, notwithstanding differences of opinion, which the Congress movement subsequently gave rise to. He presided at the Civil Service meeting at Aligarh, which accepted the Calcutta Resolutions, among which was one in favour of simultaneous examinations. It is worthy of note, however that, as a member of the Public Services Commission of 1887, he signed the report of the majority, and did not join Sir Romesh Chunder Mitter and Rai Bahadur Nulkar in their support of simultaneous examinations.

It can serve no useful purpose to recall at this distance of time the memory of controversies that are now past and well-nigh forgotten. We lost his championship and the great weight of his personal influence and authority in the controversies that gathered round the Congress movement. His Patriotic Association was started in opposition to it. But even the greatest amongst us has his limitations. The Patriotic Association has disappeared; the Congress has continued to live and flourish. But let bygones be bygones. Let us not forget the debt of gratitude that Hindus and Mohamedans alike owe to the honoured memory of Sir Syed Ahmed. For the seeds that he sowed are bearing fruit; and to day the Aligarh College, now raised to the status of a University, is the centre of that culture and enlightenment which has made Islam in India instinct with the modern spirit, and aglow with that patriotic enthusiasm which augurs well for the future solidarity of Hindus and Mohamedans.

The success that had attended my efforts in Northern India encouraged my friends to depute me on the same mission to Western, and Southern, India. I started for Bombay in the winter of 1878. The Bombay leaders had already been informed of my mission; and they received me with kindness and cordiality. Mr. Vishanarain Mandlik, Mr. Kashinath Trembuck Telang, and Mr. (afterwards Sir) Pherozshah Mehta, were the leaders of Bombay public opinion. All of them are now, alas, dead and gone. A public meeting was held in Bombay, and the Civil Service Resolutions and Memorial were in substance adopted. I then proceeded to Surat, and Ahmedabad, the capital of Gujarat. Civil Service meetings were held and the Calcutta Resolutions were adopted in both places. I then returned to Bombay, and from Bombay I proceeded to Poona, where I was the guest of the late Mr. Ranade.

Mr. Ranade was then a Subordinate Judge, but his official position never overshadowed his instincts or interfered with his duties as a citizen. He was a constant figure on the Congress platform as a visitor, and he was the power behind the throne, guiding, advising and encouraging the Congress leaders in their work. His simplicity, the charm of his manners, his intellectual eminence, and his genuine and all-consuming love of country, fascinated all who came in contact with him. I was his guest at Poona, and he treated me as a member of his family.

From Poona, where a meeting was held and our Resolutions were adopted, I proceeded to Madras, where I became the guest of Dr. Dhanakatu Raju. I called on the Madras leaders, including Mr. Chensal Row, the Hon'ble Humayoon Jah Bahadur, and others, and I urged them to hold a public meeting to discuss the Civil Service question. For some reason or other a meeting could not be held; and we had a conference of leading men at Pacheappa's Hall, at which our Memorial and Resolutions were adopted. Madras to-day, so instinct with the public life of India, is very different from what Madras was in 1878. To-day it is fully on a line with the rest of India as regards its public spirit and its efforts for the public good. In 1878, it was the only place in all India where I found it impossible to hold a public meeting upon a question of vital interest to our people, and in regard to which there was practical unanimity all over India.

I returned home from my tour as quickly as I could, for I had important work in Calcutta. Our programme was, after securing absolute unanimity of opinion all over India, expressed through public meetings at various centres, to carry on the agitation in England and make the voice of India heard there, through our chosen representative, belonging to our own people and uttering our sentiments. Mr. Routledge, late Editor of the *Friend of India,* writing about this novel departure, said that it was 'an inspired idea'. We claimed for it no special illumination. It was prompted by love of country, as pure and as warm as ever glowed in any human breast, and the sequel proved that it was a golden idea, fruitful of a rich harvest.

It may not be out of place here to pause for a moment, to consider the net result of the tour I had undertaken all over India. For the first time under British rule, India, with its varied races and religions, had been brought upon the same platform for a common and united effort. Thus was it demonstrated, by an object-lesson of impressive significance, that, whatever might be our differences in respect of race and language, or social and religious institutions, the people of India could combine and unite for the attainment of their common political ends. The lesson thus learnt was to be confirmed and deepened by subsequent events to which I shall refer later on, and it found its culminating expression in the Congress movement. The ground was thus prepared for this great national and unifying movement. The public men of the time were not forgetful of the lesson thus taught; and a deputation of the Puna Sarvajanik Sabha, which visited Calcutta in 1878, pointedly referred to it at a conference held in the rooms of the British Indian Association, as opening the way for the united political efforts of an awakened India.

Sir Henry Cotton in his book, *New India,* which at the time created a unique sensation, thus referred to my tour:

'The educated classes are the voice and brain of the country. The Bengalee Babus now rule public opinion from Peshawar to Chittagong; and, although the natives of North-Western India are immeasurably behind those of Bengal in education and in their sense of political independence, they are gradually becoming as amenable as their brethren of the lower provinces, to intellectual control and guidance. A quarter of a century ago there was no trace of this; the idea of any Bengalee influence in the Punjab would have been a conception incredible to Lord Lawrence, to a Montgomery, or a Macleod; yet it is the case that during the past year the tour of a Bengalee lecturer, lecturing in English in Upper India, assumed the character of a triumphal progress; and at the present moment the name of Surendra Nath Banerjea excites as much énthusiasm among the rising generation of Multan as in Dacca.'

The All-India Memorial on the Civil Service question was addressed to the House of Commons. It was a memorial that sought to obtain a modification of the orders of the Secretary of State for India, by raising the limit of age for the open competitive examination to twenty-two years, the maximum limit now in force, and it contained a further prayer for simultaneous examinations in India as well as in England. The Memorial might have been despatched by post to the House of Commons as had been done in similar cases in the past. But a new idea had taken possession of the public mind. We had brought all India upon the same platform upon a public question that concerned the entire educated community; and we felt that so unique a demonstration should find its suitable expression through the voice of an Indian representative explaining to British audiences this pressing grievance of his countrymen. I was asked to be our delegate to England. I had to decline it for reasons that were apparent on the surface. In England, in view of my antecedents, my advocacy for the wider employment of my countrymen in a service from which I had been removed, would be liable to misconstruction. The choice of the Indian Association fell upon Mr. Lalmohan Ghose, and Mr. Lalmohan Ghose's phenomenal success in his mission fully justified the selection. His marvellous gifts of oratory were unknown to us, for he had never before taken to public life as a serious occupation; and when they were displayed in a manner that extorted the admiration of his audience, among whom was the greatest of living orators, John Bright, the revelation was a bewildering and an agreeable surprise. Carnot took credit for discovering Napoleon while the latter was yet an unknown young subaltern. The leaders of the Indian Association warmly congratulated themselves on having discovered one who was the first Indian to stand for Parliamentary honours, and who was destined to occupy a leading place in the ranks of our public life.

But a deputation to England was a costly affair. There were of course the prophets of evil who, Cassandra-like, told us that the money would be wasted and that the deputation would prove futile. Our success in the Civil Service agitation all over India had inspired us with confidence; and we were in no mood to listen to the counsels of timidity. I applied myself to the task of collecting subscriptions; and in less than six months' time I had raised the necessary funds, chiefly among our middle class people.

The only substantial sum that we obtained was from the Maharani Swarnamoyee. I fortified myself with a letter from Babu Bankim Chunder Chatterjee, the great Bengalee novelist, who evinced the utmost sympathy with the whole movement. Armed with this letter and accompanied by my indefatigable friend, Babu Dwarakanath Ganguli, we called upon Rai Rajib Lochan Rai Bahadur, manager of the Maharani Swarnamoyee's estate, at his house at Berhampore. The old man received us with kindness, but he promised us only one-half of what we wanted. We thanked him, of course, though we made it clear that we expected more. We took leave of him, and, as we were about to step into the street from his house, he summoned us back and said, 'I have reconsidered the matter and promise the whole amount you want'. We thanked him very heartily and left his house, blessing him and the Maharani Swarnamoyee. This was the first and last time that I met Rajib Lochan Rai. The present generation knows him not. Soon his memory will pass out of the public recollection. But if the Maharani Swarnamoyee was, during her lifetime, known as the 'Lady Bountiful' of Cossimbazar, Rai Rajib Lochan was the inspirer of her beneficence, the power behind the throne. He it was who rescued the Cossimbazar Estate from forfeiture, and under his wise counsels the Maharani Swarnamoyee applied its vast resources to acts of private charity and public usefulness, which during her lifetime made her name a household word in Bengal.

I feel tempted to quote in this place an instance that illustrates the catholicity of her beneficence, which rose superior to all considerations of creed and colour. An Afghan merchant from Ghazni came and sought my help to recover certain moneys that he claimed from Government for supplying camels during the Afghan War of 1878. He came to me as a pauper and indeed a ruined man. He had lost his case and he had not even money enough to enable him to return home. I estimated the cost of the return journey to Ghazni at Rs. 150; and I applied to the Maharani for the money, telling her the whole story. She sent me Rs. 150, and the poor Afghan returned home, rejoicing and blessing the Maharani.

The money having been raised for the purpose, Mr. Lalmohan

4

Ghose was placed in charge of the Civil Service Memorial to Parliament, and was deputed to England as the representative of the Indian Association.

Mr. Lalmohan Ghose's work may be said to open a new chapter in our history, in the potentialities it disclosed of what might be done by Indian deputations to England. He set to work with resolute energy, and he received valuable help from Mr. Chesson, Secretary of the Aborigines Protection Society, and from Sir David Wedderburn, brother of Sir William Wedderburn, who is perhaps less known to the present generation than his distinguished brother, though he was one of the earliest to suggest representative government for India, and I had the honour of corresponding with him on the subject. A great meeting was held at Willis's Rooms under the presidency of John Bright. Mr. Ghose spoke with a power and eloquence that excited the admiration of all, and evoked the warmest tribute from the President.

The effect of that meeting was instantaneous. Within twenty-four hours of it, there were laid on the table of the House of Commons, the Rules creating what was subsequently known as the Statutory Civil Service. Under the Parliamentary Statute of 1870, the Government of India were empowered, subject to rules that were to be framed, to make direct appointments of natives of India of proved merit and ability to the Covenanted Civil Service. For over seven years the Government of India had slept over the matter. But so great was the impression created by the demonstration at Willis's Rooms, having behind it the sentiment of united India, that the Rules, which were only four in number and had been delayed for seven years, were published within twenty-four hours of that meeting.

Thus the deputation of an Indian to England voicing India's grievances was attended with an unexpected measure of success; and the experiment was in future years tried again and again, confirming the wisdom and foresight of those who had conceived the idea and carried it out. Indeed, Mr. Lalmohan Ghose was, soon after his return to India, again deputed to England by the Indian Association. It was during his stay on this occasion that he stood as a candidate for Parliamentary election in the Liberal interest; and if it were not for the Irish vote that went against him, almost at the last moment, he would have been entitled to the high distinction reserved for India's Grand Old Man, Mr. Dadabhai

Naoroji, of being the first Indian Member of Parliament. At any rate he prepared the ground and was a pioneer in the cause.

Long afterwards, in 1890, when I visited Deptford, Mr. Lalmohan Ghose's constituency, to address a public meeting upon Indian questions, I found that there was a kindly remembrance of him, among his old friends and supporters. His genius and eloquence had made an abiding impression upon all who had heard him or had come within the reach of his personal influence. To the people of India the early death of such a man was a catastrophe. I had known him since 1869, and for forty years we were united by ties of the closest friendship. In later years, ill-health and his growing infirmities had somewhat weaned him from public life; but his interest in public affairs never waned, and, whenever he took part in them, his judgment was as clear and his utterance as emphatic as ever.

6

Reactionary Government and its Consequences

Lord Salisbury Secretary of State – the Vernacular Press Act – the silence of Lord Lytton – Dr. K. M. Banerjee – a letter to Gladstone – strong convictions a bar to promotion – Lord Ripon and local self-government – a broader vision and a higher platform.

IN THESE MEMOIRS I have not always followed the chronological order in developing the incidents of my life. Taking up a particular chapter, I have sometimes found it more convenient to close it and begin a new one, some of the events related being of prior date. The reduction of the age limit for the Indian Civil Service examination was but a part of a reactionary policy in relation to India that was associated with the administration of Lord Salisbury as Conservative Secretary of State for India. India is said to be beyond the pale of party politics. In the opinion of educated India it is a misfortune that it should be so; for we cannot forget it was because India was a potent factor in determining the issues of party politics that Warren Hastings was impeached, and that for the first time, to quote the language of Lord Morley in his Life of Burke, 'it was definitely proclaimed that Asiatics had their rights and Europeans their obligation under British rule'. The moral result of that impeachment was a striking gain for India. But since then things have changed, and both Liberals and Conservatives have, from the front benches, uttered the shibboleth that India lies outside party considerations. Sir Henry Fowler, when Secretary of State for India, declared from his place in Parliament that every member of Parliament was a member for India. The sentiment was greeted with cheers, it was palpably so noble and so instinct with the consciousness of duty to an unrepresented dependency. In India, however, it evoked a smile of incredulity. For we all know that what is everybody's business is nobody's business, and each year the truth is painfully impressed upon our minds when we read the accounts of the debates on the Indian Budget in the House of Commons and of the empty benches to which the oratory of the speakers is addressed. Both parties have been scrupulously impartial in their attitude of indifference towards India.

A great deal, indeed, depends upon the personality of the Secretary of State for India. The policy pursued in relation to India is dominated by his personal character and his personal sympathies, and is only partially moulded by the general drift of the policy of the party to which he belongs. Each minister is more or less supreme in his department, subject to the public opinion of the country as reflected in the prevailing tendencies of Parliament. That is our reading of the situation. It was Lord Derby, a Conservative Secretary of State, who gave us the great Proclamation of 1858. It was Sir Stafford Northcote (afterwards Earl Iddesleigh) who founded the State scholarships for the encouragement of Indian students seeking to complete their education in England. It was again a Liberal Secretary of State, the Duke of Argyll, who abolished them. It was a Conservative ministry that laid the beginnings of popular representation by giving us the reformed and expanded Legislative Councils under the Parliamentary Statute of 1892. Latterly, however, the Liberal party have really tried to be more or less true to their principles in the Government of India, and the most notable illustration of this view is afforded by Lord Morley's Reform Scheme of 1909, the modification of the Partition of Bengal, and the pledge of provincial autonomy given by the Despatch of August 25, 1911.

Lord Salisbury's regime as Secretary of State for India was distinctly reactionary. He was responsible for sending out to India as Viceroy, Lord Lytton, of whom the Marquis of Hartington (afterwards Duke of Devonshire) said, from his place in Parliament, that he was the very reverse of what an Indian Viceroy should be. His son, however, the present Lord Lytton, Governor of Bengal, is a ruler of a different type. Professing to be a Conservative, he is really an advanced Democrat, with genuine sympathy for Indian aspirations. Many years later, in the nineties of the last century, Lord Salisbury, when Prime Minister, sent out Lord Curzon, and the story of his viceroyalty is one that all the ingenuity of Mr. Lovat Fraser of *The Times* has failed to whitewash.

But I am, perhaps, anticipating coming events. I have already referred to the reduction of the limit of age for the Indian Civil Service and the agitation to which it gave rise. Lord Salisbury's Viceroy, Lord Lytton, gagged the Vernacular Press, and disarmed the population of British India. These two measures, the Arms Act and the Vernacular Press Act provoked widespread agitation, in which I took my humble share.

In the dark days of the Indian Mutiny, when the British Empire in India was really exposed to serious danger, Lord Canning and his advisers did not think it necessary to disarm the Indian population. The Afghan War in Lord Lytton's time (which, by the way, was a grievous blunder, the whole policy that dictated it having been undone) caused no serious excitement in India, none at any rate among the Hindu population, and little, or hardly any, among the Mohamedans, except perhaps on the frontiers. The Arms Act was unnecessary in the sense that it was not required as a measure of protection against internal revolt; it was mischievous because it made an irritating and invidious distinction between Europeans and Indians, a distinction that has recently been done away with. It inaugurated a policy of mistrust and suspicion, utterly undeserved and strongly resented by our people, and it imposed upon us a badge of racial inferiority. We protested against it at the time. We appealed to Mr. Gladstone, and he supported our protest and condemned it and the Vernacular Press Act in his speeches in the Midlothian campaign; but, unhappily, when he became Prime Minister he did us only partial justice – he repealed the Vernacular Press Act, but the Arms Act he left untouched.

The Vernacular Press Act was passed at one and the same sitting of the Imperial Legislative Council in April, 1878. The measure was deemed to be so urgent that the country was not given time to discuss it. The rules of business of the Council were suspended, and it was passed on the very day that it was introduced. In times of excitement bureaucracy is sometimes apt to avoid discussion in the belief that publicity would be fatal to its pre-ordained policy, and that a measure, once passed into law, and embodied in an administrative arrangement, would be regarded as a settled fact, never to be unsettled. Recent events have dissipated the delusion; and our present-day officials have in a variety of ways shown that they have a better conception of the potency of public opinion. The Vernacular Press Act itself has been repealed; the Partition of Bengal, the most settled of settled facts, has been unsettled. When an unpopular measure is passed, the public for the moment submit as to the stroke of an inevitable fate. They bide their time; they gather their forces; they renew the attack, and the idols of the bureaucracy are swept away from their places of worship, and remain only as enduring monuments of administrative unwisdom and the waste of administrative energy and resource.

The Vernacular Press Act came upon the educated community as a bolt from the blue; but that something of the kind was coming had long been anticipated. To the Delhi Assemblage of 1877 the Press was invited. I attended the Delhi Assemblage as the correspondent of the *Hindoo Patriot,* then the leading Indian paper in Bengal, under the editorship of that prince of Indian journalists, Kristo Das Pal. I was not connected with the Press at this time in any definite capacity, but, when I was in London in 1874-75, I had acted as the London correspondent of the *Hindoo Patriot.* To me it was a labour of love, a discipline and a training, and also an opportunity of showing my admiration and gratitude to one to whom I was bound by the ties of personal kindness and public duty. At Delhi I organized a Press Association consisting of all the members of the Indian Press who attended the Assemblage, and we waited in deputation upon the Viceroy with an address. I was the youngest member of the Deputation, but I represented the greatest Indian paper in the country. I stood upon my rights, as there was some difference of opinion as to who should be our spokesman; and to me was accorded the position of the head of the Deputation. I read the address. We had no casket, for we could get none made at Delhi within the time allotted. In the address we made a pointed reference to the report about the coming restrictions on the Press, and we expressed the hope that the liberties so long enjoyed might be continued. The Viceroy, as might have been expected, was reticent and said nothing in reply to this part of the address. We felt that we had done our duty in communicating our hopes and fears, and for the time the matter ended there.

Within less than fifteen months, the Vernacular Press all over India, save that of Madras, was muzzled. In the Council Chamber not a single dissentient voice was raised. Maharaja Sir Jotindra Mohon Tagore, who was then a member of the Imperial Legislative Council, had been, so the report went, sent for and spoken to by the Viceroy, and he voted with the Government. The *Hindoo Patriot* wrote against the measure, but not with the warmth that usually characterized its patriotic utterances. Maharaja Sir Jotindra Mohon Tagore was one of the most prominent members of the British Indian Association; and his vote hampered the independent judgement of that body. They could not disavow him, one of their most trusted colleagues. I have no desire to justify the Maharaja's vote on that occasion. But in judging of a public man acting in circumstances of extreme difficulty we must endeavour to place ourselves in his position and recognise his difficulties and his environment. Be it noted that public opinion was not so strong then as it now is, and that, so recently as during Lord Minto's Viceroyalty, the Indian members of the Imperial Legislative Council, with two honourable exceptions, supported a Press Act (now repealed), in one sense a far more drastic measure than the Act for which the Maharaja had voted. Nor should the fact be overlooked that the Maharaja, subject to the limitations of his position, was thoroughly patriotic and supported public movements whenever he could. His vote at the Council meeting was no doubt indefensible, but it admits of palliation. In judging of the honoured dead, let us weigh the good with the evil; in his case the good certainly preponderates.

Be that as it may, the educated community in Bengal was roused to a sense of anxiety and alarm at the Vernacular Press Act, and the manner of its enactment. The feeling was deepened by the inaction of the British Indian Association and of some of our leading men. It was fortunate that the Indian Association had been formed five years before, and that there was this organization to voice the sentiments of the middle class. We were resolved to do all that lay in our power to bring about the repeal of the Press Act. I went about personally canvassing our leading men. I well remember the discouragement I met with from more than one quarter. A Brahmo leader who shall be nameless said to me, 'Mr. Lethbridge, the Press Commissioner, has seen me on the subject. We had a long talk. I have a responsible position to maintain; I cannot join you'. Another leading man, whom I saw, said to me, 'I wish you all success; but we cannot help you'. Such was the cold reception that we met with amongst those upon whose help and co-operation in this matter we felt we had a right to count.

Far different was the attitude of some of our Christian friends, including Dr. K. M. Banerjee and the Rev. Dr. K. S. Macdonald of the Free Church of Scotland. From the very first, they were with us and encouraged and helped us. The Rev. Krishna Mohan Banerjee (better known as K. M. Banerjee) was among the earliest Indian converts to Christianity. A scholar and a man of letters, it was not till late in life that he began to take an active part in politics. He was associated with the Indian League and subsequently became President of the Indian Association. Once thrown into the vortex of public life, he was drawn into its deeper currents. He joined the Corporation and became an active member of that body. He was then past sixty; and though growing years had deprived him of the alertness of youth, yet in the keenness of his interest, and in the vigour and outspokenness of his utterances, he exhibited the ardour of the youngest recruit to our ranks. Never was there a man more uncompromising in what he believed to be the truth, and hardly was there such amiability combined with such strength and firmness.

It is this type of character that I am afraid is fast disappearing from our midst. The suavity and old-world manners of our people are becoming rare, while the militant aggressiveness of the West is usurping its place. Dr. Banerjee threw himself heart and soul into the movement, and his association with it and that of the Rev. Dr. Macdonald gave it a non-sectarian and cosmopolitan character. The cry of political movements being seditious had not then been raised; but it was a distinct source of strength and inspiration to us that we had with us these two highly-honoured representatives of the Christian community of Calcutta in what was the first great political demonstration of the middle class community in Bengal.

The Town Hall was secured, and the day of the public meeting was fixed. Here an incident occurred that is worth recording. On the day fixed for the public meeting, information was received in Calcutta that, in view of the possibility of the outbreak of War with Russia, Disraeli, who was then Prime Minister, had directed the despatch of six thousand Indian troops to Malta. As a matter of fact, war did not break out, but this was one of those political fireworks in which the imaginative genius of the semi-Oriental Premier delighted to indulge. The announcement made a great impression in Calcutta. It was the talk of the town and of the Calcutta Bar Library. It was seriously suggested to Mr. Ananda Mohan Bose by his lawyer friends of the Bar Library that the Town Hall meeting should be postponed. A hint was given to him that serious consequences might follow, and a suggestion of a criminal prosecution was made, if we persisted in holding the meeting, in spite of the uncertain situation in Europe. Mr. Ananda Mohan Bose hurried to my house. It was then three in the afternoon; the meeting was to be held at five o'clock. We discussed the matter. I said that it was one of the first great demonstrations of the Indian Association and of the middle class party in Bengal, and that, if it were to be postponed, it would never again be held. The people would lose faith in us, and it would mean the beginning of the end. I added that our constituents were the people. As for the consequences, my friend, who was a lawyer, and I agreed that nothing serious need be apprehended, so long as we were moderate and kept within constitutional bounds. We decided to hold the meeting and face the consequences, whatever they might be.

It was one of the most successful meetings ever held in Calcutta. It sounded the death-knell of the Vernacular Press Act, and, what is even more important, it disclosed the growing power of the middle class, who could act with effect for the protection of their interests, even though the wealthier classes were lukewarm, and official influence was openly arrayed against them. It was a lesson that the middle class of Bengal never forgot, and which they have since utilized in many useful directions. It indeed marked a definite and progressive stage in national evolution; and was the creation of the builders of the Indian Association.

The agitation against the Vernacular Press Act was continued. The Indian Association addressed a letter to Mr. Gladstone, expressing their gratitude to him for his support of the liberty of the Press in India. The draft of the letter was mine. The Rev. Dr. K. M. Banerjee revised it. It elicited an autograph reply from the Right Hon. gentleman, which is still preserved among the archives of the Association. When in 1909 I visited the Oxford Union along with other members of the Imperial Press Conference, I was shown a record of the proceedings of the Union in Mr. Gladstone's own handwriting. He was then Secretary or President of the Union, I forget which. The writing was fine, clear and bold. The letter in the possession of the Indian Association is altogether a different specimen of handwriting, bearing traces of the change that age had wrought.

One of the earliest acts of Lord Ripon's administration was the repeal of the Vernacular Press Act. It is interesting to notice how some of those who had zealously upheld the measure were now equally zealous in supporting its repeal. The discipline of the Civil Service is one of its notable characteristics. Consistency is no part of its creed. It obeys the lead given by its seniors and elders with scrupulous fidelity. We have had a recent and somewhat notable illustration of this in its attitude in regard to the modification of the Partition of Bengal. The modification of the Partition was strongly resented by the Bengal Civilians. It was felt more or less as a blow aimed at the prestige of the Service. But among those who signed the Despatch of the 25th August, 1911, recommending the modification, was a prominent Bengal Civilian who had identified himself with the working of the Partition and with a well-known circular letter, which was one of the earliest indications of the birth of the reactionary policy that followed the Partition. The popular leaders have no quarrel with these tergiversations. But they note them as showing that strong convictions are perhaps a clog to official advancement in India, and those who change as the ruling official mind changes have the best prospects of official preferment.

Lord Ripon's assumption of the Viceroyalty was a relief to the Indian public. The reactionary administration of Lord Lytton had roused the public from its attitude of indifference and had given a stimulus to public life. In the evolution of political progress, bad rulers are often a blessing in disguise. They help to stir a community into life, a result that years of agitation would perhaps have failed to achieve. They call into being organized efforts which not only sweep away their bad measures, but create that public life and spirit which survives for all time to come, and is the surest guarantee of future and abiding progress. Lord Lytton was a benefactor, without intending to be one; and, more recently, Lord Curzon was a benefactor in the same sense, but perhaps on a larger scale.

We in India knew little or nothing about Lord Ripon or his antecedents. There were two circumstances that were in his favour. He was the nominee of Mr. Gladstone, who had thoroughly indentified himself with the popular view in India regarding the Vernacular Press Act, and he was a convert to Roman Catholicism and had suffered for his faith. We remembered what *The Times* wrote of him, when, giving up his great position in the social and public life of England, he deliberately faced the prospect of ruin by embracing the Roman Catholic faith. I was in England at the time and I remember the great stir it caused. I imagine differences of creed gave rise to stronger feelings in those days than they are now apt to evoke. *The Times* had a leading article in which it prophesied that Lord Ripon was a lost man. But in those days educated India, following the dictum of Cobden, approved what *The Times* disapproved; and we welcomed Lord Ripon as a ruler who had suffered for the faith that was in him. Events showed that we were fully justified; for one of the very first things that he said on assuming his great office was that he had it in charge from Her Majesty the Queen-Empress to look to the municipal institutions of the country; for there the political education of the people really began.

This declaration of a great policy was an open invitation to those who were working for the uplift of their country to co-operate with the Government for its realization. We of the Indian Association at once set to work. We issued a circular letter, and we sent round delegates inviting the rate-payers of our mofussil towns to move the Government for the re-organization of their municipalities upon a popular and elective basis. I myself visited various parts of Bengal, including Bhagalpore, Monghyr (now in Behar), Rajshahi, Bogra and Pabna. Public meetings were held in these places, at which I spoke. Our delegates visited many other centres in the interior. In those days there was no Criminal Investigation Department and the police did not think that it was a part of their duty to dog the footsteps and watch the movements of political workers. Our work was therefore easy; and our countrymen everywhere received us with open arms.

Political work in the mofussil was then a new thing, and the new-born enthusiasm for political progress that we were able to evoke in the most distant parts of the province is one of the most pleasant and enduring reminiscences of my life. Everywhere the Bar lent us firm support, and the zemindars hardly ever failed us. The truth is that political work in those early days was not regarded with suspicion by the official classes; and the people, left to their own impulses and unhampered by the spirit of Non-co-operation, did their duty. Of course, it was impossible to visit every town or to send delegates to every considerable place in Bengal. From such places as we could not visit we obtained written opinions on the subject of Local Self-government. Having thus ascertained the views of the country on the Viceroy's proposals, we drafted a memorial and convened a public meeting at the Town Hall.

We took advantage of this demonstration to thank the Viceroy for the repeal of the Vernacular Press Act, and to press for the abolition of the Arms Act. I moved the resolution on the subject of Local Self-government, which was in these terms:

'That this Meeting feels deeply grateful to His Excellency the Viceroy, for his recent Resolution, which seeks to confer upon the people of this country the inestimable boon of Local Self-government; and ventures to express its earnest and confident hope that the measures adopted by His Excellency for the purpose will be of such a character as to secure a fair and satisfactory working of the scheme. And with this view this Meeting would respectfully beg to make the following recommendations: (1) That the constitution of the Local Boards and of the Municipalities should be based on the elective system; (2) that their Chairman should be an officer elected by them, and on no account be the Magistrate-Collector of the district; (3) that the functions and powers vested in the existing Committees should be increased in view of their amalgamation in the proposed Local Boards.'

It will be seen that the views set forth in this resolution formed the main features of the resolutions on Local Self-government issued by Lord Ripon. They urged (1) the constitution of the local bodies upon a popular and elective basis, (2) the enlargement of their powers, and (3) the election of their chairman by the local bodies themselves. These were the basic principles of the Resolutions of the Government of India. The meeting was held on February 18, 1881; the resolutions of the Government of India were issued in October, 1881, and May, 1882. Here was a conspicuous instance of almost perfect accord between the official and the popular view, and be it noted that it was Lord Ripon who soon after, as Chancellor of the University of Calcutta, declared that the time was fast approaching when popular opinion even in India would become the irresistible and unresisted master of the Government. No Viceroy did more to promote this blessed consummation. The impress of his policy has left its enduring mark upon Indian administration, and more than one Viceroy has essayed to walk in his footsteps.

But the question of Local Self-government formed only a part of the larger movement for the strengthening of public opinion and the enthronement of the popular view. Even before we had taken up the question of Local Self-government, the attention of the Bengal leaders had been drawn to what indeed is the most vital of our problems, namely, representative government for India. The Indian Association had appointed a committee, and I had already placed myself in communication on the subject with Mr. Shaw, late of the Bombay Civil Service, and Sir David Wedderburn.

In this connexion it may not be altogether out of place to notice the steady development of our national aspirations. In the sixties of the last century, and even earlier, the efforts of our national leaders were directed to securing for the people of India an adequate share of the higher offices of trust and responsibility under the Government. The Queen's Proclamation of 1858 had stirred their ambitions in this direction, and in season and out of season they pressed for the redemption of the pledges contained in that message. In Western India, the movement was led by Mr. Nowroji Furdoonji and Mr. Dadabhai Naoroji, India's Grand Old Man. In Bengal, the movement was represented by the British Indian Association, and found ardent advocates in men like Kristo Das Pal, Rajendra Lal Mitter, Romanath Tagore, Degumbar Mitter, and others.

But the ground was now to be shifted. A higher platform appeared in view, and a brighter vision presented itself to the gaze of educated India. There is evolution in all things, even in the slow movements of public life. The efforts of the last few years had stirred a strange and hitherto-unfelt awakening among our people, and had created new hopes and aspirations. It was not enough that we should have our full share of the higher offices, but we aspired to have a voice in the councils of the nation. There was the bureaucracy. For good or evil, it was there. We not only wanted to be members of the bureaucracy and to leaven it with the Indian element, but we looked forward to controlling it, and shaping and guiding its measures, and eventually bringing the entire administration under complete popular domination. It was a new departure hardly noticed at the time, but fraught with immense potentialities. Along with the development of the struggle for place and power to be secured to our countrymen, there came gradually but steadily to the forefront the idea that this was not enough, that it was part, but not even the most vital part, of the programme for the political elevation of our people. The pursuit of high ideals has an elevating effect upon the public mind. Great as is the gain when the object is attained, its indirect results, in the widening of our vision, in the strengthening of our moral fibre, in the all-round impulse that it communicates to national activities, are even more enduring, more pregnant with unseen and undreamt-of possibilities for the future. The demand for representative government was now definitely formulated, and it was but the natural and legitimate product of the public activities that had preceded it.

7

Journalism

Kristo Das Pal and the *Hindoo Patriot* – I become proprietor and editor of the *Bengalee*, January 1, 1879 – Ashutosh Biswas – Sir Ashley Eden.

HERE I MUST INTERRUPT for a moment the narrative of these political activities, in which I had my part and share, to refer to a personal undertaking which I believe greatly helped our political work.

The Press in India in the seventies of the last century was not as vocal or as powerful as it is to-day; but even then it was a great instrument of propagandism. I felt that an organ of our own was needed to help us in our political work. I had before me the example of the *Hindoo Patriot*, which, under the editorship of Kristo Das Pal, had become the first Indian newspaper in Bengal, and perhaps in India, exercising great influence over the people and the Government.

I could start an independent paper of my own or take up an old one. I preferred the latter. I have always preferred to build upon old foundations. Throughout my life and in all my undertakings, I have fought shy of the new. My faith, perhaps an inherited Brahminical instinct, is inveterate in the old. I have always taken my stand upon old foundations. I have never indeed deemed them perfect, but I have preferred remodelling the old to starting new organizations.

A chapter of accidents favoured me in providing myself with an organ of my own. The *Bengalee* newspaper was at that time under the editorship of Babu Bacharam Chatterjee. He was also its proprietor. The paper had gone down very low, the number of subscribers not being over two hundred. Negotiations were opened between him and myself through a common friend, the late Babu Romanath Law. Babu Romanath Law's name is now wellnigh forgotton. But he was a well-known solicitor of the High Court during the sixties and the seventies of the last century. We have now a crowd of Indian solicitors of the High Court; but in those days it was Girish Chunder Banerjee (Mr. W. C. Bonnerjea's father) and Romanath Law, who vindicated the capacity of our countrymen for this branch of the legal profession. He was as good a lawyer as he was a true and an earnest friend; and through him the negotiations were brought to a successful termination and I became the proprietor and editor of the *Bengalee* from January 1, 1879. I paid Rs. 10 to Babu Bacharam Chatterjee, as consideration money for the goodwill of the paper. I owe it to his memory to say that he would not ask for more nor accept more. Indeed, he wanted to make a free gift of the paper, but, as Babu Romanath Law pointed out that some money had to be paid in order to give legal validity to the transaction, he accepted the small pecuniary consideration to which I have referred. I paid Rs. 1,600 for the press, borrowing from a friend Rs. 700 for the purpose, which I repaid after a couple of years without interest, as my friend would charge none. I mention these facts, trivial as they may seem, in order to record my appreciation of the good wishes and the unspoken blessings of many, amid which the *Bengalee* newspaper came under my charge.

Not the shadow of a desire to start a business transaction was present in my mind. All that I had in view, the sole inspiring impulse, was to serve the public ends with which I had completely identified myself. Indeed, having become the proprietor of the paper, I offered it to the Indian Association, undertaking to edit the paper for nothing, the Association paying all other expenses. As the *Hindoo Patriot* was the property of the British Indian Association, the Indian Association might, I thought, place itself in the same relation in regard to the *Bengalee*. But the difficulty was that the paper was a losing concern, and the Association, young as it was and limited as to its funds, felt that it would be inexpedient to incur the pecuniary liability of managing the *Bengalee*. Judging in the light of subsequent events, I must say that the decision of the Association was a wise one. No political organization with its own special work and its multifarious duties could have controlled with anything like efficiency a newspaper with the wide and increasing circulation of the *Bengalee*. But I am anticipating events.

When I became editor and proprietor of the *Bengalee* in January, 1879, it was a weekly newspaper. With the exception of the *Indian Mirror*, all our newspapers in Bengal, including the most influential, were weekly. The craving for fresh news was then not general; and Indian readers for the most part were content to have a weekly supply of news and comments thereon. I remember speaking at the time to the head master of a Government high school, a man of education and culture, who said to me that it took him a week's time to go through the *Bengalee* (then a weekly paper), and that if it were a daily paper he would not know what to do with it. That represented the temper of the Bengalee mind, say, thirty years ago. The daily paper is a more recent development, but it has so completely superseded the weekly that the latter has no chance of a wide circulation except as an adjunct to a daily paper.

In the early stages of my journalistic venture I was greatly assisted by the disinterested labours of my lamented friend, the late Ashutosh Biswas. I discovered him at a public meeting held at the London Missionary Society's Institution at Bhowanipore, where I delivered an address on Chaitanya. He spoke at that meeting. I was greatly impressed with what he said. The words were few; but they were eloquent, to the point, and came straight from the heart. They disclosed the man and the stuff that was in him. I invited him to see me; and our first acquaintance was the beginning of a friendship that only his tragic end dissolved. He called me his *guru;* it was no lip-deep profession. He was indeed a veritable disciple, following me with a fidelity and devotion rare in these days.

The paper used to be issued every Saturday morning, and we had to work during a good part of Friday night, correcting proofs, writing out copy if necessary, and giving directions to the printers. My friend was my companion, my colleague in this somewhat dreary work, from 1879 to the early part of 1884, when he began to help the *Guardian,* a weekly paper, which had just been started at Bhowanipore. Now that he is dead and gone, the victim of a tragic crime, I gratefully testify to the debt I owe to his memory.

With his rising practice at the Bar, my friend's interest in journalism became less keen and persistent than before, and latterly he ceased to have any connexion with it. But our personal relations continued to the last to be friendly and cordial, and, whenever I had need of legal help, I turned to him for advice and it was always cheerfully given. In politics he belonged to our party, and, while yet connected with the *Bengalee,* he went on a tour in Northern India to help the work of the Indian Association. It was the irony of fate that he should have been the victim of an anarchical outrage. The head and front of his offence was that, being engaged on the side of Government, he was helping the prosecution of the accused in what is known as the Alipore Bomb Case. He was one of the cleverest criminal lawyers of his day, and the accused had good reason to dread his legal skill and acumen. It is possibly this feeling that inspired the tragedy which

5

cost him his life, when an anarchist (who, by the way, was hardly able to use one of his arms) shot him dead within the precincts of the Magistrate's Court at Alipore. He had received threatening letters, and the authorities had offered him police protection. But he declined it, believing, fatalist that he was, that it was not in the power of any human agency to save him from what destiny had decreed.

Acute lawyer and sagacious man of the world that he was, there was in him a strange medley of orthodox and heterodox beliefs. Every Sunday he was a frequenter of the temple of Kali, where he performed his devotions; yet he never hesitated to dine with unorthodox people, and, if a dish were laid before him with a mixture of forbidden food, he would accept the unorthodox portion of the food without any objection. I mention this fact to show the sort of compromise that we meet with in Hindu society sometimes, when the forces of othodoxy are compelled to fraternize with those of the opposite school, and in a manner that would have been abhorrent to the men of the same faith in the last generation. The spirit of liberalism is marching apace even in an atmosphere of rigid and inflexible formulae. Hindu society is moving, steadily moving, adapting itself, though very slowly, to its environment.

However that may be, it was my pleasing duty and privilege to have been of some service to his family after his death. I personally introduced his sons to the late Sir Edward Baker, who was then Lieutenant-Governor, and was partly instrumental in securing from the Government a suitable provision for the family. Sir Edward Baker took the matter up with the generous warmth that always distinguished him when he had to deal with individual cases where a wrong had to be redressed or the generosity of a great Government had to be exhibited in an impressive manner.

My friend, Babu Ashutosh Biswas and myself continued to edit the paper. We made no profit, but we were able to pay our way. It was no longer a losing concern. It ceased to be so from the year I took it up. We paid off the small debt we had incurred in purchasing the printing-press, plant, etc., and we followed the usual journalistic rôle – criticizing, commenting, making friends, and not infrequently creating enemies. There is perhaps one event that I may notice before the occurrence of the contempt case in which the *Bengalee* was involved in 1883. Sir Ashley Eden was about to retire from the Lieutenant-Governorship of Bengal, and it was proposed by some of his friends and admirers to hold a demonstration in his honour at the Town Hall. Sir Ashley Eden was one of the ablest of the Lieutenant-Governors of Bengal. He was a Haileybury man and an official of the old type. He had many friends among the aristocracy and the Bengalee leaders of his time. He was on familiar terms with Maharaja Jotindra Mohon Tagore, and held Kristo Das Pal in great esteem. Let it also be said to his credit that in social life he made no distinction between Europeans and Indians, and it was during his time that Mr. B. L. Gupta of the Bengal Civil Service, who was then Presidency Magistrate of Calcutta, submitted the note that became the genesis of the Ilbert Bill controversy. If he had continued to be Lieutenant-Governor, I believe, he would have kept the Civil Service well in hand and the Bill would have had a different termination.

All this was to his credit, but he was a bureaucrat to the marrow of his bones, and had a profound distrust of all progressive institutions. Mr. Buckland tells us in his *Bengal under the Lieutenant-Governors* that Lord Ripon said of him that he had never known a man less likely to be led away by vague sentiment or mere theory than Sir Ashley Eden. This was only a euphemistic way of saying that he was singularly free from the domination of ideals, and that he had no higher conception of the duties of an administrator than to do the day's work and be satisfied with it. He was a strong supporter of the Vernacular Press Act and had no love for a free Press, or free institutions.

Of representative govenment he said that it was a sickly plant in its own native soil, and as to its being tried in India, that was out of the question.

A ruler with such ideas could not command either the affection or the esteem of the new school that had risen in Bengal, and which looked forward to the birth of a new India, with free and progressive institutions. To his personal friends he had endeared himself by bestowing on them, or on others on their recommendation, titles, distinctions and public offices. They were grateful to him. Their desire to honour him was natural; but they had no right to speak in the name of the community, who saw nothing in his administration to entitle him to the honour of a public demonstration. It was this line that I took up in the *Bengalee* and wrote ▪ series of articles. I made it quite clear that if a public meeting were held, there would be a protest against the public character of the demonstration. The hint was taken; and the Town Hall meeting, which was to have been called in the name of the public, resolved itself into 'a meeting of friends and admirers'. To this there could have been no objection, and there was none. The 'friends and admirers' of the retiring Lieutenant-Governor were at liberty to do what they pleased; and the public had no right to interfere or to protest. This was a notable triumph of middle class educated opinion in Bengal, which, it was evident, had now become a living force and had to be reckoned with.

8

The Contempt Case: Imprisonment

The leaderette in the *Bengalee* – prosecuted for contempt of court – public excitement – the trial – condemnation and imprisonment – demonstrations of sympathy; attitude of the *Statesman* – 'Good cometh out of evil' – a national Fund – my life in prison – my release.

THE NEXT INCIDENT in my journalistic career that I think should be placed on record is the Contempt Case, for which I was sent to prison for two months. I claim the honour (for such I deem it) of being the first Indian of my generation who suffered imprisonment in the discharge of a public duty. The Swarajists now make imprisonment a qualification for public service. Well, I claim that I possess it, even from their standpoint, and that I was qualified long before any one of them.

The facts of the Contempt Case are these. On April 2, 1883, the following leaderette appeared in the *Bengalee*:

'The Judges of the High Court have hitherto commanded the universal respect of the community. Of course, they have often erred, and have often grievously failed in the performance of their duties. But their errors have hardly ever been due to impulsiveness, or to the neglect of the commonest considerations of prudence or decency. We have now, however, amongst us a judge, who, if he does not actually recall to mind the days of Jeffreys and Scroggs, has certainly done enough, within the short time that he has filled the High Court Bench, to show how unworthy he is of his high office, and how by nature he is unfitted to maintain those traditions of dignity which are inseparable from the office of the judge of the highest Court in the land. From time to time we have in these columns adverted to the proceedings of Mr. Justice Norris. But the climax has now been reached, and we venture to call attention to the facts as they have been reported in the columns of a contemporary. The *Brahmo Public Opinion* is our authority, and the facts stated are as follows: Mr. Justice Norris is determined to set the Hooghly on fire. The last act of *zubberdusti* on his Lordship's part was the bringing of a *saligram*, a stone idol, into court for identification. There have been very many cases both in the late Supreme Court and the present High Court of Calcutta regarding the custody of Hindu idols, but the presiding deity of a Hindu household had never before this had the honour of being dragged into Court. Our Calcutta Daniel looked at the idol and said it could not be a hundred years old. So Mr. Justice Norris is not only versed in Law and Medicine, but is also a connoisseur of

Hindu idols. It is difficult to say what he is not. Whether the orthodox Hindus of Calcutta will tamely submit to their family idols being dragged into Court is a matter for them to decide, but it does seem to us that some public steps should be taken to put a quietus to the wild eccentricities of this young and raw Dispenser of Justice.

'What are we to think of a judge who is so ignorant of the feelings of the people and so disrespectful of their most cherished convictions, as to drag into Court, and then to inspect, an object of worship which only Brahmins are allowed to approach, after purifying themselves according to the forms of their religion? Will the Government of India take no notice of such a proceeding? The religious feelings of the people have always been an object of tender care with the Supreme Government.

'Here, however, we have a judge who, in the name of Justice, sets these feelings at defiance and commits what amounts to an act of sacrilege in the estimation of pious Hindus. We venture to call the attention of the Government to the facts here stated, but we have no doubt due notice will be taken of the conduct of the Judge.'

The leaderette was based on information that appeared in the now defunct newspaper, the *Brahmo Public Opinion*. The *Brahmo Public Opinion* was edited by the late Babu Bhubon Mohan Das (Mr. C. R. Das's father), a well-known solicitor of the High Court. As no contradiction appeared, I accepted the version as absolutely correct, especially in view of the fact that Babu Bhubon Mohan Das, being a solicitor and an officer of the Court, might naturally be presumed to be well informed on all matters in connexion with the High Court. I reproduced the substance of what appeared in the *Brahmo Public Opinion* and commented upon it.

Soon after I received a writ from the High Court to show cause why I should not be committed for Contempt of Court. The writ was served on me on May 2 and May 5 was fixed as the day for the hearing. The time was short; and my difficulty was that I could not get any barrister to take up the brief on my behalf. Mr. Monomohan Ghose was ill and confined to bed. Mr. W. C. Bonnerjea at last undertook to defend me, but on the distinct understanding that I should apologize and withdraw the reflections I had made on Mr. Justice Norris. As the comparison which I had suggested in the incriminating paragraph between him and Scroggs and Jeffreys was unfair and indefensible, written in a moment of heat and indignation, I readily consented.

On May 5, the case came on before a Full Bench consisting of five judges, among whom was Sir Romesh Chunder Mitter, and was presided over by the Chief Justice, the late Sir Richard Garth. I had moved from Calcutta to Barrackpore in 1880 and was living there at the time. I came down to attend the High Court that morning from my residence at Barrackpore. I told my wife when taking leave of her that I was likely to be sent to prison, and I came prepared for it with my bedding and the books that I wanted to read during my enforced leisure.

I was in Court by about half past ten. The Court premises and the environments were swarming with a surging crowd; and a large body of police, European and Indian, were in attendance. The student community had mustered in strong force, and among them I noticed some who rose to high distinction as servants of the Crown. In the demonstration that followed the passing of the sentence they took a leading part in a fashion common among young men all over the world, smashing windows and pelting the police with stones. One of those rowdy youths was Ashutosh Mukherjea, subsequently so well known as a judge of the High Court and as Vice-Chancellor of the Calcutta University. Another young man who was rowdy and broke the law was sent to prison for a week. His cell in the Presidency Jail was opposite mine; and every day he would make it a point to catch my eye in the early hours of the morning and salute me with a *pranam*. The young man, I understand, afterwards became a Sub-Registrar. Neither the Government nor he was the worse for this episode in his life. The mistake that is so often committed is to magnify such incidents and read into them a purpose and a meaning that they do not bear. Rowdyism of this kind committed now by a young man would, I fear, condemn him to lifelong exclusion from the service of Government. The struggle for equal rights had then just begun, and official feeling was perhaps somewhat more generous and less unrelenting than now. There are, however, happily growing signs of a return to the old days.

But from the streets adjoining the High Court let me turn to the Court-room where the judges were to assemble. It was densely crowded. Not an inch of space was left on the floor or in the galleries. I had to elbow my way along with my counsel. It was past eleven o'clock; but the judges had not yet come. They were closeted in the Chief Justice's room in close conference. We came to know afterwards what the conference was about. There was an eager discussion about the sentence to be passed. The majority of the judges, and they were Europeans, were for sentencing me to imprisonment. Mr. Justice Romesh Chunder Mitter insisted upon a fine only. The day before, so the report went, the Chief Justice had seen him at his private residence and had talked to him and argued with him, with a view to persuading him to agree with the majority, but all in vain. At the conference the arguments were repeated with the added weight of the personal authority of the other judges. But Mr. Justice Mitter remained unconvinced, relying on the precedent created in Taylor's case, where the Chief Justice, Sir Barnes Peacock, had deemed the infliction of a fine sufficient.

At last, when it was past half past eleven, the five judges appeared and took their seats on the Bench. The Chief Justice read out the judgment on behalf of the majority of his colleagues, putting in a slip, which was evidently a later production, that he and his colleagues disagreed with Mr. Justice Mitter. Mr. Justice Mitter then read out his dissenting judgment, after which the judges left the Court. The crowd in the Court-room slowly followed.

Outside in the streets, among the thousands that were gathered together, there were signs of excitement and even indignation. The prison-van was at the Court-gate ready for me; but, in view of the attitude of the crowd, I was conveyed in a private carriage, leaving the Court by the judges' entrance, and was taken by a roundabout way to the Presidency Jail. Mr. Larymore, the Superintendent of the jail, was present, expecting my arrival. Mr. Larymore was a warm-hearted Irishman. He and I were friends, for we had sat round the same table as Municipal Commissioners of Calcutta. He treated me with all the courtesy that his official position permitted.

At the time when I arrived at the Presidency Jail, it was not known whether I should be lodged in the civil or criminal side of the jail. Mr. Larymore was waiting for orders, but he had already given me to understand that, in case I had to be in the criminal jail, he would give me a separate cell and would not insist upon my putting on prison-dress. But these difficulties were soon set at rest. The order arrived that I was to be a civil prisoner; and Mr. Larymore gave me comfortable quarters in the upper storey of the civil jail. The same afternoon my friend, Mr. B. L. Gupta, who was then Presidency Magistrate of Calcutta, called on me to express his sympathy and to make me comfortable so far as lay in his power.

It is due to the prison authorities to say that, while in no way relaxing their rules, they treated me with courtesy and due regard to my feelings. I was never asked to go down to the muster, which was held in the yard every afternoon. It was sufficient for me to stand in the verandah. Visitors were allowed free access to me, and they were counted by scores every day, and my letters and telegrams were duly delivered to me. They were so numerous that, Mr. Larymore told me, he had to employ a special messenger for the purpose. My wife once came to see me, escorted by the venerable Robert Knight, editor of the *Statesman*. The *Statesman* wrote a series of articles condemning the sentence of imprisonment passed on me. The *Statesman* valiantly championed the cause of right and justice, and the Indian public showed their appreciation of Mr. Robert Knight's services by holding a public meeting and raising a fund to help him when involved in a defamation case brought against him by the Burdwan Raj. I was a speaker at that meeting.

The news of my imprisonment created a profound impression not only in Calcutta, and in my own province, but throughout India. In Calcutta, on the day of my imprisonment, the Indian shops were closed and business was suspended in the Indian part of the town, not by order, or by an organized effort, but under a spontaneous impulse which moved the whole community. The students went into mourning. The demonstrations held in Calcutta were so large that no hall could find space for the crowds that sought admittance: the bazaars were utilized for the purpose. Then was first started the practice of holding open-air meetings, and these were demonstrations not confined to the upper ten thousand or the educated classes: the masses joined them in their thousands. Hindu feeling had been touched. A Hindu god had been brought to a court of law; and, whatever the legal merits of the case might have been (and with these the general public do not usually trouble themselves), the orthodox Hindu felt, rightly or wrongly, that there had been an act of desecration. The educated community, though sympathizing with their orthodox countrymen, were impelled by motives of a different order. The Ilbert Bill controversy, in which Mr. Justice Norris had unfortunately taken a prominent part, unbecoming his judicial position, had roused them to a fever-heat of excitement. They further felt that a sentence of a fine, as in the Taylor Case, cited by Mr. Justice Mitter, would have been sufficient, and they scented in the punishment of imprisonment inflicted on me a flavour of party feeling unworthy of the traditions of the highest Judicial Bench.

In the whole course of my public life, I have never witnessed, except in connexion with the agitation for the modification of the

Partition of Bengal, an upheaval of feeling so genuine and so wide-spread as that which swept through Bengal in 1883. Public meetings of sympathy for me, and of protest against the judgment of the High Court, were held in almost every considerable town. So strong was the feeling that in some cases even Government servants took part in them and suffered for it. But these demonstrations were not of the evanescent order. They left an enduring impress on the public life of the province.

When the public mind has been roused by some great event, it struggles for expression in all directions, in melodious songs, in passionate utterances in the Press and from the platform, and in enterprises which bear on them the ineffaceable mark of daring and originality. This is illustrated in the great events of history, in the stimulus to national life and enterprise that was witnessed in the Elizabethan epoch. Poetry, original research, commercial and naval enterprise for the discovery of new worlds, all went apace. The soul of England was bodied forth in them all. The beginnings of such a stimulus, though on a much smaller scale, were witnessed in the upheaval that sprang from the Contempt Case. It gave an impetus to journalism. The *Sulava Samachar* had been started as a pice paper by the late Keshub Chunder Sen, but the movement for cheap journalism had languished. Now, however, it received an awakened impulse in the passionate desire for news. Babu Jogendranath Bose started the *Bangabasi* as a pice paper. His example was followed by Babu Kristo Kumar Mitter. The *Bangabasi* and the *Sanjibani* still continue to hold an important place in the journalistic world of Bengal.

As our public meetings now began to be attended by thousands, so our cheap vernacular papers for the first time counted their readers by thousands. But there were indeed wider developments which followed in the track of this great outburst of public feeling. One of them was an object for which I had striven so hard, and which educated India had begun to place in the forefront of its programme. The Contempt Case, as it was called, operated as a unifying influence, strengthening the growing bonds of fellowship and good feeling between the different Indian provinces. Meetings of sympathy with me in my misfortune were held in many of the great towns of India – Lahore, Amritsar, Agra, Fyzabad, Poona, and other important centres. A well-known writer under the *nom de plume* of Setji Sorabji thus referred to these demonstrations in an open letter addressed to *Gup and Gossip* of June 18, 1884:

'Last year, at one of the public meetings held in Upper India for your liberty, I heard a Kashmiri pundit, a man of years and honours, but incapable of construing one word of English into his mother-tongue – heard this grave and elderly man sob while he referred to your imprisonment. Tears, salt and bitter tears choked his utterance as he cried, "What have they done with our dearest brother? Our Surendranath is in jail." And a like passion of agony was wrung from every Indian heart, and universal mourning was observed throughout the land.'

The late Ananda Mohan Bose, referring to the political consequences of my imprisonment, thus observed in the Report of the Indian Association for 1883:

'That "good cometh out of evil" was never more fully illustrated than in this notable event. It has now been demonstrated, by the universal outburst of grief and indignation which the event called forth, that the people of the different Indian provinces have learnt to feel for one another; and that a common bond of unity and fellow-feeling is rapidly being established among them. And Babu Surendranath Banerjea has at least one consolation, that his misfortune awakened, in a most marked form, a manifestation of that sense of unity among the different Indian races, for the accomplishment of which he has so earnestly striven and not in vain.'

Babu Tarapada Banerjee of Krishnagar started the idea of a National Fund as a memento of my imprisonment. It was a fruitful conception, for since then other national funds have been started for national purposes. The amount collected came to about Rs. 20,000; and the subscribers at a meeting decided to make it over to the Indian Association of Calcutta for the promotion of political work. The amount is small, but it has been found helpful to have a permanent fund at our disposal, a sort of nucleus drawing to it funds from other sources and inspiring public workers with the belief that the sinews of war would never be wanting. This fund was most useful in the anti-Partition agitation, when the attitude of Government and the doctrine of the 'settled fact', paraded *ad nauseam,* had the effect of deterring our wealthy men from contributing to a cause with which in their heart of hearts they sympathized, but which they dared not openly support for fear of incurring the displeasure of the authorities.

It is right and proper that I should stop here for a moment to pay a tribute to the memory of an old friend and co-worker, Babu Tarapada Banerjee. For years together he was the most prominent figure in the public life of Krishnagar, the supporter and sometimes the inaugurator of public movements in that ancient town. His death was a heavy loss to the national party, and it will be long before a successor appears, wielding his influence and fired with his courage and enthusiasm. It is not always that a public man, living in a provincial town, is able to rise to fame and distinction, or acquire for himself a name beyond his parochial or local limits. But the history of nation-building in Bengal would be an inadequate record if it omitted to mention the work accomplished by men like Tarapada Banerjee, Ambika Churn Majumder, Baikuntanath Sen, Aswini Kumar Dutt, Anath Bandhu Guha, Ananda Chunder Roy, Kissory Mohan Chowdhury and others. They may not all be known to fame in the same degree; but they have all worked in the national cause in spite of many difficulties and drawbacks, and some have suffered. They have laid their contemporaries under a heavy obligation, which should at least be duly acknowledged by those who were their colleagues.

My term of imprisonment began on May 5, 1883; and I was released on July 4, a great day in the world's history, the day of American Independence, of which my friends took the utmost advantage. I suffered as a 'defender of the faith'. It was quite well known that orthodox Hinduism did not appeal to me, that my ideals were progressive, and that my social life was in conformity with those ideals. That one with my views and convictions should stand forth in defence of the cherished feelings of my orthodox countrymen and should suffer for it, was deemed to be an act of no mean merit. The sentiment was indeed universal. When a great wave of feeling sweeps overs the public mind, it breaks its barriers and rushes into channels beyond its scope. The educated community, restive and uneasy, swayed by the feelings evoked by the Ilbert Bill controversy, and perhaps not unmindful of my own public services, shared the general indignation. My personal friends were grieved and mortified. The sentence of imprisonment seemed to them to be the climax of a wrong done to me. My friend, Mr. B. L. Gupta, was then Presidency Magistrate of Calcutta. As soon as he heard the sentence, he stopped the work of the Court and came straight to the Presidency Jail to see me. Sympathy, so open and undisguised on the part of so high an officer of Government, with its implication of tacit disapproval of the judicial sentence of the highest Court in the land, was the subject of talk and even of public comment. One of the leading newspapers, which then enjoyed the reputation of a semi-official publication, called attention to this incident. But these little things never disturbed the equanimity of my friend, Mr. Behari Lal Gupta; and with confidence undimmed and his bright eyes fixed on the radiant side of life, he trudged along the path of official preferment till he became an officiating judge of a High Court in British India and Prime Minister in an Indian State.

In prison, I was treated as a first-class misdemeanant. I was allowed to read and write as I liked. I continued writing for the *Bengalee*. My letters and telegrams were delivered to me unopened, and were allowed to pass the prison-gates without inspection. There was no restriction as to the number of visitors who were to see me. Presents of fruits (for it was the mango season) and eatables were passed on to me without any objection of any kind, and the Superintendent did all he could to alleviate the hardships of my confinement. After the muster-roll had been called, the gates were closed and visitors were not allowed. I passed the evenings in conversation with fellow-prisoners detained for their debts. They offered to entertain me with music, but, as I ascertained that it would be contrary to the jail regulations, I declined it. Except that it was a bit tiresome, I rather enjoyed my detention. For it was to me a comfortable spell of rest such as I had not enjoyed for many long years; and when I felt the jail I found that I had added to my weight by several pounds.

I was released from prison early on the morning of July 4. The day before, Mr. Stevens, the Magistrate of the 24-Parganas, who afterwards officiated for some time as Lieutenant-Governor of Bengal, saw me in prison. The cause of this somewhat surprising visit was soon apparent. I lived at Manirampore near Barrackpore, which was within his jurisdiction. He apprehended that there would be a demonstration on my return home, and he was anxious that I should take measures to prevent it. I did not see my way to falling in with his views. I told him what was intended by my friends and neighbours at Barrackpore, for they had placed themselves in communication with me, and he tried to discourage the movement. I said that there would be no music or procession in the streets, but that a meeting would be held to welcome me home at the house of my friend, Babu Hara Kissen Sircar, near the railway station. It was his private residence and not a public place. I added that an Englishman's house was his castle, and that as British subjects we had the same privileges, and I did not see my way to discouraging the proposal of my friends. Mr. Stevens did not further press his point, and when taking leave of me said that he would be present at the railway station at Barrackpore to see that everything passed off well. I thanked him and said, half in jest, that I deemed it a great honour that the official head of the district should be at the station to receive me. And so he was awaiting my arrival at the railway station when I returned to Barrackpore on the evening of July 4. A Bengalee Assistant Superintendent of Police followed me in a separate carriage all the way to my house, a distance of nearly three miles from the station.

I afterwards learnt that the military force stationed in the cantonment of Barrackpore was kept ready the whole day for fear of any eventualities. The officers of the regiment were mostly Indians, some of them Gaur Brahmins like myself. They came and saw me afterwards. Their interest in my case was quickened by the orders of Government, and they wanted to know more of it than they did before. Bureaucracy is at times nervous and distrustful. In this case it sought to prevent a public demonstration. The very preparations that in its unwisdom it made, helped to spread the story of my imprisonment among a class of people notoriously indifferent to what is taking place in the world outside their own.

The same solicitude on their part to prevent any demonstration in my honour was shown in the little device that was planned to release me from jail, when the period of my imprisonment terminated. Prisoners are released at six o'clock in the morning, at least that used to be the case in 1883. I was roused from sleep by the jailor at 4 a.m. and was put into a hackney carriage and driven through various parts of the town till six o'clock, when the jailor dropped me at the *Bengalee* office. All this was done to avoid a demonstration. But the policy was truly ostrich-like. It helped to create two demonstrations instead of one. The crowds that, in the early hours of the morning had surged round the Presidency Jail to witness my release, came all the way to the *Bengalee* office. The trick only served to redouble their enthusiasm, there being thus a demonstration in front of the jail and another near the *Bengalee* office. Wisdom comes late, if indeed it comes at all, to those who, firm in their omniscience, refuse to open their eyes to the growing and irresistible forces of time.

9

Political Activities, 1883-1885

The First Indian National Conference – a second tour through Upper India; an appeal for unity – Lord Dufferin Viceroy – Sir Henry Harrison – drunkenness and the outstill system – public meetings.

ON MY RELEASE FROM PRISON, and after my enforced leisure, which, as I have already observed, I greatly enjoyed, owing to the complete rest it gave me, there lay before me heavy public work. I took up the movement for the creation of a National Fund. A great meeting was held on July 17, 1883, attended by over ten thousand people, at which it was resolved to raise a national fund to secure the political advancement of the country by means of constitutional agitation in India and in England. The Contempt Case and the growing movement for Indian unity and solidarity had opened wide our vision, and we invited the other provinces to co-operate with us. The Civil Service agitation had disclosed the essential unity of Indian aims and aspirations, the Contempt Case had accentuated the feeling, and we now began to look beyond our own province, and to seek for strength and invigoration by the moral support and active co-operation of united India. The moral transformation which was to usher in the Congress movement had thus already its birth in the bosom of the Indian National Conference which met in Calcutta, and to which representatives from all parts of India were invited.

The Ilbert Bill controversy helped to intensify the growing feeling of unity among the Indian people. The Anglo-Indian community had formed their Defence Association with its branches in different parts of the country. They had raised over a lakh and fifty thousand rupees to protect what they conceived to be their interests, and to assert their special privileges. Their organization and their resources had secured success to their cause. The educated community all over India watched the struggle with interest. There was the Ilbert Bill agitation with all its developments taking place before their eyes. They could not remain insensible to the lesson that it taught, of combination and organization; a lesson which in this case was enforced amid conditions that left a rankling sense of humiliation in the mind of educated India. It was, however, fruitful of results. It strengthened the forces that were speeding up the birth of the Congress movement; and, as I have observed, before the year was out the first National Conference was held in Calcutta. In its organization I had no inconsiderable share – *quorum pars magna fui*. It was the reply of educated India to the Ilbert Bill agitation, a resonant blast on their golden trumpet. The Conference met for three days, from December 28 to 30.

The questions that even now substantially form the chief planks in the Congress platform were taken up for discussion. They were Representative Councils, or Self-government, Education, general and technical, the separation of Judicial from Executive functions in the administration of Criminal Justice, and, lastly, the wider employment of our countrymen in the public service. Mr. Wilfrid Blunt, the great friend of Oriental nations, was then touring through India. He was present at the sittings of the Conference, and he gives the following account of his impressions in his *India under Ripon*:

> 'Then at twelve, I went to the first meeting of the National Conference, a really important occasion, as there were delegates from most of the great towns – and, as Bose in his opening speech remarked, it was the first stage towards a National Parliament. The discussion began with a scheme for sending boys to France for industrial education, but the real feature of the meeting was an attack on the Covenanted Civil Service by Surendranath Banerjea. His speech was quite as good a one as ever I heard in my life, and entirely fell in with my own views on the matter. The other speakers were less brilliant, though they showed fair ability, and one old fellow made a very amusing oration which was much applauded. I was asked to speak, but declined, as I don't wish to make any public expression of opinion till my journey is over. But at Bombay I shall speak my mind. I was the only European there, and am very glad to have been present at so important an event. The proceedings would have been more shipshape if a little more arrangement had been made beforehand as to the speakers. But on the whole, it went off very creditably. Both Banerjea and Bose are speakers of a high order. The meeting took place upstairs in the Albert Hall, and about one hundred persons were present. Before the speaking commenced a national hymn was sung by a man with a strong voice, who played also on an instrument of the guitar type.'

In 1884, I undertook another tour through Upper India. My duties in the college gave me no leisure except during the summer, when we had our long vacation. I left Calcutta about the middle of May. The excessive heat in Northern India and the Punjab greatly added to the discomforts of the railway journey. I was accompanied by Babu Govind Churn Das, a dear friend now, alas! dead, who was practising as a pleader in the High Court and was also associated with the teaching staff in the Ripon Collegiate School.

We visited Lahore, Amritsar, Multan, Rawalpindi, Ambala, Delhi, Agra, Aligarh, Lucknow, Cawnpore, Allahabad, Benares and Bankipore. The heat of Multan is a recollection that haunts me still. We started with a cry, but the central idea was the promotion of unification between the different Indian peoples and provinces, and of a feeling of friendliness between the people of Bengal and the martial races of the North. We counted for nothing in those days. It was constantly dinned into our ears that our political demands, whatever they were, came from the people of the deltaic Ganges, who did not contribute a single soldier to the army, and who were separated from the sturdier races of the North by a wide gulf of isolation, if not of alienation. We wanted to dissipate this myth. To-day it stands exploded by the creation of the Congress and the long train of united and patriotic endeavours which have marked the solidarity of the life of modern India.

Our cry on this occasion was the same as that which a decade ago had united all India. The prayer of united India on the Civil Service question had not yet been granted. The maximum limit of age for the open competitive examination had not yet been raised, though a slight and doubtful concession had been made by the creation of the Statutory Civil Service. The prayer was now repeated at the public meetings held in the great towns of Northern India, from Allahabad and Cawnpore to Rawalpindi and Multan. Coupled with this appeal to the Government, there was an appeal to ourselves, namely, that we should help to create a national fund, such as had been started in Bengal, to promote our political work. It was not long before our agitation bore fruit. Soon came the response from the Government. A unanimous despatch was addressed to the Secretary of State by the Government of India, recommending the raising of the limit of age for the Indian Civil Service. A Public Services Commission was appointed the following year, and as the result of its recommendations the age for the Indian Civil Service was raised to the present limit.

The year 1884 witnessed the departure of Lord Ripon from India, and it was the occasion of popular demonstrations unparalleled in Indian annals. The Anglo-Indian official living in isolation and detachment from the people now began to realize the birth of a national movement, of which he had not the faintest conception. 'If it be real what does it mean ?' exclaimed Sir Auckland Colvin, the Indian Finance Minister, with passionate bewilderment, in a pamphlet of that name which at the time created quite a sensation and was largely read. The demonstrations were a revelation to the bureaucracy; and they extended from Calcutta to Bombay; and town after town through which the retiring Viceroy passed vied with the others in displaying its love and gratitude to their benefactor. The vivid and picturesque language of the scriptural text was put into requisition to describe this all-embracing movement. 'The dry bones in the open valley', said Sir Auckland Colvin, 'had become instinct with life.'

Those who had eyes to see, witnessed in these demonstrations the beginnings of a united national life, the birth of a new spirit of co-operation among the Indian people, destined to have a profound influence on their future evolution. It was not that Lord Ripon had been able to do much; but the purity of his intentions, the loftiness of his ideals, the righteousness of his policy, and his hatred of racial disqualifications, were an open book to the people of India. They read it and poured out their heart's gratitude to the Englishman who, in the midst of his chilling bureaucratic surroundings, realized the great mission of England in India, and sought to fulfil it, through good report and evil report. In Calcutta we organized a huge demonstration in which I had my part and share. Indeed, in the year preceding we got up a similar demonstration, though it was of an informal character. The evening party at the Belgachia Gardens was attended by crowds of people from the highest to the lowest. Anglo-India saw at that function that the Viceroy whom they had denounced had won the people's love and esteem such as no other Viceroy had ever done before.

Lord Dufferin succeeded Lord Ripon as Viceroy. I had known Lord Dufferin in England. During the days of my troubles, when I had been rejected by the Civil Service Commissioners, he had very kindly sent for me and interested himself in my case. Quite unexpectedly and of his own motion he wrote inviting me to see him, and after a long conversation with me said that he would speak to the Duke of Argyll, who was then Secretary of State, about my case. We were all prepossessed in his favour; and on his arrival in Calcutta, the Indian Association waited upon him with an address of welcome in which, among other things, the new

Viceroy's attention was prominently called to the need of reconstituting and reforming the Provincial Legislative Councils. This address, which, I may add, was drafted by me, was presented on December 24, 1884, a year before the birth of the Indian National Congress. The passage in the address that refers to this subject is worth reproducing. After referring to the recently-conferred boon of local self-government, the address went on to say:

'In this connexion it would not be out of place to observe that the reconstitution of the Provincial Legislative Councils is one of those reforms which public opinion seems to demand with increasing urgency. This is not the time or the place to enter upon the consideration of so vast a subject. But this may safely be asserted, that the Provincial Legislative Assemblies, as at present constituted, without the right of interpellation or any share in financial management, with their official majorities, for the most part, and the non-official members owing their appointment entirely to nomination, admit of little room for the successful expression of popular opinion, and fail to command that degree of confidence which is so needful for their efficient working. Even in the neighbouring Crown Colony of Ceylon, the Legislative Council is based upon a more popular model.'

As I am on this question of the reform and enlargement of the Councils, I may refer to some of the early efforts that led to the inauguration of this great reform. The year 1887 was the year of the Queen's Jubilee, and it was celebrated in a befitting manner in India and in all parts of the Empire. Mr. (afterwards Sir Henry) Harrison was at that time Chairman of the Calcutta Corporation. He was placed in charge of the arrangements in Calcutta, and he very kindly asked me to assist him in organizing the function to be held on the Maidan, and to look after the delegates who were invited from the different mofussil municipalities.

Here I may pause for one moment to pay my tribute of respect and affection to the honoured memory of a friend who was one of the ablest, as he was one of the most sympathetic, of English officials that I have met. In my mind the memories of Sir Henry Harrison and Sir Henry Cotton are indissolubly linked together. They were twins in their political views as regards India. Both were men of high intellectual eminence. Sir William Turner, late Chief Justice of Madras, said of Sir Henry Harrison that he had mistaken his vocation, and that if, instead of becoming a member of the Indian Civil Service, he had joined the English Bar, he would have become Attorney-General. He was the very Rupert of debate.

Brilliant, fascinating, with an extraordinary command of the finest vocabulary, he was one of the best debaters that I have seen. The Indian Civil Service, so far as I know, has not yet produced his like in this respect. In his college days, he was, I understand, President of the Oxford Union. As Chairman of the Corporation, and president of its meetings, he had the last word in every discussion; and it was difficult to obtain a vote against him. So we hit upon the device of altering the rules and giving the last word to the mover of the resolution. But, in the discussion of this resolution, he had under the existing rules the last word, and we were defeated. His supremacy remained unchallenged; but it was a supremacy that was exercised with the cordial, and at times the admiring, support of his colleagues.

When the Corporation of Calcutta was threatened by a clique, at the head of which was a High Court Judge who dabbled in sanitation, Sir Henry Harrison boldly stood out for the Corporation and fought the Government with a courage and fearlessness of consequences that extorted the admiration of friends and foes alike. In the darkest days of the Ilbert Bill controversy, when the atmosphere was electric and racial feeling ran high, Sir Henry Harrison and Mr. Cotton got up a dinner in their house in Kyd Street, to which they invited the leading Indian and European gentlemen, and Mr. Cotton made a speech breathing the spirit of equality as between Europeans and Indians. In 1885, when after the Panjdeh incident we started a movement for the enlistment of Bengalees as volunteers, Sir Henry Harrison wrote a pamphlet, strongly supporting it (though he knew that the Government was against it), and urging that the legitimate aspirations of the educated community should be gratified. Of the educated Indians, he spoke as follows:

'Agents, guides, instructors, and purveyors of information to the Indian nation as the educated natives already are, very little reflection ought to satisfy us that the India of the future will infallibly think and act as that section of the community, in whose hands are their schools, their presses, their courts and their public offices, may instruct them. It is clearly destined to be the voice of India and the brain of India, the masses will be its hands and will reflect its teaching. In dealing with young India, therefore, as it is sometimes called, it is the gravest mistake to suppose that we are politically (as we are obviously militarily) dealing with an insignificant section of the community; the sentiments which are now fermenting in the minds of two hundred thousand persons will flow out, nay, are flowing out, into the hearts of two hundred millions. The greatest blunder which can possibly be made is to suppose that the effect of our dealing with the educated natives can be made to begin and end with that class.'

In similar terms Sir Henry Harrison wrote in the *Quarterly Review* when he went home in 1886. 'Repress', said he, 'the educated natives, their ambitions and their aspirations and you turn them into a solid phalanx of opposition against the Government. Gratify their ambitions, and you make them the allies of the Government.'

Such was Sir Henry Harrison, one of the finest Englishmen I have set eyes upon, one whose friendship, terminated by an early death, it was my proud privilege to enjoy.

As I was entrusted by him to look after the arrangements in connexion with the delegates who had been invited to the Queen's Jubilee from the mofussil municipalities, I was resolved to make the most of the situation. I thought it was a splendid opportunity to put in the forefront that which I considered the problem of problems at that time, namely, the reform and reconstitution of the Legislative Councils on a popular basis. The mofussil municipalities were each to present an address. I took care that every one of these addresses should contain a prayer for the reform and enlargement of the Councils. I addressed a circular to the mofussil municipalities on the subject and met with a cordial response. I reproduce a passage from one of these addresses (they all followed the same lines):

'Through the wise initiation of the late Viceroy, a system of local self-government has been established throughout the country; and it has, on the whole, been attended with such a measure of success that a feeling has been universally expressed in favour of a further extension of the principles embodied in these local institutions; and on this auspicious occasion of the Jubilee we may be permitted to express the hope that it may be the high privilege of the people of India to witness, under the auspices of Your Majesty's beneficent and glorious reign, the birth, though it may be only in a partial form, of those representative institutions which have always followed in the train of English civilization, and which have constituted the noblest monument of English rule.'

Lord Dufferin gave a suitable reply. 'Glad and happy should I be', said he, 'if during my sojourn among them (the people of India), circumstances permitted me to extend, and to place upon a wide and more logical footing, the political status which was so wisely given, a generation ago, by that great statesman, Lord Halifax, to such Indian gentlemen as by their influence, their acquirements, and the confidence they inspired in their fellow-countrymen, were marked out as useful adjuncts to our Legislative Councils.'

Mr. George Yule, afterwards President of the Congress at Allahabad, who was sitting next to me, said, as these words were uttered, 'You will get the reform in five years' time'. The words were prophetic. They were uttered in 1887, we got the reform in 1892, just five years after. It is curious that Lord Dufferin, who encouraged the idea of an Indian National Congress and sympathized with its aspirations at the outset, should have, before he laid down the reins of office, described the educated community as a 'microscopic minority'. Indeed, while he was condemning the Indian National Congress at the St. Andrew's Dinner in Calcutta, he was writing a secret despatch supporting its recommendations for the reform of the Councils. Strange are the ways of statesmanship. Nevertheless we can forget and forgive much in the case of a Viceroy who first recommended a scheme for the reconstitution of the Legislative Councils upon a popular basis. His confidential despatch, which I was the first to publish in the *Bengalee* in March 1889, formed the basis of the Parliamentary Statute of 1892.

I may here state that Lord Dufferin, before he submitted his despatch on the reform of the Legislative Councils, consulted several persons, including Sir Henry Harrison, Mr. Cotton, and, I believe, one or two others. I was invited to Government House and had a long conversation with His Excellency. I urged that the Councils should be reconstituted upon an elective basis, with the right of interpellation and of control over the budget. It was a frank and friendly conversation, and at the end of it he took me to his private secretary's room, and, introducing me to Sir Donald Mackenzie, said in terms of great kindliness, 'Give Mr. Surendranath Banerjea whatever information he may ask from you'. I repeated the conversation to Sir Henry Harrison, who, I found out, had already seen the Viceroy on the subject, and he said to me, 'Surendranath, there will be a Council of which you will be a member'. The prophecy has been fulfilled. The words of the good and the true never fail of their effect.

The year, upon the events of which I am now dwelling, was for me in many respects a year of hard and strenuous work. For the sake of revenue, what is known as the Outstill System was introduced into the Hughli district. It cheapened the sale of country liquor and reduced its price by nearly one half. This reduction naturally stimulated consumption. Drunkenness spread among the lower classes of the rural population with alarming rapidity. I live on the opposite side of the Hughli district, and within a stone's-throw of my house on the river bank is a liquor shop. I heard tales of drunkenness, of demoralization and ruin that were confirmed by reports which I received from the interior of the district. But I was not content with these reports. I visited a liquor shop at Haripal, and the sight I witnessed there was one that I shall never forget. I saw half a dozen men and women lying dead drunk on the floor of the shop. Another band of about a dozen men and women, all belonging to the lower classes, in varying stages of drunkenness, began dancing around me in wild delirious excitement. I apprehended violence and I slowly and cautiously retraced my steps from the shop, resolved that, so far as in me lay, this thing must cease.

I returned home with a load of sadness on my mind. I felt that a sustained and organized effort had to be made to save the people from the terrible effects of cheap liquor. The work was of a twofold character. We were to appeal to the people to avoid drink and to the Government to abolish the Outstill System. We gave precedence to the popular appeal and put it in the forefront of our programme. For we felt that, when opinion had been organized, our appeal would be irresistible. We worked upon this line; and the result proved the soundness of our programme. It was a guide to future work conceived and carried out on the same lines.

We began the campaign by organizing a series of mass meetings in the Hughli district. They were meetings of the poorer classes, attended by thousands and held in the open air, sometimes amid drenching rain. The language employed in addressing the meetings was the common language of the people, simple, unornate, free from the literary flavour of a more laboured diction. I had never before been accustomed to address public meetings in Bengalee, but with a little preparation I felt myself quite at home in my efforts in this untrodden path. They were to me a valuable training, which proved highly useful when later on I had to address numerous public meetings in connexion with what is known as the '*Swadeshi* agitation'. These meetings were accompanied by *Sankirton* parties, which paraded the villages singing songs suited to the occasion, to the accompaniment of the *khol* and the *kartal.* The effect was very great. The people swarmed in crowds, sometimes from villages far away, and they followed us, they attended our meetings and heard our addresses. Music played an important part in these demonstrations. We had read Vaishnava literature to some purpose, and *Sankirton* has ever since then formed a prominent feature as an instrument of popular and political propagandism in Bengal. We took the fullest advantage of it, and with admirable results. Babu Barada Prosanna Roy was the sweet singer of our party. He composed his own songs and sang them with thrilling effect. It is to be borne in mind that not one of those who were engaged in this work received any remuneration of any kind. It was to them entirely a labour of love; and from week to week and from month to month they were engaged in it, at great personal sacrifice and inconvenience.

The names of these worthies deserve to be commemorated. First and foremost amongst them was Krishna Kumar Mittra, then in the prime of life, but still retaining, despite age and heavy domestic bereavement, a superb enthusiasm for public work. A saintly character, he will, I hope, be remembered by after-generations, if they care to treasure the memories of the good and the true, as one of the worthiest and most selfless among his contemporaries. Essentially a man of religion, politics is a part of his religion. He leavens every sphere of his public work with the devout spirit of religion. He reminds one of the old Puritans. Ascetic in his temperament, unbending in his convictions, careless of the good things of life, and remorseless in his hatred of shams and shows. But he differs from the Puritans of old in the sweet amiability that suffuses his nature. Every good endeavour finds a responsive echo in his heart. There was no stauncher friend of the *Swadeshi* movement, or more unflinching opponent of the Partition of Bengal, than Krishna Kumar Mittra; and he suffered for his devotion to the cause of his country by his deportation. In his case deportation was the unkindest cut of all; for he had always been a firm supporter of constitutionalism and a thorough-going opponent of revolutionary movements. At the interview I had with Lord Morley at the India Office in 1909, I told him that Krishna Kumar Mittra's deportation was a grievous blunder; and this view, I believe, is now admitted even by the officials themselves. The fact demonstrates, if indeed any demonstration were needed, how unsafe and dangerous it is to punish men upon *ex-parte* police statements, which the party concerned has had no opportunity of explaining. But perhaps I am anticipating events that will receive fuller consideration later on.

I go back to the mass meetings, and to my friends who were associated with them. Babu Kali Sunkar Sukul was another worker. He was a brilliant student of the Calcutta University and was the Cobden Scholar of his year. He was not a Bengalee, but came from the United Provinces, from somewhere near Cawnpore. He was, however, thoroughly acclimatized, if I may use that word. He was a Bengalee to all intents and purposes; he was married to a Bengalee lady and spoke Bengalee with the easy familiarity of one born to the language. I rather think that he spoke Hindi, which was his mother-tongue, somewhat indifferently, and at a meeting at Cawnpore, at which he addressed the audience in Hindi, he said to me afterwards that he had made many grammatical mistakes. I first came in contact with him at a meeting in 1876, when I delivered an address on Indian Unity. He rose up from among the crowd of students and spoke. It was an effective little speech, which made an impression on the audience. I thought the young man had stuff in him, and I was right. Our acquaintance, which thus began, ripened into a warm friendship. He took part in the Outstill agitation, and accompanied me to Upper India, along with Babu Krishna Kumar Mittra, in one of my visits to that part of the country in connexion with the Civil Service movement. Latterly business prevented him from close association with our work; but we continued to be friends to the last.

Babu Barada Prosanna Roy was an inhabitant of Barisal. Private circumstances soon compelled him to give up public work. It is a pity that there should be no public fund to ensure the continued services of men like him. We held quite a number of meetings in the Hughli district. There was then no C.I.D. to shadow our steps and to interfere with our work. There was no unpleasant sensation of being secretly espied, while we were doing this good work alike in the interests of the Government and of the people. I believe our public meetings now no longer suffer, except on special occasions, from the embarrassing presence of the police official.

We followed up our public meetings with an appeal to the Government to abolish the Outstill System. The appeal was successful; for it had behind it the voice of the country; and we were fortunate enough to enlist the sympathies of the Temperance

Association headed by the late Mr. W. S. Caine. He saw me at the *Bengalee* office during one of his visits to India, and said to me, 'You have done the spade work. A final kick is all that is needed. We will help you in that' – and he put forward his leg as if in the act of kicking. In response to our appeal, the Government deputed Mr. Westmacott, who was then Magistrate of Howrah, to enquire into the Outstill System in the Hughli district. He held meetings and took evidence. I was present at some of them, and helped him in the investigation. As the result of the enquiry, the system was abolished, and the poorer classes in the Hughli district were saved from the grip of a terrible scourge.

Many years have passed since then; but I look back upon my efforts in this connexion as among the most pleasant memories of my life. It was indeed hard, rough work – tramping along trackless areas, living in malarial countries, and eating strange food. On one occasion I found a big centipede, which of course was dead, in the curry served out to me with dinner. But, being hungry, I ate the curry, of course without the centipede, and cannot say that I felt the worse for it, or that I dreamt of it at night. But these are little troubles that are a part of the game, and when recounted may serve to amuse and delight friends. Nevertheless it was work instructive to a degree, for it brought me into close touch with the peasant life of Bengal and helped to broaden my outlook and my sympathies. For me it was an education that proved highly useful.

10

The Indian National Congress

First sittings at Bombay – the genesis of Provincial Conferences – the first Calcutta Congress, 1886 – Congress in Madras, 1887 – the late Maharaja of Vizianagram – the Allahabad Congress, 1888 – Mr. Bradlaugh's visit to India.

IN DECEMBER, 1885, we again held a National Conference, the second of its kind, to the first of which I have referred as having been held in 1883. It was like its predecessor a conference of all-India held upon the same lines. But in the meantime the ideal had made headway. This time the Conference was convened by the three leading Associations of Calcutta – the British Indian, representing the landed interest, the Indian, the Association of the middle classes, and the Central Mohamedan Association, of which Mr. (now the Rt. Hon. Mr.) Ameer Ali was Secretary.

The Conference met for three days, on December 25, 26 and 27, 1885. Not only was Bengal represented, but delegates attended from several towns in Northern India such as Meerut, Benares and Allahabad. Bombay was represented by the Hon. Mr. Vishnarain Mandlik, the Indian member for that presidency in the Imperial Legislative Council. The Conference voted the urgency of the reform of the Legislative Councils, and appointed a committee to consider what steps should be taken to bring about its satisfactory settlement.

While we were having our National Conference in Calcutta, the Indian National Congress, conceived on the same lines and having the same programme, was holding its first sittings at Bombay. The movements were simultaneous; the preliminary arrangements were made independently, neither party knowing what the other was doing until on the eve of the sittings of the Conference and of the Congress. Mr. W. C. Bonnerjea, who presided over the Bombay Congress, invited me to attend it. I told him that it was too late to suspend the Conference, and that as I had a large share in its organization it would not be possible for me to leave Calcutta and attend the Bombay Congress. This and the one at Karachi are the only sittings of the Indian National Congress that I missed over the long period extending from 1885 to 1917, when, for reasons set forth later on, the Moderate Party definitely seceded from the Congress.

It appears that while we were organizing our National Conference at Calcutta, some of our friends headed by the late Mr. Allen Hume had met at Madras for a similar purpose. Mr. Kashinath Trembuck Telang wrote to me from Bombay requesting me to send him some notes about the first National Conference held in 1883. The two Conferences met about the same time, discussed similar views and voiced the same grievances and aspirations. The one that met in Calcutta was called the 'National Conference' and the other, which assembled at Bombay, the 'Indian National Congress'. Henceforth those who worked with us joined the Congress and heartily co-operated with it.

We in Bengal started another movement upon lines parallel to those of the Congress, but less comprehensive in its scope, and dealing only with the affairs of the province. We held in 1888 the first Provincial Conference for Bengal. The National Congress, being a convention of India, could not take up for discussion questions affecting any particular province, unless such questions had assumed the proportions of a national problem. But there were provincial considerations of the utmost importance upon which it was necessary for public opinion to make definite pronouncements. Problems of sanitation, education and even local self-government differed in the different provinces, and it was for the representatives of the province in conference assembled to discuss and to deal with them. Such were the reasons that determined the holding of the first provincial conference in Bengal.

The other provinces have followed the example of Bengal. Provincial conferences are now a recognized institution and are held in almost every part of India. They have indeed been followed by still further developments, and district conferences are held in some parts of India. They are specially popular in the Madras Presidency.

In Bengal, the provincial conferences have attained enormous proportions; on occasions their numerical strength has exceeded that of the Congress. Sometimes they are followed by social conferences enlivened by animated debates on the burning social questions of the day. In Bengal, social considerations are no longer dead. They have passed the purely academic stage and are beginning to awaken a living interest among the educated community. I have more than once presided at these provincial social conferences and can bear witness to the genuine interest that the discussions evoked. The two questions of absorbing interest are the re-marriage of Hindu widows and the raising of the marriageable age of Hindu girls. With regard to the latter there is a practical unanimity of opinion; dissentient voices are seldom if ever heard at the conferences.

Far otherwise, however, is the case with the question of the re-marriage of Hindu widows. In this connexion, I am afraid, public opinion has not advanced to the stage that is necessary or desirable. A future Vidyasagar is needed to sound the death-knell of a usage that has darkened many a Hindu home and has blasted the life of many a Hindu widow. I well remember an animated discussion that took place at the Comilla Social Conference in 1914, when after a heated debate a division was taken and it was found that in a house of more than three thousand people there were only about half a dozen dissentients. Most of those who voted for the reform would not, I am afraid, have the courage to carry out the resolution that they supported. Between profession and practice there is still a wide gulf; but opinion is steadily veering round to the right standpoint; and when the moral transformation has taken place it will not be long before Hindu society abolishes the system of compulsory widowhood. The educated community are beginning to realize that the custom is one that is abjured by the rest of the civilized world, and perpetrates a monstrous injustice upon the weaker sex. We may not indeed live to see the change, but the signs and portents all point to its near approach, and, when a man of the social position and avowed orthodoxy of Sir Ashutosh Mukherjea championed the cause by having his own daughter re-married, we may be sure that we are within measurable distance of the consummation of this great reform.

I had occasion once or twice to advertise in the *Bengalee* newspaper for bridegrooms for the re-marriage of Brahmin widows; and the response that I received was surprising. I showed the replies to some of my orthodox friends, and they were even more amazed than myself. In one case I received more than 150 applications, and among them were some from pundits with titles that denoted their orthodox character. Great, silent forces are indeed working in the bosom of society, to us invisible and perhaps unperceived. They will work out their destined end in their own good time. Nabadwipa and Bhatpara and Bajrajogini may thunder forth their anathemas and quote all the Shastric texts of which they may have a plentiful supply in their armoury; but the march of progress will not be arrested; and the time will come when perhaps our descendants will wonder what possessed their revered ancestors to perpetuate a custom so cruel and unjust to the womanhood of their race. The future is closed to us; but the past is an open book, and the past tells us that in the great seat of orthodoxy, while Raghunandan was unfolding his marvellous system of Hindu Law and jurisprudence, there rose almost contemporaneously with him the greatest reformer that Bengal, or India, has ever produced, the prophet of Love (*Bhakti*), Lord Chaitanya, who would have no distinction between man and man, or between man and woman, who treated the Brahmin, the Chandal and the Moslem alike, and enfranchised our women from the bonds of enforced widowhood. Who knows that in the years to come, in the whirligig of time, there may not arise a second Chaitanya, the Saviour of the Hindu widow, in those great centres of Sanskrit learning where the academic air stirs contemplation and carries the mind forward to brighter visions of future happiness ?

I fear I have been somewhat anticipating coming events, but they were so linked with what I was describing that the transition from the present to the future was natural. In the year 1886, the Indian National Congress met for the first time in Calcutta, and great was the popular enthusiasm. All parties combined to welcome the delegates who came from different parts of India. We of the Indian Association and belonging to the middle class were all Congressmen; but what was remarkable was that the British Indian Association, representing the landed interest, and what I may call the conservative conscience of the community, threw themselves heart and soul into the matter. Such enthusiasm this venerable body had never before, and have never since, displayed for the Congress cause. The illustrious Raja Rajendralal Mitter, more a scholar than a politician, was elected Chairman of the Reception Committee, and Babu Joy Kissen Mookerjee, the Nestor of the Bengal zemindars, then in his seventy-ninth year, proposed the election of Mr. Dadabhai Naoroji as President of the Congress. It was altogether a Congress of old men, and it brought out in striking relief the great fact that young and old, the middle class as well as the landed aristocracy, indeed all sections of the Indian community, were united on the Congress platform.

Raja Rajendralal Mitter, Kristo Das Pal, Raja Degumbar Mitter, and Maharaja Jotindra Mohon Tagore formed what I may call the political group of the British Indian Association. Kristo Das Pal was their leader; but Rajendralal Mitter was the literary genius of the group. Degumbar Mitter and Kristo Das Pal were now dead, and the leadership of the political wing devolved upon Raja Rajendralal. Young as I was, I enjoyed the confidence and even the friendship of every member of this brilliant coterie. I knew them well and knew them in all their strength and perhaps in all their weakness. Raja Rajendralal Mitter was a good speaker and an effective writer. He was pre-eminently a scholar and a literary man, but he had likewise a great grasp of public questions and was undoubtedly one of the foremost public men of his generation. I often heard him speak. His style was simple, conversational, with a touch of humour in it. In his later life, he was somewhat hard of hearing. In the debates at the Corporation meetings, he used to sit next to Kristo Das Pal, who supplied him with brief notes of the speeches, and thus enabled him to take part in the discussions. To the last he retained his interest in public affairs and continued to enjoy the esteem and regard of the community. The practice of throwing overboard our veterans, of calling them men of yesterday, had not yet begun. The traditional veneration for the services of a past generation still had a firm hold on the public mind.

At the Calcutta Congress, and in all future Congresses until the boon was obtained, I moved the Resolution on the Reform and Enlargement of the Councils. To me it was a topic of absorbing interest. I could hardly think of anything else. Call it weakness, or call it strength, call it by what name you please (and I trust I shall be excused for this self-revelation) I have through life been under the periodical domination of a single overmastering ideal. It was the Civil Service question, or Local Self-government, or the expansion of the Councils, or *Swadeshi,* with which was linked up the modification of the Partition, that filled the whole of my mental horizon, fired my enthusiasm, and absorbed my soul. For the time being I lived in my ideal. In all other spheres, my movements were more or less mechanical. I persuaded myself that it was the one thing to be achieved, priceless above all others, and I had no difficulty in persuading others. It took a little time for me to warm up. But when the process was accomplished I was proof against all dissuasion, I lived in a world of my own, an atmosphere of my creation, impervious to external influences. So when, during the anti-Partition controversy, it was again and again dinned into the ears of the people of Bengal that the Partition was a settled fact and could not be unsettled, and when all appearances pointed to the same conclusion, I remained obdurate. I had no ears to hear, no eyes to see, what all others thought was the plainest truth. I saw with the eye of faith what seemed impossible to men of little faith.

I will now pass on from this self-introspection to the events of the year 1887, in which I had my part and share. The year was the year of the Queen's Jubilee and it was celebrated in Calcutta, which was then the Imperial capital, with befitting splendour and *éclat.* To these ceremonies I have referred in a preceding part of these reminiscences. We, who were working by slow and steady stages towards the evolution of self-government, took the fullest advantage of these celebrations to give an impetus to the movement, and we claim that we did not work in vain. For we obtained from the Viceroy (Lord Dufferin) a declaration (the full text of which I have given elsewhere) in favour of the reform and expansion of the Legislative Councils.

The Congress this year was held in Madras. We chartered a steamer from the British India Steam Navigation Company, and a large number of delegates from Calcutta proceeded to Madras. Among them were Sir Rash Behari Ghose and Raja Kissori Lal Gossain, who afterwards became the first member of the Executive Council of Bengal. The sea-trip was thoroughly enjoyed by us. Pleasure and business were combined; and the meeting of so many of us for several days talking of nothing else but the Congress, and the future of the Congress, and of the country, served to impart an added impetus to the infant movement. The representatives of the generation assembled on board that steamer, the pilgrim fathers bent upon an errand fraught with great potentialities, have nearly all passed away, but their spirit endures. Though the first flush of enthusiasm has died out (and to many it may seem that the Congress is now sailing over uncharted seas) the public conviction remains unabated, that the Congress must continue its work until India has achieved her destiny as a self-governing community.

Arrived at Madras, we were treated with a cordiality the memory of which still lingers and which has become the accepted tradition of all Reception Committees of the Congress. Day and night, the Congress Volunteers, young men of respectable families, following respectable callings, were in attendance, rejoicing in their self-imposed task. We formed friendships that have endured through life. Viraraghava Chariar, G. Subramanya Iyer, Ranga Naidu, Ananda Charlu, and others, almost too numerous to be named, became as dear to us as friends in Bengal. The social side of the

Congress is not by any means the least attractive feature of the movement. A common platform is provided, where the leaders of Indian opinion meet and by the mutual interchange of views help to remove misunderstanding and promote friendly feeling.

Among the friendships that I formed at Madras on this occasion was one to which I think I must make a special reference. I made the acquaintance of the late Maharaja of Vizianagram, 'Prince Charming', as he was rightly called by Sir Mountstuart Grant-Duff, then Governor of Madras.

The incidents of our first meeting are as vivid now as if they had taken place yesterday. I was coming out of the pavilion, after I had spoken on the reform of the Legislative Councils, when he approached me and warmly shook me by the hand. We exchanged a few words of mutual compliment, and then was formed the beginning of a friendship that ended only with his premature death in 1897. He was a frequent visitor to Calcutta, where I had ample opportunities of meeting him; and I will say this of him, that I have hardly ever come across a warmer or more generous-hearted man. He was not only the pattern of courtesy, which all our princes are, more or less, but he was something more. His ample resources were always responsive to the impulses of his generous nature. The Rajas of Bhukoylas and he were hereditary friends. They were in pecuniary difficulties. He afforded them substantial monetary assistance. The same helping hand was stretched out to an English firm. Race, colour or creed was no barrier to the play of his generous affections, and he was the liberal patron of public movements and of public institutions, whether in Madras, in Bengal or the United Provinces. I approached him with a request for a subscription in aid of the building fund of the Indian Association. He wanted to know from me how much money was required and how much I had already secured. I put the figure at the modest sum of twenty thousand rupees; and I said I had obtained promises of five thousand rupees, among the donors being the Maharani Swarnamoyee, who had subscribed two thousand rupees. He said to me, with that warmth so characteristic of him, 'Suren Babu, what is the good of your going to this man and that man, and wasting your time, which might be otherwise usefully spent? I will pay you the balance of fifteen thousand rupees.' His word was his bond; and with this princely gift we secured for the Indian Association a name and a habitation. We asked permission to hang his oil-painting in the hall of the Association. He sent us a small portrait.

One more incident will illustrate the generous impulses of the man. On the occasion of the visit of Prince Albert Victor to Calcutta in 1889, a great controversy took place as to how the money that had been raised should be spent. There was a strong party, and they represented the wealth of the city, who wanted to confine the demonstrations mainly to *tamashas* and entertainments. We were in favour of a permanent memorial in the form of a leper asylum in commemoration of the visit. I moved an amendment at the Town Hall meeting embodying this view. The amendment was carried, to the great disgust and indignation of the official party and their friends. A Maharaja, as he was leaving the meeting, happened to meet me, and exclaimed, 'Lo and behold! here is your work. You have wrecked the meeting and insulted the Lieutenant-Governor.' The Lieutenant-Governor, Sir Stewart Bayley, was evidently not of that view, nor felt himself insulted; for he encouraged the idea of a permanent memorial in honour of the Royal Visit. However that may be, I was soon made to feel the weight of official displeasure. A deputation was to wait upon Prince Albert Victor in connexion with the permanent memorial. My name was submitted as a member of the deputation, but it was eliminated by the officials who had the manipulation of the arrangements. Further, I learnt that my name had been sent up to the Government of India for nomination as a member of the Senate of the Calcutta University. Then came the incident of the Albert Victor Memorial meeting; and my name was omitted from the list.

The vote in favour of the permanent memorial at a meeting presided over by the Lieutenant-Governor of the province, organized under official auspices, and backed by the authority of the European Chamber of Commerce, was a triumph of middle class public opinion too marked to be mistaken. Those who had a leading part in this vote incurred the full measure of official and semi-official displeasure. But the vote was there, and the question was, where was the money for the permanent memorial to come from? Those who had money to spare would not subscribe a pice. The Maharaja of Vizianagram came to our rescue. He was the first to offer ten thousand rupees for a permanent memorial. He wrote a letter to me offering this sum, almost immediately after the meeting was over. We raised Rs. 25,000 in all, and we made it over to the Leper Asylum, this being named after Prince Albert Victor. I was made a member of the governing body; and, when I retired several years later, I nominated Babu Bhupendra Nath Basu as my successor. I had a principal hand in selecting the present site of the Leper Asylum.

Though the Maharaja and myself were great personal friends, in politics we did not always worship in the same temple. Sometimes we agreed to differ, and on one particular occasion the difference was acute. The Maharaja and Sir Charles Elliott, late Lieutenant-Governor of Bengal, were great friends. Sir Charles Elliott was about to retire, and the Maharaja proposed to raise a public memorial in his honour. He wanted me to be associated with it, and, somewhat diplomatically (for there was considerable shrewdness and sagacity behind his frank and cordial manner) suggested to me that one of the purposes to which the memorial fund would be applied would be the endowment of a professorship in the Ripon College. Notwithstanding this somewhat seductive allurement, I flatly declined to be associated with the movement. I said, 'Maharaja, Sir Charles Elliott has wrecked his reputation by the Jury Notification. The public cannot honour such a ruler. To join such a movement would be for me to commit political suicide.' For me the matter ended there. I heard no more about it. But this difference did not in the smallest degree interrupt the cordiality of our relations or chill the warmth of our friendship.

The Madras session of the Congress of 1887 deserves to be recalled to mind for an animated discussion about the Arms Act, which is not wholly without a bearing upon that question as it now stands. A resolution was moved that the Arms Act be repealed. The Arms Act and the Vernacular Press Act were twin measures that were passed by Lord Lytton's Government. They were part and parcel of that policy of mistrust which was so conspicuously in evidence during Lord Lytton's administration, and which his great successor, Lord Ripon, did so much to undo. As I have already observed, Mr. Gladstone in his Midlothian campaign vigorously denounced both these measures. When he came into power as the result of the general election, the Vernacular Press Act was repealed, but the Arms Act was allowed to remain a part of the law of the land. It was always a source of irritation. There was always a sore feeling in connexion with the Act, which found repeated expression in the resolutions of the Indian National Congress. At the Madras Congress, an amendment was moved by the late Dr. Trailakyanath Mitter, an eminent lawyer, who, if he had not been cut off by an early death, would possibly have been a Judge of the Calcutta High Court. The amendment did not seek the repeal of the Act, but urged its more liberal administration, recommending that all persons who were certified by local and municipal authorities should be authorized to carry arms. A heated discussion took place, in which I took part. I opposed the amendment. The original proposition was carried, subject to the modification that a person or a class might be debarred from the right of carrying arms by Government for reasons to be recorded in writing. The attitude of the Congress with regard to the Arms Act has undergone a modification. The Congress no longer calls for the absolute repeal of the Act, but a modification of it so that all racial disabilities should disappear. Lord Chelmsford, when Viceroy, recognized this principle, and it has in substance been given effect to.

The Congress of 1887, which assembled in Madras, was the third of its kind. The constitution of the Congress was yet in the making. Conventions and rules of procedure were being developed as the result of experience. In this formative period, a question of great difficulty and delicacy was started. Raja Sashi Sekhareswar Roy of Tahirpore in Bengal gave notice of a resolution urging the prohibition of cow-slaughter. At any time, in any circumstances, a resolution of this kind in a mixed gathering of Hindus and Mohamedans would have been inopportune. It was especially so then. The Mohamedan community, under the leadership of Sir Syed Ahmed, had held aloof from the Congress. They were working under the auspices of the Patriotic Association in direct opposition to the national movement. Our critics regarded the National Congress as a Hindu Congress, and the opposition papers described it as such. We were straining every nerve to secure the co-operation of our Mohamedan fellow-countrymen in this great national work. We sometimes paid the fares of Mohamedan delegates and offered them other facilities.

The resolution therefore served to add to the difficulties of our position. What was to be done? We found a solution that was fair to all interests, was accepted by all parties, and has since been the recognized convention of the Congress. We decided that if any resolution affecting a particular class or community was objected to by the delegates representing that community, even if they were in a minority, it should not be considered by the Congress. The only other case in which I remember this rule being enforced was in relation to the Punjab Land Alienation Act, which was raised at a meeting of the Congress held at Lahore.

I have a distinct recollection of the Congress of 1888, the first Indian National Congress held at Allahabad. Those were the early days of the Congress; and the interest that the novel demonstration excited in a place that had never witnessed anything like it was great. It was stimulated by certain incidents. Nothing is so helpful to an infant cause seething with enthusiasm as opposition. Sir Auckland Colvin, who in 1884, on the eve of Lord Ripon's departure for England, had recognized the birth of a new life in India, now fiercely assailed the Congress, which was typical of that life. He was a pupil of Lord Dufferin. Lord Dufferin had, just before he vacated the Viceroyalty, denounced the Congress and its programme, and referred to the educated community as a 'microscopic minority'. Indian officialdom took its cue from him. Mr. Hume's stirring pamphlets appealing to educated India to rally round the Congress provoked the ire of the Lieutenant-Governor of the United Provinces, who not only wielded his pen in a wordy controversy, but threw many difficulties in the way of the holding of the session of the Congress at Allahabad. Pundit Ajodhyanath, the leader of the Congress movement in the United Provinces, and Chairman of the Reception Committee, was, however, a host in himself. A brilliant lawyer, a warm-hearted patriot, a great organizer, he overcame all difficulties, and the session of the Congress at Allahabad in 1888 was in one sense the triumph of popular opinion over the solid opposition of the bureaucracy.

Raja Shiva Prosad of Benares, the trusted friend of the officials, entered the Congress pandal as a delegate. That he should have joined the Congress was a marvel. But it was a diplomatic move. His object was soon disclosed in the course of the speech that he delivered. He came not indeed to bless, but to curse, and he received the retort courteous from Mr. Eardley Norton in a speech of withering scorn and indignation.

Mr. George Yule was the President of the Allahabad Congress. He was the first non-Indian President. He was a Calcutta merchant, the head of the great firm of Andrew Yule & Co. I had hardly come across a Calcutta merchant with broader and more liberal views or with more genuine sympathy for Indian aspirations. He was a hard-headed Scotchman who saw straight into the heart of things, and never hesitated to express himself with the bluntness in which a Scotchman never fails, if he wants to show it. Throughout, he remained a staunch friend of the Congress cause, to which he rendered valuable service by helping the Congress Deputation that visited England in 1890. After his retirement he became a member of the British Committee, the Congress organization in London, and I well remember his active interest in the work of the Committee. His premature death was mourned by all friends of the Congress as a heavy loss to our propagandism in England.

The year 1889 was a memorable year in the history of the Congress movement. It was the year of Mr. Bradlaugh's visit to India, which imparted a new impetus to the Congress cause. Next year, Mr. Bradlaugh introduced in the House of Commons his Bill for the reform and the expansion of the Legislative Councils. While at Bombay he made a point of consulting the more prominent Indian leaders, and the Bill embodied the views of the educated community. I had a bit of work to do in this Congress apart from the Resolution which I had to move. To me was entrusted the task of appealing for funds. I made the appeal. The effect was striking. A wave of enthusiasm passed over the vast gathering that was assembled; and in an hour's time a sum of Rs. 64,000 was subscribed; and more than Rs. 20,000 was paid on the spot. The incident is unique in the annals of any public movement. There were ladies present at the meeting who gave away their watches, and even their jewellery. The memory of that day will always remain one of the most grateful reminiscences of my public life. On two other occasions I made similar appeals, one in 1892 at Allahabad, and again in 1909 at Lahore, on the last occasion for funds for British Indians in South Africa. But nowhere was the appeal more generously responded to than at Bombay. Mr. Bradlaugh was a witness to the scene, and the impression that he then formed must have been no small incentive to his disinterested labours for the political advancement of a people so full of real patriotism.

11

The Congress Deputation to England

Each member pays his own expenses – first meeting at Clerkenwell – interview with Gladstone; the elective principle – members of the Deputation – the debate at the Oxford Union – return to India; the Ripon College controversy.

BY ONE OF THE RESOLUTIONS adopted at the Bombay Congress a deputation to England was appointed 'to represent the views of the Congress and to press upon the attention of the British public the political reforms which the Congress advocates'. The 'political reforms' here referred to meant the beginnings of representative government by the expansion and reconstitution of the Councils. That, indeed, had always been in the forefront of the Congress programme, and at the Bombay Session, a skeleton scheme was drawn up and accepted, suggesting the broad outlines upon which the Councils should be reconstituted. Mr. Bradlaugh was requested to introduce a Bill in Parliament upon those lines. The members of the Deputation were appointed by name, and among them were Mr. Hume, Sir Pherozshah Mehta, Mr. Monomohan Ghose, Mr. W. C. Bonnerjea, Mr. Sharifuddin, Mr. Eardley Norton, Mr. R. N. Mudholkar, and myself.

Each member of the Deputation was to pay his own expenses. We learnt that even in England this would be considered an unusual proceeding, but we did not demur. Of the financial position of the other members of the Deputation I knew nothing. Mine was far from being satisfactory. The sum total of my worldly wealth consisted of Rs. 13,000 of Government securities, which were invested in the name of my wife. It was estimated that the cost would be Rs. 4,000 for each member. In other words, I was required to spend nearly one-third of what little reserve fund I had been able to lay by. I did not grudge the sacrifice, and I owe it to the adored memory of my wife to say that she willingly joined me and made over the securities for the purpose for which they were wanted. Not a farthing of the expense did we derive from any source except our own. We paid all travelling and hotel charges from the moment of our starting till we returned to our homes. This was true of every member of the Deputation. This was the first Congress Deputation to England, and its mission was to press for the inauguration of a reform that was to culminate in the establishment of self-government in India.

The Deputation created great interest at the time. It would be no exaggeration to say that it went forth upon its errand amid the benedictions of the people. We started for England in March, 1890, and arrived in London early in April. The British Committee of the Indian National Congress organized our meetings, the first of which was held in Clerkenwell Road, Mr. Dadabhai Naoroji's constituency, under the presidency of Sir William Wedderburn. I well remember the day, and what preceded and what followed the meeting. We dined at the National Liberal Club as the guests of Mr. George Yule, and proceeded to Clerkenwell. The arrangements were very much those of an ordinary Indian meeting, such as I had been accustomed to. There was the platform where the speakers and the principal men of the locality were assembled, and there was the body of the hall where the audience sat.

I met Mr. H. E. A. Cotton at the meeting. He had been deputed by his father, Sir Henry Cotton, to see me and communicate his good wishes. I was a little nervous, as the audience was one to which I had not been accustomed. Mr. George Yule told me, as we were going to the meeting, that there was not much difference between an Indian and an English audience. Both hated long speeches and dry details; both were moved by appeals to the feelings that are a part of their inherited instincts, which it was for the speaker to discover and to play upon. I soon made the discovery. In fact, my acquaintance with English literature and history had given me an idea as to what the tenor of my speeches should be; and, on the whole, my efforts were not unsuccessful. Englishmen are not frightened by a dark man addressing them in their own language. At first they are perhaps a bit puzzled and amused. Presently they begin to appreciate, and even to admire, as the speaker proceeds; and, if he knows his business, he is able to develop in them a genuine vein of sympathy and perhaps of interest in the redress of grievances for which they are partly responsible. After I had addressed a meeting of the Chamber of Commerce at Manchester, a gentleman stood up and said, 'I have never been so deeply moved as now in regard to Indian affairs'. There is a vast field of work awaiting us in England, and a great opportunity of which we have not taken the fullest advantage. On several occasions after we had addressed public meetings, we were asked to repeat our visit. Mr. Augustine Honey, the organizer of the public meetings in the south of England and Wales, wrote thus in the official report submitted by him to the British Committee of the Indian National Congress:

> 'At all the meetings the demand was that Mr. Banerjea should visit them again; and I would point out to you the great advantage the movement would gain by his presence, as that alone would ensure overflowing audiences in the towns already visited. I would strongly urge the importance of this fact upon your Committee, as I have already urged it upon Mr. Banerjea himself as well as Mr. Hume; and in confirmation of this I would remind you that, immediately after the Cardiff meeting, Mr. R. N. Hall on behalf of the South Wales Liberal Federation, of which he is the secretary, entreated Mr. Banerjea to revisit Cardiff before leaving for India, to address a meeting of the representatives of the constituencies in South Wales in the largest hall in Cardiff, at which he promised there would be an audience of several thousands of persons to hear the claims of India. I will make a similar promise for Plymouth.'

Unfortunately, a deputation to England on the scale of 1890, backed by the organization and the resources then at our disposal, was never repeated, though the results achieved by that Deputation were unique in the history of the Congress movement. We addressed meetings in many of the great towns of England, Wales and Scotland, and the Deputation fittingly finished its labours with an interview with Mr. Gladstone, at which the impression was left on our minds that he would speak at the second reading of Lord Cross's Bill on the Expansion of the Councils and support the elective principle. Our anticipation proved true. For on the occasion of the second reading of the Bill, Mr. Gladstone urged that what should be conceded was a real and living representation of the people of India. The elective principle as such was not indeed conceded, but a definite advance towards it was made. Under regulations framed by the Government under the Parliamentary Statute of 1892, municipalities and district boards were permitted to return members to the local Councils, subject to confirmation by Government, and the non-official members of provincial Councils were allowed the privilege of returning members to the Imperial Legislative Council. The right of asking questions was conceded, and the annual discussion of the Budget was allowed. Thus the first notable step towards securing representative government was taken, and mainly through the efforts of the Congress and the Deputation of the Congress. The Act of 1892 was still further liberalized by the Statute of 1909, but the foundations of representative government had been well and truly laid by the previous Statute.

I have so far said nothing about the members of the Deputation; but I feel no hesitation in alluding to the work of honoured colleagues whose services, I fear, have not been sufficiently recognized. Mr. Allen Hume, the father of the Indian National Congress, was with us throughout the campaign. As a member of the Civil Service, he had spent his life in desk-work and had few opportunities of public speaking. But when he spoke at our meetings in England, he showed the capacity and resourcefulness of a practised debater. I well remember the crushing reply he gave to a critic of the Congress who had urged at the Birmingham meeting that social reform must precede political reform, and that the Congress must wait for the fulfilment of its programme till social evolution had achieved its work in India. The son of a great father (Joseph Hume), his association with us inspired confidence.

Mr. Mudholkar joined us after we had begun our work. But he threw himself heart and soul into it. His mastery of facts, his clear presentment, and his intense earnestness made a deep impression upon British audiences. Mr. Syed Ali Imam, afterwards Sir Ali Imam, was with us at Plymouth. He had then just been called to the Bar. His cold, clear vein of rationalism was even then conspicuous, and has helped to bring him back, through many deviations, to the fold of the Congress. Mr. Dadabhai Naoroji and Sir William Wedderburn occasionally helped us with their presence and their speeches. Mr. Eardley Norton was another member of the Deputation. He joined us late but did good service. On the occasion of the debate at the Oxford Union he moved the Congress Resolution, 'That the House views with regret the non-recognition of the elective principle in the Bill now before the House of Commons'.

That debate was a memorable one. The Oxford Union is a stronghold of Conservatism. It was here that Mr. Gladstone made his first mark as a debater; and it was under the influences of his Alma Mater that he became 'the rising hope of the unbending Tories' in the early part of his great career. We entered the debating hall of the Union, Mr. Hume, Mr. Norton and myself, with the almost certain belief that the motion would be lost in that gathering of young Conservatives. I met there Mr. Wilson, then a Professor in the Presidency College and one of the founders of the Calcutta University Institute. I felt sure from what I knew of his political views that he would vote against the motion; and on questioning him about it I found that my anticipation was correct.

We began the fight hopeless of success, but determined to make the best of a bad situation. Mr. Norton moved the Resolution in a speech of great power. The opposition was led by Lord Hugh Cecil. It devolved on me to reply to him. I had partly anticipated, and with accuracy, the line of argument he would follow, and I was prepared with facts and figures to meet him. Our educational backwardness was the deadliest arrow in his quiver. I pointed out in reply that the number of schools in England in 1821 was only 18,467 and the scholars 650,000, and it was not until 1881 that they reached the number of schools and scholars in India. And yet in 1881, England had full-fledged parliamentary institutions, and we were asking for much less. No reply was possible to this array of facts. Young Mr. McGhee, son of the Archbishop of York, a fine speaker, a chip of the old block, supported us in an eloquent speech, in the course of which he paid a high compliment to me. The division was taken, and to our great astonishment it was found that the majority of votes was on our side. The Resolution was declared carried. The vote was a memorable achievement of the Congress Deputation. It demonstrated that the Congress programme of reform was so moderate as to commend itself even to the most conservative section of the British public.

There was one passage in my speech at the Oxford Union which Mr. Norton, half in jest and half with a touch of friendly approval, was never tired of repeating. I may, perhaps, reproduce it here:

'The statement has been made in the course of this debate that the Indians before the advent of the English were a pack of barbarians or semi-barbarians; I believe that was the language that was used. Let me remind this House that they come – the Hindus of India, the race to which I have the honour to belong – (loud cheers) – they come from a great and ancient stock; that at a time when the ancestors of the most enlightened European nations were roaming in their native woods and forests, our fathers had founded great empires, established noble cities, and cultivated a system of ethics, a system of religion, and a noble language which at the present moment excites the admiration of the civilized world. (Loud cheers.) You have only to walk across the way, and place yourselves in the Bodleian library, to witness the ancient records of Indian industry, Indian culture, and Indian ethics; therefore it seems to me the remark is somewhat out of place. (Cheers.) If the remark was made to prejudice the claim which we have now the honour to put forward, to prejudice our claim for representative institutions, never was it more misplaced, for the simple reason that self-governing institutions formed an essential feature of the civilization of the Aryan race, and we come from the Aryan stock. (Cheers.) The hon. opposer of the motion is pleased to refer to the authority of Sir Henry Maine in reference to certain quotations he has made. I am prepared to bow to that authority, and accept him as an authority on Indian matters. What does he say in reference to India? "The first practical illustrations of self-governing institutions are to be found in the early records of India. Their village communities are as old as the hills." (Cheers.) When we ask for representative institutions, or a partial concession of representative institutions, we ask for something which is in entire accord with the genius and the temper of the people of India, in entire accord with the traditions of their history, and in entire accord with the tenour of British rule in India.'

I concluded my speech with the following peroration:

'Representative institutions are a consecrated possession, which in the counsels of Providence have been entrusted to the English people, to guard that possession, to spread it, and not to make it the property of this people or that people, but the heritage of mankind at large. England is the home of representative institutions; from England as the centre, representative institutions have spread far and wide until this country has justly been called the august mother of free nations. The people of India are children of that mother, and they claim their birthright, they claim to be admitted into the rights of British citizens and British fellow-subjects. I am perfectly certain that such an appeal made to the English people can meet with but one response – a response of sympathy, and a readiness to grant it. (Cheers.) I plead before this House for justice; I plead for liberty not inconsistent with the British connexion, but tending to consolidate its foundations; and I am perfectly convinced that, so long as these words, these sacred words, have any weight, any meaning, any signification, amongst Englishmen, and in this House, you will record, by an unanimous vote, an emphatic vote, your sympathy with our aspirations, our desire that India should be governed according to those eternal principles of justice and liberty, which are engraved deep in the hearts, the convictions, and feelings of Englishmen, to whatever party, to whatever creed, to whatever sect they might belong.' (Loud and prolonged cheering.)

I returned to Bombay on July 6, 1890, and on the evening of the same day a monster meeting was held at the Framji Cowasji Institute, to accord me a welcome. At Allahabad and Calcutta, where similar meetings were held, I repeated the burden of my song, namely, that the work which had been begun should be continued, and that deputations should be sent to England from time to time. Unfortunately this was not, and could not be, done for various reasons. The idea was always present to the mind of the early Congress leaders; but it was not possible to give effect to it.

As for myself, I found that on my return home I was involved in serious difficulties in connexion with the Ripon College. While I was away, materials were being got ready for a deadly blow at the College. It was found that a student, who had passed the B. L. Examination from the Ripon College, had been marked present on the rolls of the College, when as a matter of fact he was absent. An enquiry was started, and, by a resolution of the Syndicate, the Law Department of the College was ordered to be disaffiliated for one year. It was a serious thing for the College. If the resolution were given effect to, it would mean the financial ruin of the College; for in those days the Arts Departments of the independent colleges derived substantial aid from the surplus revenues of the Law Departments. The situation was critical. For me the joy of the good work that I was able to do in England was gone. My friends vied with one another in giving me parties and entertainments; but the central idea in my mind all the while was 'how to save the College from impending ruin'. I had built it up with my life-blood. It was a highly efficient and successful institution. I was now confronted with a crisis of the gravest magnitude.

The order for disaffiliation was, however, a recommendation which had to be confirmed by the Government of India. Therein lay our hope of relief. We were prepared to give every reasonable guarantee to prevent a recurrence of what had happened; and with the pledge of such a guarantee we approached the Government of India. The matter was sent back to the University for reconsideration. The guarantees were accepted by the Senate. They were loyally given effect to; and the unhappy incident was allowed to terminate. The Ripon College, partially remodelled, continued its career of increasing usefulness.

I cannot take leave of this controversy without referring to the services of some of those who helped the College on the occasion of its greatest peril; and first and foremost among them was the late Sir Taraknath Palit. We had been friends since 1868. He had known my father and admired his genius and his personality. We first met in England and we formed a friendship, which, now that he is dead, is with me a sweet and sacred memory. He was one of the most warm-hearted men that I have ever met, strong in his likes and dislikes. A man of great strength of character, he never hesitated to express his opinions with clearness and emphasis, and sometimes without reference to the feelings of others. Generous to his friends, he was rigid in exacting what was due to him. I have hardly ever met a man who was so singularly free from the conventionalities which mar the happiness of so many of us. He was throughout life the warm friend of all patriotic movements; and his love of his countrymen found its culminating expression in the princely gift which he made, of all that he possessed, for the promotion of scientific education. He took up the case of the Ripon College with all the warmth of his generous nature, and was mainly instrumental in inducing Sir Romesh Chunder Mitter to interest himself in the matter.

Sir Romesh Chunder Mitter's help and co-operation were most valuable. I was then brought into close and intimate touch with him; and the more I saw of him, the greater was my admiration for the man. Strong, honest, with an uncommon fund of that rarest of all commodities, common sense, I always felt that he was one of the finest types of our race. He was not only a great judge, but a great man.

Monomohan Ghose was another friend who helped me on this occasion. Of him also I should like to say a word or two. He did not indeed possess the great gifts of his illustrious brother, Lalmohan Ghose; but the human side was even more largely developed in him. A great lawyer, he was an even greater public man. He was the friend of all who were in need; and many an innocent man owed his life and liberty to his merciful and unpaid advocacy. I heard a story that still lingers in my memory. My friend, who repeated it to me, had gone to see Monomohan Ghose. Monomohan Ghose was not in, but an old man was seated in his office room, with whom my friend fell into conversation. The old man said that he had been charged with murder and that he had been saved from the gallows through the efforts of Monomohan Ghose. He was a poor man who could pay nothing; and nothing was demanded of him. But year after year he visited the great advocate, the benefactor who was to him a second father, and laid at his feet the offering of his heart's gratitude; and, when after his death the visit was repeated, the poor old man sobbed like a child. The news threw him into a paroxysm of grief, and for a few moments he was inconsolable.

Where is the lawyer now who can claim this rich possession over the hearts of clients whom he has served or saved? I remember Monomohan Ghose working in some of these cases without any reward or prospect of remuneration, and with an enthusiasm that lifted him high above the plane of the mere professional lawyer. As a successful advocate, he made money, though he was not as rich as some of his friends at the Bar; but he gathered together a treasure of priceless value in the heartfelt gratitude of those whom he served, too often poor men, the victims of an unscrupulous police.

He followed a plan of his own in defending prisoners in criminal cases. He recognized that the public Press was the bulwark of popular freedom; and whenever he was engaged in an important criminal case, he was careful to take with him a newspaper reporter so that the proceedings might be fully reported. He thus became the terror of wrong-headed mofussil magistrates; and it would be a fitting tribute to his memory to say that he had a sensible share in reducing their vagaries. His unique experience as a criminal lawyer impressed him with the urgent need for the separation of judicial and executive functions in the administration of criminal justice. In season and out of season did he advocate this reform; and it is mainly due to him that the question came within the range of practical politics. The pathos of his early death consecrates the undying interest he felt in this reform.

I will here repeat the incidents connected with the fatal stroke of apoplexy that carried him off. He was at his country house at Krishnagore, which he had rebuilt and embellished, and had converted into a palatial mansion. He was preparing to start for Calcutta on his way to Madras, to see his only son, who was a member of the Madras Civil Service. The morning was passed in a somewhat heated discussion over Sir Charles Elliott's article on the separation of judicial and executive functions, which had just then appeared in one of the English reviews. His interest in the subject was keen. He felt that he could give a full and satisfactory rejoinder to Sir Charles Elliott's criticisms. It preyed upon his mind and worked him up into a pitch of unusual excitement; and in this state, while in his bath, he was seized with an apoplectic fit that proved fatal. The news came upon the educated community like a bolt from the blue; and they mourned the death of one so good, so true and so patriotic. Years have elapsed since October, 1896, but the name of Monomohan Ghose is never uttered in an assembly of his countrymen without evoking the deepest emotions.

In connexion with the Ripon College controversy, it is only right that I should add that I was greatly indebted to the friendly services of Sir Henry Harrison and Sir Henry Cotton. I had known Sir Henry Cotton for a period of over forty years, and Sir Henry Harrison for nearly twenty years, since he became Chairman of the Calcutta Corporation, of which I was at the time a member. The relations between English officials and our countrymen are for the most part formal, though I must say they are improving; but both Sir Henry Cotton and Sir Henry Harrison occupied a large place in my esteem and my affections, and they were to me as good friends as any I ever knew. Both were indefatigable in their efforts to save the Ripon College; and it was chiefly through their influence that Sir Coomer Petheram, the then Chief Justice, was persuaded to interest himself in the matter. The presence and support of the Chief Justice at a meeting of the Senate, especially in those days, meant a great deal. The vote of the legal element in the Senate was largely in favour of accepting the guarantees offered and rescinding the order of temporary disaffiliation.

The strain and worry through which I had to pass in connexion with the Ripon College controversy, coupled with the work for the Congress, which was to meet in Calcutta in December, 1890, brought on an attack of pneumonia. It was so sudden and I was so little prepared for what was coming that I had actually ordered my carriage to be got ready to take me to a dinner-party, to which I had been invited by Mrs. Sarala Ghosal, the gifted wife of the late Mr. Janokinath Ghosal, and a well-known authoress. Just as I was about to start for the dinner, I felt feverish. A local doctor was brought in. He felt my pulse and said that I had fever. Within half an hour I experienced a sense of difficulty in breathing. My friend, Dr. Debendranath Roy was sent for. He came and examined me and said it was a case of acute bronchitis. I was ordered to bed; and for over a month I lay there, a helpless patient, suffering from pneumonia, while my colleagues were working hard to ensure the success of the approaching session of the Congress. To the physical pain and weakness from which I suffered was superadded the agony of a bitter disappointment, that I should be shut out from the joy of work that was so congenial to me. They held a Town Hall meeting, but I was not there. There was another fellow-sufferer whose absence was severely felt by Congress-workers. That was Mr. W. C. Bonnerjea, who, too, was confined to a sick-bed, prostrated with rheumatic fever.

I recovered sufficiently to be able to attend a meeting of the Congress and to make, under the peremptory mandate of the

President, who fixed for me the limit of time, a speech that did not exceed half a dozen lines. I owed my recovery on this occasion to the affectionate care and watchfulness of the late Dr. Debendranath Roy. I had known him since 1868. He was then ready to proceed to England with me, to compete for the Indian Medical Service. But there was a difficulty in his way. Mr. Monomohan Ghose, our non-official protector of emigrants, as Michael Madhu Shudan Dutt styled him, would not help him without his brother's knowledge and consent; and his brother, Rai Jadunath Roy Bahadur, the leader of public opinion in Krishnagore, objected to his visiting England. Caste prejudices against sea-voyages were then strong, and Rai Jadunath Roy Bahadur did not feel himself equal to overcoming them. But my friend, Dr. Debendranath Roy, graduated from the Calcutta Medical College and rose to distinction in the service of Government; and, when on his retirement he settled down in Calcutta, he commanded a large and lucrative practice. Skilful as a physician, his geniality as a man was even more remarkable. He was himself the victim of diabetes and asthma; but they were never permitted to mar his cheerfulness or disturb his optimism; and the hope and confidence that radiated from his glowing eyes were a source of never-failing comfort to his numerous patients. His premature death in 1909 was mourned by a large circle of friends and admirers. He was not only a distinguished physician but an active educationist, and as a member of the Senate he rendered good service to the Calcutta University.

12

My Legislative Council Work

Expansion of the Legislative Councils, 1892 – my election to the Bengal Legislative Council – Sir Charles Elliott – the Bengal Municipal Act – Sir Edward Baker – the House of Commons and simultaneous examinations.

The Legislative Councils were reformed and expanded by the Parliamentary Statute of 1892, and the reformed Councils met for the first time in 1893. The Regulations framed by the Government under the Statute of 1892 were much less drastic than those under the subsequent Statute of 1909, when the Councils were still further expanded and liberalized. The elective principle having been definitely recognized and larger powers having been conferred upon non-official members, the Government assumed authority to interfere with the elections. Dismissed servants of Government and persons bound down for good behaviour under section 110 of the Indian Criminal Procedure Code were disqualified; and, above all, Government assumed a general power of declaring a person disqualified whose election would, in the opinion of the Governor or the Governor-General, be contrary to the public interest. It was not indeed necessary to reserve these powers in 1893, for the Government was the final authority in accepting or rejecting an election made by a constituency.

It has been, I fear, a traditional policy with the Government, when making a concession to popular demands, to fence it round with safeguards, promoted by a spirit of caution and sometimes in excess of what may be deemed necessary by the exigencies of the case. In the old days before the Councils were reformed, official members were permitted considerable freedom of action to vote as they thought fit; and the annals of the Bengal Legislative Council bear testimony to the fact that the President of the Council, the Lieutenant-Governor of the province, was defeated by the voice and vote of the Council, a majority of whom were officials, when, in the course of the debate in connexion with what became the Calcutta Municipal Act of 1876, he supported the motion for three-fourths of the members of the Corporation being elected. A remnant of that freedom still lingered when the Councils were reconstituted in 1893, and I remember my lamented friend, Mr. R. C. Dutt, then Commissioner of the Burdwan

Division, who was for some time a member of the Bengal Legislative Council, and Mr. Cotton, Chief Secretary, voting against the Government. But all that is now a matter of the past. The official members must vote with the Government, unless released by the authority of the President. The only occasion within my recent experience when this order of relaxation was given was in connexion with the debate on the resolution I moved in the Imperial Legislative Council regarding the Chancellorship of the Calcutta University. On that occasion every official member was allowed to speak and vote as he thought fit; and, I may add, the fullest advantage was taken of the privilege.

There was another point in which the Regulations under the Statute of 1892 compared favourably with those of 1909. No special electorates, representing class or commercial interests, were created. The constituencies were the district boards and the municipalities, the former representing rural, and the latter urban, interests. The middle class received the measure of prominence to which they were entitled, but this was taken away from them by the extraordinary Regulations of 1910. In 1892, although there were no separate electorates and special constituencies, no class interests suffered. The Maharaja of Natore, the Raja of Tahirpur, Nawab Serajul Islam, the two former representing the interests of the land-holding, and the latter, those of the Mohamedan, community, found no difficulty in getting themselves returned to the Council. It is true that the Rajas and Maharajas had partly to depend upon the support of the middle class, and the Mohamedan candidates upon that of their Hindu fellow-subjects. But nobody in Bengal, so far as I know, ever made it a matter of complaint. The Hindu-Mohamedan question is of more recent date, and was accentuated, if not indeed created, by the partition of Bengal; and even to-day, notwithstanding the official acceptance of class representation, there is really no cleavage of interest between the landed aristocracy and the great middle class; and so prominent a member of the landed interest as the Maharaja of Burdwan delights to call himself a member of the educated community and to be associated with them in their public movements. Class representation is the retort courteous of the bureaucracy to the middle class, who clamoured for the reform of the Councils and got it. It seriously curtailed the power which they exercised over the elections under the Statute of 1892; and the whole trend of the Regulations of

1909 was to assign to them a back seat in the new system that was largely their creation.

The Councils having been reformed in 1892, and there being no legal bar in my way, I offered myself as a candidate for election to the Bengal Legislative Council by the Corporation of Calcutta, of which I was then a member. There were two other candidates, Babu Kalinath Mitter and Babu Joygovind Law. Babu Kalinath Mitter was the undoubted leader of the Opposition in the Corporation and the foremost representative of the rate-payers. As such, when the Calcutta Municipal Bill, which subsequently became the Municipal Act of 1888, was under consideration, he was nominated by the Government as a member of the Bengal Legislative Council, to represent the interests of the rate-payers. He performed his duties on that occasion with conspicuous zeal and ability. As a member of the Corporation (which he served from 1876 to 1899, when he resigned along with twenty-seven other municipal Commissioners) he was noted for his industry, his capacity, and his absolute candour and honesty of purpose. Babu Joygovind Law, though less distinguished as a member of the Corporation, was respected by his colleagues for his quiet, business-like ways, and his genuine interest in the affairs of the Corporation. We were all friends and we fought as friends. No misrepresentation, no word uttered in anger or in malice was permitted to mar the contest or to leave an unpleasant memory behind; and, when the elections were over, we were as good friends as ever and continued to be helpful colleagues, working in close co-operation so long as we remained members of the Corporation.

What a change now from those times – what a deterioration in the public life of the province, when mendacity and malice are the weapons, offensive and defensive, employed by those who call themselves the apostles of self-government and promise *Swaraj* to their countrymen! *Swaraj* means self-restraint in the great books of the Hindu religion where the word is first used. It means, as now employed by a certain class of people, license to use the meanest of mean tricks for the furtherance of their ends. If this is what we are to have in the green, what may we not expect in the dry?

I was returned at the head of the poll, the first representative of the Calcutta Corporation to the first reformed Legislative Council. What told in my favour it is difficult to say; for Babu Kalinath Mitter was undoubtedly a more distinguished member of the

Corporation. Possibly it was felt that my interests as a public man were wider, and that I had in part contributed to the reform and expansion of the Legislative Councils. I felt it a great honour that I should be the first representative of Calcutta, the city of my birth, in the new reformed Council, for the creation of which I had done what little I could. I applied myself to my legislative work with all the zeal that I could muster. Of that work it is not for me to speak. Good or bad, it is there in the records of the Bengal Legislative Council. All that I claim is that I did my best with the opportunities that lay before me.

After my first term of office, the Corporation again honoured me by electing me as their member. For the third and fourth terms I was returned a member of the Bengal Legislative Council, through the Presidency Division in Bengal, first by the municipalities and then by the district boards, so that I was a member of the Bengal Legislative Council for eight consecutive years, from 1893 to 1901, a period which for length of service is unique in the records of the reformed Legislative Council of Bengal.

In 1897 I was elected by the District Boards of the Presidency Division when I was away in England as a witness before the Welby Commission. It was my esteemed friend, the late Babu Ashutosh Biswas, whose tragic death we all mourned, who was mainly instrumental in securing my return on that occasion.

In 1899, the Government intervened to find a constituency for me. Under the Regulations of 1893, the number of seats open to election being few, the constituencies (the district boards and municipalities) took part in the elections by rotation. There was no constituency by which I could be returned in 1897. The Calcutta Municipal Bill was then under discussion. I had taken a prominent part in it, in pressing for a modification of the Bill upon more liberal lines. Both the Government and the public were of opinion that my presence in the Council, while the Bill was being considered, was absolutely necessary. Sir John Woodburn, the then Lieutenant-Governor, expressed the same view. He had, under the regulations, the power of changing the order of rotation. It was now the turn of the Dacca Division to return a member. The Lieutenant-Governor, in virtue of the discretion vested in him, transferred the privilege to the Municipalities of the Presidency Division for the elections of 1897. I stood as a candidate; there was no contest, and I was unanimously returned.

The two measures of the greatest importance that came up for consideration before the Council in my time were an amendment of the Bengal Municipal Act and a complete revision of the Calcutta Municipal Act. The former was pending when the reformed Council was formed, the latter was introduced in 1897. They both referred to local self-government and the municipal institutions of the land, with whose practical working I was quite familiar. I had been chairman of a mofussil municipality since 1885 and a member of the Calcutta Corporation since the introduction of the elective system in 1876. In dealing with these measures I was on familiar ground and commanded a degree of experience that was very helpful to me in my legislative work. The amendment of the Bengal Municipal Bill was the work of Sir Charles Elliott, then Lieutenant-Governor of Bengal. From 1893 till his retirement I was in close touch with him. Personally our relations were friendly and even cordial. I had the amplest opportunities of knowing the man and the ruler. He came from the United Provinces and was somewhat unfamiliar with the ways and methods of the people of Bengal. But his industry was marvellous; his mastery of detail, which would have been admirable in the Collector of a district, was somewhat out of place in the ruler of a great province. His too close touch with details interfered with his clear vision of principles. Unfamiliar as he was with Bengal, he had the good sense to summon Mr. Henry Cotton to fill the office of Chief Secretary.

No member of the Bengal Civil Service enjoyed in an equal measure the confidence and esteem of the people, and the appointment was welcomed as a good augury. That the hopeful anticipations entertained were not realized was not Mr. Cotton's fault; for he had to deal with an administrator who was a typical bureaucrat. Sir Charles Elliott had a profound faith in the Civil Service and an unshaken conviction that the Government of the country by the Civil Service was the best that could have been devised by the genius of man. As a necessary corollary to this belief there was a feeling, more or less pronounced, which ran through all his measures, that the people could not be trusted to manage their own affairs. As between Indians and Englishmen, however, he made no distinction in social amenities, or in official employment. But he had an unswerving faith in the saving virtues of the Civil Service, as an all but infallible controlling agency for the administration of the country. This distrust of the people and of popular institutions lay at the root of the two most prominent measures of his administration, namely, the Bengal Municipal Bill and the Jury Notification.

As I have observed, an amendment of the Bengal Municipal Act was pending before the Government when the Council was reconstituted under the Statute of 1892. The measure was reactionary, prompted by the official distrust of municipal institutions. Once a municipality was invested with the right of electing its own chairman, the right, under the law in force, could not be withdrawn. It was now proposed under the amending Bill to vest in the Government the power of depriving a municipality of this right. Again, under the present Municipal Act, there can be no subdivision of a municipality without the consent of the Commissioners. They are the final authority in this matter. It was now proposed under the Bill to deprive them of this power and make Government the judge and arbiter in regard to these questions.

Outside the Council I had done my best to get these provisions condemned. I had protested in the Press, I had organized public meetings against them, I had personally interviewed some of the Indian members of the Council; but all in vain. At last the idea of an appeal to England occurred to me. I wrote a long letter to Mr. Allen Hume, urging my reasons and requesting him to see Lord Ripon, who was then a member of the Cabinet. Mr. Hume forwarded my letter to him. Lord Ripon wrote back to say that each member of the Cabinet was supreme in his department, but that he had sent my letter to Lord Kimberley, who was then Secretary of State for India. I heard no more about it; but it had the desired effect. Sir Charles Elliott came to the Council one morning and before opening the proceedings declared that he had received a communication from the Secretary of State on the subject of the Bengal Municipal Bill, and that what he had decided, as the result of a careful reconsideration, was in entire agreement with the views of the Secretary of State. He and the Secretary of State had agreed that the provisions to which exception had been taken should be dropped. All is well that ends well. I was in the Council listening to these observations, and my feelings may well be imagined. The diplomatic conversion of the Local Government to our views was welcomed by the public; and we did not care to examine whether the Lieutenant-Governor had carried out a mandate from the Secretary of State, or had come to the same decision as the result of his own independent review of the situation.

For the time, the interests of local self-government in the mofussil were saved.

The other measure affecting local self-government that came on for consideration while I was a member of the Bengal Legislative Council – and here I am anticipating events that took place much later – was what was known as the Mackenzie Bill. Its genesis has so often been told that I need not repeat it here. Sir Alexander Mackenzie, who succeeded Sir Charles Elliott as Lieutenant-Governor of Bengal was the author of the measure, and its scope and object were further amplified by Lord Curzon. It is an irony of fate that the Lieutenant-Governor over whose signature as Home Secretary the great Resolutions on local self-government had been issued, should have been instrumental in forgoing a deadly weapon against the institution of local self-government in the capital of British India. But perhaps as Home Secretary Sir Alexander Mackenzie was merely carrying out the orders of superior authority, and as Lieutenant-Governor he was the master of his own policy.

A successful Civil Servant has often no convictions; or, when he has any, he never allows them to interfere with his official advancement. Sir Richard Temple was the friend of local self-government in Calcutta, and to him we are indebted for the recognition of the elective system in the constitution of the Calcutta Corporation. But in England he sat on the Tory benches of the House of Commons, and conveniently forgot his liberal predilections. Sir Alexander Mackenzie had been the pupil and assistant of Sir Ashley Eden in the Bengal Secretariat, and Sir Ashley Eden had once said, in derision of representative institutions, that they were a sickly plant in their own native soil. Sir Alexander Mackenzie, in his famous speech at the opening of the Pumping Station at Palmer's Bridge, said of the Calcutta Corporation that it was an armoury of talk and an arsenal of delays. The Commissioners talked *ad libitum;* he wanted to curb their loquacity, to reduce their brake power and to add to the vigour of executive authority. The head of the municipal executive was to have independent powers, no longer subordinate to those of the Corporation; he was to be a co-ordinate authority, and the supremacy of the Corporation was to be emasculated. The Commissioners could talk as much as they liked; but, within his own sphere, the Chairman would act as he pleased with little or no responsibility to the Corporation. The authority of the Corporation was to be further restricted by creating a General Committee, another co-ordinate and independent authority. The majority of the representatives of the rate-payers in the Corporation was still maintained; but it was left for Lord Curzon, after the Bill had passed the Select Committee stage, to issue the crowning mandate that was to officialize the Corporation, directing the reduction of the elected members, and placing them numerically on the same footing as the nominated element. This, coupled with the fact that the president was an official, gave a standing majority to the official element. Thus was the officialization of the Corporation completed.

As a protest against this arbitrary action on the part of the Government of Lord Curzon, twenty-eight Commissioners, including all the men of light and leading, tendered their resignation. Sir John Woodburn, the Lieutenant-Governor, threatened to resign, but as a matter of fact held on to his office. The Bill was introduced in 1897; it was passed in 1899; and it became the law of the land on April 1, 1900.

I was a member of the Select Committee; and for three months, and from day to day, we were hard at work until we submitted our Report. The Council held daily sittings for over a fortnight to consider the report and the amendments that were moved. The sittings of the Council often extended from 11 A.M. to 5 P.M., with an interval for lunch. For many years I was a member of the Council, but I never had such hard work to go through. It reminded me of the time when I was competing for the Indian Civil Service. Often I would be at work till one o'clock at night, preparing myself for the work of the Council, which was to meet at eleven o'clock on the following day. After the work and the excitement were over, there came the reaction, and I was prostrated by an attack of brain-fever, one of the severest illnesses from which I have ever suffered. The last day of the debate, when the Bill was passed by the Council, was September 27. It was the anniversary of the death of the great Raja Ram Mohun Roy. As I was ascending the steps on my way to the Council Chamber, an invitation to attend the anniversary meeting was put into my hands. It raised in me the saddest emotions; and for the last time, in opposing the Bill, I said:

'Just as I was coming to this Council this morning, I received a letter, which reminded me that to-day was the anniversary of the death of Raja Ram Mohun Roy. It seems to me to be most fitting that the anniversary of the death of the greatest Bengalee of modern times should correspond with the date which will be remembered by future generations of Bengalees as that which marks the extinction of local self-government in that city where he lived and worked, and which was the city of his love.'

Before I leave this subject, it is only right and proper that I should say a word or two about the distinguished member of the Civil Service, Mr. E. N. (afterwards Sir Edward) Baker who was in charge of the Bill. I had known him ever since 1890, when he was Magistrate of the 24-Parganas. I was Chairman of the North Barrackpore Municipality, and we had some differences. I saw him, and our little dispute was settled in half an hour. The acquaintance thus begun ripened into a warm, personal friendship that was not marred by even acute differences of opinion. Our respect and esteem for each other was reciprocal. He was indeed a bureaucrat, but an Englishman with warm, generous and liberal sympathies. He wrote against the Jury Notification; and, as a member of the Viceroy's Executive Council, he was the life and soul of the reform movement which culminated in the Minto-Morley Scheme. He had been for many years a member of the Calcutta Corporation and was thoroughly familiar with the working of the municipal law. His sympathies were really with us, and he did not at all like the Bill; but he had to carry out orders and to get on in the Service. The Bill had originally been introduced by Sir Herbert Risley, then Municipal Secretary; but on his translation to the Government of India as Home Secretary, Mr. Baker was placed in charge of it. Throughout he was fair-minded, and consistently with his instructions was willing to make concessions to the opposition. But, of course, he could not go beyond a certain point.

Before I made my last speech in the Council, he came round to me and said, 'Surendranath, don't burn your boats', meaning that I should say nothing that would commit me to an absolute refusal to take further part or share in the work of the Corporation after it had been reconstituted under the new Act. I said, 'That is impossible'; and have remained outside the Corporation ever since September 1, 1899, when the twenty-eight Commissioners tendered their resignation. Once or twice I was pressed to reconsider my decision, by men like Narendranath Sen and Nalin Behari Sircar; but I remained obdurate; and to me it fell by a strange irony of fate to revise the Mackenzie Act and to democratize the constitution of the Corporation.

The year 1893 witnessed what may be regarded as a notable event in our political history. On June 2, 1893, Mr. Herbert moved a Resolution in the House of Commons in favour of Simultaneous Examinations for the Indian Civil Services. Mr. Dadabhai Naoroji, who was then in Parliament, supported the Resolution, and it was carried. The acceptance of the Resolution by the House fell like a bombshell upon the official world here. The India Office lost no time in repudiating it. Sir Henry Fowler was at that time Secretary of State for India, the selfsame politician who declared amid the cheers of the House that every member of Parliament was a member for India, a declaration which we here in India understood to mean that what is everybody's business is nobody's business. He held that it was a snatch vote, that it did not represent the sense or judgment of the House of Commons, and that the Government was not bound by it. But there was the vote; and the Secretary of State sought to get over it by a reference to the authorities in India. The opinion of the Government of India and of the Local Governments was invited. Everybody knew what that opinion would be. With the exception of the Government of Madras, every Local Government was opposed to the vote. Nor was this the only occasion when Madras won pre-eminence by the liberality of its views. In the days of Lord Lytton, when the Vernacular Press Law was enacted, the Government of Madras under the Duke of Buckingham objected to the measure, and it was not extended to that Presidency.

When the reference was under discussion, Sir Anthony MacDonnell was officiating as Lieutenant-Governor of Bengal, Sir Charles Elliott having taken leave for six months. He sent for me, and I had a long conversation with him at 'Belvedere'. Let me reproduce, as far as I can, the substance of the conversation. Perhaps a dialogue would best represent what passed between the Lieutenant-Governor and myself.

The Lieutenant-Governor: Why is it, Mr. Banerjea, you are so keen about simultaneous examinations?

Mr. Banerjea: Because, your Honour, we have lost all faith in nominations, and because we think that simultaneous examinations alone can give us our fair share of appointments in the Indian Civil Service, and redeem the Queen's Proclamation.

The Lieutenant-Governor: But, under the recommendations of the Public Services Commission, a number of listed appointments have been thrown open to your countrymen in the Provincial Service, and you can also compete in England.

Mr. Banerjea: Your Honour, I repeat, nominations by Government cannot, and will not, satisfy us. By the Statute of 1870, it was provided that Indians of proved merit and capacity would be appointed to the Civil Service under rules to be framed for the purpose. It took half a dozen years to frame as many rules, and even after that you proceeded at snail-pace to comply with the requirements of the statute.

The Lieutenant-Governor: But you are now a power both here and in England. You have organized Indian public opinion, and you have a British Committee in London to represent your interests.

Mr. Banerjea: Despite all that, Indian opinion is impotent in the counsels of the Government. Our rights are dependent upon sufferance, and our privileges are more or less a matter of grace and favour.

This conversation took place in 1893. When I had an interview with Lord MacDonnell in London in 1909, he had, as it appeared to me, partly modified his views and was inclined to support simultaneous examinations. That was after the Curzon-Wyllie murder, and he was of opinion that it was unwise to encourage the steady flow of Indian students into England, and that both the examinations for calls to the Bar and for the Indian Civil Service should be held simultaneously in India as well as in England.

13

The Indian National Congress, 1894-1896

The Madras Congress – 'should students discuss politics?' – president of the Poona Congress, 1895 – preparation for the presidential speech – reflections on oratory – Sir Romesh Chunder Mitter – development of the Congress movement.

In 1894, the Indian National Congress met at Madras. We chartered a steamer, and the Bengal delegates all went in a body. The steamer party was most useful, for the delegates were thrown together for several days; and, apart from the solidarity of life and thought that this promoted, it helped the discussion of public questions in a friendly and informal way, which is often a more effective, and certainly a less irritating, method of solution than formal debates.

On board the steamer we came to a most important decision affecting the holding of our Provincial Conferences. The Provincial Conferences are offshoots of the Congress, and, as Dr. Mohendralal Sircar observed while presiding over one of them, they are tributary streams which flow on to swell the great volume of the Congress movement. Hitherto our Provincial Conferences used to be held in Calcutta, but the movement was languid and did not seem to gather force or volume. We decided upon a change; and we came to the conclusion that it was desirable to alter the locale of the Provincial Conferences from year to year, and to hold them in different mofussil centres in different years. We resolved to invest the Conferences with the peripatetic character that belonged to the Congress. Babu Baikuntanath Sen of Berhampore, who was one of the delegates present, agreed to invite the Conference to Berhampore in 1895. The change gave a new impetus to the movement; and the Berhampore Conference of 1895, the first of its kind held in a mofussil town, was a great success. Since then the experiment has been repeated with increasing success; and, as I have observed in an early part of these Reminiscences, the Provincial Conferences in point of numbers and enthusiasm reflect the character of the great Congress gatherings.

Mr. Webb, an Irish Member of Parliament, presided over the

Madras Congress of 1894. I believe that his election as President of the Congress did not meet with the approval of Mr. W. C. Bonnerjea. The latter's view was, and it is held by many, that the President of the Indian National Congress should, save in exceptional cases, be an Indian.

I moved the Resolution on the Civil Service question. It was, and had been, my practice in the Congress to stick to the two questions in which I felt the deepest interest, namely, the wider employment of our countrymen in the higher offices in the public service, and the establishment of representative institutions. I felt that they lay at the root of all other Indian problems, and their satisfactory settlement would mean the solution of them all. If power were vested in us to legislate, and to control the finances, and to carry on the administration, through and by our own men, in accordance with principles laid down by our representatives, we should have self-government in the truest sense, and possess the amplest facilities for developing our powers and faculties and taking our legitimate place among the nations of the earth. Our goal was not power for the sake of self, but power for the accomplishment of the high destiny assigned to us by an Almighty Providence.

In Madras I was invited to address a students' meeting. I gladly responded to the invitation. The topic was 'Should students discuss or take part in politics?' The subject, owing to recent events, had assumed an importance all its own. It gave rise to an animated discussion in which Pundit Madan Mohan Malavya and Mr. Khaparde took part. Both of them opposed me at the time. That Mr. Khaparde should have expressed the views that he did, seems extraordinary in the light of his subsequent utterances. I expressed the view, and have stuck to it through life with the strength of a growing conviction, that students should certainly discuss politics, and may even, subject to proper control and guidance, take part in political work. I have never wavered in this opinion, even when it was fiercely assailed by high official authority and eminent public men. I have noticed with pleasure, and with pride, that some of those who sang a different tune have come round to my views. When the Calcutta University Institute was started I was asked to join it. At the first anniversary meeting I was invited by the Secretary, the late Mr. Wilson, to move the first Resolution proposing the adoption of the report. I said I would gladly do so, but subject to one condition, namely, that students should be allowed to discuss politics in the Institute. The matter was laid before Sir Charles Elliott, and he vetoed it. As a result I did not move the Resolution, nor did I join the Institute. The Institute does not indeed encourage the discussion of political questions, but high officials like Mr. Lyon and Mr. Cumming have from its platform expressed their views upon the great problems of Indian administration and self-government.

The unwisdom of excluding students from the discussion of political questions is being recognized. Some sort of politics, good or bad, they are bound to have; and if you will not teach them the right sort of politics, and by discussion with them lead them to it, you must make up your mind for the wildest vagaries among them, in a matter of vital concern to the student community. In the Unions of Oxford and Cambridge political questions are not tabooed, and political leaders are invited to open discussions. India is not England; but the student mind is the same all the world over; and the discipline of knowledge and of healthy discussion is bound to be as fruitful in the East as in the West.

While I hold this view, I deprecate all demonstrations of rowdyism on the part of some of our young men, who have displayed an unpardonable intolerance of views opposed to their own. Tolerance has been the immemorial creed of the Hindu race; and discipline is the soul of student-life. These deviations from ancient practice and the deep-rooted instincts of the Hindu student constitute a serious menace to our orderly political progress. I am afraid that both in our homes and in our educational institutions the bonds of discipline have been relaxed, and a spirit of disorder is gaining ground. I can only hope that it is a temporary phase, a short-lived development, which will pass away with the exciting causes that have given rise to it.

We returned home from Madras by the British India Steam Navigation Company's steamer *Rewa*. My friend, Mr. B. L. Gupta of the Indian Civil Service, and Miss Muller, who had adopted an Indian student, Mr. Ghose, were our fellow-passengers. Kali Prosanna Kabyavisarad, editor of the *Hitabadi*, was one of our party, and he used to entertain the European passengers on board with his card-tricks and his feats of jugglery. Visarad, whose versatility was wonderful, was a past master in this art. One of the most genial of men, a brilliant Bengalee writer, a poet of no mean order, a composer of songs of exquisite beauty and pathos, which thrilled the audiences at our *Swadeshi* meetings, it will be necessary for me to refer to him and his work at greater length later on. I was pressed by my fellow-passengers to address them on the subject of the Congress. My Indian friends joined in this request, and I gladly responded to their invitation. I spoke for over half an hour in the saloon, which was crowded with passengers, Captain Hansard, the captain of the steamer, presiding. There were a good many passengers who were not Englishmen; and I concluded my speech with an earnest appeal to them in the following words:

> 'To those who are not Englishmen I would also appeal with confidence to help us in the work in which we are engaged. For do they not belong to the brotherhood of civilized humanity? I venture to claim for the Congress that its work does not belong to India alone. It has a wider scope and a deeper significance. It concerns the interests of human freedom and the progress of human civilization; and the political enfranchisement of a great people on the banks of the Ganges would be welcomed as glad tidings of great joy throughout the length and breadth of the civilized world.'

In the year 1895, I was for the first time elected President of the Indian National Congress. The Congress was held that year at Poona, the capital of the Deccan, and an important intellectual centre in the western presidency. Early in November, I received a wire from Mr. Mahadeo Govind Ranade offering me the Presidentship of the Congress. I replied the same day thankfully accepting the offer. In those days there was no eager competition, no canvassing for the honour. The Reception Committee selected the President, and their decision was acquiesced in without demur. If I remember rightly, it was in 1906 that the first signs of a contest for the Presidentship showed themselves. They culminated in the break-up of the Surat Congress in the following year, and the unhappy schism that followed. The contest was synchronous with the development of strong differences of opinion in the Congress camp soon after the Partition of Bengal, and the apparent failure of constitutional methods.

Mr. Ranade was, in regard to all public movements in the western presidency, the power behind the throne. A public servant, loyal to the Government, with that true loyalty, not born of personal motives, or of passing impulses, but having its roots in the highest considerations of expediency and the public good, he was the guide, philosopher and friend of the public men of the western presidency; and all public movements, were they political, social or religious, bore the impress of his masterful personality. I came in contact with him while quite young in my career as a public man.

When I went to Poona in 1877 in connexion with the Civil Service question I was his guest. I was as much impressed by his great talents and his ardent patriotism, as by the simplicity of his domestic surroundings, and the lovableness and nobility of his personal character.

Having accepted the Presidentship, I applied myself to the task of preparing the presidential speech. It was Herculean work; and on both occasions – for I was honoured twice with this high office – I found it to be so. I had my professorial duties in the College. I was in sole charge of the *Bengalee* newspaper. I had my municipal work to attend to, for I was then a member of the Calcutta Corporation. I followed a simple plan. I used to return home to Barrackpore every day by two o'clock in the afternoon, and start writing my speech. I would allow no interruption of any kind to divert me from the steady pursuit of this programme. I would ruthlessly say 'No' to every intruder. Save only once. I remember my friend, Ashutosh Biswas, coming up to me at Barrackpore while I was engaged in this work, to canvass for my vote for a gentleman who stood as a candidate for the Vice-Chairmanship of the Calcutta Corporation. I could refuse nothing to Ashutosh Biswas. I said I could give him only ten minutes, and he did not take more than five.

For two hours every day, and from day to day, I was absorbed in this work, alone in my house, for my family were at the time at Allahabad owing to my boy's illness; and the speech grew until it became, I fear, one of the biggest ever delivered from the presidential chair of the Congress. After two hours' hard work at the speech I used to have my regular constitutional walk on the riverside for three-quarters of an hour, when the whole of what I had written would be thought over, repeated and corrected, and the corrections subsequently embodied in the manuscript. This work was continued for six weeks without interruption, with my mind centred on the performance with all the power of concentration of which I was capable. I delivered the whole of my speech without referring to any notes, except perhaps when there was a long string of figures. The delivery took over four hours, and I think I was able, during the whole of that time, to keep up, undiminished and without flagging, the attention of a vast assembly of over five thousand people.

I have often been asked to explain the secret of my being able to make long speeches without reference to a single note, and even to reproduce passages that I have thought over in my mind. Perhaps it is an incommunicable secret; the speaker himself hardly knows. Much depends upon the arrangement and upon the construction of the sentences. If the order be natural, logical and consistent, it is an aid to the memory. If the sentences are rhythmical, they imprint themselves on the mind, the cadence helping the memory. Lord Salisbury used to say that his finest sentences, as they occurred to him while preparing his speeches, burnt themselves upon his mind. That I believe is true of all who have practised the art of public speaking. After all, preparation is the great thing. It is indeed the one thing needed. Genius, as Carlyle has truly observed, is an infinite capacity for taking pains. A speech is not worth listening to, John Bright used to say, unless it has been carefully prepared. The great English orator would absent himself sometimes from Cabinet meetings, when preparing his more important speeches. It is constant preparation that fits you for the impromptu debate, that gives you the command of words, the readiness of resource, in a word the mental equipment of the accomplished debater. A successful debater is not necessarily a great orator. The qualifications of the orator are moral rather than intellectual. It is the emotions that inspire the noblest thoughts and invest them with their colour and their distinctive character.

Let no one aspire to be an orator who does not love his country, love her indeed with a true and soul-absorbing love. Country first, all other things next, is the creed of the orator. Unless he has been indoctrinated in it, baptized with the holy fire of love of country, the highest intellectual gifts will not qualify him to be an orator. Aided by them, he may indeed be a fluent debater, an expert in the presentment of his case, a fascinating speaker, able to please, amuse and even to instruct; but without the higher patriotic or religious emotions he will not possess the supreme power of moving men, inspiring them with lofty ideals and the passion for the worship of the good, the true and the beautiful. The equipment of the orator is thus moral, and nothing will help him so much as constant association with the master-minds of humanity, of those who have worked and suffered, who have taught and preached great things, who have lived dedicated lives, consecrated to the service of their country or of their God.

Addressing a body of young men, many, many years ago, on the art of public speaking, I said to them, 'You must live in a high and holy atmosphere fragrant with the breath of the gods. Burke, Mazzini, Jesus Christ, Buddha, Mohamed, Chaitanya, Ram Mohun

Roy, Keshub Chunder Sen, must be your constant companions. Your souls must be attuned to the pathos and the music of the *Bande-Matarama.*' All that is best and truest must form a part of the moral composition of the orator. Let him have it – in whatever measure he can, but he must have it – and the words will come gurgling from the fountains of the heart. His intellectual equipment, though important, is subsidiary. The moral takes precedence.

Among the intellectual qualifications to which I attach the utmost importance is the power of concentration. Gladstone possessed it in a pre-eminent degree. It is useful in all walks of life. To the orator, who can always live in the midst of his thoughts, arranging them for impressive presentment, the quality is especially valuable. I have zealously cultivated it through life and have found it a valuable aid to all my efforts. When a boy of only eleven years of age, I remember coming down in a boat to Calcutta from Manirampore near Barrackpore, our ancestral home. My father, my eldest brother, my cousin, the late Dwaraka Nath Banerjee, barrister-at-law, and one or two others were in the boat. They were engaged in a boisterous conversation. I had a lesson to prepare for my class; it was a verse consisting of a dozen lines, which I had to commit to memory. I sat in one corner of the boat, heedless of the talk that was going on, and by the time we reached Calcutta I was ready to repeat the verses. Every faculty grows with cultivation; and now when I am at work I am absolutely absorbed in it, insensible to all distraction, unless I am directly spoken to.

I may here be permitted to relate an incident in this connexion known only to myself and to some members of my family. When Queen Victoria died, I was invited by Lord Curzon, through my esteemed friend, Mr. Greer, then Chairman of the Corporation, to take part in the memorial meeting, which was to be held at the Town Hall. The Viceroy himself was to preside. Permission was given to me to select my own Resolution. The preparation of the speech, which in my opinion was one of the best I ever made, took me about an hour and a half. I sat down the evening before, at a table in one corner of a room about sixteen feet by twelve, at the other end of which were my children, playing and frolicking with all the ardour of children. Their frolics did not at all disturb me. I was absolutely insensible to their prattlings, and when I had finished the preparation of the speech I joined them.

My professorial work greatly helped me in my public speeches, for I had to teach the classics of the English language. Among them were the speeches and writings of Burke, Froude, Lord Morley, and others. I thus lived in constant association with the great masters of the English language and in close familiarity with their vocabulary and methods of thought, and to none do I owe a greater debt than to Edmund Burke, whose political philosophy has so largely moulded my own views about government and society. One of the most extraordinary things that the Calcutta University ever did was to interdict the writings of Burke. The ban has now been partly removed. I suppose the idea was, at least in the minds of some, that Burke taught revolutionary doctrines, and a learned counsel in the Dacca Conspiracy Case actually referred to Burke's *Reflections on the French Revolution* in that light, forgetting that the book is the strongest and the most reasoned protest against revolutions of all kinds.

On my way to attend the Congress at Poona I halted for a day at Allahabad and stayed with my son-in-law, Colonel Mukerjee, who was then in medical charge of an Indian regiment, and who is now so well known as the author of *A Dying Race*. I repeated to him the peroration of my Poona presidential speech. He heard it and said, 'That speech has been twenty years in the making'. The remark struck me as one of extraordinary shrewdness and more or less of general application. It meant that my laborious performance covered a period of time far beyond what was actually taken up by the work. No improvisation is, or can be, productive of any really great effort, for there are no short cuts either in nature or in art. Even when there is improvisation in a great achievement in public speaking, it will often be found to have its roots in laborious efforts in a kindred field of work. The orator has laid by in the chambers of his mind a storehouse of noble thoughts and a fine vocabulary, ready at his command to form varied combinations. They move forward in serried procession, for him to pick and choose, or modify, for the deliverance of his message. Nature and his prepossessions predispose him to live and move and have his being in company with the immortals of the earth, breathing an atmosphere fragrant with their breath. His training and equipment are moral rather than intellectual. His heart inspires, his intellect obeys. Carlyle has observed that all great thoughts spring from the heart; and through the heart they work round the brain. It must be so in a special degree in the orator's work; for here heart speaks to heart and is the centre of the emotions which flow out to the audience and overwhelm them. Oratory indeed is reason incandescent with passion. It is love of country, love of humanity, decked forth in the fervid light and effulgence of the soul. It is the words that burn and glow and sparkle that alone can set the soul on fire; and it is the heart that touches the tongue with the celestial fire.

The presidential speech at Poona elicited warm encomiums. Sir Herbert Risley, himself an accomplished writer, wired to me to say that he greatly admired its perfect finish. The ovation that I received at Poona and elsewhere made a great impression in Calcutta. That a schoolmaster and an agitator should have been so honoured outside his own province, touched the gods of the official hierarchy. I myself was greatly moved by the cordiality of my reception. I can never forget the scene that took place at the pandal when I had finished my last concluding speech. I was familiar with Congress proceedings, and was ready with a speech that I intended to deliver at the termination of the session. I found that the atmosphere had become electric, seething with an exuberance of feeling for which even I was not prepared. I grasped the spirit of the situation; I cast aside the speech that I had prepared, and threw myself heart and soul into the full flood of the emotions that were swaying that vast audience. I was moved and carried away by the surging current. It was no longer a speaker inspiring an audience. It was the audience that moved and inspired the speaker. Truly a galvanic current was established between them and myself, and as I sat down, after my improvised speech (for here there was real improvisation) – as I sat down, the younger section of the audience rushed up the platform and were at my feet, eager to touch them and take the dust off them. For the moment glancing through the great past, the genius of which seemed now to stand revealed to me, I could realize the spirit that moved the ancestors of those young men, to found the greatest Hindu Empire of modern times. The memory of that day will never be effaced. It was one of the proudest in my life.

I returned to Calcutta, breaking journey at Allahabad, where my boy was dangerously ill. My friends, headed by Raja Benoy Krishna Deb Bahadur, had arranged a great demonstration for me at Sealdah railway station. I changed at Hughli and arrived at Sealdah via Naihati. The rush at the station was so great that the Raja fainted away, and it was with the utmost difficulty that I could get to my carriage.

Raja Benoy Krishna was a great friend of mine. My father and his, the late Maharaja Komal Krishna, were schoolfellows, and an hereditary bond of friendship subsisted between his family and mine. His brother, Maharaj Kumar Neel Krishna, and he were in one sense my political pupils. They early joined the Indian Association, took an interest in its proceedings, and developed a considerable aptitude for political work. Maharaj Kumar Neel Krishna, whose sincerity of purpose and nobility of character had raised high hopes in the minds of his friends, died early, to the great loss of his country, and the regret of his friends and of those who knew him. Raja Benoy Krishna, with intervals of interruption, followed in his brother's footsteps. He took a leading part in the agitation against the Calcutta Municipal Bill of 1897. He was the founder of the *Parisad,* or Academy of Bengalee Literature, and of that philanthropic institution known as the Benevolent Society. For me he had always a feeling of genuine kindness and affection. He helped me to start the daily *Bengalee,* in raising funds for the Ripon College building, and in all undertakings in which I sought his help. With the limitations imposed by his position and the traditions of his family, which rendered opposition to Government a matter of considerable difficulty, he was a valuable member of the Bengalee community, and his death in the prime of life was a grievous loss to me and the many interests with which he was associated.

The Indian National Congress was to be held in Calcutta in 1896, and we had heavy work before us. A Reception Committee was formed with Sir Romesh Chunder Mitter as its Chairman. It was a great thing to have secured the services of the eminent judge, who had now retired. He needed no persuasion, no pressure to join the Congress ranks. His sympathies with us were open and undisguised, though, like the late Mr. Justice Ranade, he was not able while still on the judicial Bench to associate himself closely with the Congress movement or to influence its deliberations. As Chairman of the Reception Committee, Sir Romesh Chunder Mitter made a notable speech. He asked me for some notes, which I gladly supplied him with; but his speech was his own in every sense, bearing in every line the impress of his views and of his personality. One of the most notable declarations made by him (and coming from him it had a value all its own) was that the educated community represented the brain and conscience of the country, and were the legitimate spokesmen of the illiterate masses, the natural custodians of their interests. To hold otherwise, said Sir Romesh Chunder Mitter, would be to presuppose that a foreign administrator in the service of the Government knows more about the wants of the masses than their educated countrymen. And he went on to add that it was true in all ages that 'those who think must govern those who toil; and could it be' he asked, 'that the natural order of things was reversed in this unfortunate country?' This claim is now practically admitted; and I need not waste words to justify it. But in those days it was still a matter of controversy, and the vigorous pleading of so eminent a man as Sir Romesh Chunder Mitter, who showed no partisan bias even in the advocacy of public interests, was necessary and useful. The trouble now, however, is of a different kind. The Indian public man, in the exuberance of his love for his own views, is apt to mistake his own opinion for that of the country, and his voice for the trumpet-organ of the masses. He too frequently talks of the country, all the while meaning himself and nobody else.

The year 1896 witnessed a further development in the Congress movement. Coming events cast their shadows before, and the industrial upheaval that was soon to find expression in the *Swadeshi* movement was heralded by a new departure for which the Congress was indebted to the foresight and organizing capacity of Mr. J. Chaudhuri. Mr. J. Chaudhuri may be regarded as the pioneer of the industrial movement in Bengal. He suggested (and I cordially supported his recommendation) that there should be an Industrial Exhibition in connexion with the Congress. The idea was started somewhat late, but we decided to give effect to it; and we did our best in the circumstances and with the resources at our disposal. We appealed to the Government for help, and I personally requested the Lieutenant-Governor, Sir John Woodburn, to open the exhibition. I represented to him that it was a purely industrial movement, that an Englishman like Mr. Woodroffe, Advocate-General, had joined it, and that the Government might lend it their moral support by His Honour's opening the Exhibition. Such was the official attitude with regard to the Congress movement in those days that Sir John Woodburn did not see his way to complying with our request. He said, 'Mr. Banerjea, after all, your Exhibition is an annexe of the Congress. The political flavour is strong in it. I am sorry I cannot undertake to open your Exhibition.' The function was performed by the Maharaja of Cooch-Behar in a neat little speech.

Ten years later, when the Congress was held in Calcutta, an exhibition, also an annexe of the Congress, and organized on a much larger scale, was opened by Lord Minto, then Viceroy.

Between 1896 and 1906, in the course of a decade, a marked change in the attitude of official opinion in regard to the Congress had taken place. We have seen how frankly hostile that opinion was to the movement in 1888. In 1890, the Bengal Government had circularized, directing that its officers should not attend the sittings of the Congress in Calcutta even as visitors, and that circular had to be withdrawn at the instance of the Government of India, to which an appeal was made by the Congress authorities. In 1891, when the Congress was held at Nagpore, the Chairman of the Reception Committee had approached Sir Anthony MacDonnell, then Chief Commissioner of the Central Provinces, to ascertain his attitude with regard to the Congress. Sir Anthony MacDonnell, who was an official out-and-out, but was not devoid of liberal instincts, said to him, 'Mr. —— I shall not think the better or the worse of anybody who attends the Congress.'

The same Sir Anthony MacDonnell, when the Congress was held in 1899 and he was Lieutenant-Governor of the United Provinces, would not, as a plague measure, allow the Congress to be held anywhere in or near Lucknow, but located it at a distance of seven or eight miles from the city, amid sugar-cane and rice fields, where the delegates were tormented by flies during the day and by wild boars during the night. Visitors to Lucknow were not excluded from the city, nor segregated in this way. They were allowed access and residence, subject to the ordinary measures of precaution. But for some reason or other the delegates to the National Congress coming from plague-stricken areas could not be dealt with in this way. For safety, physical as well as, we presume, moral, they were excluded, isolated and segregated in this fashion. I lived at Barrackpore, which was not a plague-stricken area, but I had dear and esteemed friends among the delegates and I did not wish to be separated from the general body of my co-workers, but preferred to participate in their hardships and inconveniences. Kali Prosanna Kabyavisarad was suffering from fever; Kali Churn Banerjee was not in the best of health; Ambika Churn Majumder was one of our party. We were all in the same tent, and we tried to make the best of a bad and trying situation.

It is a different atmosphere now. One naturally enquires, what was it that contributed to bring about this change in the official mind and temper? The Congress had not changed its programme. Its ideals and its methods remained the same until its recent adoption of the principles of non-co-operation. It has never allowed itself to be sullied by intemperance of thought or language. It has always been conspicuous for dignity and self-restraint. In 1888, when it was fiercely assailed by official critics, as in 1906 when it was honoured by the Viceroy opening its Exhibition, it was the living organ of the legitimate aspirations of the Indian people, voiced by their chosen representatives with moderation and dignity. I again ask, what was it that contributed to the change in the official mind? I have no hesitation in saying that, apart from the general causes which make for what is true, it was the attitude of Lord Morley and his statesmanlike appreciation of the new spirit in India, that helped to clear the official atmosphere and to allay the prejudice in the official mind. The Civil Service is noted for its sense of discipline, its subordination of heart and soul to superior authority. An order issued or a principle laid down, or an opinion expressed by superior authority, is accepted by the rank and file with implicit acquiescence. The efficiency of the machinery of the Civil Service, almost semi-military in its temper and complexion, depends upon this quality. It is also perhaps its weakness. Speaking from his place in the House of Commons on the occasion of the Indian Budget debate in 1906 Mr. Morley said:

> 'Then there is the Congress. I do not say that I agree with all that it desires. But, speaking broadly of what I conceive to be at the bottom of the Congress, I do not see why anyone who takes a cool and steady view of Indian government should be frightened. I will not at once conclude that, because a man is dissatisfied and discontented, he must be disaffected. Why, our own reforms and changes have been achieved by dissatisfied men, who were no more disaffected than you or I.'

In the same vein and perhaps with greater emphasis he spoke of the new spirit in India of which the Congress was the expression. 'Every one', said he, in the same speech from which I have quoted, 'every one – soldiers, travellers and journalists – they all tell us that there is a new spirit in India. Be it so. How could you expect anything else? You have now been educating the people for years with Western ideas and literature. You have already given them facilities for communication with one another. How could you suppose that India could go on just as it was when there was little higher education, when the contact between one part and another was difficult and infrequent? How could you think that all would go on as before? We should be untrue to the traditions of Parliament and to those who have from time to time and from generation to generation been the leaders of the Liberal party, if we were to show ourselves afraid of facing and recognizing the new spirit with candour and consideration.'

Views such as these, expressed by the highest Indian authority, coupled with the growing power of Indian public opinion; and the persistent moderation of the Congress leaders, could not but produce a profound influence upon official opinion in India; and the changed attitude was confirmed and strengthened by the whole tenor of Lord Hardinge's administration. In 1911, Lord Hardinge received a Congress deputation which had been refused by Lord Curzon a few years before, and in 1914 Lord Pentland visited the Congress in Madras.

14

Two Clouded Years

Evidence before the Welby Commission – British public addressed on Indian questions – my return to India: elected to the Bengal Council – the Congress of 1897: case of the Natu brothers – famine, plague, and deportations – Lord Curzon assumes office – the Madras Congress: Mr. Ananda Mohan Bose.

In 1897, I was invited to give evidence before the Welby Commission appointed to enquire into Indian Expenditure and the adjustment of the financial relations between England and India. Lord Welby was President of the Commission, and among the members were Sir William Wedderburn, Mr. W. S. Caine, and Mr. Dadabhai Naoroji. I was invited as the Indian witness from Bengal, the other witnesses from India being Mr. Gokhale and Sir Dinshaw Wacha from Bombay, and Mr. G. Subramanya Iyer from Madras.[1]

I made up my mind to accept the invitation and began to prepare myself for my examination; and here I must record my grateful acknowledgments to the Bengal Secretariat and to the memory of the late Sir Herbert Risley, then in charge of the Financial Department, for the help I received. I believe Sir Alexander Mackenzie, the Lieutenant-Governor, was doubtful as to whether I should be able to stand the test of a severe cross-examination in Finance; but I made up my mind to do my best, and I did not, I think, fare badly. I got up the details of provincial finance and the system of provincial contracts after careful study; and the labour I bestowed and the pains that I then took were helpful to me in my work as a member of the Legislative Council.

I arrived in London early in May and found that my friends had already been examined. I had to prepare a memorandum for submission to the Commission upon which I was to be examined by them. The preparation of the memorandum took me about a fortnight; and it was hard and strenuous work. I used to begin work at ten o'clock in the morning after breakfast and stop at about five o'clock, with a short interval for lunch, which I often had in my own room. The memorandum has been printed by the British Committee of the Indian National Congress along with

---

1. See Appendix B.

those submitted by the other Indian witnesses, in a separate volume, as a Congress blue-book.

It is worthy of notice that Mr. Dadabhai Naoroji, although a member of the Commission, submitted himself for examination.

My examination lasted for a whole day, from eleven o'clock in the morning till about four o'clock in the afternoon, with an interval for lunch. Sir Louis Peile, who was a member of the Commission and of the India Council, severely cross-examined me with regard to that part of my evidence which related to the wider employment of Indians in the higher offices of the Government. 'Have you read the Public Services Commission Report?' he asked me. 'Very thoroughly' was my reply, and I think I was able to turn the tables against him. I especially protested against the practical exclusion of our countrymen from the higher offices in the Educational Service. Mr. Gokhale, who was present during my evidence in cross-examination, said, 'It was brilliant'.

Immediately after my examination I went to a function where I met Sir Charles Elliott. He warmly shook me by the hand and invited me to dinner. Notwithstanding wide differences of opinion, our relations were friendly and continued to be so till 1909, when he wrote to me during my visit to England as a member of the Imperial Press Conference, asking me to disavow my sympathy with anarchical crimes, and offering me in return the honour of his hospitality. I showed this extraordinary epistle to several of my friends, including Sir Henry Cotton. I declined to take any notice of it, and did not reply to it. But this little cloud, which darkened our relations, had not then appeared, and we were good friends, glad to meet one another.

The Calcutta Municipal Bill was then before the Legislative Council, and I had a talk with him about the matter. Sir Charles Elliott was no friend of Local Self-government, but I found that in the free atmosphere of England and as the result of his contact with the institutions of Local Self-government, a change had taken place in his ideas. He was a member of the London School Board and he said to me, 'Now that I have seen how these things are worked in England, I think more about your Corporation than I ever did before'. He was not in sympathy with the drastic changes that had been introduced in the Calcutta Municipal Bill. He had the inclination, and if he had had the power, he certainly would have helped us.

After my examination as a witness, I had a little time to spare before leaving for India, and I utilized it in addressing public meetings upon Indian questions. We had a very successful meeting at Sunderland, Sir Henry Fowler's constituency. Mr. Dadabhai Naoroji was present and spoke.

With Sir Henry Fowler I had a most interesting conversation about Indian affairs. The talk turned upon the employment of our countrymen in the public service. He said, and with perfect candour, as he was then out of office, 'We are opposed to simultaneous examinations for political reasons'. I said, 'I think I can understand your hesitation so far as the Indian Civil Service is concerned, but why do you object to simultaneous examinations for what are called the Minor Civil Services? There are no political reasons here.' He had no answer to give. I promptly followed up my question with the observation, 'Sir Henry, when you are again Secretary of State, you must be prepared to receive a representation from us urging this view'. We then parted, both laughing heartily.

I thought that I had at last got to the bottom of the official mind in its objection to simultaneous examinations. Sir Henry Fowler spoke as an honest, straightforward Englishman, without the reserve of office, and he laid bare his mind. All that talk about the necessity of maintaining the English character of the administration in India by insisting upon an irreducible minimum of Englishmen in the Civil Service (as if Indians could not be thoroughly imbued with Western ideas of government) is 'moonshine' and is a diplomatic mask put on to hide the real motive. It is political and not administrative considerations that have so long operated as a bar to the wider employment of our countrymen in the higher offices of Government.

I returned to Bombay about June 12, and learnt on my arrival that a terrible earthquake had occurred in Bengal, causing serious loss of life and property. The earthquake was specially disastrous in North Bengal; and the Bengal Provincial Conference, which was then being held at Natore, had to be broken up while it was in session. I got down at Serampore, instead of at Howrah, where my friends were waiting to welcome me. Having heard all about the earthquake, I was anxious about my people at home and hurried across the river from Serampore to my Barrackpore residence. It was *Moharrum* time when the earthquake occurred, and my children had all gone to see the fun. They were in the open, and the carriage and horse reeled under the shock. My wife was left alone in the house, and she hurried out to the garden. There were cracks in the house, but no serious damage was done.

On my return home I learnt that I had in my absence been elected a member of the Bengal Legislative Council by the District Boards of the Presidency Division. In those days the elections to the Councils were less exciting, and less open to the influence of personal canvassing. The District Boards and municipalities elected delegates to vote for the candidates at the final elections. The delegates were chosen men, the pick of their class, above corruption and the influence of personal pressure.

The Congress met at Amraoti in December, 1897. Amraoti is the capital of Berar and was the headquarters of my late friend, Mr. Mudholkar, to whom I have already had occasion to refer. A more selfless and less ostentatious friend of the national cause it would have been difficult to find. With great capacity and common sense he combined a geniality and a modesty of character that made him one of the most lovable of men. He invited me to live with him as a guest; but my party included my friends, Upendranath Sen, Kali Prosanna Kabyavisarad and Taraprosanna Mitter (manager of the *Bengalee*), better known as T. P. Mitter. They were looking after me with the affectionate care of devoted friendship, and I could not separate myself from them. I lived with them in the quarters provided for the delegates and was happy in their company.

I was asked to move the Resolution proposing Mr. Sankaran Nair as President of the Congress, a duty that I have often since performed. I said that times were critical, and we needed the guidance and leadership of such a man as he. Mr. Sankaran Nair was then an advocate of the Madras High Court, and he had already attained a distinguished position at the Bar. Subsequently he became a Judge of the High Court and a member of the Viceroy's Executive Council. His presidential speech was a strong and masculine utterance, worthy of the man and suited to the times when the forces of reaction were so strongly in evidence. 'It is impossible to argue a man into slavery in the English language' said he; and his was a vigorous plea for free institutions as the true cure for degradation and misery, and racial and credal conflicts.

I was entrusted with the Resolution regarding the deportation of the Natu brothers of Poona. The Natu brothers were Sirdars of the Deccan, whose ancestors had taken an important part in the events which led to the establishment of British power in Western India, and were themselves men of light and leading in the capital of Maharashtra. When I was at Poona as President of the Congress, I was treated by them with courtesy, and along with other delagates was the recipient of their hospitality. The Congress movement was then still under a cloud of official suspicion, but they were not afraid to join it openly.

The Plague, the forced segregations, the compulsory domiciliary visits, had created a feeling of panic and alarm among the population at Poona. Mr. Gokhale, then in England, had received accounts of what had taken place; and his publication of them had brought him into trouble. There is nothing that touches our people so deeply as interference with their household arrangements and invasion into the sanctities of their domestic life. The excitement was intense and it culminated in the unhappy murder of Mr. Rand, President of the Plague Committee, and Lieut. Ayerst. There are always extremists among the organs of public opinion. They called for a gagging act, for deportations and other familiar methods of repression.

The Natu brothers as leading citizens had formally appealed to the Government to interfere. Soon after they were deported under an old, obsolete regulation (Regulation XXV of 1827 of the Bombay Regulations, corresponding to the Bengal Regulation, III of 1818), and their property was taken charge of by the Government. Was it the reward of their efforts for their countrymen, or was it a bureaucratic device to strike terror into the hearts of the people? Whatever it was, it was useless and superfluous – in the language of Edmund Burke, 'a waste of the precious treasure of human suffering'. For the murderers of Mr. Rand and Lieut. Ayerst were soon traced. They were tried, convicted and hanged. The Natu brothers had been five months under detention when the Congress met.

The Congress Resolution on the subject, which I was asked to move, deprecated the exercise of the extraordinary powers vested in the Government by the Regulations at a time of peace and quiet, though the Congress recognized that circumstances might arise in which it might be necessary to put them into force. The Congress recommended that, upon the appearance of such conditions in any province or a specified area, the fact should be notified that the Government intended to take action if necessary under the

Regulations, and that in no case should the period of detention without trial exceed three months.

The question of the deportations under the Regulations assumed a wider interest when in 1907 and 1908 under Lord Minto's administration the Regulations were vigorously worked. Lala Lajpat Rai and Sirdar Ajit Singh were deported from the Punjab, while in Bengal Babu Krishna Kumar Mittra, Babu Aswini Kumar Dutt, Babu Syam Sunder Chakervarti and several others were similarly dealt with. It is a melancholy chapter in the history of my province to which I shall have to refer later on. A bad law in the hands of rulers owing no responsibility to the people is apt to be worked in a manner that often creates grave public dissatisfaction. In times of excitement, when deeper and more permanent remedial measures are needed, it affords a short cut for meeting the situation, leaving behind bitter memories that take years to efface.

The year 1898 opened with dark clouds rolling over the political horizon, with popular unrest followed by repression. Famine and plague cast their shadows over the land. The popular excitement was aggravated by the plague measures so ruthlessly enforced at Poona. Upon their heels came the murder of two European officers, the deportation of the Natu brothers, and the alleged disclosure of the existence of secret conspiracies in the western presidency.

It was when the atmosphere was so charged with the forces that make for unrest that Lord Curzon assumed the Viceroyalty of India. In India we had known him as a brilliant parliamentarian and as one of the coming leaders of the great political party to which he belonged. We were expectant, but not confident; and we acted as men in that attitude of mind would often do. When we met in Congress in Madras in December, 1898, which was synchronous with his assumption of the Viceroyalty, we gave him credit for qualities which we hoped he would display in the government of India. I was entrusted with the Resolution according him a hearty welcome, and we proceeded to add in the Resolution the hope and trust that the policy of progress and confidence that had characterized the best traditions of British rule would be followed during his Lordship's tenure of office.

In supporting my Resolution I quoted from Lord Curzon's speeches delivered immediately after his appointment as Viceroy of India. In one of them he said: 'I love India, its people, its history, its government, the complexities of its civilization and life.' In another speech delivered about the same time he observed that the essential qualifications of a Viceroy of India, were 'courage and sympathy'. Courage he had in abundance, the courage to defy public opinion and to exalt his personal ideals above those of the community he governed; of sympathy he had but little. He loved the people of India after a fashion that they did not appreciate, which excited their resentment, and prepared the way for those difficulties and embarrassments from which the Government long suffered.

The message of the Congress was communicated by the President, and Lord Curzon thanked him and the Congress for the welcome.

In February, 1899, the Indian Association presented him with an address of welcome. As Secretary, I introduced the deputation and read the address. An incident took place which is worth mentioning. We were assembled in the throne room awaiting the arrival of the Viceroy. An aide-de-camp came a few minutes before His Excellency entered the room, apparently with a view to satisfying himself that all the arrangements were in proper order. He noticed that two of the members of the deputation had Indian pump-shoes on. They were asked to take them off and appear without shoes, or retire from the deputation. They chose the latter course. The incident created a painful impression, and one or two other members of the deputation wanted to follow the retiring members; but it was felt that it would be discourteous to the head of the Government, and perhaps in the long run prejudicial to the interests that we represented.

There were only two occasions when I personally came in contact with Lord Curzon in India. I was never bidden to his presence by his command; and his policy and his public measures never inspired me with the desire to solicit an interview with him for conversation on public questions. The deputation was the first opportunity I had of meeting Lord Curzon. I was impressed by the pomp and grandeur of the viceregal surroundings, so different from the days of Lord Ripon, and the stately and sonorous periods of the viceregal reply. We were beginning to feel unhappy; and the order of the Government of India with regard to the Calcutta Municipal Bill caused the gravest disappointment and anxiety about the future.

The second time I met Lord Curzon was at the public meeting held at the Town Hall in honour of Queen Victoria's memory,

10

when he presided and I spoke. Bishop Weldon on that occasion sat next to me, and, after my speech was over, shook me by the hand and said, 'Well done'. Sir Walter Lawrence, the Viceroy's Private Secretary, who was present, congratulated me and said, 'I hope we shall meet often'. We, however, never met at all.

Before I leave the Madras Congress of 1898 it is only right and proper that I should refer to Mr. Ananda Mohan Bose's presidential speech. It was a masterly performance, one of the greatest orations ever heard from a Congress platform. Perhaps the voice of the orator was not equal to the occasion, but this was fully made up for by the inspiring earnestness and the penetrating conviction that lay behind every utterance; and, when it is borne in mind that Mr. Bose's health was not good at the time, one marvels at the performance.

Mr. Ananda Mohan Bose, with his great intellectual and moral gifts, did not combine that physical robustness which sets them off to the best advantage, nor, I have to add regretfully, did he take that great care of his health which I regard as the first and foremost duty of all our public men. Their lives are to the community an invaluable possession; and length of days must invest their judgments with a maturity, their utterances with a weight, their personalities with a halo of reverence, almost an air of sanctity, that should make them national assets beyond all price. This is a consideration that I fear our public men do not always bear in mind, and we have had so often to mourn their premature loss.

Immersed in his multifarious public duties, social, religious and political, Mr. Bose was careless of his health, and suffered for it. He had been to England in 1898 and returned home in September. We gave him a public reception at the Town Hall. I made a speech proposing the adoption of the address to him. He rose to reply, but, after he had uttered a few sentences, he completely broke down and fell back into his chair. The meeting had to be broken up. While he was in this weak state of health, an invitation was addressed to him by the Madras Reception Committee to preside at the Congress. His friends hesitated; his doctors shook their heads; but his sense of duty overmastered him; he responded to the call and delivered the magnificent address to which I have referred.

In his noble life, there was a still nobler instance of self-surrender and of thrilling devotion to the cause of country to which it will be my duty to call attention later on.

15

The Struggle for Recognition

Simultolla's attractions – tragic death of Dr. Suresh Chunder Sircar: 'grievous hurt' by British soldiers – Lord Curzon's policy: Local Self-government in danger – Congress at Lucknow: making India known in England – my Congress tour in the Punjab: inter-racial concord: Kali Prosanna Roy – officialdom and the movement – exclusion of Indians from higher appointments – W. C. Bonnerjea.

IN JANUARY, 1898, my house at Simultolla was completed and I began to take that annual rest (and this was for some time repeated twice a year) to which I attribute much of the health and vigour that I possess at a time of life when so few in India are fit for work. Simultolla is a health resort, 217 miles from Howrah on the Chord line. In 1894, when my son, then a boy of about eight months, was ill, Rai Kedarnath Chatterjee Bahadur, a well-known medical practitioner at Serampore, recommended for him a change to Simultolla. I took his advice and came to the place with the boy and the other members of my family.

At that time there was in the station only one house, which belonged to Babu Sarat Chandra Mitter, who very kindly placed it at my disposal. My brother, who was suffering from malarious fever, accompanied us. The house was insufficient for our accommodation, and we had to remove to Allahabad. I was charmed with the beauty of the scenery and was benefited by the salubrity of the climate. I made up my mind to be on the look-out to secure if possible a site whereon to build a house and make it an annual resort for rest and change.

Nothing in England had impressed me so much as the annual migrations during the summer to the seaside towns and the European Continent; and, while yet a mere youth, I wrote to my father in 1868 noticing this feature of English life and complaining of its absence among our people. Madhupur had not then become a health resort; and our people during the great *Durga Puja* vacation stayed at home, celebrating the Pujas and enjoying the festivities, but neglecting the golden opportunity that the holidays presented for rest and change. Later on a change to Madhupur and Baidyanath, and sometimes to Darjeeling, grew to be popular, and I had the proud satisfaction of strengthening the popular feeling and the popular movement by helping to make Simultolla a health-resort for the middle classes.

In 1897, my friend, the late Babu Hem Chunder Roy, whose early death we all deplore as a loss to his family and the national party, obtained for me a plot of land on the ridge, one of the finest sites at Simultolla. It was part of a plot secured by the late Babu Behari Lal Chatterjee, then practising as a pleader at Baidyanath. He distributed the plot, which covered the whole of the ridge, among his friends, including Sir Rajendra Nath Mookerjee, the late Babu Pulin Behari Sircar, and others. Having got the site, I started the building without loss of time, and it was ready for occupation in January, 1898.

Mine was the first house built and within the last twenty years Simultolla has become a highly popular health resort. Lord Sinha, Sir Rajendra Nath Mookerjee and others have all built houses there, where they occasionally reside. To many it has given health and life. The late Bhabanath Sen, a well-known municipal contractor and a leader of the Kayastha community in Calcutta, while in the grip of a deadly malady prolonged his life by residing here for six months every year.

I have always looked forward to my stay at Simultolla with interest and expectancy, and have always been benefited by the change. It is not that I pass my days in idleness, gazing upon the beautiful scenery around or reflecting upon the memories of the past. Here I composed my presidential speech for the Ahmedabad Congress of 1902. Here I wrote more than one-third of these reminiscences. Freed from the distraction of visitors, canvassing for appointments or soliciting advice, I pursue my work amid conditions of health and ease which are a comfort and a stimulus. Here I take rest, but enjoy it all the more with the leaven of work. I do not believe in absolute idleness, with the intellect lying fallow or in a condition of *comatose torpor*. Moderate intellectual work even in times of absolute rest has been with me a physical tonic, a bracing stimulant which has sent the blood coursing through the veins, chasing away all impurities, stimulating the flow of life and the vital energies through the obscurest corners of the physical system. I believe in a rest-cure, diversified by moderate work. I do not believe in hurried peregrinations from place to place, so popular with so many of our health-seekers.

The year 1898 was marked by a grim tragedy, which at the time roused a considerable measure of public attention among the Indian community, especially in Bengal. The tragedy to which I refer was the murder of Dr. Suresh Chunder Sircar of Barrackpore. Dr. Suresh Chunder Sircar was a medical man with a large practice. He was held in great esteem for his skill and his kindness to his patients. He had also some European patients. They too recognized his worth and his skill. He had a dispensary near the Barrackpore station. One night in April, 1898, while he was about to leave for home, after finishing his day's work, three European soldiers, more or less the worse for liquor, called at his dispensary. His carriage was ready, and he was about to start. Some words were interchanged; an altercation ensued; and the European soldiers brutally attacked him. He had to be removed to hospital, where he died within twenty-four hours.

After the murderous attack upon the doctor, his assailants ran away, chased by a crowd whom the shouts and the shrieks of the doctor had brought to the spot. They ran as fast as their legs could carry them. The excitement of drunkenness had apparently passed away, amid the horrors of the scene which they had helped to create. The doctor lay weltering in a pool of blood, but there were some among the crowd who chased the soldiers. Two of them ran back to the barracks, leaving a helmet behind, which the pursuers picked up; and a third, fortunately for the ends of justice, took shelter inside a mosque, which was immediately closed from outside. The police were informed and brought in. They caught the man red-handed within the mosque.

The doctor was my family physician, a dear and esteemed friend. I heard the details of the tragedy with grief and indignation. The doctor lay in the hospital close to my house; but in my eager desire to bring the offenders to justice I hurried off, without seeing my dying friend, to Alipore, a distance of sixteen miles, to interview the magistrate with a view to moving him to take prompt action for the punishment of the perpetrators of this dastardly outrage. For cases of this kind, having regard to the temper of European juries in those days, had to be carefully attended to even from the start.

The magistrate was Mr. Charles Allen, an officer of great promise, who, if he had been spared, would probably have risen to the highest offices in the service. He was a personal friend. We had known each other while he was at Chittagong on settlement work. The late poet, Nobin Chunder Sen, who was a Chittagong man and knew him well, spoke of him as one who some day would become Lieutenant-Governor. He had called at my house at Barrackpore, a compliment rarely paid in those days to Indian gentlemen by European officers; and we corresponded upon public questions. I gave him the first information about the occurrence, he had not heard of it before; for the doctor was then still alive. I explained to him the facts of the case. He fully shared my indignation, and said that he would do his best to bring the culprits to justice. I suggested that Babu Ashutosh Biswas, Public Prosecutor, one of the ablest criminal lawyers of his time, should at once be instructed to take up the case. Mr. Allen agreed. Instructions were issued and Babu Ashutosh came up to Barrackpore to look after the case.

I did not stop there. I sent a message to the newspaper *India* in London by wire, giving the facts of the case, with the result that a question was asked in Parliament about the matter. I called upon Sir John Woodburn, the Lieutenant-Governor, and spoke to him about the case. He expressed the utmost abhorrence of the crime, and told me that His Excellency the Viceroy (Lord Elgin) was taking an interest in the matter. I gathered from the conversation that a message had come from the Secretary of State, as the result of the interpellation in Parliament.

The case was committed to the High Court Sessions. Mr. Justice Jenkins, who was then a Puisne Judge, presided over the ordinary criminal sessions. But the Chief Justice himself, Sir Francis Maclean, sat to try the case with a special jury, the majority of whom were Europeans. The charges against the accused were those of murder, culpable homicide not amounting to murder, and grievous hurt. The jury brought in a unanimous verdict of guilty of grievous hurt, acquitting the prisoners on the more serious charges. What the Chief Justice thought of the verdict might be inferred from the fact that he inflicted upon the prisoners the highest punishment under the law.

Mr. W. S. Caine, Member of Parliament, commenting upon this case, said that all three should have been strung up on a tree. If indeed it was not an act of deliberate murder, it was certainly a case of the infliction of such grievous bodily injuries as were likely to cause death. It is difficult to see how it could be otherwise than a case of culpable homicide. I have not yet met a high European official who has not expressed his unqualified condemnation of these cowardly assaults, which unfortunately are now and then committed by Europeans upon Indians.

I interested myself in another case of this kind in which one Gurdit Maiti was assaulted by two Europeans, because he happened to be riding a horse while they were standing. He was an old man and died from the injuries inflicted. The subordinate court had let them off with a fine. It was a bad case and needed condign punishment. I wrote in the *Bengalee* newspaper and I personally moved Sir John Woodburn. An application was made for enhancement of the punishment. One of the accused could not be found as he had left for South Africa to fight in the Boer campaign. The other accused was sentenced to four months' imprisonment as the result of a re-trial. He was employed in the Public Works Department under the Government, and I interested myself after his release, and with success, to get him re-appointed.

The subordinate courts in these cases too often reflect an unhappy racial feeling. But the higher we mount the purer becomes the atmosphere. I thankfully note the fact that there has been a distinct advance in European opinion in this direction, which is bound to grow with time and the development of closer relations between the two communities.

The death of Dr. Suresh Chunder Sircar left his family helpless and penniless. He was the head of the family, its sole bread-winner. He had an extensive, but by no means lucrative, practice, as his patients for the most part belonged to the poorer middle class. His sons were young, one of them studying in a medical school. I approached the Lieutenant-Governor, Sir John Woodburn, for help. Sir John Woodburn was a man of generous instincts, and he warmly responded to my appeal. He said to me, 'Mr. Banerjea, if the young man (naming Dr. Suresh Chunder Sircar's son) had passed the Matriculation examination, I would have made him a Deputy Magistrate. I am fettered owing to his not possessing suitable qualifications, but I will appoint him a sub-registrar.' He got this appointment, and later on, when the burden of a growing family made his position financially difficult, Sir Edward Baker, who was then Lieutenant-Governor, was good enough at my request to appoint his brother a sub-registrar.

At the Congress of 1898, we had expressed our gratitude to Lord Curzon for his words of sympathy, and our hope that he would follow a policy of progress and confidence in the people. The events of the following year served to dissipate whatever expectations the most optimistic among us might have formed. The reactionary policy of the Viceroy and his disregard of Indian public opinion was evidenced by the orders he passed in connexion with the Calcutta Municipal Bill after it had emerged from the Select Committee stage. To those orders I have already referred in a previous part of these reminiscences. They served to officialize the Calcutta Corporation. They were so unexpected that it was widely reported that Sir John Woodburn had threatened to resign. Why he did not, we do not know. They threw Calcutta into the vortex of an agitation that was only surpassed by the anti-Partition demonstrations, which also were due to Lord Curzon's policy. People were rapidly losing confidence in the Viceroy, and the popular sense of mistrust found expression in a Resolution of the Lucknow Congress of 1899, which I had to move. The Resolution was in these terms:

'That this Congress expresses its disapproval of the reactionary policy, subversive of Local Self-government, as evidenced by the passing of the Calcutta Municipal Act in the face of the unanimous opposition of the people, and by the introduction into the Legislative Council of Bombay of a similar measure, which will have the effect of seriously jeopardizing the principle of Local Self-government.'

The Calcutta Municipal Bill was a local measure, but it had an all-India interest as it affected the principle of Local Self-government, in the growth and development of which all India felt a concern. It used to be in those days the standing practice of the Congress to take up and discuss provincial questions in which the interest and the feelings of all India had been roused. In discussing the Calcutta Municipal Bill, the Congress did not act in contravention of its traditional practice. Similarly, the Provincial Conferences often included in their programme questions which affected the whole of India. Such a procedure served to keep the public life of the province in touch with that of the rest of India, and contributed to the solidarity and the growth of national life.

There was a peculiar fitness in Mr. R. C. Dutt's presiding at the Congress when the question of the disfranchisement of the Calcutta Corporation was discussed. He was in England when we started the agitation against the Calcutta Municipal Bill. I placed myself in communication with him. It was chiefly through his efforts that the great debate on the Bill in February, 1897, was organized when Mr. Herbert Roberts, now Lord Clywd, pressed for a commission of enquiry, and Sir Henry Fowler, then in opposition, declared that he had discovered no evidence to show that the elected Commissioners had failed in their duty.

The debate led us to hope that some modification of the Bill would take place. The hope proved illusory. Lord Curzon's influence prevailed; and the Bill was passed into law with all the reactionary provisions that had excited comment and criticism. It was the first of a series of reactionary measures which revealed the policy of an administration that was destined to create widespread unrest and excitement.

At the Lucknow Congress we recorded a resolution urging 'the appointment of an agency in England for the purpose of organizing in concert with the British committee public meetings for the dissemination of information on Indian subjects, and the creation of a fund for the purpose'.

I moved the Resolution and made an appeal for funds. I cannot say that the appeal was successful; nor was indeed any immediate action taken to give effect to this Resolution. The Resolution remained a part of the standing programme of the Congress; but the efforts made to carry it out were spasmodic and not persistent.

In 1900, the Congress was to meet at Lahore. The invitation to Lahore was made by Lala Muralidhar, a veteran worker of the Congress cause. Old Congressmen still remember the wit and humour with which he used to enliven the Congress when his health and strength permitted him to attend its meetings. Though borne down by age and its infirmities, his interest in the Congress movement remained unflagging.

Lala Jaishi Ram extorted from me a promise at Lucknow that I would, before the Congress met at Lahore, visit some of the towns in the Punjab and address public meetings. He thought that was necessary in order to rouse an interest in the Punjab in the Congress cause. It was a call to duty to which I gladly responded. I broke my annual *Durga Puja* holidays, which I was enjoying at Simultolla, and started for the Punjab in October, 1900. Our first meeting was held at Delhi, where Sirdar Guru Chand Singh, barrister-at-law, joined me and accompanied me throughout the tour. I addressed public meetings at Delhi, Amritsar, Lahore and Rawalpindi. At Lahore, at the request of the Reception Committee, I opened the Bradlaugh Hall, which was raised in honour of the memory of the late Mr. Bradlaugh, and where the Congress was to meet. The Hall was subsequently destroyed by fire; but it has since been rebuilt.

While I was at Rawalpindi I heard of the unexpected death of Lala Jaishi Ram. He was, in the words of the late Babu Kali Prosanna Roy, Chairman of the Reception Committee of the

Lahore Congress, 'the light and life of the Congress movement in this province (the Punjab)'. The burden and responsibility of the Congress arrangements had for the most part devolved upon him; and to his untiring and devoted energy and careful forethought much of the success of the Lahore Congress of 1900 was due. The death of such a man in the very prime of life, before he had emerged from his manhood, was an irreparable loss to the cause and the country, and cast a shadow over the approaching session of the Congress.

It is significant that a Bengalee pleader should have been elected Chairman of the Reception Committee at Lahore. It is evidence, if evidence were needed, of the good feeling between Bengalees and Punjabis. It disproves the calumny that the martial races hold in contempt the people of our province. Babu Kali Prosanna Roy was the Indian leader of the Punjab Bar, and was held in respect by Europeans and Indians alike, for his capacity as a lawyer, his public spirit as a citizen and the thorough probity and integrity of his life, public and private. The general impression at Lahore was that, but for his independence and his association with the Congress movement, which was distasteful to the local authorities, he would have been elevated to the Bench of the Punjab Chief Court.

The idiosyncrasies of the official temper vary in the different provinces. While association with Congress in some provinces was a disqualification for high judicial office, it was not held as such in others; and certainly not in Bombay or in Madras. The President of the Lahore Congress of 1900 was Mr. (afterwards Sir) Narayan Chandravarkar. He had already received his appointment as Judge of the High Court, in succession to the late lamented Mr. Justice Ranade, when he was invited to occupy the presidential chair of the Congress. He consulted the Chief Justice of the Bombay High Court, Sir Lawrence Jenkins, who raised no objection. It was Sir Lawrence Jenkins who, as Chief Justice of the Calcutta High Court, offered a judgeship to Mr. Ashutosh Chaudhuri, a staunch Congressman, and persuaded him to accept it. Mr. Chandravarkar, after presiding over the Lahore Congress, joined his office as Judge of the Bombay High Court. His appointment as a High Court Judge was well known at the time when the Congress met. I was asked to propose him to the chair; and I said in moving the resolution that the presidential chair of the Congress had proved too often to be the royal road to the High Court Bench.

At the Lahore Congress I moved a resolution regretting the

practical exclusion of Indians from the higher appointments in the minor Civil Services, namely, the Police, the Customs, the State Railways, the Opium, the Public Works, the Survey, and other departments.

I can never forget the conversation I had with Sir Henry Fowler in the House of Commons in regard to this matter, and the idea had sunk deep in my mind that our exclusion was indefensible from every point of view, and that we had an overwhelmingly strong case. On my return to India, I submitted, as Secretary of the Indian Association, a memorial to Government. The departments of Government, wedded to old-world ideas, move slowly. I cannot say that the result of our efforts was satisfactory, or that we got what we had a right to expect; but the representation had a quickening effect upon the departments. It is slow work to move the Government; but patience is the first and last qualification of public workers.

At the session of the Congress held in Calcutta in 1901 I moved what was substantially the same resolution, urging at the same time that effect should be given to the Resolution of the House of Commons of June 2, 1893, regarding the holding of Simultaneous Examinations for the Indian Civil Services.

This session of the Congress was the last in which Mr. W. C. Bonnerjea took part. Ill-health compelled him to leave for England early in 1902. Though stricken down by disease, he never lost his interest in the Congress. He stood as the Liberal candidate for Walthamstow; and all accounts say that he had a good chance of being returned. But Providence had willed otherwise. His failing health compelled him to withdraw from the parliamentary contest; and soon after his countrymen learnt with a sense of profound sorrow the news of his death in England.

Mr. W. C. Bonnerjea was one of the leading members of the Calcutta High Court Bar in his time; and, though enjoying a wide and lucrative practice, he took a keen and active interest in the work of the Congress. In his time, it would be no exaggeration to say, he was the leader of the Congress movement in Bengal. He was not an agitator in the ordinary sense – and the word stinks in the nostrils of some of our officials. His association with the movement gave it a dignity and an air of responsibility in official eyes which otherwise it would not perhaps have possessed.

It cannot be said that Mr. W. C. Bonnerjea was throughout his life a public man. Immersed in the engrossing work of one of the most exacting, and, be it added, one of the most lucrative, of professions, he had not, in his early days, the time nor perhaps the inclination, to turn to public affairs. But the Ilbert Bill controversy was to him, as to many others, an eye-opener, and revealed, in its grim nakedness, our real political status. No self-respecting Indian could sit idle under the fierce light of that revelation. It was a call to a high patriotic duty to those who understood its significance; and Mr. W. C. Bonnerjea enthusiastically responded to the call. He had closely identified himself with the Congress since its birth, and the Bar felt the impulse of his lead in this matter. As a speaker he was perhaps outdistanced by some of his contemporaries; in point of enthusiasm some of his colleagues might be said to have been fired with the warmth of apostolic fervour; but in the calm, clear recognition of the situation, in the adaptation of means for a given end, in wise and statesmanlike counsel and guidance, he was without a peer amongst those whose privilege it was to work with him. His place in the Bar as a public leader to-day remains void. Mirabeau is dead. There is none to fill his chair; and Bengal mourns in silence the loss of one of the worthiest of her sons. The death of such a man was a heavy loss to the country, and especially at a time when Bengal was in the throes of the greatest agitation that convulsed the province since the establishment of British rule.

The year 1906 was a year of heavy misfortune for Bengal and India. W. C. Bonnerjea, Budruddin Tyabji, Ananda Mohan Bose, and Nalin Behari Sircar, followed one another in close succession to that land from whose bourne no traveller returns; and Bengal was then in mourning over the partition of the province.

16
1900—1901

Rise of the *Bengalee*: a devoted manager: journalism in India – I am again President of the Congress: successful Ahmedabad meeting – the Coronation Durbar – Viceregal profession and practice – Commission on Universities: abolition of law classes in colleges.

I CANNOT PASS AWAY FROM THE YEAR 1900 without referring to the further expansion of the scope of my journalistic work. I took up the *Bengalee,* as Editor and Proprietor, in 1879. It continued to be a weekly newspaper from 1879 to February, 1900, when it was converted into a daily. The proposal to make it a daily paper had been suggested to me more than once, but I thought it would interfere with my other public activities. I soon discovered, however, that a weekly English paper in Bengal advocating Indian interests was fast becoming an obsolete institution. Public life was growing, and the demand for early news was increasing. The weekly newspaper was rapidly falling into disfavour, losing influence and popularity. I had to yield to the great law of adaptation and the pressure of circumstances.

The proposal was pressed upon me by the late Raja Benoy Krishna Deb, who always took a friendly and even an affectionate interest in all my undertakings, public or private. Babu Upendranath Sen, of Messrs. C. K. Sen & Co. and part proprietor of the *Hitabadi* newspaper, and myself entered into a partnership agreement for ten years, and the *Bengalee* became, and now is, a daily paper. Ours was the first Indian newspaper to subscribe to Reuter's Agency, and we never regretted having done so.

What measure of success the *Bengalee* achieved while it was under my control, it is not for me to say. But whatever position it attained was largely due to the rare devotion and businesslike capacity of Taraprosanna Mitter, its late Manager. Taraprosanna Mitter was the life and soul of the paper. He trained himself to the work that he was called upon to perform, and by a combination of tact, devotion and organizing power he built up the paper. He worked hard, worked incessantly – he literally sacrificed himself in the service of the *Bengalee;* and, now that he is gone, his memory is a cherished possession with those who had the privilege of working with him and under him.

I have learnt one great lesson from his life and that of the Superintendent of the Ripon College, the late Amrita Chunder Ghose, and that is, that the one quality which, more than any other, ensures the success of an institution or of a business concern is absolute and unstinted devotion, combined with honesty and a moderate fund of common sense.

I was connected with journalism for over forty years, and I may say as the result of a somewhat long experience, that the success of a newspaper depends much more upon the manager than upon the editor. The personality of the editor counts for much; it is an asset that is not to be despised. But even more important to the newspaper is the efficiency of its management. Indeed, the two functions sometimes overlap; at any rate the editor and the manager must be in the closest correspondence and touch with one another. The editor must indeed guide and lead public opinion, though he cannot go violently against it and incur the risk of unpopularity, which would mean loss of subscribers, loss of advertisements and loss of revenue.

In my work as a journalist I tried to avoid sedition and libel and personal recriminations. I was never charged with sedition formally, or informally, though I fear some of my writings in the *Bengalee* were considered as making a very near approach to it; and when the question regarding my disqualification for election to the Imperial Legislative Council was under consideration by the Government of India, the files of the *Bengalee* were sent for in order to discover whether any allegation of sedition could be substantiated against me. I presume that it was found to be a hopeless task, and the files were sent back to the Imperial Library, from where they had been borrowed. I confess that I wrote strongly, very strongly when the necessities of the situation and the demands of public feeling required it – I confess that in the days of the anti-Partition controversy, when the public mind was thrown into a state of unusual excitement, by the adoption of a policy that no British Government had followed before, it was difficult to write with reserve or restraint.

Our rulers often complain of strong writing in the Press, but they sometimes conveniently forget the provocation that they give for such writing. As for libels, no newspaper writer can always avoid them. Sometimes in the public interest he has deliberately to take the risk of uttering libellous matter and to face the consequences. Sometimes it is a reporter who lets him down and he has to pay the penalty. Nominally, the editor is responsible for the whole of what appears in his paper; in reality his true responsibility does not extend beyond a few columns of editorial matter, which he can personally supervise, or what his subordinates who work under his general instructions may bring to his notice. But in the eyes of the law he is responsible for the whole publication.

Let me explain what I mean by reference to a case in which I was personally concerned. In May, 1911, I was charged with contempt of court upon a writ issued by Mr. Justice Fletcher upon a motion of the Advocate-General. This was the second case of contempt in which I was involved. Some comments had appeared in the *Bengalee* upon evidence given in a pending case by Mr. Weston, who was Magistrate of Midnapore at the time of the Midnapore Conspiracy Case. The leaderette containing the comments was written by Babu Kalinath Roy, sub-editor of the *Bengalee,* and now editor-in-chief of the *Tribune* newspaper. In my written statement I took upon myself the entire responsibility for the publication. Babu Kalinath Roy was too high-minded to permit this. He wrote me an official letter, absolving me of all responsibility, and urging that, if anybody were to blame, it was he. I had no desire to take advantage of his avowal, for I had already definitely assumed all responsibility for the leaderette, but at his request I showed his letter to my counsel, Mr. A. Chaudhuri, who afterwards became a Judge of the High Court. We made no use of it for the purpose of the case, but he showed it to the Advocate-General, who was the counsel on the opposite side. I do not know what impression it made upon his mind or what influence it had with him. The Judge, I presume, knew nothing at all about it. The case was dismissed upon another and a wholly technical ground.

As a public man and as editor of the *Bengalee* I was often exposed to personal attacks. Every one taking part in public affairs must be prepared for them. They are an incident of his position, and he must submit to them with all the patience that he can muster in the hope, which is not always realized, that the game of personal recrimination is not even profitable to those who start it.

In India the atmosphere is sometimes leavened with racial bitterness or personal rancour. Kristo Das Pal was described by Sir Rivers Thompson, Lieutenant-Governor, as dishonest and dishonourable. I was told by a leading newspapers after my failure at the Imperial Council elections that I had ceased to be a representative man on July 31, the date of my failure, though I imagine I was one the day before. Such puerilities are beneath contempt. I never took any notice of personal attacks unless there were misconceptions that needed explanation, or unless public issues were involved.

After the expiration of ten years, I became the sole proprietor of the *Bengalee*. I continued to be so till January, 1919, when I entered into an agreement with the Maharaja of Cossimbazar, by which he became joint proprietor with me under conditions which were to convert the concern into a limited liability company within a specified period of time. Events happened which compelled me to withdraw from the *Bengalee* altogether, with which I have now no concern, nor does it represent me or my policy in regard to public affairs.

In 1902 I was again invited to accept the Presidentship of the Congress to be held at Ahmedabad in the Bombay Presidency. I was at Simultolla in October, 1902, when the invitation came. My friend, Sir Dinshaw Wacha, wrote to me unofficially on the subject. I replied begging to be excused and urging the claims of Mr. Kali Churn Banerjee. Sir Dinshaw wrote back to say that there was the great Delhi Durbar of 1902; a counter-attraction, and a counter-influence had to be set up; and Sir Pherozshah Mehta and the Reception Committee were of opinion that I should preside. In declining the honour I had said in my letter, 'If the worst comes to the worst I am your man'. I was pinned fast to this conditional promise. For me there was no escape and I accepted the office, though I should have greatly preferred Mr. Kali Churn Bannerjee to occupy my place.

The session of the Congress at Ahmedabad was a great success. The reception that was accorded to me by the people of Ahmedabad was right royal in its proportions and in its enthusiasm. I said in my closing speech that a victorious prince returning to his capital from the field of his triumphs could not have been more enthusiastically welcomed than I had been as President of the Congress, and I added that it was not a tribute paid to me or to my personal worth, but to the great cause which I had the honour to represent. The presidential speech took me about six weeks to prepare. I began it at Simultolla on October 7, and finished it on November 27. The beautiful scenery, the fine climate, the delightful weather, the all-pervading sense of restfulness prevailing over the place, all had their share in helping my work. The speech took me two hours to deliver. The physical effort was great, seeing that I had to address an audience of over five thousand people. I followed my usual practice and spoke without notes.

The Coronation Durbar was to take place within a few days of the meeting of the Congress. Educated India had protested against this expensive show; but all in vain. I echoed in my speech the sense of my educated countrymen, but, as the Durbar was bound to be held, I urged that, like the previous Durbars of 1858, 1877 and 1887, it should be commemorated by a suitable boon. The Durbar was held, but no boon was announced. The memory of it lingers, if at all, in the flashy rhetoric of the hour, and in the wasteful expenditure, which might have been avoided.

The most important topic of the day, which necessarily found a large place in the presidential speech, was the question of University Education. I had been an educationist all my life, and I naturally felt a deep interest in the educational problem. Of the many disservices which Lord Curzon had done to India, his so-called reform of the universities was the most far-reaching in its consequences. Under the plea of efficiency he had officialized the Calcutta Municipality; under the same plea he now proceeded to officialize the universities, and to bring the entire system of higher education under the control of Government. Efficiency was his watchword; popular sentiment counted for nothing, and in his mad worship of this fetish Lord Curzon set popular opinion at open defiance.

In 1901 Lord Curzon held an Educational Conference at Simla, to which only European educationists were invited. It was a secret conclave, its proceedings have not yet been published, and yet at this very conference Lord Curzon declared, 'Concealment has been no part of my policy since I have been in India, and the education of the people is assuredly the last subject to which I should think of applying such a canon'. Never was there a greater divergence between profession and practice. And the effrontery of it lay in the emphatic denunciation of secrecy at the very time, and in connexion with the very subject, in regard to which the speaker had deliberately made up his mind to violate the canon that he had so eloquently proclaimed. But that was Lord Curzon's method, and we Orientals regarded it with a feeling of amusement, as coming from one who had extolled the ethics of the West above the baser morality of the East.

The Educational Conference was followed by the appointment

of a Universities Commission, which, when its personnel was first announced, did not include a single Hindu member. Yet the Hindus had the largest interest in the educational problems that were to be considered. I raised a vigorous protest in the columns of the *Bengalee* against this ostracism of the Hindu element. The organs of Indian public opinion were unanimous in this view, and as the result Mr. Justice Gurudas Banerjee was subsequently added as a member of the Commission.

The report was submitted in less than five months' time, whereas the Education Commission of 1882 had taken eighteen months to make their recommendations; and the report itself was a startling performance. It would be no exaggeration to say that it convulsed educated India from one end of the country to the other. The report was felt as a menace to the whole system of higher education in India. It reversed the policy of the Education Commission of 1882. It recommended: (1) The abolition of the second-grade colleges (and they formed the bulk of the colleges in Bengal); (2) the abolition of the law classes; and (3) the fixing of a minimum rate of college fees by the Syndicate, which really meant the raising of the fees. In order to raise the standard of efficiency the area of high education was sought to be restricted.

The feeling against Indian lawyers, which the report of the majority disclosed, was open and undisguised. 'To do away with the law classes' said the report, 'will in many cases increase the expense of the law students' education; but the central school will have the scholarships; and, even if the net result should be to diminish the number of lawyers in India, we are not certain that this would be an unmixed evil.' The aversion to law and lawyers is a permanent feature of the official mind in India, and found expression on an important occasion in the columns of the *Pioneer*, which commented unfavourably on the fact that the legal element predominated among the nineteen signatories to the scheme of post-war reforms submitted by nineteen elected members of the Imperial Legislative Council.

It is worthy of remark that the Commissioners themselves admitted that the effect of their proposals would be to narrow the popular basis of high education, and to restrict its area.

It need hardly be said that Mr. Justice Gurudas Banerjee recorded a strong dissent, traversing the points to which I have referred. A vigorous agitation was set up against the recommendations contained in the report. A Town Hall meeting was organized;

and a memorial, which I had a large hand in drawing up, was submitted to Government.

The agitation was not without its results. The Government of India partially accepted the popular view. In a letter issued by the Home Department, in October, 1902, the Government declared that 'the second-grade colleges occupy a definite place in the educational machinery of the country and fulfil a useful function'. As regards the abolition of the law classes, the Government of India were of opinion that 'a central Law College should be established in each province, but that it should be a model, and there should be no monopoly'. Whatever the spirit of the Government declaration may have been, the law classes in all the Calcutta colleges were abolished, excepting those of the Ripon College. The Government was silent with regard to the question of the minimum college fees.

Upon the basis of the recommendations of the Universities Commission, a Universities Act was passed. The Universities (I speak specially of the Calcutta University) have assumed in a large measure the function of teaching in the higher branches of Arts and Science, with results that are commendable. An impetus to higher learning and culture has also been imparted by regular lectures delivered by University Readers and Lecturers. But, all the same, the expense of higher education has increased with no sensible increase in the resources of the middle class, from whom the bulk of our college students come.

17
The Universities Act

Ripon College made over to trustees: from proprietor I become President of Council: public appeal for funds – farewell to teaching: what I taught – my membership of the Senate: an inexplicable election rule – English literature without English history – Mr. Justice Ashutosh Mukherjea as Vice-Chancellor – I cease to be a member of the Bengal Legislative Council.

THE UNIVERSITIES ACT WAS PASSED IN 1904, and a Committee was appointed to frame the regulations under the Act for the University of Calcutta. On the passing of the Universities Act I divested myself of my proprietory right over the Ripon College and made over to a body of trustees the college and the school, which is an adjunct to it, with the library, the laboratory and all property belonging to them, together with a sum of Rs. 5,000 in cash. I myself remained one of the trustees, reserving to myself no interest, pecuniary or otherwise, save the right of nominating my successor.

Having thus made over the college and the school to the public, I applied myself to the task of providing a permanent habitation for them. We had never had funds for so large an undertaking. So long as I was proprietor I could not appeal to the public for subscriptions in aid of an institution which was mine. But, now that the college was a public concern, no such scruples stood in my way, and I opened a subscription list for the college building, the foundation-stone of which was laid by Sir Edward Baker, Lieutenant-Governor of Bengal, in August, 1910.

Sir John Rees attacked him for thus publicly associating himself with an institution with which I was so closely connected. Sir Edward Baker, having read the article, wrote to me, requesting me to see him at 'Belvedere'. He showed me the article. He said, 'I mean to give a reply to it'. 'My reply' he added, 'is a further grant of Rs. 5,000 to the Ripon College. Write to the Accountant-General and he will give you the money.' That was the character of the man: strong, generous, impulsive, he was one of the staunchest friends of the Ripon College; and it is no exaggeration to say – and I owe it to his honoured memory – that, but for his powerful intervention, the law classes of the Ripon College would not have been saved. Our law library was not well equipped. He made a present of law reports, the gift of the Bengal Government, worth several thousand rupees.

We were asked at one stage to show cause why the law classes should not be disaffiliated. Subsequently the attitude of the Syndicate was modified and the affiliation of the law classes was continued on our complying with the requirements of the University. I was invited to a meeting of the Syndicate and was subjected to a rigorous cross-examination, which ended in a compromise acceptable to both parties, the Syndicate and the Ripon College authorities. In all these negotiations, in the change of temper that was manifest; the influence of the Rector (Sir Edward Baker) was throughout apparent.

The work of collecting subscriptions for the college building was one of no ordinary difficulty. To obtain money for a public purpose from the general body of the public, except when the feelings of the community have been deeply stirred, must always be a matter of considerable labour and trouble. In India the task is beset with peculiar difficulties. Our people are not rich. Those who are rich are not always willing or patriotic enough to pay. It is the same men who are every time called upon to subscribe. We have a limited circle from which to draw public subscriptions, and the yield is more or less unsatisfactory.

Sir Edward Baker having gone home on leave, I appealed to Sir William Duke, who was officiating for him, to help us with Government money and influence. He promised to assist, and very kindly came over to inspect the buildings. We had then made very little progress in paying off the contractors' bills. He said, 'Mr. Banerjea, you have been building upon faith'. I said, in reply, 'Your Honour, faith removes mountains'; and my faith was abundantly justified by the result. The estimates had originally been fixed at Rs. 1,14,000. They mounted up, as Sir Edward Baker had prophesied, to Rs. 1,44,000. Government contributed Rs. 60,000; and the balance I raised from the public and only a small sum from the college funds. I made an appeal to the ex-students of the Ripon College, some of whom had obtained their education free at the college. The response, however, was unsatisfactory and disappointing.

We have now cleared off the debt; we have added a fourth storey to the college building, and have laid by a reserve fund of over a lakh of rupees. The college, with the school department, is one of the largest educational institutions in the country, with students numbering about 2,500, and it is the only private college with a law department affiliated to the University. The financial control of the college is vested in a body of trustees, while the college and the school are administered by a council with me as President. The constitution of the Board of Trustees and of the College Council was settled by me in consultation with the Syndicate of the University.

I ceased to take part in professorial work in February 1913, when I was elected a member of the Viceroy's Legislative Council, and when my absence from Calcutta at Delhi and Simla made it impossible for me to be regularly associated with the work of teaching. It was with a wrench that I withdrew from duties that had been the pleasure of my life, and in which I had been engaged for over thirty-eight years. I look back with the utmost satisfaction upon my work extending beyond the lifetime of a generation, among the youthful section of my countrymen. I loved the students, and they loved me; and I claim to have had a considerable share in moulding their minds and stimulating their aspirations. I have been charged with diffusing political ideas among them, and so I have done, and they were political ideas of the right kind, the strongest safeguards against revolutionary principles.

I have preached patriotism coupled with orderly constitutional progress. I have preached self-government within the Empire as our goal, and constitutional and lawful methods as the only means for its attainment. If to-day revolutionary principles have found acceptance among some young men in Bengal (and their number is a handful) the fact is traceable to conditions economic and political, which are more or less independent of all propagandism. The teacher or the preacher may incite, but he cannot create the nursing-ground from which the revolutionary draws his inspiration and his support. The writings of the pamphleteers would have fallen upon barren soil, if the conditions in France, political and economic, had not prepared men's minds for the acceptance of revolutionary ideas.

However that may be, it was with me always a pleasure to be in the class-room with young men, teaching, guiding, inspiring them. In their company I felt rejuvenated, and now, if in the evening of my life my optimism remains unabated, I attribute it largely to my close and constant association with young men, and the living interest I felt in them and in their welfare. The class-room was to me a training-ground. If I tried to teach the young to be good and true and patriotic, they in their turn imbued me with their juvenescence, their youthful ardour and their radiant outlook on life. I always returned from the class-room with an added stock of youthful qualities, which, controlled and regulated by my contact with affairs, was a superb asset in the daily struggle of life.

Frederick the Great would not appoint a schoolmaster to any administrative post, and a Lieutenant-Governor of Bengal, as the great Vidyasagar once told me, followed the same rule. But a schoolmaster, in living touch with affairs, ought to possess the qualities that are most valuable in life. More than one President of the United States had been a school master. I can scarcely exaggerate the benefit I derived from close association with the young for a period of nearly forty years. As President of the College Council, I am in touch with the administration of the college, though I have ceased to be a teacher. My interest in the college and in the cause of education will only cease when I have ceased to take an interest in all mundane affairs.

For five years I was a member of the Senate. I owed my seat not to nomination by Government, but to the votes of my fellow-graduates. The new Universities Act had given to registered graduates the right of returning five members to the Senate, who should be graduates of not less than ten years' standing. I stood as a candidate and was returned at the head of the poll.

Before the enactment of the new Universities Act a modified sort of election was allowed, but it was only M.A.'s and B.A.'s who had graduated in or before 1867 who could stand as candidates for election. Why the year 1867 was fixed, why no one who had graduated in or after that year could stand as a candidate, is one of those riddles that the official sphinx has not chosen to solve, and which at the time evoked considerable comment and criticism. The graduates of 1868 were under no special ban. They could not by any means be considered an inferior set as compared with the graduates of previous years. Why then were they excluded from standing for the election? If the rule had been that only graduates of twenty or even twenty-five years could be eligible, there would be some sense in it as having in view the return of only experienced graduates. But such a rule, my friends said, would not have served the purpose of its framers; for their view was that the rule was especially framed to exclude me, the year of my graduation being 1868.

So unreasonable was the restriction that a public meeting was held at the Albert Hall, attended by many leading graduates of the Calcutta University, urging its modification, but all in vain. The rule continued in force until the Universities Act, which definitely conferred the right of election upon graduates of ten years' standing.

The most important work done, during the period I was a member of the Senate, was the framing of the regulations for the consideration of the Government. I was on the Committee. We had hard work. I cannot say that our recommendations were all accepted. In one important matter they were rejected. We recommended that the history of England should be a part of the curriculum for the Matriculation Examination. This recommendation was negatived by a committee of the Government, which finally settled the regulations. How it is possible for a student to study English literature without a knowledge of English history is one of those enigmas that the framers of the regulations and the Government of India must solve as best they can.

When I became a member of the Senate, Sir Alexander Pedler was Vice-Chancellor. He had a leading hand in the framing of the Universities Act. He engineered it in the Legislative Council; and in the fitness of things he was placed at the head of the University of Calcutta, for which the Universities Act was chiefly meant. He was succeeded by Mr. Justice Ashutosh Mukherjea. His long familiarity with the Calcutta University, his wide grasp of educational problems and his extraordinary capacity for dealing with them, made Sir Ashutosh the most commanding figure in the University. During the time he was Vice-Chancellor (and he held the office for several years) he ruled the University with a supreme sway; and it is but right to say that he enforced the regulations with a measure of discretion, a regard for all interests, that partly allayed the suspicion and anxiety they had created in the mind of the educated community of Bengal. It was during his Vice-Chancellorship that Sir Taraknath Palit and Sir Rash Behari Ghose made their princely gifts to the University for a College of Science. They had faith in his capacity, and they doubtless felt that under his able guidance the foundations of the institution, which they had contributed to build up, would be well and truly laid. A vice-chancellor with less devotion and capacity would not probably have inspired their confidence. University teaching in the higher departments made a great stride during his Vice-Chancellorship.

One of the features of his administration that provoked comment and criticism was the abolition of the law classes in the private colleges, with the exception of those of the Ripon College. His underlying idea perhaps was the creation of a central law college that would serve as a model of efficiency fit to compare favourably with the great law colleges in England and America, but this might have been done by insisting upon a higher standard of efficiency in the law classes in the private colleges, and without their actual disaffiliation. A healthy competition contributes to educational efficiency, and anything approaching a monopoly is injurious to the public interests.

It is impossible to leave this reference to Sir Ashutosh Mukherjea's work as a member of the University without lamenting the grievous loss which the cause of education in Bengal and India has sustained by his early death, almost immediately after his retirement from the Bench. He was a unique figure in the educational world of Bengal and it will be difficult to fill his place. The numerous demonstrations held in his honour, all over the province, bore testimony to the universality of the national sorrow.

In 1901 I ceased to be a member of the Bengal Legislative Council. I stood for a seat in the Imperial Legislative Council the same year. The rival candidate was the present Maharaja of Darbhanga. I was defeated. The circumstances that led to my failure were peculiar. There was a tie between the Maharaja and myself, each counting five votes. The matter went up to the Government of India. Under the Council Regulations, the Government was bound to pass orders within two months of the polling. The Government of Lord Curzon violated this rule. It did nothing for three months, and ordered a re-election when I had ceased to be a member of the Bengal Council and could not record my vote in my favour.

It was a piece of diplomatic strategy, opposed to the rules in force and to all considerations of fairness, the effect of which was to exclude me from the Governor-General's Council. I had stood for a seat in the Imperial Legislative Council several times before, but I had always been defeated; and I fear that official influence was exerted against me. A friend of mine, who came from Behar and whom I helped to be returned to the Bengal Council, assured me that he would have voted for me, but that he could not disregard the request of a high official who had spoken to him on the subject. I think the fact was published at the time in the newspapers, without, of course, the names of the parties concerned.

18
The Partition of Bengal

A former Partition – the Civil Service case for further division – the energy of Lord Curzon: his visit to East Bengal – contempt of public opinion: the secret despatch – astonishment and indignation of Bengalee-speaking public; we make our plans.

THE YEAR 1905 is one of the most memorable in the history of Bengal. It would be no exaggeration to say that it was an epoch-making year, leaving a profound and far-reaching influence on the public life of Bengal and the future of the country. It was the year of the Partition of Bengal.

There had been for some time a general feeling in official quarters that Bengal was too large a charge for a single ruler, and that the partition of the province was necessary in the interests of administrative efficiency. It was in pursuance of this idea that the province of Assam was separated from Bengal in 1874, and made a separate administrative unit under a Chief Commissioner. The separation did not, at the time, excite much criticism, although in the province thus separated from Bengal there were three Bengalee-speaking districts, namely, Sylhet, Cachar and Goalpara. Public opinion was not then much of a power, and the solidarity of the Bengalee-speaking people and their growing sense of unity had not become so pronounced a factor in the public life of the province. The change was acquiesced in without demur; possibly it was welcomed by the people of Assam, who hoped that special attention would be paid to their interests.

But there is growth in all things, good or bad – nothing stationary in administration or in other human concerns. Soon the bureaucracy discovered that a further expansion of the scheme of partition was required, in the interests of efficiency as well as of the Service. Assam had no cadre of its own. The Civil Service appointments for the province were too few to justify a special cadre. Civil servants from Bengal and sometimes from the United Provinces took up appointments in Assam, but after a term reverted to their own provinces, the high appointments being few and the prospects limited. The interests of the Civil Service, with which undoubtedly the interests of the province were to some extent bound up, demanded that Assam should be a self-contained province.

The idea of a further partition for the creation of a greater Assam loomed large in the official view. The proposal was made, that the Chittagong Division, comprising the districts of Chittagong, Noakhali and Tippera, should be withdrawn from Bengal and tacked on to the Province of Assam. The proposal elicited a strong protest from the people of the Chittagong Division, supported by the public opinion of Bengal. The reformed Legislative Council had come into existence. Public opinion was becoming a growing power and could no longer be altogether ignored. The proposal was dropped in view of the strong public protest; but it was never completely shelved. It lingered in the subterranean depths of the official consciousness, to emerge into view in more propitious circumstances.

Lord Curzon was now at the head of affairs. His energy was feverish. He was upsetting and unsettling things. The question of boundaries attracted his attention. The map of India was to be recast, but by pacific methods and with the impress of his genius and superior personality stamped thereon. Here was this unsettled question. It was taken up and its scope further expanded. The proposal now assumed the form of the separation from Bengal of the whole of the Chittagong Division, to which the districts of Dacca and Mymensingh were to be added, and this area was to be incorporated into Assam.

It was in this form that the proposal came up for discussion before the public of Bengal. It roused strong opposition among all sections of the community – Hindus and Mohamedans alike. It was an opposition that the Government could not ignore. The Government sought to persuade and to conciliate by conferences with the leaders of East Bengal. These conferences were held at 'Belvedere' under the presidency of the Lieutenant-Governor, Sir Andrew Fraser. They were organized by the newly-formed Landholders' Association, of which the life and soul at that time was Mr. (afterwards Sir A.) Chaudhuri. I was asked by Mr. Chaudhuri to attend these conferences. I said it was not necessary, as the arrangements were in such excellent hands. I watched the proceedings as an interested spectator, eager to know and to help, but took no personal part or share in them.

I was under the impression, wholly unfounded, as the sequel proved, that the Government, as the result of these conferences, would bow to public opinion and withdraw from an untenable position. But this was not to be. Lord Curzon visited East Bengal, ostensibly with the object of ascertaining public opinion, but really to overawe it. He was so hopelessly out of touch with the new spirit that his own reactionary policy had helped to foster, that he thought that his presence would serve to bring the leaders of East Bengal round to his views. He was greatly mistaken. At Mymensingh he was the guest of the Maharaja Surya Kanto Acharya. Among the Zemindars of Bengal there never was a finer or a stronger personality. He received Lord Curzon with all the honours of princely hospitality; but he told him with quiet and dignified firmness that he would regard the Partition of Bengal as a grave disaster, and that he was opposed to it; and throughout he remained a prominent leader of the anti-Partition agitation.

It was in the course of this tour that the scheme of Partition underwent a further expansion. It was now proposed, and for the first time, to include the whole of North Bengal and the districts of Faridpore and Barisal in East Bengal, in the new and expanded project.

The revised scheme was conceived in secret, discussed in secret, and settled in secret, without the slightest hint to the public. The idea of submitting it to a representative conference was no longer followed. 'The final scheme' said Lord Morley from his place in Parliament, 'was never submitted to the judgment of anybody in Bengal.' And why not? What became of that pretended deference to public opinion, of the solicitude to consult it, so conspicuous in the early stages of the discussion, when the East Bengal leaders were invited to conferences at 'Belvedere' under the presidency of the Lieutenant-Governor?

The truth is that there never was any real desire to defer to public opinion and abide by its decision. Lord Curzon and Sir Andrew Fraser had hoped to persuade the leaders to acquiesce in their views; when they failed, they set public opinion at defiance, but not with the inborn courage of real statesmanship. For the scheme, as finally settled, was embodied in a secret despatch of which the public knew nothing. Indeed, so complete was the lull after Lord Curzon's visit to East Bengal and before the storm actually burst, that the idea gained ground that the project of a partition had been abandoned. Had we the faintest idea of what had been secretly decided, a deputation would have gone to England along with the despatch, with a view to procuring the annulment of its recommendations. I would have gladly joined such a deputation.

It is abundantly clear from the despatch of the Secretary of State that he accepted the Partition of Bengal with hesitation, for he suggested an alternative scheme to afford relief to the administration by creating a province on the model of Sind in the Bombay Presidency; and when I had an interview with Mr. Brodrick in London in the summer of 1909 and we discussed the Partition of Bengal, he did not seek to justify it. It is my deliberate conviction that, but for the profound secrecy observed with regard to the final scheme, and our inaction owing to the absence of all information, the Partition of Bengal would not have been sanctioned by the Secretary of State. A timely deputation to England would have sealed its fate. But it is no use speculating as to what might have been.

On July 20, 1905, the announcement was made that Bengal was to be partitioned, and the public were informed of the details of the Partition. For the first time they learnt that North Bengal with all its historic associations was to be separated from the old province. The announcement fell like a bomb-shell upon an astonished public. But in our bewilderment we did not lose our heads. We made up our minds to do all that lay in our power, with the aid of the constitutional means at our disposal, to reverse, or at any rate to obtain a modification of, the Partition.

We felt that we had been insulted, humiliated and tricked. We felt that the whole of our future was at stake, and that it was a deliberate blow aimed at the growing solidarity and self-consciousness of the Bengalee-speaking population. Originally intended to meet administrative requirements, we felt that it had drawn to itself a political flavour and complexion, and, if allowed to be passed, it would be fatal to our political progress and to that close union between Hindus and Mohamedans upon which the prospects of Indian advancement so largely depended. For it was openly and officially given out that Eastern Bengal and Assam was to be a Mohamedan province, and that credal distinctions were to be recognized as the basis of the new policy to be adopted in the new province.

We lost no time in taking action. We held a conference at Maharaja Jotindra Mohon Tagore's palace at Pathuriaghatta. The Maharaja was present and took an active part in the deliberations. Among those who attended was Mr. H. E. A. Cotton, then practising as a barrister in Calcutta, and now President of the Bengal Legislative Council. He was in the deepest sympathy with the movement for the reversal of the Partition; so was Mr. Ratcliffe,

Editor of the *Statesman,* and so was Mr. Fraser Blair, then Editor of the *Englishman.* Anglo-Indian opinion, which generally supports the official view of things, condemned the partition through its accredited organs. The attitude, however, did not long continue; but that was the view of the Anglo-Indian Press in the early days of the anti-Partition agitation.

At the conference, it was decided that the Maharaja should send a telegram to the Viceroy praying for a reconsideration of the orders passed, and urging that, if the partition were unavoidable, owing to administrative reasons, the Bengalee-speaking population should form part and parcel of the same administration. It is significant that the form of partition that was subsequently adopted by Lord Hardinge's Government was definitely foreshadowed at this conference, and was embodied in the telegram despatched to the Viceroy.

To have divided Bengal into two provinces, keeping the Bengalee-speaking population together in one province, and the rest in the other, would have removed all administrative inconveniences, whatever they were, and gratified public opinion. But this would not suit Lord Curzon and his Government. For, as we believed, there was an underlying political motive, which would not be satisfied with such a division of the province as was suggested by the Maharaja. Lord Hardinge's Government fell in with our views, but their policy and aims were different from those of Lord Curzon.

The Conference at the Maharaja's palace was followed by almost daily conferences held in the Indian Association Rooms or at the house of Maharaja Surya Kanto Acharya of Mymensingh. It was resolved to hold a public meeting at the Town Hall on August 7, a day that was destined to become famous in the history of the anti-Partition controversy. Letters were sent to the mofussil, inviting delegates to be present at the meeting. The response was unanimous and enthusiastic. My friend Babu Anath Bandhu Guha wrote to me from Mymensingh, requesting a postponement of the date of the meeting so as to give the mofussil people more time for organization; but, having regard to the strength of the feeling that had been roused, and the eagerness to fire the first shot without delay, I wrote back, after consulting friends, that time was an important element, and that the first great demonstration should be held early, so as to give the movement a lead and a direction which would co-ordinate its future development and progress throughout the province.

The resolutions to be adopted at the meeting of August 7 were the subject of anxious and prolonged discussion at the various conferences, which were attended by leading men from East and North Bengal. It was felt that mere public meetings would be of no use. Lord Curzon's Government had shown a systematic disregard of public feeling, and had treated public demonstrations with undisguised contempt. Something more was necessary – something that would be a fitting embodiment of the intense feeling that lay behind the whole movement. I remember the various suggestions made at the meetings held almost daily in the rooms of the Indian Association. One of them was that we should resign all our honorary appointments, such as those of Honorary Magistrate, and membership of district boards and municipalities. The obvious objection to the resignation of our seats on the local bodies and the Magisterial Bench was that they afforded an opportunity of serving our countrymen, and that they were a source of local influence which would be useful in the coming struggle. Further, it was doubtful whether the whole country would be with us, in such a view. A partial failure on the threshold of a great controversy would be disastrous, and the idea was therefore abandoned.

19

The Boycott and 'Swadeshi' Movement

Genesis of the Boycott – new note of practicality in agitation – how the *Swadeshi* movement spread: enthusiasm of the student community – industrial revival.

WHILE THESE DISCUSSIONS WERE IN PROGRESS, the idea of what was afterwards called the 'Boycott Movement' was in the air, and thrust itself into prominence in our deliberations. Much has been written and said about its genesis. From whose fertile brain did it spring – when did it first see the light? Both these questions it would be difficult to answer with anything like accuracy. When the public has been roused by any stirring event, its hidden springs touched, and its slumbering forces set in motion by some great calamity or by the passionate desire to work out a cherished ideal, promising to unfold a new chapter in a nation's history, the moral atmosphere becomes fruitful under the pressure of new ideas; for the mind of the whole community is at work and makes its contribution to the sum total of national thought.

In my younger days, I had read Macaulay's graphic account of the condition of English society on the eve of the Civil War between Charles I and his Parliament – how the coming struggle overshadowed all other considerations, how it penetrated the homes of England and became the subject of conversation round every fireplace, how it leavened thought and moulded aspirations. Something of the same absorbing interest was roused by Lord Curzon's Partition of Bengal. The whole community felt a concern about a matter affecting their province such as they had never experienced before. The community was writhing under a sense of surprise and indignation, accentuated by the farce of a conference at 'Belvedere', with its seeming deference to public opinion. It was in this state of the public mind that the idea of a boycott of British goods was publicly started – by whom I cannot say – by several, I think, at one and the same time. It first found expression at a public meeting in the district of Pabna, and it was repeated at public meetings held in other mofussil towns; and the successful boycott of American goods by the Chinese was proclaimed throughout Asia and reproduced in the Indian newspapers.

The feeling was further emphasized by the stirrings of an industrial movement that was beginning to fasten its hold on the public mind. The *Swadeshi* movement had already come into existence. At any rate the *Swadeshi* spirit was abroad. It was in the air. There was a growing party among the educated community who espoused it. Our industrial helplessness was attracting attention in an increasing measure; and it was readily perceived that the boycott would be a double-edged weapon, industrial and political, in its scope and character.

The idea of a boycott was anxiously discussed for days together at our conferences. There was, as the result of these discussions, a pretty general unanimity of feeling amongst us. It was recognized that in the state of public feeling which then prevailed the movement would meet with general support; and the result fully justified this anticipation.

The only objection that was felt and seriously discussed was, how it would affect our English friends. Would they approve of it? Would they sympathize with it? Might they not regard it as an open avowal of ill will? For, as I have already observed, there were many Englishmen in Calcutta who strongly disapproved of the Partition, and of the form and the manner in which it was carried out. They were helping us with their advice and the weight of their moral support. We were anxious that we should do nothing to alienate them, and that we should continue to receive their sympathy, which proved so helpful. Further, our appeal lay to the British public against the decision of the Government of India. We knew that Lord Curzon and the India Office would do all that lay in their power to prevent a revision of the orders passed. We felt some doubt as to how the movement would be viewed by the British public.

Thus the movement was not anti-British in its origin, nor even in its subsequent developments, though our official critics tried to make out that it was so; and we wanted to know what the British standpoint was likely to be, from Englishmen who might be presumed to be in closer touch than we could be with the temper and opinion of their countrymen at home. How foolish it would have been to have made an appeal to the British public for the reversal of an order of the Government of India by starting an anti-British movement! The organizers of the movement were presumably men of common sense, and they were not going to begin business by an act of folly that would make the British public turn a deaf ear to their appeals.

The terms of the resolution on the subject adopted at the Town Hall meeting demonstrated their anxiety to proceed with caution and care, and to offend no interest that might be enlisted in their favour. I was commissioned to consult some English friends as to whether they would advise such a resolution and what should be its form. As the communications were confidential, it would not be right to disclose their names even at this distance of time. But, one and all without a single exception, they advised the adoption of the course that had been suggested. A final conference was held at the house of Maharaja Surya Kanto Acharya of Mymensingh, when it was definitely decided to accept the following resolution:

> 'That this meeting fully sympathizes with the resolution adopted at many meetings held in the mofussil to abstain from the purchase of British manufactures so long as the Partition Resolution is not withdrawn, as a protest against the indifference of the British public in regard to Indian affairs and the consequent disregard of Indian public opinion by the present Government.'

It will thus be seen that the boycott was a temporary measure adopted for a particular object, and was to be given up as soon as that object was attained. Its only aim and purpose was to call the attention of the British public to Bengal's great grievance, and, when the partition was modified and the grievance was removed, the boycott was to cease. That pledge was redeemed.

That the boycott sometimes led to excesses no one will dispute; but all constitutional movements suffer from this inherent weakness, which springs from the defects of our common human nature. All causes – the purest and the noblest – will have their moderates and their extremists. But the excesses, more or less incidental to all constitutional movements, have never been held as an argument against the adoption of constitutional methods for the redress of public grievances. If such a view were held, some of the noblest chapters of human history would have been left unwritten, and we should have been without the inspiration of self-sacrifice and patriotic devotion, which have so often been associated with the struggle for constitutional freedom. Who will say that because there is unhappily a revolutionary propaganda in Bengal, undoubtedly limited and insignificant in the circle of its influence, all constitutional efforts should be given up? The enemies of Indian advancement would wish for nothing better. The friends of Indian progress would view it as a calamity.

The Boycott Resolution was entrusted to Babu Narendranath Sen. It would have been impossible to have found among the ranks of Bengal leaders one who by his moderation and patriotism was so well qualified for the task. Babu Narendranath Sen was then at the height of his fame and influence. He was the editor of the *Indian Mirror*, the only daily newspaper at the time in Bengal under Indian management and control. He had long fought the battles of his country with constancy and courage; and his character for sobriety and self-restraint made him respected even by those who did not view Indian aspirations with a friendly eye. It were much to be wished that to the last he had maintained his hold over the affections of his countrymen. But, alas! the closing chapters of his life dimmed the lustre of that great popularity which at one time made him a power in the counsels of his countrymen. The unhappy anarchical developments in Bengal somewhat unhinged a temperament in which the emotions played so prominent a part. He viewed them with concern and dismay, and this champion of a free Press went so far, in his solicitude to support the authorities, as to consent to receive a subsidy from the State for the publication of a vernacular newspaper.

It was an un-English and unwise policy for the Government to pursue, for such a paper could command no influence; but it was a matter of national regret that Babu Narendranath Sen should have lent the weight of his name and influence in support of a journalistic enterprise that was so thoroughly condemned by his countrymen. This, however, was the solitary flaw in a career of exceptional brilliancy and usefulness; and the historian of our times will accord to Narendranath Sen his rightful place among contemporaries, as a fearless champion of the public interests, and a warm and devoted worker in the cause of Indian progress. If his wary footsteps gave way in a position of exceptional difficulty, who amongst us is so blameless, so far removed from human failings, that he can afford to throw the first stone at him?

I remember Narendranath Sen in the days of his sturdy manhood, when age and disappointment had not worked their havoc upon his noble temperament, when he was the terror of evil-doers, and when the enemies of his country shrank from his virile presence. I saw him the day before his death. It was a hot day in August; Narendranath Sen lay prostrate on his bed. He was weak, scarcely able to speak, but still in full possession of his faculties. Not a word passed between him and me. We exchanged glances.

He looked at me with a look on which, as it seemed to me, were imprinted the memories of the past. Tears flowed down his cheeks. I returned the sad and loving glance, my eyes dim with tears, which I tried to check as best as I could, amid the grim surroundings of that chamber of death. I came away with a heavy heart, feeling that my honoured colleagues were one by one passing away, leaving 'the world to darkness and to me'.

It is worthy of remark that the Boycott Resolution did not elicit any marked sense of disapproval from the European Press, certainly not the strong resentment that it subsequently provoked. All that the *Englishman* newspaper said about it was that 'the policy of boycott must considerably embitter the controversy if it is successful, while in the opposite event it will render the movement and its supporters absurd'. The *Statesman* was inclined to ridicule the whole movement, but there was not a trace of any resentment on the ground that an anti-British agitation had been inaugurated.

> 'Those who were responsible for the Boycott Resolution (said the *Statesman*) have doubtless been fired by the example of the Chinese, and they are optimistic enough to assume that a boycott of European goods could be made as effective and as damaging as the Chinese boycott of American goods has to all appearance been. The assumption will cause a smile on the European side for more reasons than one. But all the same it would be unwise for the Government to assume that the whole movement is mere froth and insincerity. On the contrary, it has been apparent for some time past that the people of the province are learning other and more powerful methods of protest. The Government will recognize the new note of practicality which the present situation has brought into political agitation.'

I have dwelt at some length on the attitude of Anglo-Indian opinion with regard to the Boycott Resolution, in order to indicate that the subsequent change that took place was but the reflex of the official bitterness which the success of the movement evoked. Bureaucracy is always unequal to a new situation or to an unexpected development. So long as things go on in the normal groove, bureaucracy, deriving its light and leading from precedent and from ancient and dust-laden files, feels happy and confident. But when the clouds appear on the horizon and when there is the ominous presage of stormy weather ahead, the bureaucratic mind feels restive; the files afford no guidance; the bureaucrat is disturbed; he loses his equanimity; his uneasiness slides into resentment;

and, imagining dangers where there are none, he adopts heroic measures, which engender the very troubles that wiser and more pacific counsels would have averted.

A boycott movement in India had never before been thought of or attempted. It was a bold conception; and the first impulse of all spectators, as in the case of the *Statesman,* was to treat it with ridicule. But the success that it soon attained disclosed the volume of public sentiment that was behind it. Without a more or less universal feeling supporting it, the boycott was bound to fail. Its success was a revelation to all; it outstripped the anticipations of its inaugurators. But the bureaucracy in those days would learn nothing that was not in its files and was not consecrated by the dust of the Secretariat shelves. It was amazed at the ebullition of public feeling – it was indignant – it lost all self-control; it sought to repress where tactful handling and conciliatory measures would have been more effective, and it thus added to the intensity of the flame.

The course of events during the whole of the controversy in connexion with the Partition of Bengal bears out what I have just observed. There was throughout a persistent attempt to suppress the expression of public feeling in the name of law and order; and, as always happens in such cases, the attempt at repression recoiled upon its authors. More repressive measures were requisitioned; and the more signally did they fail; and the public excitement and unrest grew apace.

Undoubtedly the student community were deeply moved, and in the exuberance of their zeal they were sometimes betrayed into excesses. When a great impulse stirs the heart of a community it is the young and impressionable who feel the full impact of the rising tide. At all times and in all ages it is to the young that the preachers of new movements have addressed themselves. ' Suffer little children to come unto me ' were the words of the divinely-inspired Founder of Christianity. In Greece, in Italy, in America, in Germany, all over the world, when a new gospel was preached, charged with the message of a new hope, it was the young who enthusiastically responded to the call.

I appealed to the young to help us in the great national movement. I knew how deeply they were stirred when I was sent to prison for contempt of court, and I felt that they would help to create a body of public opinion without which we could not hope to succeed. I addressed them at numerous public meetings, and warm was the response. It had its roots in economic rather than in political causes. The Partition had indeed moved their deepest feelings, but they were more concerned with the spread of the *Swadeshi* movement than with the political propaganda that sought to reverse the Partition of Bengal.

Their enthusiasm was roused to a pitch such as I had never before witnessed. It was positively dangerous for a schoolboy or a college student to appear in a class or lecture room in clothes made of a foreign stuff. The students would not submit to exercise books being circulated for their class examinations with paper that had been manufactured abroad. I remember a schoolboy appearing in the fourth form of the Ripon Collegiate School with a shirt made of foreign cloth. As soon as the discovery was made, the shirt was torn off his back, and he narrowly escaped lynching. Let me here relate one more incident of a similar character. At an examination of the Ripon College students, the college authorities supplied foreign-manufactured paper upon which the answers were to be written. The students in a body refused to touch the blank books that were supplied. So strong was the feeling that it was thought not safe to ignore it. Country-made paper had to be substituted, and the examination then proceeded in the usual way.

It was the fervour of the students that communicated itself to the whole community and inspired it with an impulse, the like of which had never been felt before. It was a strange upheaval of public feeling. The *Swadeshi* movement invaded our homes and captured the hearts of our women-folk, who were even more enthusiastic than the men. A grand-daughter of mine, then only five years old, returned a pair of shoes that had been sent to her by a relative, because they were of foreign make. The air was surcharged with the *Swadeshi* spirit, and it is no exaggeration to say that our young men were the creators of this stupendous moral change.

I have not witnessed a revolution in my time, nor by an effort of the imagination can I conceive what it is like. But, amid the upheaval of the *Swadeshi* movement, I could, I think, obtain some idea of the transformation of public feeling and of the wild excitement which must precede a revolutionary movement. A strange atmosphere is created. Young and old, rich and poor, literate and illiterate, all breathe it, and all are swayed and moved and even transported by the invisible influence that is felt. Reason halts; judgment is held in suspense; it is one mighty impulse that moves the heart of the community and carries everything before it. An eminent doctor told me that in the height of the *Swadeshi* movement a girl-patient of his, not more than six years old, cried out in her delirium that she would not take any foreign medicine.

How was it that every one was so moved? The visible and outward conditions do not suffice to explain it. But after all, the element of mystery, if there is any, vanishes before the gaze of the earnest student of history. The *Swadeshi* movement did not come into birth with the agitation for the reversal of the Partition of Bengal. It was synchronous with the national awakening which the political movement in Bengal had created. The human mind is not divided into watertight compartments, but is a living organism; and, when a new impulse is felt in one particular direction, it affects the whole organism and is manifest throughout the entire sphere of human activities. When the Congress movement was started in the early eighties of the last century it was, and is even now, a common enough remark among a certain class of writers, perhaps not friendly to Indian interests, that it would have been far better, and a more natural course, to have commenced with the vital problems of social reform than with political considerations, which might have been more usefully dealt with later on, after our social and domestic institutions had been placed on a better and more satisfactory footing. The whole course of our national evolution has belied this confident assertion. Social reform, industrial revival, moral and spiritual uplift, have all followed in the track of the great national awakening, which had its roots in the political activities of our leaders. Once again the truth was established, that all reforms are inter-linked and interdependent, and that they act and react upon one another, and strengthen one another by their mutual interaction. The activities of Iswar Chunder Vidyasagar helped Keshub Chunder Sen by enabling him to appeal to instincts and tendencies broadened by the spirit of reform. His work, in its turn, helped that of Kristo Das Pal and others; and the new school of politicians, fresh from their contact with the West, familiar with Western methods and imbued with the Western spirit, left the beaten track and extended the scope of their work by direct appeals to the educated community and even to the masses. The new ideals and the new methods moved the people, and imparted to them an impulse that bore fruit in the manifold activities of an awakened national life.

Industrial revival followed as a matter of course, and devoted men, instinct with the new spirit, applied themselves to the development of our indigenous industries. One of the earliest pioneers in this field was Jogesh Chunder Chaudhuri. He belonged to a highly capable family, one of the members of which, Sir Ashutosh Chaudhuri, became a Judge of the High Court of Calcutta. Mr. Jogesh Chunder Chaudhuri is a member of the Calcutta High Court Bar, and is the founder of the *Weekly Notes,* a law journal which has a recognized and authoritative place among legal publications. But he is no mere lawyer; and the development of the indigenous industries of his country had an irresistible fascination for him. He it was who first started an Industrial Exhibition of *Swadeshi* articles as an annexe to the Indian National Congress. That was in 1896, and a similar exhibition on a much larger scale was again held under his management in 1906, in connexion with the Calcutta Congress of that year.

Thus when the anti-Partition controversy arose, the ground for a *Swadeshi* movement had already been prepared, and the political enthusiasm of our people was linked with the fervour to uplift our industrial status. The *Swadeshi* movement was in spirit a protectionist movement. Only, as we had not the power to make laws, which was in hands other than our own, we sought to surround our domestic industries with a tariff wall not raised by the mandate of the legislature, but by the determined will of our people. Such a movement could only succeed among a highly emotional people, swayed by an impulse that was universal.

The European Press viewed the whole thing as a huge mistake, and was confident that it would soon disappear as a nine days' wonder. That it lasted much longer and was in fairly vigorous operation during the six years that the Partition was in force, was the wonder of foreign visitors, accustomed to the economic conditions prevalent in the Western world. That the people of Bengal should continue, and that for several years, to purchase home-made things at a higher price when similar or even superior articles, imported from foreign countries, could be had cheaper, was a striking testimony to their devotion and self-sacrificing spirit. In this they have never been wanting when the occasion required it, but to this quality, I fear, justice has not always been done.

A powerful, overmastering impulse soon breaks its prescribed bounds and penetrates into the many-sided relations of life. It soon becomes a social force. Swadeshism during the days of its potency coloured the entire texture of our social and domestic life. Marriage presents that included foreign goods, the like of which could be manufactured at home, were returned. Priests would often decline to officiate at ceremonies where foreign articles were offered as oblations to the gods. Guests would refuse to participate in festivities where foreign salt or foreign sugar was used. So great was the pressure of public opinion that no Bengalee would think of purchasing a foreign-made *dhoti* or *saree;* and, if he wanted to do so for its cheapness, it had to be done during the hours of darkness, when no eyes would watch him, or, if watched, he would elude observation under the friendly covering of night.

20

Swadeshism and 'Bande-Mataram'

Non-Co-operation: a comparison – my ideals in public life – campaign in the country: roughing it for the cause – Kabyavisarad: journalist, composer and patriot – beginning of repression: Government circulars – *Bande-Mataram* forbidden – a pan-Indian cry: its meaning and origin.

We have heard a great deal about the Non-Co-operation movement. To-day the vernacular Press is far more widespread in its influence than it was at the time of the *Swadeshi* movement; and the vernacular Press in its utterances distinctly leans towards Non-Co-operation. But the truth cannot be gainsaid that Non-Co-operation is nowhere as compared to the influence that Swadeshism exercised over our homes and our domestic life. Non-Co-operation, even in its strongest centres (and they are not many in Bengal), is not a social force, such as Swadeshism was in the days of its power and influence. There are innumerable villages in Bengal where the *charka* and the *khaddar* are unknown. I wish it were otherwise; but the truth must be stated. An industrial movement linked with a political controversy may receive a momentary impulse which may send it far forward, but in the long run it suffers by such association. An industry must be conducted on business lines; and business considerations must, in the long run, guide and dominate its course and progress. Capital, organization and expert knowledge – these constitute the basic foundations of an industrial enterprise. A patriotic impulse will certainly help it; but only for a time, and will cease to be operative when normal conditions are restored.

It is sometimes said that our public movements are soulless, and that they are so because we do not always take the masses of our people with us. This is perhaps neither the time nor the place to discuss this question. The masses do not actively associate themselves with any public movement unless their own particular interests are vitally concerned. All great movements originate with and are guided and controlled by,. the intellectual leaders of the community, the masses more or less sympathizing with them and lending them the weight of their moral support. They are vocal only on great occasions, demonstrative and sometimes uncontrollable when their deeper feelings have been roused, and the memories of past wrongs, or the sense of present oppression, are kindled in their breasts. The *Swadeshi* movement appealed to their personal interests. They had sense enough to perceive that the movement, if successful, would herald the dawn of a new era of material prosperity for them.

When I entered public life nearly fifty years ago, I had three ideals, which have never failed to inspire me, and to which I always, amid the many vicissitudes of my political life, endeavoured, according to my opportunities, to give effect. They were : (1) The unification of the various Indian peoples upon a common platform for the advancement of our common political interests; (2) the establishment of friendly and fraternal relations between Hindus and Mohamedans as the first indispensable condition of Indian progress; and (3) the uplifting of the masses and their association with us in our public movements. It was for the realization of the first two of these ideals that I toured all over India in 1876 and 1877, spoke upon the question of Indian unity at numerous public meetings, and sought to unite all India in a common demand for the redress of a great national grievance. To me the *Swadesh* movement opened out a splendid opportunity for the realization of one of the ideals of my life, and I embraced it with alacrity and enthusiasm.

Swadeshi meetings were held all over the country, even in places beyond our own province. I was present addressing as many meetings (mostly in Bengalee) and in as many places as I could, and as my health and strength would permit. It was a time of unusual excitement and strenuous work. None spared himself. Every one did his best. We travelled to places strange and unknown, often difficult of access. We ate strange food. We minded nothing. We complained of nothing. We put up with the severest hardships and inconveniences in our journeys to distant places. We faced the risks of malaria and cholera. Our enthusiasm was our protection. Our faith in our immunity from danger and disease was a moral inoculation that never failed.

There was one comrade to whom I cannot help referring in this connexion, and I do so all the more readily, as he has long been lost to us. I mean Pundit Kali Prosanna Kabyavisarad, editor of the *Hitabadi* newspaper. In ill-health, suffering from a fatal ailment (Bright's disease), he was present at every *Swadeshi* meeting to which he was invited. He introduced a new element into the *Swadeshi* meetings, which is now largely employed in our public demonstrations. They usually begin with some patriotic song, appropriate to the occasion. Kabyavisarad had a fine musical talent.

He himself could not sing, but he composed songs of exquisite beauty, which were sung at the *Swadeshi* meetings and never failed to produce a profound impression. He had a natural gift for musical composition, and, though he had an imperfect knowledge of Hindi, his Hindi song (*Deshki e kaya halat*) was one of the most impressive of its kind. It was a fierce denunciation of the passion for foreign goods in preference to domestic articles, and, when it was sung at the great Congress at Calcutta in 1906, attended by thousands of our people, it threw the whole audience into a state of wild excitement.

Kabyavisarad was always attended by two musical experts, who opened and closed the proceedings of *Swadeshi* meetings with their songs. They were taught, paid and maintained by him; and, though by no means rich, he sought no extraneous assistance for their upkeep. He was not much of a speaker, but as a writer he was the master of a vigorous and caustic style which he ruthlessly employed against the enemies of Indian advancement. A devoted patriot, he never spared himself in the service of the motherland; and I remember his attending the Lucknow Congress of 1899, with fever on him, and a warrant in a defamation case hanging over him. He was reckless of health and life; strong-willed, and even obstinate, above all advice and remonstrance. He was rapidly sinking into his grave. Those near and dear to him thought that the best way to improve his health and to save him from the consequences of his fanatical devotion to the *Swadeshi* cause was to send him away from the scene of his loved labours. A friend was going to Japan as a doctor on board a passenger ship; and his relations persuaded Kabyavisarad to accompany him, believing that rest and sea-voyage would do him good. Somehow the idea never found favour with me. A presentiment haunted me. Possibly public considerations were working in the inner depths of my consciousness, and coloured my judgment. However that may be, I tried to dissuade Kabyavisarad. He called me his political *guru*; but so did many others without his fervour or devotion, and who are too ready to fling mud at their *guru*. He at one time made up his mind not to go, but at last yielded to pressure. He took leave of me in front of the Howrah railway station, as we returned from a *Swadeshi* meeting at Mugkalyan on the Bengal-Nagpur line, a few miles from Calcutta. He took the dust of my feet. I blessed him. Alas! we were destined never to meet again, for he died at sea on the return voyage.

Thus was lost to Bengal one of the ablest and most patriotic journalists, who wielded the resources of our language with a power that made him the terror of his enemies and of the enemies of his country. He was not indeed above personalities, the bane of a species of vernacular journalism from which unhappily we have not yet emerged; and some of his sallies into the domain of domestic sanctities we must all deplore and condemn. But his fiercest personal attacks were directed against the enemies of Indian advancement, too often masquerading in the guise of friends and well-wishers. The news of his death was received in Calcutta on July 7, 1907; and when, a fortnight later, the District Conference of the 24-Parganas was held at Baraset, and the proceedings were opened with his *Swadeshi* songs, there were few in that audience who could withhold the tribute of their tears to the memory of one who, despite his faults and failings – and he had many – served his country with fidelity and devotion, and with a courage that never flinched.

But though a great *Swadeshi* worker had passed away, the cause did not suffer. All great movements, however much they may be indebted to personal initiative and genius, are largely independent of even commanding personalities. These sow the seeds, which fructify in the birth of men who, though not always their equals, are yet capable of bearing their burden and carrying on their work. Kabyavisarad's enthusiasm was but a reflex of the fervour that was so widely prevalent.

The Government was alarmed at the upheaval of public feeling, and it adopted the familiar methods of repression, which only served to stimulate such feeling. Agricola is reported by Tacitus to have made the shrewd observation that the government of a household is more difficult than that of an empire. When an explosion takes place in a family, the healing influences of time and good sense, aided by friendly counsels, help to bring things to their normal condition; and generally they are found to be effective. But a bureaucracy armed with omnipotent power is tempted to follow short cuts in dealing with an unforeseen situation. Repression is handy and promises to be effective. The heavy price that has to be paid, the disastrous moral result that it produces in the long run, are lost sight of in the eager desire to do the thing quickly. Temporary success is perhaps achieved, but permanent injury is done, and the seeds of future troubles are sown.

The students, as I have already observed, and young men who

were not students, had taken a prominent part in the *Swadeshi* movement. Their zeal had fired the whole community. They had become the self-appointed missionaries of the cause. It was thought necessary to curb and control their activities. A circular was accordingly issued by District Magistrates to heads of educational institutions, in which they were told that unless the school and college authorities and teachers prevented their pupils from taking public action in connexion with boycotting, picketing and other abuses associated with the so-called *Swadeshi* movement, the schools and colleges would forfeit their grants-in-aid and the privilege of competing for scholarships, and the University would be asked to disaffiliate them. The circular was addressed to schools in the mofussil.

The circular made a distinction between students in Calcutta and those in the mofussil, but the Calcutta boys were just as enthusiastic in the *Swadeshi* cause as their mofussil brothers. Day after day, during the height of the excitement, a number of students used to stand at the corner of the Maidan, watching those who entered Whiteaway, Laidlaw's premises, begging Indians not to purchase foreign goods, or, if the purchase had been made, appealing to them not to repeat their offence. It was reported to me at the time, that some of these young men threw themselves at the feet of a fashionable Bengalee lady, as she was coming out of Whiteaway, Laidlaw's shop, and begged of her to promise not to purchase foreign goods when similar home-made articles were available.

The circular only served to add to the excitement, and it evoked universal condemnation even among organs of opinion that usually supported the policy and measures of Government. The *Statesman* newspaper, commenting upon the circular, used language that the *Statesman* has since banished from its columns, except when denouncing really bad measures. ‘We should really like to know’ exclaimed the *Statesman*, ‘the name of the imbecile official at whose instance the Lieutenant-Governor sanctioned this order. The Government, there can be no doubt’ added the same authority, ‘has been misled by some person who is either grossly ignorant of the situation, or has allowed himself to be frightened by the fantastic scares of the last few weeks’; and the paper concluded by observing, ‘Government has blundered apparently into a childish and futile policy which can only have the effect of manufacturing an army of martyrs’. That was the language of a leading English newspaper when the first circular of a restrictive character was issued affecting students. But circular after circular followed, each one adding to the prevailing excitement, and aggravating the evil which it was intended to cure.

The *Bande-Mataram* circular was one of them. It was issued by the new Government of Eastern Bengal, and it declared the shouting of *Bande-Mataram* in the public streets to be illegal; and an authority in the person of a high European official, supposed to be versed in the ancient lore of our country, was found, who went so far as to assert that it was an invocation to the goddess Kali for vengeance. Where he got this idea from it is difficult to know. The opening lines of the *Bande-Mataram* are the words of a song, full of love for, and devotion to, the motherland, expatiating upon her beauty and her strength. 'I salute the mother, the mother of us all, namely the motherland' – that is the plain meaning of the words. But amid the excitement which prevailed in official circles a sinister meaning was read into this very innocent formula, and a circular was issued by the Government of East Bengal suppressing the cry in the streets. We took legal opinion, and the legal opinion (that of Mr. Pugh, an eminent advocate of the Calcutta Bar) was in our favour, and against the legality of the circular.

At the Barisal Conference the cry had an almost historic bearing, to which I shall refer later on. In the meantime let me thankfully note that the official angle of vision has, in this respect, undergone a change, and the national standpoint has been accepted. At one of the recruiting meetings that I attended in North Bengal, I saw British officers standing up with the rest of the audience as the great national song was sung, and soldiers of the Bengalee regiment, wearing the King's uniform, were received by their countrymen, in the numerous towns that they visited, with shouts of *Bande-Mataram*! And when they spoke at the recruiting meetings, some of them declared within the hearing, and with the full approval, of their officers that nothing would give them greater pleasure, or fill them with more patriotic pride, than to attack the German trenches with the cry of *Bande-Mataram* on their lips.

The cry, at one time banned and barred and suppressed, has become pan-Indian and national, and is on the lips of an educated Indian when on any public occasion he is moved by patriotic fervour to give expression to his feelings of joy. What is equally important to note is that it is no longer regarded by officials as the rallying cry of seditious men, intent on breaking the peace or on creating a disturbance.

The song of which '*Bande-Mataram*' are the opening words occurs in Bankim Chunder Chatterjee's well-known novel, *Anandamatha.* It is a Bengalee song, but so rich in Sanskrit vocabulary that it is understood in every part of India by educated men. Its stately diction, its fine musical rhythm, its earnest patriotism, have raised it to the status and dignity of a national song, and it forms a fitting prelude to the business of great national gatherings. Bankim Chunder Chatterjee could hardly have anticipated the part which it was destined to play in the *Swadeshi* movement, or the assured place it was to occupy in all national demonstrations. Dante, when he sang of Italian unity, had no conception of the practical use to which his song would be put by Mazzini and Garibaldi, or the part it would play in the political evolution of the Italian people. Men of genius scatter their ideals broadcast. Some of them fall on congenial soil. Time and the forces of Time nurse them. They ripen into an abundant harvest fraught with unspeakable good to future generations.

21

By-issues of the 'Swadeshi' Movement

A stimulus to journalism – industrial activity: Government's neglected opportunity – the Banga Luxmi Cotton Mill – banking and insurance – public inauguration: the ball set a-rolling.

THE SWADESHI MOVEMENT gave an impetus to all our activities, literary, political and industrial. Literature felt the full impact of the rising tide of national sentiment, which bodied itself forth in prose and verse. Journalism received a stimulus such as it had not felt for a long time. The speeches made in Bengalee at *Swadeshi* meetings, under the inspiration of the new ideas, were models of eloquence and it is a pity they have not been preserved. Where do we see the like of it in the Non-Co-operation movement, at least in Bengal? Where is the universal movement of uplift throbbing in the heart of the Bengalee, raising him to a higher plane of social and moral life? Or where now do we find in literature or in journalism the inspiration of a patriotic impulse brushing aside all that is mean or contemptible or spiteful, leading national life upwards and onwards towards the fulfilment of a nobler destiny? We see none of it. It is all words from start to finish, or ill will and hatred, robed in the garb of patriotism. Or at the best, it is separation, isolation from the larger interests of humanity. As a nation we are to live, prosper and flourish, by detachment from the wider concerns of mankind. The sap that feeds humanity is to be cut off from us, and we are to flow down the stream of life, unfed, unsupported by the culture, the art and the civilization of the rest of mankind, rejoicing in our isolation, taking pride in our aloofness. To me the thought is intolerable. It must stunt our national growth, make us dwarfs where others are giants.

But let me pass on from these reflections, and dwell upon the many-sided development of the *Swadeshi* movement in the zenith of its influence. It is, however, in the industrial line that the national activities received an unprecedented stimulus. Soap and match factories and cotton mills were started one after another. The weaving industry received an impetus all its own. The weavers were a dying class; Manchester goods had killed their trade. But now there was a revival. I went to Haripal in the Hughli district to attend a *Swadeshi* meeting. The weavers who were there in large numbers blessed us. The neatness and tidiness of their homes, which we visited, bore evidence of their revived prosperity. So it was all over the country; and the official reports testified to the fact. But in the wild enthusiasm of the hour and the eager desire to help forward our domestic industries, the preliminaries of organization were not always carefully thought out, and the need of expert knowledge was not sufficiently attended to. Capital flowed in, but capital was not always wisely employed. Failures followed, and they served to damp the *Swadeshi* spirit.

It must be regretfully noted that the Government did not take advantage of the opportunity to assist the movement. If it had placed itself at the head, and by wise guidance had led the movement into fruitful channels, it would have softened the acerbities of the political situation created by its own action, and would have taken a long step forward towards the solution of the industrial problem. But the political leaven of the *Swadeshi* movement probably determined the attitude of the Government, which was one of indifference and even of hostility. Boys were punished for boyish excesses, and quite a youthful army of martyrs was created. The seeds were thus sown of youthful dissatisfaction, which were destined to bear bitter fruits in the not very distant future, in the unhappy anarchical developments, of which, I am sorry to say, we have not yet seen the last.

But, despite the excesses of our boys and the repressive methods pursued, the *Swadeshi* movement made steady headway. Throughout, the dominating idea was to be independent of Manchester and of the foreign market for our ordinary wearing apparel, our *dhoties* and *sarees*. Bombay was partly supplying them; and the Bombay cotton mills had a highly prosperous time during the height of the *Swadeshi* movement. But it was felt that Bengal might, to some extent, supply her own needs. There was a cotton mill at Serampore on the Hughli, which had now been in existence for some time. It was resolved to buy up this mill and to extend its operations. A sum of eighteen lakhs of rupees was needed. An appeal was issued. I was one of the signatories. The money was easily found, being largely subscribed by our middle class people and even by our women-folk. The mill was purchased, extended and re-named. It was called the 'Banga Luxmi Mill', as a compliment to the gentler sex, who had shown a practical interest in the concern. The mill has had a chequered history. It has had its ups and downs.

We have to pay for our experience. This we have done, and we have gathered wisdom which I have no doubt will prove valuable. The mill has now entered upon a new career, and I hope it will be one of increasing prosperity.

From the very outset of the *Swadeshi* movement, it had been felt that banking facilities were indispensably necessary for the development of our industries. It was a matter of complaint that the banks under European management did not afford the requisite help to Indian concerns, and it was felt that we should have a bank of our own. Accordingly, the Bengal National Bank was started under an Indian directorate and Indian control and management. Its history shows that in Bengal Indian banking concerns may prove successful. But, like the Banga Luxmi Cotton Mill, it has had its vicissitudes; it was confronted with a crisis, which happily is now over.

The *Swadeshi* movement also gave a stimulus to the inauguration of insurance companies under Indian management. I had ventured to suggest, in one of my speeches on the anniversary of what is called the Boycott Movement, that this was a direction in which we might usefully employ our energies. The suggestion was taken up, and several insurance companies were started, of which the National and the Hindusthan Co-operative Insurance Companies are the best known and the most successful.

The *Swadeshi* movement was inaugurated on August 7, along with the first demonstration against the Partition of Bengal. The demonstration was an historic one. The young men of Calcutta marched in solemn procession from College Square to the Town Hall under leadership of Mr. J. Chaudhuri. The Indian shops were all closed. The Indian part of the city had a deserted look. But all was life and animation in the vicinity of the Town Hall. A huge crowd had gathered. They came rushing up the steps, filling the upper and the lower hall, flowing out into the portico, and the grounds beyond. We decided to have three meetings, two in the Town Hall, upper and lower floor, and the third on the Maidan near the Bentinck Statue. I made the announcement from the steps of the Town Hall. It was received with enthusiasm, and the vast crowd moved away to arrange themselves for the three meetings. There was no disorder of any kind, no unseemly rushing to and fro. The discipline of our people at public meetings has always in recent years, except with the rise of Non-Co-operation, been admirable, and foreign visitors who have witnessed our great demonstrations have been struck by their orderliness and the readiness of our people, even in moments of excitement, to obey authority. It is some evidence of their fitness to manage their own affairs.

I spoke at all the three meetings; the enthusiasm was unbounded, and I may here mention a little incident expressive of the prevailing *Swadeshi* feeling. It had been resolved to drape the upper floor of the Town Hall in black, as emblematic of the mournful occasion which had brought us together. An order to that effect was given to Messrs. Whiteaway, Laidlaw & Co., and it was duly carried out. Mr. Halim Ghaznavi came to me on the morning of the day fixed for the meeting, saying that if the black cloth, which was a foreign stuff, were not removed, he apprehended that there would be a disturbance. A hasty consultation was held, for there was not much time to lose; and by the hour of the meeting the whole of the drapery had been removed. Feeling was running high, and we could not ignore it. We could not afford to have a schism in our camp at the start.

The ball was now set a-rolling. The success of the first demonstration inspired public confidence and stimulated the national enthusiasm. The meeting was representative of all Bengal, more representative than any in which I have had my part and share. Never was public sentiment so outraged as by the Partition of Bengal; and Bengal, united and indivisible, thundered forth her protest through the mouths of her chosen representatives. The delegates who had attended the Calcutta meeting returned to their homes, fully resolved to continue the agitation against the Partition and in support of the *Swadeshi* cause. The two movements went hand in hand, and acted and reacted upon one other. The rising tide of the *Swadeshi* movement checked the import of Manchester goods, and Marwari merchants who dealt in them were alarmed. They made proposals to us with a view to facilitating the clearing off of the Manchester goods they had already in hand. We were willing to help them if they agreed not to import foreign goods beyond what they had already done. The negotiations were long and protracted, but they led to nothing.

22

The Settled Fact

The Partition takes effect – proposal for a Federation Hall: analogy of Alsace-Lorraine – the stone-laying: swan-song of Ananda Mohan Bose – Sir Gurudas Banerjee – our proclamation – Sir Bampfylde Fuller's administration – strictures by the High Court.

THE MONTH OF OCTOBER was rapidly approaching. The 16th October was to be the day on which the Partition of Bengal was to take effect. For Bengal it was to be a day of national mourning. We were resolved to observe it as such, and the country warmly responded to our call. The programme of mourning was fixed in consultation with the mofussil leaders, and was widely circulated. There was to be: (1) The *Rakhi-Bandhan* ceremony – the red band of brotherly union was to be tied round the wrists of all whom we welcomed as brothers. It was to be the revival of an ancient Indian custom, and was to be emblematic of the new brotherly bond between the sundered province and old Bengal. (2) The 16th of October was to be observed as a day of fasting. The domestic hearth was not to be lit; food was not to be cooked except for the sick and the invalid; the shops were to be closed, business was to be suspended; people were to walk barefooted, and bathe in the Ganges in the early morning hours for purposes of purification. It was a self-denying ordinance, but it was cheerfully accepted, and, as the sequel showed, the heart and soul of the nation were in it.

But this was not all. The day was to be marked by the inauguration of a plan of constructive work. I proposed the building of a Federation Hall, which, assuming that the Partition was not undone or modified, was to be the meeting-ground of the old province and its severed parts, the mark and symbol of their indivisible union. The idea suggested itself to me from what I saw at the Hotel des Invalides in Paris, where round the tomb of the great Napoleon are laurelled statues, representative of the different provinces. Those of Alsace and Lorraine were at the time veiled and shrouded. To me it seemed that we should have a memorial of that sort, statues of all the districts in Bengal, those of the sundered districts being shrouded until the day of their reunion. The Hall would serve other purposes of a public nature. It would keep alive the remembrance of our severance, and thus be an ever-living stimulus to our efforts to secure our reunion.

The proposal was carefully considered, and it was warmly supported by the late Sir Taraknath Palit and Sister Nivedita of the Ramkrishna Mission, that beneficent lady who had consecrated her life to, and died in, the service of India. Sir Taraknath Palit will go down to posterity as a princely benefactor in the cause of scientific education in Bengal; but he was a man of many-sided sympathies. When his soul was stirred, he was quite an active figure in our politics, helping and guarding our public interests with all the clear insight of an astute lawyer, and the warmth and enthusiasm of a generous friend. He was heart and soul with us in our efforts to undo the Partition, and, though stricken down by a fatal disease, he was with us whenever he could attend, and his clear-sighted guidance was to us a valuable help.

But laying the foundation-stone of the Federation Hall was not the only function fixed for the 16th October. The anti-Partition agitation and the *Swadeshi* movement were linked together, and it was decided to hold a great demonstration in order to raise a National Fund, chiefly for the purpose of helping the weaving industry.

Such, in short, was the programme fixed for the 16th October, 1905, the day on which the Partition of Bengal was to take place. Our workers had been out all night, looking after the arrangements for the morrow. They were tired and exhausted, but full of high spirits, cheered by the conviction that the programme would be successfully carried out. The day dawned; the streets of Calcutta re-echoed from the early hours of the morning with the cry of *Bande-Mataram,* as band after band of men, young and old, paraded the streets on their way to bathe in the river, stopping at intervals to tie the *rakhi* round the wrists of passers-by. They were often accompanied by *Sankirton* parties singing the *Bande-Mataram* and other patriotic songs. The bathing-ghats were crammed with a surging mass of men and women, all furnished with quantities of *rakhis,* which they tied round the wrists of friends and acquaintances, and even of strangers.

I was out early in the morning visiting Beadon Square, Central College, and other places, which were thronged with people, whom I addressed. Crowds of young men took the dust of my feet and embraced me. My arms were red with the *rakhis* tied round them. It was a day worth living for – a day of inspiration that perhaps comes only once in a lifetime; but it was also a day of hard and strenuous work.

The meeting for laying the foundation-stone of the Federation Hall was fixed for 3.30 p.m. Long before the appointed hour, the grounds where the meeting was to be held were filled with a surging crowd, which flowed out into the streets, now rendered quite impassable. It was estimated that at least fifty thousand people must have been present. Yet so quiet and orderly was this vast assemblage that not a policeman was required, and no policeman was to be seen. The police had mustered strong in the different police stations, but their services were not needed either to maintain order or to regulate traffic.

The function of laying the foundation-stone was to be performed by Mr. Ananda Mohan Bose. Of Mr. Ananda Mohan Bose I have spoken elsewhere and in another connexion. He came from one of the districts in the sundered province, the district of Mymensingh, and he not only regarded the Partition of Bengal as a great national calamity, but felt it as a personal grievance. He was now an invalid, the victim of a deadly disease which carried him off in less than twelve months' time. He was confined to his bed; but, as in the case of many other great men, the spirit rose above the ailments of the flesh; and, despite his weakness and the deepening shadow of his approaching end, his interest in public affairs continued unabated. We approached him. We consulted his medical advisers. They thought that under proper conditions he might be permitted to perform the function. To us it was a matter of great satisfaction that the foundation-stone would be laid by one of the noblest sons of Bengal, whose patriotic enthusiasm had been stirred by the severance, by autocratic power, of old and time-honoured associations.

The speech that he prepared on his sick-bed, amid the daily inroads of a mortal disease, is striking evidence of the triumph of mind and spirit over matter. I regard it as the greatest of his oratorical performances, and one of the noblest orations to which it has been one's privilege to listen. Indeed, judged by what happened within a few months, it was the song of the dying swan. The honour of reading the speech fell to me, for my friend was too weak to read it himself: he could not indeed stand on his legs. At the appointed hour, attended by his medical advisers and carried in an invalid's chair, he was brought to the meeting amid cries of *Bande-Mataram,* the whole of that vast audience rising to its feet, as if to salute one who had risen from the dead. For months the public had heard nothing of Ananda Mohan Bose, except the news of his illness and of his growing infirmities, which were hurrying him on to his end.

Quiet being restored, Sir Gurudas Banerjee rose from his seat on the platform and in an impressive and eloquent speech delivered in Bengalee, in which he strongly condemned the Partition, proposed Ananda Mohan Bose to the chair. The proposal was carried by acclamation. The appearance of Sir Gurudas Banerjee on the platform of a political meeting and in the rôle of a speaker was a fact so significant that it should have opened the eyes of the authorities to the deep feeling that lay behind the anti-Partition movement. A judge has no politics. According to Sir Gurudas, an ex-judge should have none. We may or may not accept this view. Some of the most distinguished of Indian judges have been of a different opinion, and after their retirement from the Bench have not hesitated to take their share in the political movements of the day; but that was not Sir Gurudas's opinion, and he stuck to it, with that quiet determination which so pre-eminently distinguished the man. On this occasion he was possibly overborne by the all-pervading influence of an irresistible public feeling, which penetrated our hearths and our homes, and captured the minds of young and old, rich and poor, men and women, alike. All bitterly resented the Partition. Some pretended to be neutral. Office-seekers and sycophants affected to be pleased.

The Chairman having been duly proposed, I read out the speech. I think I made myself heard by the vast audience that came to witness the proceedings, as I was told afterwards that the speech was distinctly heard from Mr. Ananda Mohan Bose's house, which was on the other side of the street. A Sikh priest of the highest social position, a descendant of Guru Nanak, Baba Kuar Singh, was among the audience, and he pronounced a benediction upon the function. Just before the foundation-stone was laid, Sir Ashutosh Chaudhuri read the following Proclamation in English, and Dr. Rabindranath Tagore followed him with a translation in Bengalee:

'Whereas the Government has thought fit to effectuate the Partition of Bengal in spite of the universal protest of the Bengalee nation, we hereby pledge and proclaim that we as a people shall do everything in our power to counteract the evil effects of the dismemberment of our province, and to maintain the integrity of our race. So God help us.'—A. M. Bose.

The Proclamation was settled in the *Bengalee* office, from where we started for the Federation grounds, just before the meeting was held. It was afterwards said that we had no right to issue a proclamation, that being the exclusive function of the ruling authorities. I am unable to discuss the legal aspect of the question, which certainly did not trouble us at the time. We issued the Proclamation as a fitting sequel to a function that was to commemorate by a permanent memorial the indissoluble union between East and West Bengal. The Hall was to be the living symbol of our determination to counteract the evil influences of the Partition, and to maintain the integrity of our race; and we felt that it was as well that the fact should be set forth in a clear and emphatic statement, issued on a great occasion.

We afterwards purchased the Federation grounds in order to build the Hall. But the memorial became unnecessary. The Bengalee-speaking population, with the exception of those living in what may be called an outlying area, have been re-united by the modification of the Partition. A memorial hall, which was to commemorate the dismemberment of our province and to remind us of our duty to bring about its reunion, was, therefore, not only unnecessary, but might prove hurtful by perpetuating memories of bitter controversies which should recede into the background of oblivion.

The function over, Mr. Ananda Mohan Bose was taken back under his medical escort across the road to his residence. He was none the worse for the strain and the effort. The undaunted spirit of the man and his noble fervour, which was proof against weakness and disease, bore him up. But there was something also in the moral atmosphere, in the patriotic determination and the fervid enthusiasm of that vast audience, to help and sustain him. Those near and dear to him were anxious, but they felt happy and proud that their illustrious relative had passed through an ordeal, the severest for a man in his state of health, and had performed a great function with a dignity and an eloquence worthy of the occasion.

After the ceremony, the crowd, all barefooted, wended their way to the house of Rai Pashupatinath Bose, a distance of nearly two miles. It had been decided that the collection for the National Fund, which was to help our industries, was to be made in the grounds of his palatial mansion. Due and adequate arrangements had been made for that purpose. Sir Ashutosh Chaudhuri, Mr. J. Chaudhuri, Mr. Ambika Churn Majumder and myself, along with a few other friends forming a party, walked barefooted along the flinty road. When we arrived at the house we found the grounds crammed with a vast and increasing crowd. It was impossible for me to make my way. People rushed forward to take the dust of my feet. I had better describe what happened from the columns of a daily newspaper giving an account of the scene:

'His friends, at this juncture, gathered round him and helped him out of the crush. But the people, disappointed, said, piteously, that they had come from a long way off without any food whatever, only to see Babu Surendranath and receive his blessings. Similarly, as he came into the street on his way back from the meeting, the crowd rushed round him, and it was Babu Debendra Chunder Ghose, the Senior Government Pleader of Alipore, who happened to be in his carriage near, who helped him out of the crush.'

A sum of Rs. 70,000 was collected on that day and in the course of a few hours. The amount was made up of small subscriptions. It was the gift of the great middle class of Bengal. Rajas and Maharajas indeed subscribed, but they paid small sums. There was no canvassing of any kind. It was a spontaneous gift prompted by the emotions of the hour. It was to be devoted to the encouragement of weaving and the promotion of the domestic industries. Some money was spent upon a weaving school, which, however, did not prosper and had to be closed. The balance of the money is now in the Imperial Bank under the control of trustees. Out of the interest a monthly grant is made to the Home Industries Association, established by Lady Carmichael, and to a school for the industrial training of Indian women.

The months that followed the 16th October, 1905, were months of great excitement and unrest. The policy of the Government, especially that of East Bengal under Sir Bampfylde Fuller, added to the tension of the situation. He declared, half in jest, half in seriousness, to the amazement of all sober-minded men, that he had two wives, Hindu and Mohamedan, but that the Mohamedan was the favourite wife. A ruler who could publicly indulge in a display of offensive humour of this kind was clearly unfit for the high office which he held. The Civil Service took their cue from him; and his administration was conducted upon lines in the closest conformity with the policy which he had so facetiously announced. The taint spread to the judicial Bench, and in a well-known case brought down upon the erring judge the just censure of the High

Court of Calcutta. In reversing the sentences passed upon the prisoners in the great Comilla Rioting Case in 1907, the High Court observed:

> 'The method of the learned Judge in dealing with the testimony of the witnesses by dividing them into two classes – Hindus and Mohamedans – and accepting the evidence of one class and rejecting that of the other, is open to severe criticism. The learned Judge ought to have directed his mind solely to the evidence which had been given before him, and to have excluded from his consideration all pre-conceived sympathies with either section of the population.'

This is very strong language, coming from the High Court with its great traditions of scrupulous fairness and judicial sobriety. But if preference or class bias had been the only fault of the new Government established in East Bengal, the position would not have been so grave as it soon became. The Partition was followed by a policy of repression, which added to the difficulties of the Government and the complexities of the situation. The cry of *Bande-Mataram,* as I have already observed, was forbidden in the public streets, and public meetings in public places were prohibited. Military police were stationed in peaceful centres of population, and they committed assaults upon honoured members of the Hindu community, which excited the deepest public indignation. Respectable citizens were charged with sedition for issuing a *Swadeshi* circular, and Babu Aswini Kumar Dutt, the revered leader of the people of Barisal, a man universally respected, was so charged by Mr. Jack. The accusation was baseless and Babu Aswini Kumar Dutt obtained damages against him for libel in a Civil Court. The climax was reached when the police assaulted the delegates of the Bengal Provincial Conference at Barisal in April, 1906, and forcibly dispersed the Conference.

23
Barisal

Programme of the Conference: *Bande-Mataram* a point at issue – police attack the procession: 'instructions to arrest Mr. Banerjea alone' – wounded magisterial dignity – the Conference suppressed by the police: our indignation.

TO THE NARRATIVE OF THE EVENTS of the Barisal Conference, with which I was closely associated, I will now invite the reader's attention. I had gone with some friends to Dacca, just a few days before the Conference, to settle some points at issue between our workers. Our work being over, we proceeded by steamer from Dacca to Barisal. We arrived in the evening and found that the delegates from Calcutta and other places were already there. They had not landed, but were still on board the steamers awaiting our arrival. Certain questions had arisen, which they considered to be vital, and they wanted to settle them in consultation with me before they landed. The cry of *Bande-Mataram* was forbidden in the streets of Barisal, and indeed of all the towns in East Bengal. We held the order to be illegal, and we had fortified ourselves with competent legal opinion. Were we to submit to arbitrary authority, which was not countenanced by the law? Self-respect forbade submission. But the Barisal leaders had entered into an understanding with the authorities, by which they agreed to abstain from crying *Bande-Mataram* in the public streets, in welcoming the delegates. Were we bound by this agreement? The younger and more ardent section among the delegates were in favour of shouting *Bande-Mataram* despite the agreement. A compromise, however, was effected, which was readily acquiesced in and was acceptable to all parties. It was urged that the Barisal people were our hosts, and we were their guests, and that we should, if possible, do nothing that would compromise their position. Their compact with the authorities should be respected; but it was equally binding upon the delegates to vindicate the legal right, which they undoubtedly possessed, of uttering the cry in the public streets against the arbitrary order of the Government of East Bengal. The agreement of the Barisal leaders was limited to not uttering the cry on the occasion of welcoming the delegates, it did not go further. It was therefore settled, with their full concurrence on board the steamer, that the understanding with the Barisal leaders should be respected, but that on all other occasions during the Conference we should utter the cry as if no Government order to the contrary had been issued. This being agreed to, the delegates landed in the evening.

I took up my quarters at the residence of Mr. Behari Lal Roy, Zemindar of Lakutia, who was related to me by marriage. Mr. Behari Lal Roy was never a public man. Immersed in the affairs of his own estate, he had little time or inclination to interest himself in public movements. But the Partition of Bengal drew him forth, like so many others, from his seclusion and he became, and continued to be throughout, one of the warmest supporters of the anti-Partition and *Swadeshi* movements. A man like him would naturally like to stand well with the authorities. But the public feeling was so strong that he was carried away by its resistless current and joined the national party.

The Provincial Conference was to meet on Saturday, April 14. On the morning of the 14th a conference was held at the house of Mr. Behari Lal Roy, where I was staying. All the leading delegates were there, including representatives from the Anti-Circular Society, a society recently formed with Mr. Sachindra Prosad Bose as Secretary and Mr. Krishna Kumar Mittra as President, to take necessary action against the circular issued by the Bengal Government affecting students. They formed a devoted band of *Swadeshi* workers, composed mostly of young men, who rendered valuable service to the *Swadeshi* cause. It was decided at the Conference that the delegates should meet in the compound of Raja's *haveli,* and march in procession to the *pandal* where the Provincial Conference was to be held, crying *Bande-Mataram* as they went along. It was apprehended that the police would interfere and even use force; but it was strictly enjoined that in no circumstances were the delegates to retaliate and that they were not to carry *lathis* or even walking-sticks with them. Mr. B. C. Chatterjee, barrister-at-law, asked me if he might not have a walking-stick with him. 'Not even a walking-stick', was my curt and emphatic reply. The instruction was loyally carried out.

The procession was to start at about 2 p.m. I arrived at the place about half an hour before the time. We arranged the procession and made a start. The President, Mr. A. Rasool, and Mrs. Rasool, who was an English lady, led the procession in a carriage. We were in the first line, Babu Motilal Ghose, Editor of the *Amrita Bazar Patrika,* Babu Bhupendra Nath Basu and myself. The younger men were in the rear. The police were strongly in evidence. They were armed with regulation *lathis;* an Assistant Superintendent of Police was on horseback. There was really no occasion for all this demonstration of force. It was unnecessary and inexplicable except in the light of what followed.

We were allowed to pass unmolested. It was when the younger delegates, the members of the Anti-Circular Society, emerged from the *haveli* into the public street that the whole programme of the police was developed, and the attack was begun. They were struck with regulation *lathis* (fairly thick sticks, six feet long); the *Bande-Mataram* badges that they wore were torn off. Some of them were badly hurt, and one of them, Chittaranjan Guha, son of Babu Monoranjan Guha, a well-known *Swadeshi* worker and speaker, who afterwards was deported, was thrown into a tank full of water, in which, if he had not been rescued, he would probably have found a watery grave.

These young men had done nothing; they had not even before the assault uttered what to the Government of East Bengal was an obnoxious cry, that of *Bande-Mataram.* The head and front of their offence was that they were going along the public streets in a procession, causing no inconvenience or obstruction to anybody. It was after they had been attacked that they lustily shouted *Bande-Mataram,* and the air re-echoed with the cry. It was difficult to conceive a more wanton and unprovoked assault. The processionists, if they had committed any offence, might have been arrested; and the procession itself might have been broken up if it was thought desirable; but that did not suit the authorities, and I have no hesitation in saying, and it was the verdict of contemporary opinion, that a preconceived plan had been arranged, which was a part of the policy of terrorism that was being systematically followed in East Bengal, in the hope that the agitation against the Partition would be crushed out of existence. It was a vain hope. Repression failed here, as it has failed wherever it has been tried. It served only to strengthen the popular forces and to deepen the popular determination.

While all this was going on, we were marching ahead in blissful ignorance of the unholy activities of the police. Mr. Lalitmohan Ghosal, one of the delegates from Calcutta, came running up to us with outstretched hands, saying, 'What are you doing? You cannot proceed. Your brother-delegates behind are being beaten by the police.' I turned back at once, followed by Babu Motilal Ghose and one or two others. As I was coming along, I met

Mr. Kemp, Superintendent of Police. I said to him, 'Why are you thrashing our men? If they have done anything, I am the person to be punished. I am responsible. Arrest me if you like.' 'You are my prisoner, sir', was the prompt reply of the Police Superintendent. At this stage Mr. Motilal Ghose came forward and said, 'Arrest me also'. To that Mr. Kemp's reply was, 'My instructions are to arrest Mr. Banerjea alone'. Evidently my arrest had been pre-arranged; but that is another story.

This part of the episode closed with my arrest. I was now a prisoner in police custody. Turning to Mr. Bhupendra Nath Basu, who was close by, I said, 'You had better proceed with the business of the Conference without me. Let it not be stopped or suspended.' My instructions were scrupulously followed. The excitement and indignation were great; but the Conference went on to transact the business that was before it as if nothing had happened. This display of self-restraint in circumstances so trying was no small testimony to our possessing one of the essential qualities for self-government.

In the meantime I was taken by Mr. Kemp to the Magistrate's house. We hired a *ticka gharri* (hackney carriage). Mr. Behari Lal Roy, Mr. Aswini Kumar Dutt and Pundit Kali Prosanna Kabyavisarad accompanied me. There was no room in the carriage for five of us, as Mr. Kemp, who had me in his charge, had to form one of the party. Kabyavisarad stood behind the carriage, occupying the place of the syce.

We were ushered into the verandah of Mr. Emerson's house, and stood there for a minute or so to give the magistrate time to be ready. We were then asked to enter his room. As Kabyavisarad crossed the threshold, Mr. Emerson cried out, 'Get out' in a somewhat loud voice. There was reason for this exceptional treatment of Kabyavisarad. Kabyavisarad belonged to the priestly family of the Halders of Kalighat, the keepers of one of the holiest shrines in Bengal. Usually he appeared at the anti-Partition and *Swadeshi* meetings robed in the habiliments of Hindu orthodoxy. It was not a mere whim (though Kabyavisarad had many), there was a reason for it. That dress was the symbol of priestly and Brahminical influence, and he naturally wanted to enlist on his side all the sources of power that he possessed. He was without a shirt, in plain *dhoti* and *chaddar,* with the Brahminical thread in striking evidence on his bare body. All this was meant for the delegates of the Conference, and not for Mr. Emerson or his Court. The magistrate was offended at the scantiness of his attire; and with less than magisterial dignity ordered him out of the room. Kabyavisarad had to submit, but he remained close to the door, so that he could see and hear what was transpiring in the magistrate's room, which for the time being was converted into a chamber of justice.

I entered the room as a prisoner, charged with breaking the law – no unique experience for me, as I had been in the same position some years ago, in a higher court and amid more dignified surroundings. My other two friends accompanied me into the room without objection and took their seats on the chairs that they found there. I was about to follow their example and had laid my hand on a dilapidated rattan chair, intending to take my seat when the magistrate shouted out, 'You are a prisoner. You cannot take your seat. You must stand.' I said in reply, 'I have not come here to be insulted by you in your house. I expect to be treated with courtesy and consideration.'

Mr. Emerson was angry. He forthwith drew up contempt proceedings against me, and asked me to plead. Of course, I pleaded not guilty and I prayed for time for my defence. There was sitting with the magistrate, while all this was going on, a European gentleman who, I afterwards learnt, was Mr. Lees, then Magistrate of Noakhali. He asked me to apologize and end the matter. I said, 'What have I to apologize for? I have done nothing for which I feel I ought to express my regret.' I was fined two hundred rupees for contempt.

The police case was then taken up. Mr. Kemp gave his evidence. He was, I think, the only witness in the case. I was charged with being a member of a procession which had not taken out a licence, and with uttering a cry forbidden by competent authority. I pleaded not guilty and prayed for time to cross-examine Mr. Kemp and produce witnesses. The prayer was rejected. I was again fined two hundred rupees. I had no money with me. Mr. Kemp, who throughout treated me with great courtesy, accompanied me for the realization of the fine.

The fine being paid, I returned to the Conference, which was then sitting. As I entered, accompained by my friends, we witnessed a unique scene, the whole audience rising to a man, shouting *Bande-Mataram* at the top of their voices. For several minutes the proceedings were suspended, and were resumed on our taking our seats on the platform. But the Conference was in no mood to address itself to the business on the agenda. The events of the day were too recent in point of time, too absorbing in their character, to permit the consideration of any other matter.

Presently there appeared on the platform Babu Monoranjan Guha, accompanied by his son, Chittaranjan Guha, with a bandage round his forehead, to tell the delegates the story of the assault committed by the police upon this young man. The father, who as a speaker wielded the resources of our language with wonderful power, told the story in his own inimitable style keeping the audience spellbound for the time. Chittaranjan had been attacked by the police with their regulation *lathis*, and thrown into a tank full of water. The assault was continued, notwithstanding the helpless condition of the boy, who offered no resistance of any kind, but shouted *Bande-Mataram* with every stroke of the *lathi*. It was a supreme effort of resignation and submission to brutal force without resistance and without questioning. The spectacle of father and son, standing side by side on the platform, the father relating the story, the son bearing witness to it by the marks of violence on his person, was a sight ever to be remembered; and it was afterwards transferred to canvas and was one of the most popular pictures in the Calcutta Exhibition of 1906, which was opened by Lord Minto.

The Conference broke up in the evening; and as the delegates dispersed to their homes they shouted the forbidden cry of *Bande-Mataram* in the streets of Barisal. The police did not interfere. Presumably they thought they had done a sufficient day's work, and left the delegates alone.

But the story of this act of repression, one of the darkest in the annals of the defunct Government of East Bengal, was not yet closed. The Conference met on the following day, and was transacting its business in the usual way, when Mr. Kemp, District Superintendent of Police, entered the *pandal*. He walked up to the platform and told the President that the Conference must disperse, unless he was prepared to give a guarantee that the delegates would not shout *Bande-Mataram* in the streets after the Conference was over. The President, after consulting the delegates, declined to give the guarantee. Mr. Kemp then read out the order of the magistrate directing the dispersal of the Conference under Section 144 of the Criminal Procedure Code. A wave of indignation passed over the Conference. The delegates were in no mood to submit.

Mr. J. Chaudhuri and other leaders appealed to them to respect authority, however arbitrary the fiat might seem to them, and they responded to the appeal. Throughout these exciting times, the discipline of our people and their readiness to submit to the advice of their leaders was conspicuously in evidence and largely contributed to the success of the movement.

The delegates left their seats, moving out in files into the public street, shouting *Bande-Mataram*. At every stage they sought to vindicate the legality of that cry. All left, save and except one and one alone. That was Mr. Krishna Kumar Mittra, editor of the *Sanjibani,* to whom I have had occasion to refer more than once in these pages. Like the senators of old when Brennus was entering Rome with his barbarian horde, he remained in his seat and would not move. Determination was painted upon his features; his face was red with indignation. He was prepared to face the consequences of the disobedience of authority. We argued, prayed and protested; and it was with the utmost difficulty that we persuaded him at last to leave the *pandal.*

There were about three hundred ladies who had come as visitors to the Conference. To them one of two alternatives was open, either to wait in the deserted *pandal* for their carriages, which had been ordered to fetch them home in the afternoon, or to return home almost without protection in the burning sun of April. They chose the latter, at what sacrifice it may be readily imagined by those who are familiar with the habits and temper of mind of the Indian lady. We all dispersed, somewhat amazed at the extraordinary order, which was *ultra vires* and perfectly indefensible, as no breach of the peace by the delegates could be reasonably apprehended after their quiet submission to the unbridled lawlessness of the police on the previous day. The order was couched in the following terms:

'As it appears from police reports that the breaking up of a meeting of the Conference, which is being held at a *pandal* in the town opposite to B. M. College, is likely to be followed by unruly proceedings in the streets, and noisy processions, which have been forbidden by proper authority, I hereby order that the public or any person are not to meet in the *pandal* or elsewhere for the said purpose, and the public are not to form crowds in the streets. As it also appears likely that the crowds may meet in Raja Bahadur's *haveli* and form an unlawful procession, it is hereby ordered that this is also forbidden.'

From the *pandal* many of us proceeded to the house of Babu Rajani Kanto Das, one of the leading members of the Barisal Bar. Soon a large crowd gathered there. Pundit Kabyavisarad, Mr. Bepin Chunder Pal and myself addressed them, urging them to continue the agitation against the Partition and to stick to the *Swadeshi* vow.

24
After the Barisal Conference

The *Swadeshi* vow : an inspiration – my visit to the Chakravartis of Rahamatpore : the police are foiled – Liyakat Hossain – Mr. A. Rasool, President of the Barisal Conference – Indian public opinion stirred – anarchy in Bengal : the provocation – a sinister interview – an unpopular Lieutenant-Governor – rowdyism at the Surat Congress.

THE SWADESHI vow deserves a word of mention. It played an important part in the *Swadeshi* movement. The inspiration for the vow came from me. I was its author. The idea struck me while I was addressing a *Swadeshi* meeting in a village close to Magra on the East Indian Railway line. The meeting was held in the courtyard of a Hindu temple, with the image of the god right in front of me. The atmosphere of the place was religious. Swadeshism had evoked the fervour of a religious movement. It had become part of our *Dharma*. Priests refused to officiate at ceremonies where foreign goods found a place. Foreign articles of clothing and of food, foreign sugar and salt, were eschewed with almost religious scrupulousness. The sentiment of religion is with us so all-pervading as to colour and dominate our activities even beyond its legitimate sphere. The *Swadeshi* sentiment had thus come to assume a religious hue. As I spoke and had my eyes fixed upon the temple and the image, and my mind was full of the associations of the place, in a moment of sudden impulse I appealed to the audience to stand up and to take a solemn vow in the presence of the god of their worship. I administered the vow, and the whole audience, standing, repeated the words after me. The words were in Bengalee and the speech was in Bengalee; the vow may be translated as follows:

'Invoking God Almighty to be our Witness, and standing in the presence of after-generations, we take this solemn vow that, so far as practicable, we shall use home-made articles and abstain from the use of foreign articles. So help us God.'

I had never before thought of this vow. It was a sudden inspiration prompted by the surroundings of the place; and the effect, may be better imagined than described, when a vast audience of, say, ten or fifteen thousand people rose up with one impulse, and repeated in one voice the solemn words of the vow. For a time our critics said nothing; but soon the profound impression it created became apparent, and they thundered forth their anathemas. We noted them, but heeded them not, and pursued the even tenor of our ways.

A Literary Conference was to have been held at Barisal on the following day. Dr. Rabindranath Tagore had come down from Calcutta to attend it. It was, however, abandoned, and he left for Calcutta with Mr. Bhupendra Nath Basu. On the following day I was invited to Rahamatpore, a place a few miles from Barisal, to address a *Swadeshi* and anti-Partition meeting. Our hosts were the Chakravarti Zemindars of the place; an ancient family who had thoroughly identified themselves with the *Swadeshi* movement. We were treated to a sumptuous breakfast. Caste objections were forgotten even in this out-of-the-way village in the fervour of our *Swadeshi* feeling, and we sat down to breakfast together, although I was an England-returned Bengalee.

The meeting was held after breakfast. When we had finished the police came in. They came in *ticka gharries* filled with regulation *lathis;* but they were a trifle too late. They came after the fair was over. They had no arrests to make, no meeting to report. In the meantime sensational rumours had been spread at Barisal about the movements of the police, and it was reported that they had gone down to Rahamatpore to arrest us. My relative, Mr. Behari Lal Roy, was alarmed, and he hastened to Rahamatpore to ascertain the situation and help us, if necessary. We met him on our way back near Lakutia, his ancestral home. He was delighted to meet us unhurt and with whole skins. He shewed us over his ancestral seat and grounds, the *Samadhi*, the funeral monuments of his father and brother; and we returned to Barisal with him, rejoicing that we had been able to do the day's work and elude the vigilance of Mr. Emerson and his police.

Thus closed one of the most stirring chapters of my somewhat eventful life. An English lady, when speaking to me about it, said, 'The authorities prepared a trap for you at Barisal. You got out of it. They fell into your trap. The moral victory was yours.' And she was an impartial spectator, standing wholly detached from the passions of the hour, and could take a true perspective of the situation.

After resting for a day we left for Calcutta. The return journey was one never to be forgotten. At every station where the steamer or the train touched crowds of people had gathered to see me and to take the dust of my feet. For me there was no sleep or rest during the twenty-four hours of the journey, and, when I arrived at the terminus at Sealdah before daybreak, I found that a huge crowd had assembled to welcome us. The boys of the Anti-Circular Society, with their honoured President Babu Krishna Kumar Mittra, were in the same train.

We were all taken to College Square, where, in those early hours of the morning, before Calcutta had risen from its sleep, thousands had gathered to see us and to hear us. There are always moments in the lives of men that are worth living for. For me this was one of such moments. My voice was hoarse with the speeches I had had to make so often during the past twenty-four hours. But, overborne by the enthusiasm of the hour, I again spoke, exhorting the audience to stick to the *Swadeshi* vow and to carry on the agitation against the Partition with unflinching determination, in the certain confidence that it was bound to be undone or modified.

Among the speakers on that occasion was that devoted man, Liyakat Hossain. He said that he had fasted the whole day when he heard of my arrest. Liyakat Hossain is a singular personality. He had suffered imprisonment for sedition. He was shadowed by the police; his public activities were often restrained by official authority. One may or may not agree with him, but he is dauntless and unflinching, unbending in his honesty of purpose. I fear the officials look upon him as a dangerous fanatic. But for sincerity of purpose, single-minded devotion to the interests of his country, and fearless courage in serving them, he has few peers. He is not a Bengalee; he comes from Behar and does not speak our language; but Bengal is the land of his adoption and the Bengalees are the people of his love. I have not always been able to see eye to eye with him in regard to some of his views and methods, but he stood forth as a champion worker in the *Swadeshi* cause; and for him there has always been a soft corner in my heart.

Before I take leave of this part of my reminiscences I must say a word or two about Mr. A. Rasool, the President of the Barisal Conference. Alas! death has snatched him away in his prime, on the eve of his celebrating the most notable event of his domestic life, the marriage of his only daughter. He died suddenly of heart failure, in the midst of a promising career of great public usefulness, to the infinite regret of his friends and admirers and the heavy loss of his country. Mr. Rasool was a Bengalee Mohamedan and came from the district of Comilla in East Bengal. He was a graduate of

Oxford University and was a member of the Calcutta High Court Bar. He was one of the very few Mohamedans who opposed the Partition of Bengal, after it had become an accomplished and a settled fact. He was always an unflinching advocate of the union between Hindus and Mohamedans for political purposes, and he regarded the Partition as a national calamity, in the sense that it would alienate Hindus and Mohamedans, interfere with the solidarity of the Bengalee-speaking population, and weaken their political influence. At one time, on account of these views, great was his unpopularity among his co-religionists. He outlived it all and had the satisfaction of witnessing the triumph of the opinions that he professed and unflinchingly advocated; and he lived to become a recognized leader of the great community to which he belonged. Mr. Rasool was never very strong, and the anxieties and cares of the most eventful conference ever held in Bengal were a great strain upon him; but he bore them all, sustained by the patriotic fervour that distinguished his public career.

The proceedings of the authorities in connexion with the Barisal Conference created a sense of indignation among the educated community not only in Bengal but also outside our province. In Madras a crowded and influential public meeting was held. Over ten thousand people assembled in the open air on the Esplanade. 'Long before the hour fixed for the meeting', says the report, 'people began to come in streams, shouting *Bande-Mataram*.' Bad rulers serve a useful purpose in the evolution of nations. They stir up the sleeping lion from his torpor; they stimulate public spirit and foster national unity. The recognized leaders of the people took part in the proceedings, and, on the motion of the Hon. Nawab Syed Mohamed Bahadur, seconded by Dr. Nair, the meeting recorded a resolution protesting against the high-handed proceedings of the Barisal authorities as 'a flagrant infringement of the liberties of British subjects, and a subversion of the principles of constitutional government'. A cablegram was sent to the Secretary of State for India by the meeting, calling his immediate attention 'to the arrest of a great popular leader and the dispersal by the police force of an annual conference of several thousand members, and praying for sympathetic orders for allaying excitement and the restoration of public faith in British freedom and the rights of citizenship, and the punishment of the officers responsible'.

But the centre of the storm was in Calcutta, where it raged with cyclonic force. College Square had its meetings almost daily. The mofussil were not slow in following the lead of Calcutta. Indeed, the reports of the proceedings of the Barisal police flew like wildfire and deeply stirred popular feeling. Men indifferent to public movements took the *Swadeshi* vow and practised it in their daily lives. Recluses buried amid their books emerged from their seclusion and eagerly joined the *Swadeshi* and anti-Partition demonstrations. A monster meeting, second only to that of the 16th October, was held at the house of Rai Pashupatinath Bose. It was an open-air demonstration and the spacious courtyard was filled to suffocation. Rai Narendranath Sen, the most moderate among the political leaders of Bengal, was called to the chair. He described the Barisal incident as 'hardly having any parallel in the history of British India. The Press and the platform' he said, 'are the safety-valves of popular discontent,' and he added that 'whenever they have been sought to be suppressed, anarchy has intervened.' The words were prophetic, as subsequent events have shown.

The anarchical or the revolutionary movement – the terms are somewhat loosely used as synonymous – soon after made its first appearance in Bengal. It was the culminating expression of the widespread discontent caused by the Partition of Bengal and deepened by the policy associated with it, of which the unprovoked assault on the delegates by the police and the dispersal of the Conference were the most notable illustrations. The Partition of Bengal was not only an administrative measure, but it was the symbol of a new policy unknown to the traditions of British rule. It was followed by repression. *Swadeshi* workers or preachers were often prosecuted or persecuted; public meetings in public places were prohibited; military police were stationed in quiet centres of population, and they committed assaults upon peaceful citizens. Many of the residents of Banaripara, in the district of Barisal, where Gurkha soldiers were stationed, seriously thought of migrating from the place. Respectable people were falsely charged with sedition for issuing *Swadeshi* circulars, and Babu Aswini Kumar Dutt, the recognized leader of the Barisal district, was one of them.

The climax was reached when the police assaulted the delegates and dispersed the Conference at Barisal. The anarchical movement followed immediately. The public feeling was one of wild excitement. The young in all countries are the most impressionable. In Bengal, recent events had shaken their faith in constitutional methods and had driven them to the verge of despair. An incident within my own experience enables me to fix the time of the genesis of what may be called the Revolutionary Movement. I have no hesitation in saying that the Partition of Bengal and the policy that followed it were the root causes of the movement in our province, though no doubt they were strengthened by economic conditions. It was the dispersal of the Barisal Conference with all its attendant circumstances of lawlessness and violence that brought it to a head. I am confirmed in this view by the facts to which I shall presently refer.

One evening a few months after the Barisal affair, two young men called at my residence at Barrackpore and wanted to have a private interview with me. As I entered the room and took my seat, they said that it was an exceedingly delicate and difficult matter, and they wanted the doors to be closed. Three of us were now closeted in the room, and one of the young men who, it appeared, was a medical student, began the conversation. He said, 'We have come to ask your advice upon a matter of the utmost importance. We have formed a plan to shoot Sir Bampfylde Fuller; and we are going to — to-night for this purpose. What do you say about it?' Not being prepared for it, and the proposal being so unusual, I was a little staggered. I said, 'Why do you want to shoot Sir Bampfylde Fuller? What has he done?' The young man replied with evident emotion, 'His Gurkhas stationed at Banaripara have been outraging some of our women, and we want to take revenge upon him.' I said, 'You are bound to be caught and hanged.' They said, 'We will take our chance and if need be suffer for the honour of our women.'

No position, one might well imagine, could be more difficult than mine. Here were two young men, determined to avenge the honour of their women in the belief that the law would give them no remedy, and they had to be dissuaded from their purpose. At that time, fortunately for me, there was a strong rumour, which I believed to be well-founded, that Sir Bampfylde Fuller had resigned. I said to them, 'Do you know that Sir Bampfylde Fuller has resigned? What is the good of shooting a dead man? On the other hand, your attempt would be attended with imminent risk to the public interest. We all want to get rid of him as Lieutenant-Governor. If your attempt fails – and you cannot be sure that it will succeed – his resignation is bound to be withdrawn, and he will continue in office. Do you want to do this disservice to your country?'.

That was a settler. The young men at once agreed to drop the idea and abandon the proposal. I clinched the matter by saying that they must swear to do so by laying their hands on my Brahminical feet. They readily responded to my appeal, and I heaved a sigh of relief. There was yet a difficulty. They said they must go to the place at once by the night train and stop the arrangements. But they had no money with them. I readily advanced the money they wanted. I did not know who they were; up till now I do not know who they are, for I never asked their names. But I felt I could trust them, and, sure enough, the money was refunded to me through the post office.

The incident indicated the ideas that were in the air, the deeper undercurrents that were moving, it might be unconsciously, some of the young men of Bengal. With anarchism no one can have any sympathy. Murder is murder, no matter by what name the deed is sought to be palliated, or by what motives excused. But let not the historian of the future lose sight of the atmosphere of mistrust, of hopelessness and helplessness, created by the acts of an administration which no British historian can refer to without a blush on his countenance.

Soon after the incidents which I have described at some length came the attempt to blow up Sir Andrew Fraser's train at Nursinggarh near Midnapore. Sir Andrew Fraser was Lieutenant-Governor and was one of the authors of the Partition of Bengal, and that alone made him one of the most unpopular among our rulers within living memory. He had never before held any office in Bengal. His administrative experience was confined to the Central Provinces. He was President of the Police Commission before he became Lieutenant-Governor and his recommendations excited severe criticism. He came to Bengal with no prepossessions in his favour. His administration of the province created a violent prejudice against him. The popular impression was that he came with a mandate to partition Bengal, and he naturally suffered as the chosen instrument for carrying out one of the most unpopular measures under British rule.

About the same time, almost on the same day, that this attempt was made, the District Conference that met at Midnapore was sought to be wrecked, and by some of those men upon whom there was a strong suspicion of being associated with the anarchical movement. Mr. K. B. Dutt, the President of the Conference and the recognized leader of the Midnapore District at the time, was repeatedly interrupted in the course of his speech. I was invited as a guest and was surprised to witness a spectacle so unusual. Through the joint efforts of Mr. Dutt and of myself, aided by the good sense of the audience, we succeeded at last in restoring order and resuming the business of the Conference. But what happened was to me a revelation, and it was the augury, the precursor of a similar scene enacted on a larger scale in the Surat Congress held a month later. The forces of disorder had been let loose, and by the authorities themselves, in a great and newly constituted province. The popular faith in constitutional methods was shaken; and young and ardent spirits, writhing under disappointment, but eager to serve their country, were led into the dangerous paths of lawlessness and violence, unrestrained by the voice of their elders.

It was in an atmosphere almost electric in its character that the Indian National Congress met at Surat in December, 1907. The venue of the Congress had to be changed from Nagpore to Surat, owing to demonstrations of rowdyism, which in the opinion of the Bombay leaders of the Congress rendered it undesirable to hold the Congress at Nagpore. But the disease was there, deep-rooted, having drawn its virus from the unhappy proceedings of the authorities in East Bengal. As I rose to speak there were signs of opposition from the body of the hall. As a past President of the Congress, it was my duty to propose Sir Rash Behari Ghose as President. I had often before performed this duty with the general concurrence and approval of the Congress. It was not to be so this time. The events of the Midnapore Conference, in which I had a hand as the pacifier, were remembered, and repeated attempts were made to prevent me from proceeding with my speech. This was with me an unusual experience; for my appearance on a Congress platform as a speaker was usually the signal for hushed silence after the first signs of applause had subsided.

There was a strong party in favour of the election of Mr. Tilak as President, and they would not have Sir Rash Behari Ghose to preside over the Congress. Rather that the Congress should be broken up than that Sir Rash Behari should preside. That was the feeling of this party, and the Congress was broken up. Chairs and shoes and slippers were flung at the leaders, the platform was rushed – I remained on the platform, with some of my friends forming a guard around me. I was led along with Sir Pherozeshah Mehta and others to the tent behind, and the police cleared the *pandal*. Thus closed a memorable chapter in the history of the Congress, to be followed by a new departure.

The Bengal delegates felt shocked and humiliated at the insulting treatment meted out to me. In less than an hour they held a meeting and recorded a vote of confidence in me. Nor were the all-India delegates idle. A meeting was held, and after a prolonged deliberation a constitution was drawn up, and its first article came to be subsequently known as the Creed of the Congress. It laid down that self-government within the Empire was the goal of the Congress; and that it was to be attained by purely constitutional means. It was obligatory upon every one to sign this creed before he could become a member of the Congress. For a long time those who had seceded from the Congress declined to sign it; but later on better counsels prevailed, and all wings of the Indian Nationalist party were reunited at the Lucknow Congress in 1916, when also an *entente* between Hindus and Mohamedans was established, and a scheme of constitutional reform was formulated and accepted at a joint Conference of Hindu and Mohamedan leaders, over which I presided.

25

Passive Resistance

The Congress united – entry of Mrs. Besant: her internment – the Home Rule league – passive resistance discussed at Bombay Congress: conditions not favourable for success – a Calcutta meeting forbidden for astonishing reasons – interview with Lord Ronaldshay: the true reasons – the prohibition withdrawn – my speech at the Town Hall.

ALL WINGS OF THE NATIONALIST PARTY were now united; and educated Islam joined hands with them on the Congress platform. Never did the prospects of effective and united work seem more hopeful. But the ancient divisions and methods of action which have their roots in temperament and human nature, and even in personal ambitions, were not to be effaced in a day; and they were soon apparent in the work of the Congress. Mrs. Besant, who had hitherto identified herself with the work of the Theosophical Society and the Hindu Educational movement, joined the Congress held in Madras in 1914. Her eloquence, her forceful personality, her indefatigable industry, and her power of organization, soon made themselves felt. She had a considerable hand in bringing about the union of the different wings of the Nationalist party. She travelled from one part of India to the other, held personal interviews with the different Indian leaders and was in close correspondence with some of them.

When the Congress met in Bombay in 1915, she called a meeting to consider the question of the formation of a Home Rule League. It was to be an organization to carry on propaganda work in connexion with the question of Home Rule or Self-Government. I presided at the meetings of this conference. The general feeling at the time was that such an organization would serve to overlap and perhaps weaken the Congress. The Home Rule League was not then formed. The idea, however, was not given up by Mrs. Besant, and the League was subsequently organized.

I have no desire to re-awaken the memories of events which are now well-nigh forgotten, but I must say that the League served to create the first division in the Congress camp after the reunion. I did not join it, nor did many of the ex-Presidents of the Congress. I incurred some unpopularity. But unpopularity is an inconstant factor in public life, and I was not afraid to run the risk of facing it, in comradeship with colleagues, now, alas, dead, and in what I conceived to be the best interests of the country. I had helped to build up the Congress. It was a part of my life work, my pride and my privilege, and it was not in me to do aught which, in my opinion, would weaken its influence or the position which it occupied in the estimation of the country.

Never was the pressure brought on me to join the Home Rule League greater or more persistant than after Mrs. Besant's internment. I was then a candidate for a seat in the Imperial Legislative Council. A voter, who was a friend, wrote to me that unless I joined the Home Rule League he would not vote for me. I took no notice of the offer or the threat. The Secretary of the Home Rule League wrote to me to say that if I joined the League I should be unanimously elected President of the Calcutta Branch and my election to the Imperial Council would be unopposed. In my public life, I never allowed myself to be daunted by the frowns or seduced by the smiles of power. And even when the dispensation of favour lay in the hands of friends or colleagues I acted on the same principle, and was not to be deterred from my purpose or from fulfilling the behests of my conviction, by threats or by inducements.

Great as is my reverence for Mrs. Besant and my admiration for her public work, my objection to joining the Home Rule League was not in any way minimized by her internment. But I readily and whole-heartedly associated myself with the public protests against this unfortunate measure. I presided at two protest meetings, one held at the Indian Association rooms and the other at the Town Hall of Calcutta, and as strongly condemned her internment as any Home Rule Leaguer. The internment of Mrs. Besant was the origin of the movement for her election as President of the Congress of 1917. The first visible sign of disunion among the members of the Nationalist party after the Lucknow Congress was, as I have observed, the formation of the Home Rule League and the second was the movement for the election of Mrs. Besant as President of the Congress. The internment of a gifted lady who was serving the motherland with unexampled devotion set the whole country ablaze with excitement. The general feeling was that by her internment the Government sought to aim a deadly blow at the agitation for self-government, which she had so vigorously championed; and the utterances of provincial rulers, which had a wonderful family likeness in their tone of disparagement, if not of ridicule, of our aspirations for self-government, deepened the public impression and intensified the public agitation.

It is no exaggeration to say that it was the Government that set in motion the impulse that placed Mrs. Besant in the presidential chair of the Congress. That has often been the way of bureaucracies, which, living in an atmosphere of their own and out of touch with the popular forces, have failed to gauge their strength and volume and have eventually been overwhelmed by them. Could the bureaucracy have anticipated the agitation that Mrs. Besant's internment gave rise to, it would probably have left her alone. The Madras Government had indeed an Indian member on the Executive Council. But he had been through life a bureaucrat, and his appointment as a member of the Government failed to satisfy the one condition that Lord Morley had in view in his scheme of reform, namely, to place the highest Councils of the Government in touch with popular opinion. However that may be, the mistake was committed. It was indeed a blunder; it was persisted in for a time; but, with the appointment of Mr. Montagu as Secretary of State for India, a new atmosphere was created in the India Office, and Mrs. Besant was released, attesting once again the growing power of public opinion in India. This was further illustrated in a curious fashion in Bengal by a side issue of some moment.

Mrs. Besant's internment brought to the forefront the question of passive resistance. With whom it originated it is difficult to say. Possibly the idea was Mr. Gandhi's; at any rate Pundit Madan Mohan Malavya came down to Calcutta and discussed it at an informal meeting of friends. I was not present, as I was at Ranchi for a change and rest. I understood that the sense of my Bengal friends was opposed to passive resistance as a political weapon to be now employed. At a meeting of the All-India Congress Committee held soon after in Bombay, the question was discussed. As senior ex-President, I presided. There was a fairly strong party in favour of passive resistance. Our Bengal friends, however – the majority of them, at any rate – were all opposed to it. It was a difficult situation to deal with and at a private meeting we arranged our plans. When confronted with a trying situation I have always found it useful to have recourse to Fabian tactics. I suggested the postponement of the question, referring the matter to the Provincial Congress Committees. Time would thus be gained; the prevailing excitement would pass away; and reason and common sense would assert themselves. This proved to be a wise course to have followed.

Mr. (now Sir) Provash Chunder Mitter was entrusted with the

Resolution that we drafted. The feeling was high on the day when the question first came up for discussion. I allowed full scope to the debate, which had to be postponed on account of the lateness of the hour; and, as I anticipated, the temperature was much cooler on the following morning when we met and the discussion was resumed. Speaker after speaker followed, until Mr. Tilak suggested that a committee should be appointed to consider the question. That was Sir Provash Chunder Mitter's opportunity, and he moved that the matter, in view of its importance, be referred to the Provincial Congress Committee for report. A time-limit was fixed for the report: it was to be the first week of October. The motion was carried with practical unanimity; and, as the event showed, a difficult situation was saved. Everything pointed to an early pronouncement by the Government on the question of self-government; and if the pronouncement was made before the meeting of the All-India Congress Committee in October, the excitement and irritation which lay at the root of the idea of passive resistance would be allayed.

We in Bengal, who had passed through the ordeal of fire in connexion with the anti-Partition and the *Swadeshi* agitation, knew the difficulties that surrounded a movement of defiance of authority culminating in the violation of official orders, legal or illegal. The incidents of the Barisal Conference (where we followed a policy of passive resistance), the nameless insults offered to respectable people at Sirajgung, Banaripara and elsewhere, the persecution of *Swadeshi* workers under the guise of the maintenance of law and order, were all still fresh in our minds; and we felt that passive resistance could not succeed unless there was an overwhelming body of public feeling behind it and there were many who would be willing to suffer for the cause which had provoked it. We were not sure that these conditions existed in the present case; and we were glad of a postponement, which allowed time for thought and reconsideration, and, as we hoped, for the development of a situation that would make passive resistance unnecessary and undesirable.

In the meantime in Bengal the question had assumed an acute form owing to circumstances which I shall presently relate. I have already referred to the meeting held at the Indian Association rooms to protest against Mrs. Besant's internment. It was held in a hurry and was in the nature of a preliminary conference, delegates from the mofussil not having been invited. It was therefore resolved to hold a Town Hall meeting at a subsequent date, to be convened by the Sheriff, in which representatives from the mofussil were to be asked to take part. A requisition was duly signed and presented to the Sheriff. The date of the meeting was fixed and Sir Rash Behari Ghose was to preside.

All of a sudden the public learnt that the meeting had been forbidden by the Government. The principal requisitionists were invited by the Hon. Mr. Cumming to meet him, and the orders of Government were communicated to them. One of the astonishing reasons for the prohibition of the meeting was that the orders of the Government of one province could not be allowed to be criticized by the people of another province. This new doctrine of inter-provincial amenity had never been heard of before. Everybody laughed at it; everybody knew that that was not the real explanation, which was withheld under a plea, the hollowness of which was transparent. The explanation was the subject of ridicule in the newspapers. It certainly did not improve the position of the Government, but added to the public discontent. We were at the time in Bombay attending a meeting of the All-India Congress Committee. I sent a wire urging the summoning of a conference on our return, and we hurried back as fast as we could.

The Conference was held on the day after my return to Calcutta; and it was largely attended. There was, alas, one prominent personality who was absent and who was never again to appear in our public meetings. Two days before, Mr. Rasool had died suddenly of heart failure, while he was in the thick of the preparations for the wedding of his only daughter. Many of us were thus assembled at the Conference under the shadow of a personal bereavement. I was in the chair. The excitement was great, and it grew as the discussion proceeded. Everybody who spoke vowed that he was prepared to resist the order of Government and go to jail if necessary. Obviously, if the forbidden meeting were held, a collision between the promoters and the police would be inevitable.

At last, after a good deal of animated discussion, it was resolved that six of us should retire and formulate a method of action, which was to be accepted by the Conference without demur. The gentlemen thus honoured were the elders of the Conference. They were Sir Rash Behari Ghose, Babu Motilal Ghose, Mr. Byomekesh Chakravarti, Mr. C. R. Das, Mr. Fazlul Huq and myself. We withdrew to an ante-room for about an hour, and unanimously agreed that we should wait in deputation upon Lord Ronaldshay at Dacca, where His Excellency the Governor then was, explain the situation to him, and appeal to him to cancel the order of prohibition. We felt that we should give the Government an opportunity of withdrawing from an untenable position, and that, if we failed, then and then only should we have recourse to passive resistance and hold the Town Hall meeting in defiance of the Government order.

We returned to the Conference Hall with this decision, and Mr. Byomekesh Chakravarti was charged to explain it. He did so with the tact and skill of an old and practised lawyer. But, as always happens when an audience is excited, counsels of moderation failed to impress them. We were subjected to a good deal of heckling. Our decision evidently did not commend itself to the majority of the Conference, who were all for holding the meeting and for the conflict with the police that must follow. How many would have stood the test, if the collision had actually taken place, is more than I can say. I have some recollection of those who, with bold language on their lips and defiance in their mien, ran away as fast as their legs could carry them when the police dispersed the procession in connexion with the Barisal Conference. The times have changed; nevertheless the frenzy for incarceration and the mad fury for cheap notoriety is confined to a limited class.

The Conference broke up without a decision; but it was understood that we were to go as a deputation, though without the formal authorization of the Conference. I at once placed myself in communication with Mr. Gourlay, the Governor's Private Secretary, and a day was appointed for the Deputation. We were to be received on the day immediately following a meeting of the Legislative Council to be held at Dacca. Many of the Indian members of the Legislative Council wanted to join the Deputation; but the number was limited to six, and I think it was a wise decision, regard being had to the confidential talk we had with the Governor, which perhaps a larger deputation would have prevented. In the meantime, the air was full of wild proposals of protests against the prohibition of the Town Hall meeting. One of them was that the Indian members should all abstain from attending the meeting of the Legislative Council. This idea was seriously discussed on board the steamer that carried most of the members to Dacca. Nothing could have been more unwise on the eve of a settlement and when a deputation was about to be received on the subject. I mention it only to show how extreme views are apt to find currency and even predominance when the public mind is thrown into a state of excitement by the unwisdom of the Government.

Our deputation was received by Lord Ronaldshay, at Government House at Dacca, with courtesy and cordiality. The deputation consisted of Mr. Byomekesh Chakravarti, Mr. C. R. Das, Mr. Fazlul Huq, Dr. Nilratan Sircar, Babu Surendranath Roy, and myself. The first question asked by Lord Ronaldshay was who was to be our spokesman. Mr. Chakravarti mentioned my name. The political atmosphere in Bengal had not yet become charged with the feelings which the subsequent controversy about Mrs. Besant's election to the presidency of the Congress evoked.

Lord Ronaldshay came fully prepared with all the official papers bearing on the matter. His Excellency opened the discussion, and it soon became apparent that all talk about inter-provincial amenities, about the undesirability of the people of one province criticizing the actions of the ruler of another, was moonshine. The real grounds for the prohibition were disclosed with perfect candour. They were not indeed convincing, but they were plausible enough. What prompted the order for prohibition was that at a meeting of the Home Rule League (at which, the Governor added, addressing me, 'You were not present') language was used to which the Government took strong exception; and it was apprehended that at the Town Hall meeting, the speakers being substantially the same, similar language would be employed and addressed to a much larger audience of young men; and this would do great harm. 'I have not prohibited' added Lord Ronaldshay significantly, 'the attendance of students at public meetings as has been done in other provinces.'

Lord Ronaldshay began reading out extracts from the reports of C.I.D. officers who were present at the meeting of the Home Rule league referred to above. Whether the proceedings were correctly reported or not, it is impossible to say; but, if the notes were substantially correct, the language used was highly improper. One speaker, who was often in requisition at public meetings held by the authorities themselves, was reported to have advised the young men present to adopt the tactics of the Anusilan Samiti, which had been suppressed, advocating the employment of force. This speaker, said the report, added that the English were a handful in this country, while they, the children of the soil, could be counted by lakhs; and yet this handful of foreigners were our masters. Another speaker addressing the Home Rule meeting said that he must speak in English, as he did not trust the translated reports of the C.I.D. officers. This observation seemed to me to be perfectly innocuous, and I said so, especially as the same speaker on a former occasion had to complain of an inaccurate report of his speech by the C.I.D. To this His Excellency said in reply that it meant a reflection upon the C.I.D., about which the Government felt a natural concern, as the officers of the C.I.D. had too often been singled out for the vengeance of the revolutionary party.

I said in the course of the conversation that the fact that Sir Rash Behari Ghose was to have presided was a guarantee that the proceedings of the meeting would be conducted upon moderate and reasonable lines. Lord Ronaldshay observed that they were not aware of this fact. I said that it could have been easily ascertained. His Excellency was throughout frank and reasonable; and he said that, if we gave a guarantee that no inflammatory language would be used and that the meeting would be properly conducted, he would withdraw the order of prohibition. We replied that we could give no undertaking, but that we would do our best to carry out His Excellency's wishes, and we added that there was always an implied understanding on the part of the organizers of public meetings that they should be conducted upon proper and reasonable lines. The upshot of it all was that the prohibition was to be withdrawn, subject to the assurance we gave.

We returned home gratified with our success. But I, for one, was not altogether free from doubt as to the sort of welcome that would be accorded to us. In Bengal, even the most indubitable achievement is not always a passport to unqualified public approval. When the Partition of Bengal was modified, and when all thought that the voice of dissent would be drowned in a chorus of public appreciation, there were those who regretted that Behar should have been separated from Bengal, and there were many more to whom the transfer of the capital came as a shock. I was therefore fully prepared for comment and criticism, especially in view of what had transpired at the conference, which broke up without a decision.

Our representative character was challenged, and one of those who had taken a leading part in our deliberations and had allowed himself to be nominated as a member of the Deputation, was loud in his protestations of our want of representative authority. But in this world nothing succeeds like success. The withdrawal of the prohibition was a point gained, the value of which could not be questioned. The public are not, or are only temporarily, concerned with side issues of a personal character, which may for the time being tickle their nerves, or satisfy their innate love of scandal. But the fit soon passes away and reason and common sense assert themselves as the normal attitude of the public mind. It was suggested that we should hold another conference and tell them what had passed. I set my face against it, for I anticipated a repetition of the heckling, the quarrelling and wrangling of the last Conference. I proposed a Town Hall meeting; for I felt that such a meeting would, by its size, its publicity and its representative character, minimize the play of personal passions and even of partisan prejudice. I was right in this view.

A public meeting at the Town Hall was held; it was the old prohibited meeting, with the glamour of success achieved over the obstructiveness of official authority. It was a vindication of our indefensible right to hold meetings so long as there was the fair promise of the observance of a constitutional procedure. In the absence of Sir Rash Behari Ghose, I was asked to preside, and I accepted the invitation. Mine was the only speech; none other was made. That was the universal sense of the meeting and it was cheerfully acquiesced in. I took advantage of this opportunity to explain the character of the Deputation that I had the honour to lead. I believe that what I said at the Town Hall meeting in this connexion met with general approval; and I cannot resist the temptation of quoting it here:

'My friend Babu Motilal Ghose and myself were at Bombay when the news of this prohibition reached us. We hurried back to Calcutta. A conference was held and a deputation waited upon His Excellency Lord Ronaldshay at Dacca. We as a deputation did not derive our authority from any association or public body, but from our representative character as individuals who on many critical occasions have borne the heat and brunt of battle in the service of the motherland. Our charter lay in the memory of our public services, in the purity of our motives, above all in the conviction that we enjoyed the confidence of our countrymen. At the interview with His Excellency we gave no undertaking of any kind; none was asked. We said that we should do our best to see to it that the meeting was conducted upon responsible lines. Call it an assurance if you like, but it was an assurance which is implied in all our public meetings; it is what is required by the law. There was no equivocation of any kind on our part, no compromise of any principle, no surrender of any right. We acted according to our lights, with dignity and firmness, and with due regard to the constituted authorities of the land. His

Excellency Lord Ronaldshay reciprocated our attitude. He received us with kindness and even cordiality, and treated us in a spirit of conciliatory statesmanship. The order of prohibition was withdrawn. The principle that the people of one province were not to discuss the proceedings of the authorities of another province was abandoned. This is the sum total of our work at Dacca. We are not ashamed of it; we stand by it.'

Thus was averted what threatened to be a crisis in the history of our public movements. Collisions with the Government I am, and have never been, afraid of, provided that the cause is just, that it has behind it a strong body of public opinion, and that it may not lead to a measure of repression beyond our strength to endure and which may retard our growing public spirit. The repressive measures following the anarchical movement in Bengal had a blighting effect upon the growth of our public life, because the hand of repression was too heavy for us to bear. The all-pervading influence of the police, to which our public men were subjected, the long terms of imprisonment inflicted on some of our young men, and the suppression of the *Samitis,* all had a disastrous effect upon the growth of our nascent public life. But perhaps I have travelled a little beyond the period with which I was dealing when I was led into this somewhat lengthy digression.

26
The Revolutionary Movement in Bengal

The Mozufferpore murders – deportations under Regulation III: Mr. Morley's attitude – how orders from Home have been exceeded – the Morley-Minto Reforms – the new Councils – my disqualification removed, but I decline to stand before the Partition is modified.

IN THE EVENTS OF THE MIDNAPORE CONFERENCE and of the Surat Congress following one another in close succession, in the adoption of lawlessness and violence, so conspicuous in the break-up of the Surat Congress, as a method of political warfare, impartial observers could read the beginnings of a new development fraught with peril to the orderly and peaceful evolution of our national life. Here was a portent, the full significance of which soon manifested itself. On the morning of April 1, 1908, all Calcutta was startled to learn that on the previous evening a bomb outrage had been committed at Mozufferpore in Behar, and that the unhappy victims of it were two European ladies, mother and daughter, the wife and sixteen-year old child, of Mr. Pringle Kennedy, a leading pleader of the Mozufferpore Bar.

By a bitter irony of fate Mr. Pringle Kennedy was one of the few Europeans who had identified themselves with the Congress movement, and had on one occasion presided over a session of the Bengal Provincial Conference. The bomb was meant for Mr. Kingsford, District Judge of Mozufferpore, who, as Presidency Magistrate of Calcutta, had made himself unpopular by passing heavy sentences on young Bengalee *Swadeshi* workers. Especially odious had he become by inflicting corporal punishment upon more than one respectable young man. The sentences were believed to be unjust; and it was adding insult to injury to degrade their victims by the infliction of corporal punishment. The insult sank deep into the hearts of some of the young *Swadeshi* workers; and they vowed revenge. Two young men, Khudiram Bose and Profulla Chakie were charged with the execution of the mandate of the conspirators. Both lost their lives. One was hanged; and the other shot himself when about to be captured. It was a tragedy in the fullest sense – grim, futile and purposeless. It was immediately followed by the discovery of the Moraripuker Conspiracy, the trial of the conspirators and the heavy punishments inflicted upon the leaders.

Bureaucracy was alarmed, startled at the result of its own blunders. It sought to restore the situation and to ensure the ends of peace, and of law and order, by repressive measures which followed one another in rapid succession, chilling the public life of the country, and stunting its growth and development. The liberty of the Press and of public meetings was curtailed; and an old rusty weapon which had long lain unused in the armoury of the Government was taken down to deal with public workers who had been prominently connected with Swadeshism. Regulation III of 1818 was requisitioned to deport men, some of whom were the leading spirits of the *Swadeshi* movement, honoured and respected by their countrymen. One morning in December, 1908, people learnt with astonishment that Aswini Kumar Dutt, the leader of the Barisal District, the founder of the Brojomohan College, Krishna Kumar Mittra, one of the foremost members of the Brahmo Samaj, a man held in universal respect by all who knew him, Satis Chunder Chatterjee, Sachindra Prosad Bose, prominent *Swadeshi* workers, and the wealthy and patriotic Subodh Mullick, had all been deported under Regulation III of 1818.

As regards myself, it was said that the order for deportation was ready, but that it was cancelled at the last moment through the intervention of Sir Edward Baker, who had now become Lieutenant-Governor and who knew me well. Whatever the truth might be, one evening in the first week of December, 1908, as I was about to sit down to dinner, my friend, Moulvi Abul Hossain, one of the most eloquent of our *Swadeshi* preachers, came rushing to my house at Barrackpore with the report that the C.I.D. officers were coming to arrest me and that I had better get ready. I said, 'All right, let me have my dinner, and you too have yours.' He readily agreed. We had our dinner; and we waited for a couple of hours for the police, but the police never came. So I went to bed, and my friend returned to Calcutta with his mind somewhat at ease.

As a matter of fact, I was not deported, while some of my most prominent friends and associates were. Was it ever in contemplation to deport me? I know not. The archives of the Secretariat may some day yield up the secret. While I was a member of the Government, I could have perhaps obtained this information – but I refrained. However that may be, the report of my friend Abul Hossain derived some confirmation from the fact that on the day of his visit, when he said I was to be deported, a considerable body of police and European troops had come up to Barrackpore, though it was explained that this was because the Viceroy, Lord Minto, had come to attend the races. But the Viceroy had often been known to attend races at Barrackpore without such a strong muster of troops or of police.

It is very evident from Lord Morley's *Recollections* that, radical statesman that he was, his whole soul revolted against the policy of deportation without trial, and that he yielded reluctantly to the pressure of circumstances, and to the weight of superior knowledge which the men on the spot claimed and which he could not dispute. He was so much annoyed with some of the members of the Viceroy's Executive Council that he wrote to Lord Minto: 'And, by the way, now that we have got down the rusty sword of 1818, I wish you would deport — and — (two officials); what do you say? I should defend that operation with verve.' This was said half in earnest and half in jest, but it was sufficiently expressive of Lord Morley's sense of irritation and dislike at the deportations. Who these two officials were, the public will probably never know. But officials of this class will never be wanting so long as officialism is not controlled by the popular will. That, in all countries and in all ages, has been found to be the true panacea for official vagaries.

Human nature and human conditions are not materially different in India. The fur-coat argument is the weapon of the reactionary, though it was not a reactionary who coined the phrase, and it must be allowed that, subject to the strictest scrutiny and the limitations that such scrutiny must impose, Lord Morley's sense of fairness led him to suggest safeguards which, I fear, were not always acted upon. Writing to Lord Minto on December 4, 1908, he said: 'One thing I do beseech you to avoid – a single case of investigation in the absence of the accused. We may argue as much as we like about it, and there may be no substantial injustice in it, but it has an ugly, Continental, Austrian, Russian, look about it.'

Quoting this passage from Lord Morley's *Recollections* in moving my Resolution on the appointment of an Advisory Committee in the Imperial Legislative Council on March 19, 1918, I asked the hon. member-in-charge of the Home Department of the Government of India 'if this part of the instructions of Lord Morley were being given effect to in connexion with the investigations relating to prisoners under Regulation III of 1818'. No reply was given; the obvious inference must therefore be that this very necessary safeguard was not followed. There was another equally important limitation prescribed by Lord Morley. On August 23, 1908, he said:

> 'He (an Anglo-Indian official) must have forgotten what I very expressly told him, that I would not sanction deportation except for a man of whom there was solid reason to believe that violent disorder was the direct and deliberately planned result of his actions.'

It is obvious that here again Lord Morley's instructions were not followed by the authorities out here. Had they been obeyed in spirit and essence, men like Krishna Kumar Mittra, Aswini Kumar Dutt, Satis Chunder Chatterjee, and Sachindra Prosad Bose and some others would not have been deported; for they were all strongly wedded to constitutional methods and never dreamt of doing anything which directly or indirectly was calculated to produce 'violent disorder'. Under the gravest provocation, when attacked by the police, they never thought of retaliation, and submitted to police violence without striking a blow. Here we have again a repetition of the old order of things so often observable in the remissness or the total disregard shown by the servants of the East India Company in carrying out the orders of the Court of Directors. Again and again they were told by the Court of Directors not to add to their ever-expanding dominions; but as often the temptation proved too strong and they violated the express orders of their masters; and their offences were condoned, for they helped to bring larger dividends to the shareholders and larger additions to their territories, and with them to the power and the prestige of the Company.

There are no such temptations now; possibly there are no glaring violations of orders proceeding from the India Office; but the old spirit of officialism impatient to have its own way is, I am afraid, still there. The control of a Secretary of State from a distance of ten thousand miles, despite the present facilities of communication, must be feeble. And the time has come or is in sight when the power and responsibility of the Secretary of State should be transferred to the Government of India, subject to popular control, with the necessary safeguards for Imperial unity.

By instinct and by conviction Lord Morley was opposed to a policy of repression, but was driven to it by the overmastering pressure of circumstances, which, as Minister responsible for the Government of India, he could not resist. But the revolutionary movement taught him its own lessons. The people are never interested in revolutions or in movements that are a menace to the public peace. Their whole soul is bound up with law and order. The conclusion was therefore forced upon him that everything was not right in India, that there was something rotten in the State of Denmark, and that there must be conditions in the constitution of the Government and in the administration of the country to account for the development of the revolutionary forces. It was, I believe, acting under this conviction, that Lord Morley set himself to the task of constitutional reforms which would make the Government more acceptable to the leaders of the Indian people.

No matter from whom the Reforms emanated, they found in him a warm champion, insistent in carrying them through, and reminding Lord Minto that they should not be delayed. The zeal of the philosopher-statesman was apparent in his letters to Lord Minto, who, let it be said to his credit, responded with readiness and alacrity to the instructions of his chief. The idea of having an Indian member for the Viceroy's Executive Council, and for the Provincial Executive Councils, and that of the appointment of Indian members to the India Council in London were Lord Morley's own. Friends of India like Ripon shook their heads; and even so sympathetic a sovereign as King Edward was doubtful about an experiment so novel, and so opposed to deep-rooted and traditional official ideas. But Lord Morley was nothing if not strong in his statesmanship, and he never showed this quality of strength more strikingly than in connexion with the Reforms, and his stern attitude in opposing Lord Kitchener as Viceroy of India, a proposal which had ever the support of the King.

The reform measures, known as the Morley-Minto Scheme, were welcomed as a small advance. Nobody in India was under the delusion that they meant very much. Their most important feature was perhaps the power given to non-official members to move resolutions on public questions, thus affording them an opportunity of criticizing the measures and policy of the Government, though without exercising any real control over them. Lord Morley was careful to tell the House of Lords that he was not inaugurating parliamentary institutions in any sense, though he must have realized from what small beginnings parliamentary institutions had their genesis in that great country which was the mother of all Parliaments.

A deputation waited upon the Viceroy for the boon, such as it was; and even a Town Hall meeting in Calcutta was suggested. That such a meeting was not held was due to my intervention. I told Sir Edward Baker, who was then Lieutenant-Governor, that I could join it only on the understanding that there would be a resolution against the Partition of Bengal and praying for its modification. This the official inspirers of the meeting would not agree to, and the idea was dropped.

The new Councils came into existence in 1910, and at the very first meeting the Viceroy announced that it was no longer necessary to keep in confinement the political prisoners detained under Regulation III of 1818, that they were not associated with any revolutionary movement, and that they would all be released. The deportation of Krishna Kumar Mittra, Aswini Kumar Dutt and the others was a great political blunder. It served no useful purpose, it did harm; it frightened none; it added to the political uneasiness and excitement. Since then there have been cases of deportation, but nothing like the feeling that was then evoked. When I had an interview with Lord Morley in the India Office in the summer of 1909, I made a strong representation for the release of Babu Krishna Kumar Mittra and Babu Asmini Kumar Dutt. Lord Morley listened, but said nothing. The occasion indeed was inopportune. Sir William Curzon-Wylie had just been murdered, and a strong feeling of indignation was roused in England against all suspected of political intrigue. In quieter times I might have had some chance of success. In July, 1909, I had none. To the grim tragedy of that month I shall have to refer later; but in the meantime, let me pass on to a personal reminiscence in connexion with the reformed Councils.

Under the Regulations framed under the Parliamentary Statute of 1909, a dismissed servant of the Government was not eligible for election to the Legislative Councils. Dismissal from Government service was thus made a disqualification. Under the former Regulations (under the Statute of 1892) there was no such disqualification, though I believe an attempt was made to introduce it. Thus under the new Regulations I was disqualified for a seat in the Legislative Councils, local and Imperial. It was however, a disqualification that could be removed by the head of the Government. Sir Edward Baker was then Lieutenant-Governor. He knew me well. For years together we were colleagues in public work; and we learnt to like and respect one another. Of his own motion, without any suggestion from anybody, he removed my disqualification and sent me a copy of the Government notification.

I was placed in a position of some difficulty. I had repeatedly said that I would not allow myself to be elected to the Councils unless and until the Partition of Bengal was modified. So far as the reformed Councils were concerned I had often told the leaders of public opinion in Bengal: 'Hands off till the Partition is modified.' Speaking at Sir William Wedderburn's breakfast in Westminster Palace Hotel on June 24, 1909, I said in the presence of Sir Charles Dilke, Sir Henry Cotton, Mr. Hume, Mr. Ramsay MacDonald, and others:

> 'If Lord Morley were to hold out in his right hand the gift of the Reform Scheme and in his left the gift of the modification of the Partition, and were to tell the people of Bengal, "You cannot have both, make your choice", my countrymen would, with overwhelming spontaneity, declare themselves in favour of the modification of the Partition and would allow the Reforms to come in their own good time.'

It had always struck me that one of the most effective protests that we could make against the Partition of Bengal, which Lord Morley had so often declared with nauseating insistence to be a settled fact, was, for the Bengal leaders to abstain from all participation in the work of the reformed Councils. I knew that such a self-denying ordinance would not be acceptable to all. But I had made my choice and had proclaimed my faith. For me, at any rate, there was no excuse. I had resolved upon making the sacrifice, forgoing a career, in which on a former occasion, I had, in the opinion of my countrymen, done useful work. But it was a far more difficult task to refuse what indeed was an invitation made by a friend, for whom I had great personal respect, and who was moved by a friendly and generous impulse. The invitation of the Governor of a province would have made little or no impression on me. It was the act of a friend who wanted to make the new Reform Scheme a success and who desired that I should contribute to it. To me it would have been a matter of great personal satisfaction to have been a colleague of Sir Edward Baker in the enlarged Legislative Council; for I knew how high-minded he was in all his dealings, how generous to his critics, and how affectionate and kind to his friends.

I felt the difficulty of my position and at last invited some of the leading men of Bengal to a conference to advise me as to what I should do. Among them were the late Mr. A. Rasool, Babu Ananda Chunder Roy and Babu Ambika Churn Majumder. Their unanimous opinion was that I should decline, for, if I stood for election to the Bengal Legislative Council, the people of East Bengal would lose all faith in the leaders of West Bengal and the Partition agitation would receive an irreparable blow. The political leaders of East Bengal had abstained from standing for election to the Council of the new province and they naturally expected that we should do the same. I accepted their advice. To me the modification of the Partition of Bengal was the most pressing national concern, eclipsing all others then before the public.

There was yet another serious ground of objection. Under the Regulations as passed, several prominent leaders of the Moderate party stood disqualified. How could I enter the Council with the ban of disqualification excluding my colleagues? That was the decision of a conference of some of the leaders of the Moderate party. I accepted it and informed Sir Edward Baker that, deeply grateful as I was to him for the kindly consideration which in this as in other matters I had received at his hands, I must respectfully decline to avail myself of the Government notification removing my disqualification and to stand as a candidate for election to the Reformed Council. I may here add that my refusal did not in the slightest degree interfere with the cordiality of my relations with Sir Edward Baker, whose early death I deplore and whose memory I revere.

27

My Visit to England in 1909

I am invited to the Imperial Press Conference – Ripon College in safe keeping – the first function – irrelevance of Lord Cromer: my reply and its effect – Warwick Castle; Stratford-on-Avon; Oxford – when and why I smoked – I speak at Manchester – a visit to Windsor – work after the Conference – I speak on the Partition: repression condemned – breakfast and speeches at Sir William Wedderburn's – the assassination of Sir William Curzon-Wyllie – meeting at the New Reform Club – conference at Mr. Stead's house: my 'last words' to the British public – return to Calcutta, August, 1909.

I MUST NOW GO BACK TO THE YEAR 1909, beyond which I have travelled. Early in 1909, I was invited to attend the Imperial Press Conference which was to meet in London in the June following. It was to be a gathering of the representatives of the Press throughout the Empire. I was the only member of the Indian (as distinguished from the Anglo-Indian) Press who was asked to join the Conference. The invitation was made by Mr. Lovat Fraser, formerly of the *Times of India,* and at the time on the staff of *The Times*. It was an honour done to me, and I felt it as such; but there were difficulties in my way. The administration of the Ripon College was then being organized under the new University Regulations. The College had just passed through a serious crisis in connexion with the affiliation of its Law Department. There was a time when it seemed as if the Law Department, which was the largest in Bengal, would be disaffiliated. Thanks, however, to the powerful intervention of Sir Edward Baker, and the readiness of the college authorities to comply with the requirements of the University, these difficulties were overcome; and, while every law college in Bengal, with the exception of less than half a dozen, was disaffiliated, the Law Department of the Ripon College was allowed to retain its status and position.

We were not, however, quite out of the wood yet, and I sought the advice of Sir Edward Baker. He advised me to accept the invitation, assuring me that during my absence no harm would come to the college. A similar assurance was given to me by the Vice-Chancellor, Sir Ashutosh Mukherjea, who then ruled the University with undisputed sway. I had thus the satisfaction of feeling pretty sure, before I left for England, that the Law Department would be safe. For, at a meeting of the Syndicate to which I was invited, I discussed the constitution of the college with the members of the Syndicate, and everything was satisfactorily settled. I was thus enabled to leave for England about the middle of May, free from the anxieties which my absence from India would otherwise have caused.

My lot in life made me a great traveller, but I never liked the idea of leaving home for a distant journey. The comforts and associations of home always possessed an overwhelming fascination for me. In 1897, when I went to England to give evidence before the Welby Commission, I begged Lord Welby, the President of the Commission, to dismiss me as early as possible. He very courteously complied with my request, and I hurried back to India, although my colleagues stayed on for the celebration of the Queen's Diamond Jubilee, which was to take place in a few weeks' time. Pageants and shows never possessed any attraction for me, and I was glad to get back to my home and my work.

I left home on May 15, and arrived in London on June 3. It was nearly midnight when the train steamed into Victoria Station, and my old and esteemed friend, Mr. H. E. A. Cotton, was on the platform waiting for me with a motor ready to take me to the Waldorf Hotel, where the Press delegates were accommodated. He would not leave me till he saw me comfortably lodged in my room.

And here a word about Mr. Cotton. Mr. Cotton is now President of the Bengal Legislative Council, the duties of which, under existing conditions, have become anxious and troublesome, but which he is conducting, according to all accounts, with ability, tact and firmness that have won him praise and admiration. His experience as a member of the House of Commons and his familiarity with English public life have been a valuable help to him in the performance of his present arduous task, and when, on the death of Nawab Sir Shamsul Huda, late President of the Bengal Legislative Council, Mr. Cotton was suggested as his successor, I warmly supported the proposal. His father and myself had been friends for a period of over forty years, and in my public life I received valuable advice and guidance from him. After his retirement from India in the early nineties of the last century, we used to correspond every week on questions of public importance.

The first function of the Press Conference took place on the following evening, when Lord Burnham, proprietor of the *Daily*

Telegraph, a venerable old man of eighty, but still retaining something of the fire and the fervour of early life, and Lord Rosebery, the greatest of living English orators, welcomed us in suitable speeches at a great banquet given in honour of the Press delegates. I sat at table with Mr. Nevinson and Mr. Gardiner of the *Daily News,* and altogether it was a most enjoyable function.

Our deliberations commenced almost immediately. The first meeting of the Conference was held on June 7, and the subject discussed was the reduction of cable rates. A resolution declaring that facilities for telegraphic communication should be cheapened and improved was adopted, and a committee was appointed. Dr. (now Sir) Stanley Reed proposed the committee, and it was unanimously carried. I supported the resolution, on the ground that accurate news regarding the situation in India, especially in view of the developments that were then taking place, should be readily available to the British public, and cheap cable rates would materially promote that object.

At the second day's sitting the subject discussed was the Press and the Empire. Mr. McKenna, First Lord of the Admiralty, presided. The debate turned mainly upon the question of naval defence. I made up my mind to leave the Conference, as I had a meeting of the British Committee of the Congress to attend, when quite unexpectedly and without any occasion for it, Lord Cromer threw out a challenge, addressed almost personally to me, asking whether the anarchical developments which had then taken place were not helped by the irresponsible utterances of a certain section of the Indian Press. I heard the challenge with regret and astonishment. It seemed to be so utterly irrelevant; but for me there was no escape. The invitation was almost of a personal kind, for I was the only representative of the Indian section of the Press; and to keep quiet and say nothing would be to acquiesce in the insinuation. I made up my mind to reply; I collected my thoughts and sent up my name to the Chairman as one who intended to speak. I was called to the table at once. It was a short speech and I give the full text of it:

'I am sorry to interpose with any remarks which may appear to be some what irrelevant to the considerations which are now before the Conference, but Lord Cromer has extended to us as invitation – I will not call it a challenge – that we should say whether in our opinion the anarchical developments which have recently taken place in Bengal are due to the irresponsible utterances of a certain section of the Indian Press. To this question my answer is an absolute, an unqualified, and an emphatic "No". (Hear, hear, and voice, "Bravo".) I am not here to defend everything that has been said in the Indian Native Press. I ask my brother journalists here from other parts of the Empire if they are prepared to defend everything said in their columns about questions of great public importance. Are we an infallible body? We are not. We are liable to make mistakes, and sometimes very serious mistakes. I shall, therefore, say at once that I am not going to defend the irresponsible utterances, which, unfortunately, have now and then found a place in some of the Indian newspapers; but it must be remembered that those newspapers form an insignificant minority:—(hear, hear)—their circulation is limited, and their hold upon public opinion feeble. Let there be no misconception about my attitude. I do not stand here in justification of those anarchical developments which have unfortunately taken place in Bengal. I express the sense of the better mind of Bengal, and, I may add, of all India, when I say that we all deplore those anarchical incidents. (Cheers.) My Indian colleagues and myself have condemned them in our columns with the utmost emphasis that we could command. They are in entire conflict with those deep-seated religious convictions which colour, consciously or unconsciously, the everyday lives of our people. Anarchism, if I may say so without offence, is not of the East but of the West. It is a noxious growth which has been transplanted from the West, and we hope that under the conciliatory and ameliorating treatment of Lord Morley it will soon disappear from the land. I feel tempted to enter into those considerations which have brought about these unhappy developments, but I remember that this is a non-political gathering; I will, therefore, resist the temptation, and exercise the self-restraint of the East. (Loud cheers.) We regard a free Press as one of the greatest boons that have been conferred upon us under British rule. It was conferred upon us not merely for political purposes, but as an instrument for the dissemination of knowledge and useful information. At any rate, that was the hope, the aim and the aspiration of the great liberator of the Indian Press. Lord Metcalfe, speaking in reply to a deputation that waited upon him in connexion with the emancipation of the Indian Press, said: "We are not here in India merely to maintain order, to collect the taxes and make good the deficit; we are here for a higher and nobler purpose, to pour into the East the knowedge, the culture, and the civilization of the West." I claim on behalf of my countrymen that they have used this gift for the benefit of the Government, and to the advantage of the people, and I pray that it may long endure to the mutual credit of England and India alike.' (Cheers.)'

It is not for me to speak of the effect that the speech produced upon the meeting. When I said that I would not enter into a political controversy, but would exercise the self-restraint of the East, the

House came down with uproarious applause. Sir Hugh Graham, the doyen of the Canadian Press, who was present at the Conference, said to me afterwards that it was a 'model of a debating speech'. Another member of the Press Conference remarked that 'Mr. Banerjea wiped the floor with Lord Cromer'. It was generally felt that the retort was merited and I was glad that I had the opportunity of vindicating the Indian Press before the assembled journalists of the Empire.

Every day we had business meetings supplemented by parties. It was one continuous round of work, enlivened by festivities. The English are not a demonstrative people, but they are truly hospitable, and they show their cordiality to their guests in ways that are not to be mistaken. At Sheffield every one of us was presented with a knife, the kind of work for which Sheffield is noted, and at Dempster, after we had inspected the motor works, we were asked to take with us a handsome pocket-book as a souvenir of our visit. At the dinner and luncheon tables the talk was frank, cordial, and free from reserve and restraint. At the luncheon given to us at All Souls' College, Oxford, the Regius Professor of Greek of the University (Professor Gilbert Murray), who was sitting next to me, said of Lord Curzon, who presided and spoke, 'Here is a man who could set off the most trifling commonplaces in the most superb ornaments of language.'

Visiting England after twelve years I could not help noticing some of the changes that had taken place. One thing that struck me was that both teetotalism and vegetarianism were making headway, and, what was still more remarkable, as in the case of all social movements, their indirect influence upon the consumption of meat and alcohol was appreciable. But let me proceed with my narrative.

On the fourth day of the Conference Lord Morley was in the chair, and the subject of discussion was 'Journalism and Literature'. I spoke at that meeting, and Mr. T. P. O'Connor, M. P., who followed me, paid me a high compliment. I think it was Lord Morley who at that Conference described Literature as an art, and Journalism as an industry. We were invited to Aldershot and witnessed a review of fourteen thousand troops. I was here introduced to Lord Haldane, who was then Secretary of State for War and had come down from London to receive the Press delegates. I had a short conversation with him in which I referred to the Partition and the great grievance it was to the people of Bengal.

He heard me out and finished by saying, 'Why doesn't Morley upset it? ' That indeed was the feeling of every English politician of any note whom I met in the course of this visit.

I returned home with the impression that no public man who had any influence in the country liked the Partition, they were all against it, and that if we persevered it was bound to be upset. I saw Lord Courtney, who was a great friend of Lord Morley, and Mr. Winston Churchill in company with Mr. Mackarness, that staunch and redoubtable friend whose service to India at a critical time we have not sufficiently asknowledged. The impression left on my mind was that they were convinced that we had a great grievance and both promised to speak to Lord Morley. At Manchester I had an interview with Mr. C. P. Scott, editor of the *Manchester Guardian.* His sympathies were all with us. I pressed him to write in the columns of the *Manchester Guardian,* but his difficulty was that Lord Morley was a Liberal leader, and above all a Lancashire man.

Our work in London being over, we started on our provincial tour on June 14. We went by special train to Coventry, where we inspected the motor works to which I have already referred, and then we proceeded by motor to Warwick Castle where we were entertained at lunch by the Earl and Countess of Warwick. The Countess welcomed us in a fine speech, ringing with the inspiration that belongs to the old castle, so full of the stirring traditions associated with the name and fame of the great Kingmaker. She reminded us that, where we sat and had our lunch, equipped with the arms and the military emblems of the middle ages, was the hall in which the Barons deliberated and from where they sallied forth on their military expeditions under the leadership of the Kingmaker.

As I write these lines in my quiet residence in the suburbs of Ranchi, amid the deathlike stillness of a summer afternoon, I recall with vividness the sonorous strains of her something more than womanly voice, repeating the glories of the Warwick family, in a speech that left little or nothing to be wished for, in point of force or dignity of expression. The picturesque situation of the castle, overlooking a wide tract of woody country, almost forest-like in the beauty of its landscape, deepened the impression of medieval times, and of medieval strife and conflict, which the speech awakened.

From Warwick Castle we motored to Oxford, stopping at

Stratford-on-Avon, and alighting in front of Shakespeare's house. We entered it as a place of pilgrimage. I had seen the house and its memorials, the room where Shakespeare was born, the inscriptions of Dickens and of Byron some forty years back, in 1871, while I was yet a student in London. I saw nothing new except that an oil-painting of Shakespeare had been added; and that the birthplace of the great dramatist now possessed a Shakespeare Theatre, which did not exist forty years before. At the house itself we were welcomed by the Mayor in his robes of office, and one of our delegates made a reply. All this did not take more than ten minutes, and the function was performed in the little garden attached to the house.

How mindful the English people are of the memories of their great dead! In his own lifetime Shakespeare was not the towering and immortal figure that he now is – and even a prophet is not always honoured among his own people –, yet how scrupulously and reverentially the memorials of Shakespeare were preserved by his contemporaries. How different is all this in India! We worship our gods of clay and stone in the firm faith that the Divine Spirit dwells therein; but the living gods who move about us and amongst us, doing, daring, dying for the country, are nowhere in our estimation. We persecute them when necessary for our own ends, and we invoke the holy name of religion and love of country to conceal our spite. The great Ram Mohun Roy was outcasted by our ancestors; and it was only when death had obliterated personal jealousies and bitterness, and when we could view the Raja and his work in the cool, colourless atmosphere of reason and solid achievement, that we realized his worth and hastened to raise a memorial in his honour, in the place of his birth. A nation that does not know how to honour its heroes does not deserve to have them and will not have them.

From Shakespeare's birthplace we hurried on to Oxford in the dim and disappearing twilight. The country around, nature and men, were preparing for the welcome rest of the night. We too felt tired, despite the varied enjoyments of the day; and as I entered my room in the hotel, I felt that I had done a good day's work and had earned my rest. Our programme for the following day was cut and dried. It had all been arranged beforehand. I never saw an abler or more effective organizer than Sir Harry Brittain, who was looking after us and was our guide, philosopher and friend. Ceaseless in his work by day and night, no one could perceive on his placid and immobile countenance the faintest trace of strain or worry. He organized the Conference. The conception was his. The execution was also his. He sketched out its programme, and he carried it through with an ability and devotion, tempered with a never-failing geniality which made him the most attractive personality in that historic gathering of the journalists of the Empire. It is now several years since we met, but the memory of his kindliness and readiness to serve must remain imprinted on the minds of the members of the Conference.

Our programme, as I have said, was ready, and we set to work. We began the day with a visit to New College, which was almost opposite our hotel. We inspected the college building, almost every nook and corner of it, the lecture-rooms, the common-room, the smoking-room, and even the wine-cellar. To an Indian educationist like myself, bred in the puritanic ideas of our educational system, I confess the sight of the smoking-room and the wine-cellar gave a shock. No Indian educational institution or hostel has either of these appurtenances. Smoking among our students we dislike and discourage, and drinking among them, even in moderation, we abhor. There may perhaps be nothing immoral, the feeling is perhaps not based upon reasoned judgment; but our educational ideas have their roots in the Brahminical system of old, which was rigidly austere in its character and ascetic in its complexion, and in its outlook upon men and affairs. Poverty, purity, total contempt of wordly luxuries, are the basal ideas which built up the ancient educational system of India, and moulded its culture and civilization. The Brahmin has an instinctive dislike of both smoking and drinking, though sometimes, in imitating the failings of a civilization not his own, he takes to both.

I have throughout my life been a non-smoker. Often my friend, the late Mr. Turnbull, one of the most genial of men, pressed me to have a smoke with him, without success. At last he had recourse to a dodge. He made me a present of a fine cigarette-holder which he had purchased at the Paris Exhibition. I could not refuse the gift, coming from a friend so kind and so courteous. Equipped with this beautiful cigarette-holder, I took to smoking. But the practice was short-lived. It lasted for three or four days. I could endure it no longer. I felt the stench through every pore of my body. I put away the cigarette-case then and for ever; and I felt greatly relieved when I learnt that a thievish servant of mine had stolen it.

At Oxford we were treated to a luncheon in the Library of All Souls' College. Lord Curzon, as Chancellor of the University, received us in the garden of the College, and afterwards presided and spoke at the lunch. There was nothing very striking in the function or in the speech. From Oxford we proceeded to Sheffield, where we were entertained by the Mayor, and were taken round the works of Messrs. Vickers, Maxim & Co., the world-famous manufacturers of arms. To me, and, I imagine, to most of the delegates, it was a bewildering sight. We gazed, we wondered – that was all. At Sheffield the suggestion was made that I should speak. I demurred, and preferred to hold myself in reserve for Manchester. I think I was right in this decision.

We arrived at Manchester on June 18. At the entrance to my hotel there were my Indian friends, headed by Mr. Dube, a resident of Northern India, to welcome me. They garlanded me and decked me with flowers, while some of my colleagues of the Press Conference looked with no little curiosity on this novel sight. Among the spectators was Mr. Mackenzie, the correspondent of the *Daily Mail*. As I noticed him I said, 'This is what you called my coronation in the *Daily Mail*. This is what is usually done every day to honoured friends in India.' He laughed; and I entered the hotel, making over my flowery appendages to Sir Harry Brittain for presentation to Lady Brittain.

At Manchester I was selected to speak at a luncheon at the Town Hall presided over by the Lord Mayor. The Lord Mayor proposed the toast of 'The Imperial Press', coupling it with my name. I have taken the liberty of printing this speech in an appendix because in that speech I tried to voice, as effectively as I could, our aspirations for self-government as 'the cement of the Empire', the strongest guarantee of Imperial unity, and the most powerful bulwark against the machinations of the enemies of England. We are now within measurable distance of the fulfilment of that for which I then ventured to plead. For the beginnings of responsible government have been inaugurated, which I hope, notwithstanding the clouds that now darkly frown, will, in the fulness of time, make India an equal partner in the British Commonwealth. In the last sentence of my peroration, I said:

'India in the enjoyment of the blessings of self-government, India prosperous, contented and happy, will be the most valuable asset of the Empire, the strongest bulwark of Imperial unity. And the

Empire, thus knit together upon the basis of common civic rights and obligations, may bid defiance to the most powerful combination that may be formed against it, and may gaze with serenity and confidence upon those vicissitudes which, as all history tells us, have wrecked the fortunes of States and thrones which relied upon the security of physical rather than upon the paramountcy of those moral laws which represent the index-finger of Divine Providence in the dispensation of human affairs.'

This was said in 1909, and when in 1914 we stood face to face with the most formidable combination that had ever been formed against the Empire, our rulers discovered that in a prosperous and contented India, secured by the inauguration of responsible government, lay one of the strongest guarantees of Imperial unity and strength. If the truth had been earlier recognized and practised, our man-power and money-power would have been even more freely available in the service of the Empire.

The speech was received with warmth and even enthusiasm by the audience; and a Press delegate sitting next to me said as I resumed my seat, 'If there are two hundred men like you in India, Mr. Banerjea, self-government ought to be granted tomorrow.' I said, 'There are twice two hundred men like me in India.' The function being over, as I was leaving the hall, the caretaker came up to me and said, 'Will you, sir, write down your name in this book?' And as I was writing he said to me, 'Sir, let me tell you this, that such a speech has not been delivered in this hall since it was built.' It may have been the language of high-pitched admiration, but it certainly represented the feelings of the man, for he spoke with evident warmth and sincerity.

The Manchester Press, whose representatives were all present at the function, wrote in appreciative terms. The *Manchester Courier*, an organ of Conservative opinion and not always very friendly to Indian aspirations, said of the speech: 'It was the most dramatic incident of the Press delegates' visit to Manchester. . . . On the Manchester citizens whom the Lord Mayor had invited to meet the guests, the effect of the speech was almost electrical. To find themselves addressed in their own language by a native of India with a fluency that must have been the envy of all present, and with the impassioned utterance that only a born orator can attain, was an experience that happens only once in a lifetime.'

I left Manchester almost immediately after the function as I had to attend a dinner party in London at the house of Mr. (afterwards

Sir William) Byles, M.P. I arrived late for the dinner; but it was a pleasure to have made the acquaintance of Mr. and Mrs. Byles – such good friends of India were they. The Press delegates returned to London the same day and on June 19 we were at Windsor Castle to witness the presentation of colours to the Territorials by His Majesty the King. On the terrace where we were stationed I met Mr. Ameer Ali. There was a bleak, cold, east wind blowing, and Mr. Ameer Ali, who was dressed in Windsor uniform with the badge of a Companion of the Indian Empire on his breast, was almost shivering with cold. His first words on approaching me were, 'You are very wise, Mr. Banerjea, to have put on that overcoat.' I said to him, 'I never part with it if I can help it in the fickle and changeable climate of England.' My absolute immunity from colds and coughs during my stay of over two months in England was evidence that I acted wisely. On one occasion, when I had gone on a visit to Lord Midleton (Mr. Brodrick, who, as Secretary of State, had sanctioned the Partition of Bengal) his lordship came up with me to open the door. He looked hard at my overcoat, which he helped me to put on. I noted the significance of his look, and I said, 'My Lord, your climate is fickle and treacherous, and, though it is a bright day, I thought there was no harm in being extra cautious.' Lord Midleton laughed approvingly and closed the door after me.

The visit to Windsor was followed by a deputation that waited upon Mr. Asquith on the question of cable rates. I was a member of the Deputation. There were the usual speeches; but Mr. Asquith gave no pledge of any kind. This was the last function at which I was present as a member of the Press Conference.

When I went to England, as a member of the Press Conference, I did not forget the promise I had made or the responsibility I had imposed upon myself in connexion with the Partition of Bengal. On the eve of my leaving for England the Indian Association held an afternoon party in my honour, to which my colleague, Mr. Everard Digby, was invited, and I assured my friends in the speech I made that, next to my duties as a member of the Press Conference, the modification of the Partition of Bengal would claim my attention. I now applied myself to this work. The members of the Conference having finished their work in England, were now to proceed on tour to Scotland. I told Sir Harry Brittain that I must now be permitted to withdraw from the Conference. I left the Waldorf Hotel and engaged a suite of rooms at Clement's Inn, the headquarters of the Suffragist movement, with which of course I had no concern. I occupied these rooms with Mr. Kedarnath Das Gupta of Chittagong, who, let me here record, did me most useful service in helping me to move about London. He is a permanent resident and knows every corner of the great city, and was my companion in my numerous visits to persons and places.

The first function at which I spoke, and in which the Partition of Bengal was the burden of my theme, was a dinner in my honour organized by a committee of Indian residents, of which Mr. Parekh was the chairman. The dinner was held at the Westminister Palace Hotel and among the guests were many Members of Parliament, including Sir Henry Cotton, Mr. Mackarness and Mr. Ramsay Macdonald. The gathering was in one sense a unique one, consisting of representatives from all parts of India and of its varied creeds. But it was not merely an Indian demonstration. It was in truth a convention of the English friends of India assembled to hear an Indian public man engaged in one of the keenest political struggles of his generation. As might have been expected, there was the deepest sympathy and appreciation of the work done by my colleagues and myself in the fight that we carried on for the modification of the Partition.

There rang out, too, from that meeting a clear note of condemnation of the measures of repression that were for the first time employed to deal with political agitation. Punishment without trial is abhorrent to Englishmen, though it should take no harsher form than simple detention. Even Lord Morley, who sanctioned the deportations on the advice, apparently the insistent advice, of the men on the spot, disapproved of them in his heart of hearts, and was never, as would appear from his *Recollections,* reconciled to them. When referring to recent measures of legislation, I said in the course of my speech, 'Never was there a confession of a more hopeless failure. Where in the history of the world has repression been successful?' I was cheered to the echo.

Sir Henry Cotton, who followed me, said that 'if the growth of national feeling in India and of the sense of patriotism and enthusiasm for the motherland was due to any man, that man was Babu Surendranath Banerjea.' Mr. Keir Hardie, one of the best friends of India, whose premature death we all lament, spoke next. He said: 'Mr. Banerjea was one of the few, very few, whose personality was greater than his reputation.' Mr. Mackarness, one of the friends of India, whom we have lost by his translation to a Government appointment, said, that 'the speech was more than eloquent – it was statesmanlike.' Mr. Swift McNeill, an Irish Member of Parliament, whose zeal for the good of India never failed him, was the last speaker of the evening. He said: 'The Indians are happy in having such a leader as Mr. Surendranath Banerjea. I have heard many great speeches, but my heart has never been more profoundly touched than by the magnificent exposition of intellect and high character which Mr. Banerjea has brought to the discussion of these subjects.'

The public dinner was followed by a breakfast given by Sir William Wedderburn to which he invited a large number of Members of Parliament and others interested in the cause of Indian progress. Sir William Wedderburn is now lost to us. Mr. Allen Hume, Sir Henry Cotton and Sir William Wedderburn formed a band of devoted friends of India whose loss is irreparable and whose counsels would have been invaluable in the critical times through which we are now passing. No other Englishmen possessed the same measure of influence over the mind of educated India. For none showed such passionate love for India and such rare devotion to the cause of Indian progress; their lives were lives of self-dedication to the interests of the land of their love and of their adoption. When the history of these times comes to be written, to them will be assigned in varying degrees a high and honourable place among those who by their labours have contributed to upbuild the future of our nation's history. In the pantheon of our great men, these Englishmen will live surrounded by the veneration of distant generations. If they had been spared to us, what a wise and restraining influence would they not have exercised over the controversies now raging and splitting us into hostile camps! But it is idle to indulge in unavailing regrets.

Sir William Wedderburn had indeed a glimpse of the new order that was soon to be established. He had the supreme satisfaction, as he was nearing the end, of witnessing the partial success of that cause to which he had consecrated the evening of his life. He heard the message of August 20, 1917 promising responsible government to India. But he only heard it; for he died soon after when Mr. Montagu was about to start for India.

The fascination of Sir William Wedderburn's name and the delight that every Indian must feel in dwelling upon his loved memory has drawn me somewhat away from the point which I was discussing. Sir William Wedderburn's breakfast was a very successful function. Among Anglo-Indian Members of Parliament he was, I think, the most influential. The quiet assertiveness of his gentle and charming manners, the transparent sincerity of his purpose, the overwhelming power of deep conviction, which had its roots in his love for India and her peoples and his thorough mastery of Indian problems, lent to his advocacy a weight which was all but irresistible.

There was a brilliant gathering of Members of Parliament including the late Sir Charles Dilke and Mr. Ramsay Macdonald. I had of course to speak. I must say that I have never been reconciled to the English practice (I imagine it is also the European practice), of having to make speeches at festive functions. We Indians, when we are invited to a feast, go there to eat and to talk in a friendly and informal way with those whom we may happen to meet. The eating is the principal thing; the talking is a subsidiary adjunct. It is somewhat different in English public functions when there is a festive side to them. The talking is the most important thing, the eating is secondary. The result is that the dinner or the lunch is spoilt for those who have to speak. Their thoughts are centred upon the speech. The enjoyment of the dinner is gone. That is how these functions strike an Oriental. That these speeches are sometimes useful, I have no doubt. The Lord Mayor's Banquet would be shorn of much of its brilliancy and its public interest if the speeches were eliminated. I only say what has struck me. It is only a personal note, as the speeches that I have had to make at these festive functions interfered with my full and personal enjoyment of them. Nobody must imagine that speech-making costs nothing. No speech is worth listening to unless it has been thought over and carefully prepared. Demosthenes, the prince of orators for all time and countries, burnt his midnight oil in the preparation of those orations that captivated the imagination and moved the hearts of his Athenian audience.

In the speech at Sir William Wedderburn's breakfast I again spoke of the Partition and of the deportations.

Sir Charles Dilke, Mr. Ramsay Macdonald and Sir Henry Cotton followed, strongly denouncing the deportations. Mr. Allen Hume was also one of the speakers. His speech was brimful of personal recollections and kindly references to me. He said it was with very great pleasure and pride that he found himself permitted to take an active part in welcoming once more to the shores of England his old friend and tried comrade, Babu Surendranath Banerjea. It seemed to him but a few days since Mr. Mudholkar, Mr. Banerjea and himself were tramping throughout Great Britain, from Plymouth in the far south-west to Aberdeen in the north-east, everywhere pleading the cause of India, and asking the people to support a demand for those reforms in the administration, for the accomplishment of which they had all three been working for so many years. He would never forget that happy tramp; it was rendered happy, in the first place, by the apparent success of their crusade, for everywhere they were welcomed by huge audiences, which passed the strongest of resolutions in favour of the measures they advocated. But, above all, that campaign was made memorable by the unalterable good temper and amiability of their friend, and his readiness on every possible occasion to do all he could to assist them. He would never forget almost their last meeting, held at Aberdeen. It was late at night. The room was hot and stifling, and when they emerged into the cool, crystalline twilight of the North – one hardly recognized the beauty of the twilight down south – it caused them to loiter a little in one of the broad ways of the Granite City. He and Mr. Mudholkar began to discuss with a companion the probability of the resolutions passed at the meetings in the large provincial centres being effective in bringing about the reforms they were working for. But their friend Mr. Banerjea, with that eye to practical business which had always characterized him, closed the talk by saying, 'It is very late; we have to travel in the early morning; let us think about our supper.' (Laughter.) It was the clear eye and the practical nature of Mr. Banerjea which enabled him, even while eating his heart out in a prison cell, where one of their best men was now slowly dying, to carry on his great crusade with such success. (Cheers.) Since those days he (Mr. Hume) had been in constant touch with the work of their guest, and he had reason more and more to admire the tact, good temper and wisdom with which in putting forward the wrongs of his countrymen and the rights they ought to possess, he had abstained from saying or writing anything which would give his enemies an opportunity of putting in motion against him the miserable un-English laws which were associated with deportation. (Hear, hear.)

Allen Hume was not only a great organizer, but one of the most affectionate of men. With the shrewdness and the practical sense of the Scotchman he combined the generous warmth and the fiery impulsiveness of the Oriental. He loved his Indian friends: their welfare, personal and national, was the object of his keenest solicitude and they repaid his love with compound interest. No Englishman of his time excited deeper veneration or more unbounded enthusiasm among educated Indians than this ex-member of the Indian Civil Service, and it is worthy of note that among Englishmen the staunchest friends of the Congress movement in its early days were all members of the Indian Civil Service who had risen to distinction in that service. What precious opportunities the members of the Indian Civil Service had to win the affections and the regard of the people; and how seldom did they avail themselves of these opportunities to strengthen the bonds that should unite Indians and Englishmen in the ties of a common citizenship! But the angle of vision is now happily changing; and thoughtful Indians are hopefully looking forward to the time when the enjoyment of equal civic rights may create new and stronger ties of unity than now exist.

The breakfast took place on June 24. In less than a week's time an event occurred which stirred India and England alike. On the night of July 1, at the anniversary meeting of the National Indian Association, Sir William Curzon-Wyllie, Political Aide-de-camp to the Secretary of State for India, and Dr. Lalkaka were shot dead by a young Indian of the name of Dhingra. Almost at the time when this tragic event took place, we were being entertained at dinner as members of the Imperial Press Conference by Lord Strathcona. I had been invited to the anniversary of the National Indian Association, and at one time I had a mind to attend it. But, as it was getting late, I slipped off, and went to my rooms in Clements' Inn. The toasts were being proposed and speeches made, and, as I thought it would be very late for me, I quietly went away, leaving the party to enjoy their postprandial orations. My friend, Mr. K. N. Das Gupta, who was waiting to take me home, suggested that I might look in for a minute at the Imperial Institute and see how the function of the National Indian Association was going on; but I was tired and sleepy, and preferred my bed to the excitement of an evening party, little dreaming of the tragic happenings that were taking place about the very time when I was deciding as to whether I should abstain or attend.

On the following morning, July 2, almost immediately after I had finished my breakfast, a newspaper reporter called on me. He was the first to give me news of the tragic event. He said, 'Will you give me what particulars you can, of the assassination of Sir William Curzon-Wyllie?' I said in a vein of horrified astonishment, 'Assassination of Sir William Curzon-Wyllie! I know nothing at all about it. This is the first time that I hear of it.' I added 'You seem to know more about it than I do.' He gave me the particulars, so far as he knew them, and he asked me if I knew who Dhingra was. I said that from the name it was clear that was not a Bengalee; but it was difficult to say what part of India he came from. The reporter got precious little from me for copy, except a clear expression of my own personal opinion and the sense of abhorrence that all India would feel at the terrible crime. Soon after, reporters, one after another, began to pour into my room, to the infinite disguest of the liftman, who said to a friend, 'The suffragettes are bad enough' – Clements' Inn where I was residing was their headquarters – 'but this Indian (meaning me) is worse. He gives us a lot of trouble.'

Reporters' visits continued till a late hour of the evening, and were supplemented by those of Indian students who came in large numbers, soliciting my advice as to what should be done; for the situation was one of the utmost gravity. It was an Indian student who had murdered a high English official, and a countryman of his own who had rushed to his rescue. The wantonness of the crime gave a shock to English public feeling and created wide-spread indignation. Unless prompt steps were taken by the Indian students to disavow the crime and repudiate it in the most explicit terms, public indignation would spread from the individual student who had committed the deed to the class, and Indian students generally would be tarred with the same brush. It was necessary to save the situation by prompt and decisive action. Mr. D. C. Ghose and Mr. H. M. Bose, who were then in England studying for the Bar, took the lead in organizing a demonstration of students, which we decided should take place at once. The rooms of the New Reform Club were secured, and the meeting was to be held on the following day with myself as President. Fortunately for the Indian students, I had been invited by some journalistic friends to lunch with them the same day at the National Liberal Club. The tragedy of the preceding night was naturally the subject of discussion, and it was decided that I should write a letter to the Press, which – or, at any rate, a substantial summary of it – was to be published through the Press agency in every newspaper in the country. The letter was drafted and before evening it was despatched over my signature to all newpapers throughout the United Kingdom. Thus the first step was taken towards meeting a situation that threatened a crisis.

The meeting at the New Reform Club was held on the following day. The room in which it was held was not large in the Indian sense; but it was filled with an eager and earnest audience. The Indian students mustered strong, among them being Mr. Savarker, who, at a meeting held for the same purpose the next day, created a scene by his opposition to the main resolution. No untoward event, however, occurred at our meeting. Everything passed off quietly; and my speech was, on the whole, well received by the British Press, with the exception of that portion of it in which I challenged the Prime Minister's assertion that there was a widespread conspiracy in India; the implication being that Dhingra belonged to this gang. The *Times* supported the Prime Minister (Mr. Asquith), though the trial subsequently made it clear that Dhingra stood alone in this murderous deed, and had acted on his own impulse and initiative.

The murder of Sir William Curzon-Wyllie operated as a set-back to the Indian cause. My reading of the many political situations through which I have passed is that political crimes of the sensational order undoubtedly serve as a wide advertisement to political grievances, but they strengthen the Conservative elements in society, and operate in the long run as a bar to political progress. The same is true as regards the tactics of obstruction that are now being followed in our Legislative Councils. I will not refer to the history of Russian Nihilism and the measures of repression by which it was followed, the long-drawn conflict between the forces of despotism and those of revolution culminating in the enthronement of Bolshevism. The theme would be beyond the scope of these reminiscences; but I was in hopes of obtaining from Lord Morley a reconsideration of the cases of some of those who had been deported. I had especially in mind the orders passed against Krishna Kumar Mittra and Aswini Kumar Dutt. When I subsequently had an interview with him, I pleaded hard for their release, but pleaded in vain. A patient hearing was accorded; but it was not until the inauguration of the Morley-Minto Scheme of reform that the deportees were released.

In the meantime, my work, to the good effects of which, if not to its complete success, I had looked forward with some little confidence, was hampered by the assassination. I had been invited to speak at the Eighty Club, and at a full-dress debate on the Indian question at the forthcoming meeting of the Club. The club, which is an organization of the Liberal party, had fixed the day and had made the necessary arrangements for the meeting. The meeting indeed came off, and I spoke, but it was more or less a formal affair. A vote of condolence with Lady Curzon-Wyllie was passed; but the main issues upon which I had hoped to address the leaders of the Liberal party had to be left untouched. A golden opportunity was missed; the assassination of Sir William Curzon-Wyllie was responsible for it. The Chairman indeed said in bringing the proceedings to a close: 'We desire to do our utmost to further the cause of constitutional progress and development in India.' It took the British democracy ten years to make a substantial step in this direction, and possibly this would even then have been delayed, but for the war and the time-forces that it had helped to create.

The last speech of any importance that I delivered on this occasion was at Caxton Hall under the presidency of Sir Charles Dilke. Sir Charles Dilke was one of the foremost public men of his day, respected alike for the soundness of his views and his knowledge of the political situation outside Great Britain. He had a close insight into Indian affairs, combined with sympathy for Indian aspirations. It was a great thing to have got him to preside at our meeting. I spoke on the Partition of Bengal and the Morley-Minto Scheme. It may not be out of place here to reproduce what I said of the Morley-Minto Scheme in 1909, two years before the Despatch of the Government of India promising provincial autonomy, and eight years before the Parliamentary Message of responsible government. I said:

> 'The Scheme (Morley-Minto) contains no concessions which have not been in some form or other repeatedly asked for. So far from the Scheme being lavish, I will say that it does not come up to our expectations in regard to many matters of vital importance. For instance, we want the power of the purse. We want definite control at least over some of the great departments of the State: over Sanitation, Education and the Public Works Department. Are you not aware that thousands of my countrymen die every year from preventible diseases, such as malaria and cholera ? If we had an effective control over finance or at least over the sanitary measures to be employed, I am convinced that we could prevent to some extent the appalling rate of mortality which now desolates the village homes of Bengal. The expenditure on education is inadequate. As for elementary education, the less said the better. We want the power of the purse and a definite and effective measure of self-government. That we have not got. All that the Reform scheme does – and let me be perfectly candid in the matter – is to provide the machinery by which the representatives of the people would be in a position to bring to bear upon the Government not anything like direct influence but indirect moral pressure.'

The two questions to which I devoted the largest measure of attention in my address in England in 1909 were the modification of the Partition of Bengal, and the introduction of Self-Government in India; and, from the manner of the reception accorded to them by British audiences, I was convinced that both were coming, that the Partition would be modified sooner or later, and that a feeling was spreading in England that India was rapidly growing ripe for some measure of self-government. After I had spoken in Manchester in reply to the toast, several members of the Imperial Press Conference, delegates from the Overseas Dominions, from Canada and Australia, said to me, 'Mr. Banerjea, if there are men like you in India, self-government should be conceded without delay.'

The war strengthened the gathering forces, and the national awakening which was stimulated by the anti-Partition and *Swadeshi* movements and the repressive measures that followed in their train made the demand for self-government in India more vocal and insistent, until it was no longer possible to ignore it. Almost on the eve of the Message of August 20, 1917, several heads of provinces tried this impossible feat; but all in vain. Canute-like, but without his humour, they essayed to roll back the rising tide. Canute-like they failed. Their efforts recoiled on themselves; and served only to add to the volume and intensity of the rising movement.

I should not be doing justice to myself or to my English visit on this occasion, if I did not refer to a small party held at Mr. Stead's house. It was a quiet, informal gathering in which there were no set speeches, no conventionalities, where every one opened his heart and spoke out his mind without fear or favour. The idea of the gathering was Mr. Stead's. He organized it and led its deliberations. Its aim was an informal discussion of the burning topics of Indian interest. All India remembers Mr. Stead's tragic death when the *Titanic* was lost in the Atlantic in 1912. Many were his admirers in India. His puritanic austerity, his hatred of modern abominations, his sympathy for human freedom, no matter whether the persons concerned lived on the banks of the Ganges or of the Neva, raised him above the common level of humanity and excited veneration wherever his name was pronounced. Twelve years have elapsed. The same feelings continue, though perhaps in a diminished degree, for time blunts the edge of even our sharpest sorrows.

The gathering was characteristic of the man – it was Mr. Stead all over – cosmopolitan in its breadth and comprehensiveness, and direct in its aims and utterances. There were present in that company, small though it was, Americans, Canadians, and Irish; and among Indians was Mr. Bepin Chunder Pal. Mr. Stead appeared in the room with a whip in his hand, which, I presume, was typical of the axe that was to fall in two minutes' time, and he wanted my dying message to the British public on behalf of the motherland. I must say that I was not prepared, even from the dramatic point of view, for so awful a doom and so solemn and historic a message. There was, however, no escape from the position. The whip was there. It was in the hands of one of the most inflexible of men, who knew how to wield it, either to rouse the sympathy or evoke the indignation of his fellows. I addressed myself to the task as best I could, not indeed without a shuddering fear, but behind it there was the sanguine hope of enlisting the sympathies and the active co-operation of those who guide and control the public opinion of large sections of their countrymen.

The appeal made to me to utter a dying message to the British public on behalf of my motherland stirred all that was most sensitive in me, and I threw myself heart and soul into it. The whip was the outer symbol; love was the inspiring principle; and the love of the great Englishman for India's freedom awakened in me a deep and sympathetic response, which I think was shared by my audience. I can do nothing better than quote it in his own words; for it will serve the double purpose of a faithful record of my message and all that transpired, and of a memorial of love for India and her people on the part of a great and philanthropic Englishman:

'If you were under sentence of death, Mr. Banerjea, and the headsman's axe was to fall in two minutes, what is the message which you would wish to address to the British public as the last words you were able to utter on behalf of your motherland ?'

Without a moment's hesitation Mr. Banerjea replied:

'I would say this: (1) Modify the Partition of Bengal; (2) Release the deported patriots and repeal the Act which annuls Habeas Corpus in Bengal; (3) Amnesty all the political prisoners; (4) Give the people of India control of their own taxes; and (5) Grant India a constitution on the Canadian model. That is what I would say, and, having said that, I would go to my doom.'

'Good', said he. 'Now let us come to particulars. I thought you wanted the repeal of the Partition ?'

'I wish that repeal were possible, but I recognize that Lord Morley, having been challenged perhaps prematurely for an expression of opinion, took up a stand from which he can hardly now be asked to recede. I am a practical man; I ask for modification, not for repeal.'

'But I suppose you want to modify it lock, stock, and barrel?'

'What I should like is to see Bengal placed under one Lieutenant-Governor with an Executive Council of six, of whom two should be Indians. You will have to come to this, for the new province is at present placed in a position of inequality with the old, having no Executive Council. The next proposal, and one which commanded from of old time the balance even of official opinion, was to divide Behar from Bengal. The people of Behar are distinct in race and language from the Bengalees. All administrative advantages claimed for the original Partition would be secured by this arrangement without offending national sentiment. So long as the Bengalee nation is unnaturally cleft in twain by the sword of Lord Curzon so long will agitation and unrest continue.'

'Now as to the deportees?'

'They ought never to have been deported without charge and without trial. They ought to be allowed at once to return home. I hope that will not be long delayed. They are good men, upright citizens who did not deserve deportation.'

'Now as to the last article in your programme?'

'A constitution like that of Canada is our ultimate goal. But as a practical first step I claim for our people the right of financial control over the expenditure of the money raised from Indian taxpayers.'

'Humph! What about the army and railway expenditure?'

'I will exempt these two heads of expenditure for the sake of compromise. But surely we ought to control expenditure for education, for sanitation, for civil public works. The refusal or neglect to carry out sanitary works, the need for which has been admitted since 1861, has led to terrible loss of life, which might have been prevented.'

'Do you want a Duma for India?'

'If you mean an assembly representing all India, with control over the expenditure of India, I say "yes". But I would say, first give us autonomous provincial governments, with financial control over certain departments of provincial expenditure. Then build up on these provincial autonomies a central federal council or assembly. That is what we ask, and that is what sooner or later we mean to have.'

So far Mr. Banerjea. That is his programme. And 'Surrender Not' is the nearest English equivalent to the pronunciation of his name, Surendranath I do not think that he is likely to abandon any of the planks in his programme. John Morley, of the *Pall Mall Gazette* and of the life of Burke, would probably subscribe to them all. But as for Lord Morley, that is another matter.

Such is the gist of the conversation we had, as described by Mr. Stead himself. I said all this in 1909, three years before the

Partition of Bengal was modified and on the lines I suggested in my message, and eight years before Mr. Montagu's announcement in August, 1917, promising Dominion status for India. A part of my message has already been fulfilled. I have dreamt many dreams in my life. Some of them have been realized. Others are awaiting the flux of time for their fulfilment. Among them I regard our admission into the British Commonwealth, as an equal partner with an equal status, as among the certainties of the future. Mr. Stead did me the honour of writing a personal note on myself in the *Review of Reviews,* as an introduction, which, with the reader's permission, I reproduce in this place:

> 'I travelled down to Lord Northcliffe's seat at Sutton with Mr. Banerjea, when the editors of the Empire went down to lunch at that delightful place; and formed the highest opinion of his lucid intelligence, his marvellous command of English, and his passionate devotion to his native land. I had the honour of being one of the guests at the banquet given to him by his fellow-countrymen in England at the Westminister Palace Hotel, and was delighted to find in him an orator of brilliant eloquence and a statesman of comprehensive outlook, with a most practical mind. I invited him to my house, and there in company with a dozen friends – American, Canadian, Irish and Indian – Mr. Banerjea kindly submitted himself to a process of composite interviewing, the gist of which my readers will find condensed in this article. Mr. Banerjea has been twice President of the Indian National Congress; he has been once in gaol, he is the editor of the *Bengalee,* and his repute is such that he was once said to have been crowned king of Bengal as a protest against the Partition. He was the only representative of the Native Indian Press at the Conference, and none of the editors of the Empire excelled him in eloquence, energy, geniality, and personal charm.'

I returned to India in August, 1909 and was welcomed home with cordiality and enthusiasm. My reception at the Howrah station was on a scale rivalling that accorded to Mr. Dadabhai Naoroji when he came to Calcutta to preside over the Congress of 1906, and it was followed by a Town Hall meeting, one of the most enthusiastic ever held in that historic hall. In my private conversations as well as in my public utterances, I emphasized what was with me a deliberate conviction – that the Partition was not to be regarded as a settled fact, despite Lord Morley's oft-repeated declarations to the contrary, and that there was a slowly growing feeling in England that some measure of self-government must be conceded to India.

So far as the anti-Partition movement was concerned, it seemed to many, even to some of the stalwarts of our party, that ours was a lost cause and that I was leading a forlorn hope. But I never despaired, not the faintest ray of despondency ever crossed my mind. My never-failing optimism stood me in good stead. But I had also solid ground to tread upon. The great leaders of public opinion in England whom I had interviewed, belonging, I may add, to all parties, did not like the Partition of Bengal, and especially the manner in which it was carried out during its concluding stages. One of them said to me, 'Why does not Morley upset it?' It was really Lord Morley's great name and influence that propped it up; and I felt that if we continued the agitation for some time longer it was bound to go. The tide of circumstances soon began to roll in our favour. Everything comes to the man who knows how to wait. Patience and optimism are supreme qualities in public life. That has been my experience, and I bequeath it, with loving concern, to my countrymen.

28

The Anti-partition Movement

Lord Hardinge Viceroy – my first interview with him – the Delhi Durbar, 1911 – modification of the Partition – Outstanding personalities.

In 1910, Lord Hardinge was appointed Viceroy in succession to Lord Minto. I met Lord Minto several times and had fairly long interviews with him. He was an English gentleman of a fine type. Fairly liberal in his sentiments, but I fear without any large power of initiative, his name will be remembered in Indian history as the joint author of the Morley-Minto Scheme; though Lord Morley's *Recollections* leave no doubt as to where the driving power lay. India owes to Lord Minto the system of communal representation for the Legislative Councils, from the meshes of which it will take her many long years to emerge. I had in one of my interviews a long conversation with him about the Partition of Bengal. He was frank and outspoken, but obdurate in his adhesion to the 'settled fact'. He said, 'Mr. Banerjea, if my country was divided in the way your province has been, I should feel just as you do.' He spoke his mind out, but he was powerless to help us in any way. When we formally waited upon him in deputation as members of the Indian Association with a request that the Partition should be modified, he repeated Lord Morley's formula and told us in reply that the Partition was a 'settled fact'.

Some of our friends in India thought that we should not have put forward the request for its modification, in view of the repeated pronouncements of the Secretary of State. Our friends in England, including Mr. W. C. Bonnerjea, who was then in London, were of a different opinion. Their view was that, having regard to the all-important character of the Partition question, it was our plain duty to give it a prominent place in an address to the Viceroy. To have omitted all reference to it on an occasion so important was to have relegated it to a secondary place among the public questions of the day. In any case, it was clear that Lord Minto would do nothing to modify the Partition. We thought it possible, though our experience of the past was not very encouraging, that Lord Hardinge might take a more favourable view.

Lord Hardinge came out to India as a comparative stranger. He was not in the ranks of English public life; diplomacy was his profession. The Indian public received the announcement of his appointment with mixed feelings. But, before twelve months had elapsed, we realized that he would take his place in the front rank of Indian Viceroys, by the side of Bentinck, Canning and Ripon.

A new Viceroy having assumed the reins of Government, we resolved to place him in possession of all the facts and the attitude of the Indian public in regard to the Partition question. We accordingly announced a public meeting to be held in the Town Hall of Calcutta early in January to consider it. Within a day or two of the announcement I received an urgent letter from Government House inviting me to see His Excellency the Viceroy the day after. I had never before been so summoned; but I guessed the purpose of the invitation. I thought it was the proposed Town Hall meeting about which His Excellency wished to have information. I was right in my anticipation. After the usual greetings, Lord Hardinge wanted to know why we had called the meeting. I said in reply, 'In order to acquaint your Excellency with the situation in Bengal relating to the Partition.' His Excellency's answer was: 'But that can be done by a memorial without a public meeting.' I said, 'If your Excellency would look into the memorial personally and consult our leaders, the district leaders, there would be no reason for holding the public meeting.' His Excellency said he would do that and consult his officers. I said, 'My Lord, the officers of Government have again and again been consulted, and they have given their opinions. It is our leaders whose opinions should now be asked.' Lord Hardinge very kindly agreed; and the public meeting at the Town Hall was not held.

I drew up a memorial largely assisted by my esteemed friend, Babu Ambika Churn Majumder, the Grand Old Man of Faridpore, and sent it to the district leaders for signature by influential and representative men. My request was that the memorial was to be regarded as absolutely confidential, so that the other side under official inspirations might not set up a counter-agitation. My instructions were faithfully observed. The contents of the document never leaked out. In the district of Rajshahi, however, the District Superintendent of Police came to know that there was an anti-Partition memorial, which was being signed, and he wanted to have a copy of it. My friend, Babu Kissory Mohan Chowdhury, who was entrusted with the signature of the memorial in the district, asked for my instructions. I replied telling him that the document was confidential and was not to be shown to any one except the actual signatories.

We submitted this memorial, signed by representative men in eighteen out of the twenty-five districts of Bengal, about the end of June, 1911, and the Despatch of the Government of India recommending the modification of the Partition of Bengal was dated August 25, 1911; and some of the arguments that we urged in the memorial were accepted by the Government as valid reasons for the modification of the Partition, and were emphasized in the Despatch.

The Partition was modified on December 12, 1911, by the announcement made by His Majesty at Delhi. I had heard about it a week before; but from the general public and from the newspaper Press it was kept a secret. Indeed, the officials and others most interested knew nothing at all about it until the actual announcement was made, and some of them were staggered at the news. Among them was the late Nawab Salimulla of Dacca, who was the Government's right-hand man in supporting the Partition and securing the assent of the Mohamedan community of East Bengal. He got a G.C.I.E. as a solace, but to the last he remained unconvinced and unreconciled. As a gentleman, the Nawab was without an equal. As a politician, he was narrow, but shrewd, with a fund of common sense that made him a tower of strength to his supporters and the Government.

In the meantime expectation ran high in Calcutta. All eyes were centred on the Durbar at Delhi. Some announcement was expected. The King had come out to India; the King was expected to do something beneficent and to appease the excitement and unrest in Bengal. Nothing definite was indeed known. But hope builds a pyramid upon a point. The *Bengalee* office was crowded with expectant visitors throughout the day, anxious to know the news from Delhi. The hours rolled by. Disappointment was visible on the countenances of the assembled visitors. It was late in the afternoon; but there was no news about the Partition. Late in the day, the Associated Press sent a message from Delhi, but it contained not a word about the Partition. There were friends sitting near me in my editorial room, eager and anxious, but growing despondent at the absence of all reference to the Partition in the last message from Delhi. I dictated an article, which was to appear the day after, expressing profound dissatisfaction at the Partition not being modified, at the same time urging our people not to lose heart, but to continue the agitation.

Having dictated the article and revised it, I went downstairs, preparing to leave office, when I was summoned back to the telephone and heard the news that the Partition had been modified. There was quite a crowd at the *Bengalee* office at the time. The news spread like wildfire. People came in throngs to the office. A huge gathering had assembled in College Square, and I was seized by my friends, put into a carriage, and literally carried by force to College Square. There I witnessed a wild scene of excitement. It was quite dark – there were no lights – we could not see one another, but we could hear voices shouting with joy and occasionally interjecting questions. A voice from crowd cried out, 'What do you think of the transfer of the capital to Delhi?' I said at once, 'We are not likely to lose very much by it.' Subsequent events have demonstrated that I was substantially right in my impromptu answer.

I returned home from the meeting happy at the thought that for six long years my friends and myself had not worked in vain, and that our efforts to restore to the Bengalee-speaking population their ancient union and solidarity were crowned with success. The secret is told in less than half-a-dozen words. We were persistent, we were confident of success; we religiously avoided unconstitutional methods and the wild hysterics that breed and stimulate them. Even when attacked by the police, we did not retaliate. We shouted *Bande-Mataram* at each stroke of the police *làthi,* and then appealed to the constituted courts of law for redress. Passive resistance we practised. Soul-force we believed in; but we never were under the delusion that it could be employed to any useful or national purpose, except by men trained in the practice of self-restraint and the discipline of public life. It is the acceptance of naked principles, without reference to the circumstances of their application, which is responsible for many of the deplorable events that have darkened the pages of recent Indian history.

It is a pity that the Partition of Bengal was not modified in 1906, when Mr. John Morley denounced it from his place in the House of Commons as 'a measure which went wholly and decisively against the wishes of the majority of the people concerned', at the same declaring it to be 'a settled fact'. A pronouncement in which the conclusion was so wholly inconsistent with the premises only served to add to the irritation and intensify the agitation. The Partition and the policy that was adopted to support it were the root cause of the anarchical movement in Bengal, and I have no doubt in my mind that, if it had been modified just when the agitation was assuming a serious aspect and the whole country was seething with excitement, the history of Bengal, and possibly of India, would have been differently written, and our province would have been spared the taint of anarchism. Here again the psychological moment was allowed to pass by, and the modification came when it was overdue. The words, 'too late' were once more written on every line of British policy.

I cannot pass from the subject without referring to some of the prominent persons who took part in the anti-Partition and *Swadeshi* movement and shared its troubles and risks. Some of them are now dead. Among these may be mentioned Mr. Ananda Mohan Bose, Maharaja Surya Kanto Acharya Chowdhury of Mymensingh, Babu Ambika Churn Majumder and Mr. Bhupendra Nath Basu. Of Ananda Mohan Bose and Bhupendra Nath Basu I have written elsewhere and in another connexion. Maharaja Surya Kanto Acharya Chowdhury, before the anti-Partition controversy, took little or no interest in politics. He was a man of wealth, and *shikar* was the pleasure and the passion of his life. He took to it far more seriously than many people take to their business. By nature he was an enthusiast, and, when his feelings were roused, he spared neither money nor pains to attain his object. For a man in his position, in those days, to stand up against the Government, in regard to a measure upon which it had set its heart, needed no little courage and strength of purpose. It was a much more serious affair than voting against Government in the Legislative Council. Lord Curzon undertook a tour in the eastern districts, and at Mymensingh, the Maharaja's headquarters, he became his guest. The Viceroy was treated with princely hospitality: but the Maharaja never flinched in maintaining an attitude of unbending opposition to the Partition of Bengal and frankly expressing his opinion to the Viceroy. That attitude was maintained by him throughout the whole of the controversy, and even in the darkest days of repression, when the leaders of the anti-Partition movement were, in the eyes of the authorities, so many political suspects.

I well remember his attending the first boycott meeting on August 7, 1905, dressed in the roughest *Swadeshi* garb, which alone was then available. It was in his house in Lower Circular Road that many of our meetings were held and many of the most momentous decisions taken. He died just on the eve of the deportations in

Bengal, and there was some apprehension, not perhaps well-founded, that if he had lived he would have shared the fate of many of his friends and co-workers. His death has left a gap among the zemindars of East Bengal which has not been filled. For courage, virility and strength of purpose, he stood head and shoulders above the men of his class, and left behind him an enduring example for imitation and guidance.

Babu Aswini Kumar Dutt of Barisal was another leader of East Bengal who came into prominence. He was a schoolmaster and proprietor of the Brojomohan College at Barisal. It was founded in honour of his father, as a memorial of filial piety, but it was Aswini Kumar Dutt's devotion and organizing powers that made it one of the most successful educational institutions in East Bengal or in the whole of province. Aided by Babu Satis Chunder Chatterjee, a colleague of his in the Brojomohan College, he organized the whole district for the *Swadeshi* movement. These organizations rendered splendid service; and when famine broke out in Barisal Mr. Dutt was able to afford substantial help to the sufferers. The relief of the famine-stricken and the spread of the *Swadeshi* cause went hand in hand.

Those were days of conflict and controversy between the officials and the representatives of the people; and Aswini Kumar Dutt and his friends in Barisal felt the full weight of official displeasure and all that it implied. In 1908, Mr. Dutt and his friend and lieutenant, Mr. Satis Chunder Chatterjee, were deported without a trial. The reasons for their deportation will possibly remain a state secret for many long years. But, apart from the general reasons that make deportations without trial repugnant to the ordinary canons of law and justice, it seemed extraordinary that men like Aswini Kumar Dutt and Satis Chunder Chatterjee, who never harboured an unconstitutional idea or uttered an unconstitutional sentiment in their lives, should have been dealt with in this way under an old and forgotten regulation, intended to be employed against quasi-rebels. The general impression at the time was that the authorities wanted to put down Swadeshism, and they sought to strike terror among *Swadeshi* workers by this extraordinary procedure adopted against some of their most prominent leaders. But repression did not kill Swadeshism. Its decline was largely due to the failure of many *Swadeshi* enterprises, and the removal of the root cause by the modification of the Partition.

Babu Ananda Chunder Roy of Dacca must now claim attention

as one of the outstanding figures of the anti-Partition movement. The undisputed leader of the Dacca Bar, Ananda Chunder Roy occupied a position of unrivalled influence among the Hindu leaders of that city; and the whole of that influence he exerted, and with conspicuous success, for the promotion of the *Swadeshi* movement and the modification of the Partition. It is no mean testimony to his public spirit and that of the Hindu citizens of Dacca that, for the sake of maintaining the solidarity of the Bengalee-speaking population, they strenuously opposed a scheme that would have made their city the capital of a new province, with all its attendant advantages. Ananda Chunder Roy was one of the stalwarts of the anti-Partition movement, and never faltered in his opposition to the Partition. In the same category must be placed Anath Bandhu Guha of Mymensingh. As head of the Mymensingh Bar, he wielded great influence. In those days to be a popular leader was to incur the displeasure of the authorities. Anath Bandhu Guha was in their bad books. He was not indeed deported. I believe he narrowly escaped it; but he was bound down to keep the peace under section 110 of the Criminal Procedure Code. It was a gross insult to a man of his position. But with him it was not merely a sentimental grievance, for he suffered from it, as under the rules then in force he was disqualified for election to the local Legislative Council. When he applied for the removal of the disqualification, the Local Government, which had the power to remove it, rejected the application. Fortunately this rule and several others of the same character have been done away with on the recommendation of the Southborough Committee, and the range of executive discretion has been curtailed.

Last but not least among the distinguished men who identified themselves with the anti-Partition and *Swadeshi* movement and supported it throughout was Ambika Churn Majumder. He was rightly called the Grand Old Man of Faridpore (his native district) and of East Bengal. In intellectual eminence, in the possession of the gift of eloquence, and in unflinching love and devotion to the motherland, he stood in the forefront among the leaders of Bengal. He began life as a schoolmaster. He was my colleague in the Metropolitan Institution of Pundit Vidyasagar; but he early took to politics, and his interest in it was never-failing. He was associated with the Congress almost from its birth and was the President of one of the most memorable Congresses ever held, that of 1916, which adopted the Lucknow Convention and sealed the union between Hindus and Mohamedans in their efforts to secure their conmmon political advancement.

Ambika Churn Majumder felt so strongly about the Partition that he once told me that, if the Partition was not modified, he would sell off his ancestral property in the new province and settle in West Bengal, and he seriously asked me to purchase some landed property for him in the 24-Parganas. He controlled the *Swadeshi* and anti-Partition movement in the district of Faridpore, and was always ready with his advice and active assistance whenever required. So great was his influence that on one occasion, in the height of the anti-Partition agitation, when the Lieutenant-Governor arrived at Faridpore, he found the railway station denuded of coolies, and the subordinate police had to carry the luggage of the ruler of the province.

It has been said by a great writer that the public affections are but an expansion of the domestic feelings, and that patriotism has its roots amid the sanctities of the home and the tranquil surroundings of village life. Faridpore, his native district, will remember Ambika Churn Majumder as one of its greatest benefactors. He was for years the Chairman of the Faridpore Municipality, and the town of Faridpore owes its waterworks largely to his initiative and to his administrative vigour and efficiency. The Faridpore College, which has recently been established, is another monument of his public spirit, his capacity for solid achievement, and his unflinching love for the people among whom he was born and lived. Prostrated by disease, suffering from bereavements, which darkened his home, his interest in public work remained unabated, and from time to time, as occasion required, the Grand Old Man spoke out with the decisive emphasis of his younger days. In the schism that took place between the two wings of the Nationalist party over the Reform Scheme, Ambika Churn Majumder never hesitated, never wavered, but threw in his lot, with characteristic ardour, with his friends of the Moderate party with whom he had worked through life.

29

Work in the Imperial Council

Sundry Resolutions – reform of Calcutta University – Local Self-government – the Bengal Internments – Provincial Autonomy – recruiting work.

THE PARTITION OF BENGAL having been modified, my objection to joining the Legislative Councils was removed. Early in 1913, I stood as a candidate for election to the Bengal as well as the Imperial Legislative Council. I was elected for both at the head of the poll, but with me it was not all plain sailing. There was a load of prejudice against which I had to contend. I had just finished the anti-Partition campaign. It was a hard tussle; and I had made many enemies. I had to say many unpleasant things, and they were now to be brought up against me in the attempt that was made to disqualify me for election to the Imperial Legislative Council. My disqualification for the Bengal Council had indeed been removed by Sir Edward Baker, the Lieutenant-Governor; my disqualification for the higher Council on the ground of my dismissal from the Civil Service some forty years ago still remained. Lord Hardinge was then lying ill at Dehra Dun, suffering from the effects of the dastardly attempt upon his life; and Sir Guy Fleetwood Wilson, the senior member of the Executive Council, was in charge of the Government. He was known to be a man of liberal views; and he and his civilian colleagues had to deal with the question of my disqualification. An enquiry was started, and several volumes of the *Bengalee* newspaper were requisitioned from the Imperial Library in Calcutta, and carefully examined in order to discover if any element of sedition could be traced in its columns.

In the meantime, Lord Carmichael, Governor of Bengal, was growing impatient at the delay in the elections, and my friends, among whom were some Europeans in high official positions, were growing apprehensive lest the Government of India should provoke an agitation by disqualifying me. Such a decision would on the face of it be absurd; for, if I was good enough for the Bengal Legislative Council, surely I was good enough for the Imperial Council. Everybody, including Lord Carmichael himself, felt that it would be a grievous blunder. Happily, good sense prevailed in the counsels of the Government, and a blunder was averted. Almost at the first interview I had with Lord Hardinge after my election, he said to me, 'Mr. Banerjea, you owe your position in my Council to me.' I thanked His Excellency, but did not go deeper into the matter, as it might look like an attempt to ferret out official secrets.

I became a member of the Imperial Legislative Council in February, 1913, and in the following month I moved a Resolution recommending the separation of the judicial and executive functions in the administration of criminal justice. There was nothing original in the Resolution. The subject had for a long time been before the public. The most prominent Indian public worker, who took a special interest in it, and with whose name the genesis of the public agitation on this subject will be associated, was the late Mr. Monomohan Ghose. The most distinguished criminal lawyer of his generation in India, he was deeply impressed with the evils arising from this combination of judicial and executive functions. Mr. Monomohan Ghose got up a representation, which was submitted to the Secretary of State for India, signed by Lord Hobhouse, Sir Richard Garth, late Chief Justice of Bengal, Sir Raymond West, late Judge of the Bombay High Court, Mr. Herbert Reynolds, late Member of the Board of Revenue, Bengal, and others, pointing out the evils of the system and calling for its reform. The late Mr. Romesh Chunder Dutt formulated a scheme for the introduction of the reform in Bengal.

In 1908, Sir Harvey Adamson, then Home Member, had declared from his place in the Imperial Legislative Council that the Government of India had definitely decided to introduce the reform in a cautious and tentative way. Five years had elapsed since this declaration, but nothing had been done. My Resolution therefore was clearly opportune. It is worthy of remark that every non-official Indian member supported it. It was negatived by the vote of the official majority. But it was obvious that there were officials who favoured my motion; and after the debate was over, Sir Guy Fleetwood Wilson, who presided in the absence of the Viceroy, came up to where I sat, and said, 'Mr. Banerjea, if I had had two votes, an official and a personal one, I should have given the personal vote in your favour.'

The Resolution, I understand, though negatived, formed the subject of a despatch to the Secretary of State by the Government of India, who, according to my information, supported the proposal. But as it involved considerations of finance it had to run the gauntlet of the India Council, which rejected it. However that may be, the system is doomed. The Government of Bengal under the Reforms has formulated a scheme for the separation. The matter is under consideration. Finance, as usual, stands in the way.

Among other matters in regard to which I moved Resolutions were the question of the Press Act, Education, the recommendations of the Decentralization Commission relating to the expansion of Local Self-government, the appointment of an advisory committee to deal with internees, and finally the Reform proposals contained in the Montagu-Chelmsford Scheme. I pressed for a modification of the Press Act, not for its repeal; for I knew that as a matter of practical politics its repeal was out of the question. I urged that the safeguards which had been promised by the Government should be made operative and not rendered illusory, as they were declared to be by the Chief Justice, Sir Lawrence Jenkins, in the *Comrade* case. The voting on the non-official Indian side was practically unanimous; but there was again the official majority, and the motion was defeated. I had expected no better result, but I thought that it was possible that, as the result of the debate, the administration of the Press Act would follow more popular and conciliatory lines. I cannot say that that hope was realized. The complaints against the administration of the Press Act continued as loud and as persistent after the debate as before; the influence of the solid phalanx of the non-official Indian minority was powerless to modify the policy of the Government.

The Morley-Minto Councils were constituted as advisory bodies; and to the last they retained this character, even when the unanimity of Indian public opinion was expressed with unequivocal emphasis. Only on two occasions do I remember the official vote yielding to the pressure of non-official opinion. One was when a Resolution was moved for the postponement of a Bill relating to the organization of the presidency banks; the other was for the appointment of a committee to enquire into the complaints of postal and telegraph clerks and subordinates. But these were not proposals involving important questions of principle or policy.

The reform of the Calcutta University looms largely in the public view. We have before us a great measure of reform recommended by what is known as the 'Sadler Commission'. It involves far-reaching changes and heavy outlay. There was one little change in the existing constitution of the Calcutta University which I ventured to suggest from my place in the Imperial Legislative Council, in a

Resolution I moved in March, 1916. I recommended that the University should be autonomous and that the Chancellor should be the Governor of the province, instead of the Viceroy, the Calcutta University being thus placed upon the same footing as the sister universities of Madras and Bombay in respect of its relations with the head of the local Government. The Resolution was accepted by Sir Sankaran Nair on behalf of the Government.

As Education Minister, Sir Sankaran Nair was a success, at any rate from the Indian standpoint. From the judicial bench he was transferred to the Executive Council of the Viceroy. He had no practical familiarity with educational problems or those of Local Self-government. But in dealing with them he shewed capacity, judgment and firmness. Once again he has proved the truth that our best men, taken from whatever positions they fill in life, are equal to the highest executive offices. That has been the experience of all free countries. It has been repeated in India. Sir Sankaran was not an educationist, but to him we owe the Behar University Act, which breaks new ground and is one of the most advanced of its kind. Sir Sankaran Nair resigned owing to differences with his colleagues in regard to the Punjab disturbances. Whatever the merits of the controversy may have been, his resignation was evidence of the readiness of Indians in high office to retire from it for the sake of principle. Lord Sinha, when Member of the Viceroy's Executive Council, is reported to have resigned over the Press Bill in Lord Minto's time, and withdrawn his resignation only in order not to add to the difficulties of a situation created by the assassination of a Deputy Superintendent of Police. In the case of several whom I knew, the acceptance of office as a member of the Executive Council was a real sacrifice.

But while I was congratulating myself on having done a service to my university, some of those who were my colleagues were up in arms against me. They held a meeting of the Committee of the Indian Association, and I narrowly escaped censure by the adjournment of the motion, which was never taken up. And now the reform that I had pressed for, and for which I was blamed by my colleagues, is an accomplished fact. The Governor of Bengal is now the Chancellor of the University of Calcutta and the University is none the worse for it.

Such are the rewards of public life in India; but it was only a foretaste of what was to come, when no language was sufficiently strong to condemn one, the head and front of whose offence was that he had preferred duty to the vanishing fumes of an evanescent popularity. The opposition to my motion among my friends of the Indian Association was partly sentimental and partly based upon practical grounds. They did not like the withdrawal of the Viceroy from the Chancellorship. That was a point of dignity. Further, the Government of India had made large grants to the Calcutta University, and they apprehended that the flow of beneficence from the Central Government would receive a check from the discontinuance of the Viceroy's personal relationship with the University. The question of dignity never troubled me. The financial consideration was more weighty, but it was bound to be short-lived, as no exceptional treatment in administration can long endure.

In the cause of Local Self-government I have always felt very great interest. I agitated for it as an instrument of political advancement even before the Resolution of Lord Ripon of October, 1881; and ever since its inauguration I had been associated with its practical working. I felt that it was my duty to take advantage of my presence in the Imperial Legislative Council to press for its further expansion. There was no denying the fact that its growth was dwarfed by official neglect and apathy. It really meant the withdrawal of power from the bureaucracy; and bureaucracy all over the world is so enamoured of power that it resents its curtailment. As Lord Morley pointed out in one of his despatches that as there was little of real power vested in the popular members of the local bodies, they felt little or no interest in their work. In March, 1914, I moved a Resolution recommending that the Presidents of District and Local Boards be elected and that a Local Government Board should be created in each province. The Resolution was opposed by Government and was lost, as might have been expected. But I have the satisfaction of feeling that official opinion has within the last few years steadily advanced towards the acceptance of my views. The Government of India, by their Resolution of May 18, 1918, urged Local Governments to arrange for the election of the Chairmen for the rural boards wherever possible; and in Bengal, all District and Local Boards have since been allowed this right. As Minister of Local Self-government, it was my privilege to have helped this movement forward. In 1919, when I was in England as a member of the Moderate Deputation, I was appointed by the Secretary of State as a member of a Committee to enquire into the institutions of Local Self-government in the United Kingdom as regards their applicability to Indian conditions. I was convinced of the desirability of establishing in each province a Local Government Board, so far as practicable on the English model, for the co-ordination and further development of the activities of our local bodies; and I urged this view in my Report. I understand that in the main it has been accepted by the Governments of Assam and the Central Provinces, but has been objected to by the Bengal and other Governments.

In the reformed Bengal Council the question was raised by Mr. D. C. Ghose. My sympathies as Minister of Local Self-government were all with him; but financial difficulties blocked the way. Perhaps in happier times and under the pressure of a steadily progressive public opinion, we may have in Bengal a Government Board, more or less modelled upon the parent local institution in England, ensuring to our system of Local Self-government the stimulus, the concentration of effort and the co-ordination of methods, so essential to success.

Popular assemblies in all countries, subject of course to varying conditions and ever-changing limitations, have been the bulwark of popular rights. They are sometimes apt to go to extremes, and, overlooking the difficulties of Government, to ignore responsibilities of which no Government can divest itself. Nevertheless their guidance is valuable. It is through popular assemblies that popular opinion even in its extreme forms reaches the ears of Government, whose mission is that of the peacemaker, dispensing justice to all interests, making the welfare and the safety of the State its supreme concern. In Bengal in 1918 many persons were interned under an Act similar to that in operation in England at that time. Great as was the excitement, it was aggravated by mistakes inseparable from a procedure that encouraged secrecy and eschewed publicity, the strongest safeguard for the righteous dispensation of justice. An extraordinary mistake – and it was not the only one – was committed in what is known as the *Sindhubala* case. There were two *sindhubalas* in the Bankura District. Only one of them was wanted. The police authorities cut the Gordian knot by arresting both and marching them to prison through the public streets, although they were *purdanashin* ladies, who by the custom of the country were not to appear in public. But the climax was reached when, after twelve or thirteen days' detention in jail, they were both released; because forsooth there was not a scrap of evidence against them. It was a real tragedy in public affairs. There could hardly be a more grievous blunder. The policemen concerned were neither better nor worse than the class to which they belonged. They were in this case the victims of a discarded and obsolete system that reminded one of the days of the Star Chamber, and made secrecy the pivot of the whole machinery. Bengal was seething with excitement. That respectable women should have been insulted and humiliated, treated as malefactors, and that their status and position should have afforded them no protection, and all under the cover of a law that shut out the light of publicity, threw Bengal into a paroxysm of rage and indignation. I felt that here was an occasion when from my place in the Council I should voice the public sentiment of my province. I moved for the appointment of an Advisory Committee to deal with all cases of internment and deportation under Regulation III of 1818 and cognate laws. The terms of the Resolution were as follows:

'This Council recommends to the Governor-General in Council that a Committee with an adequate Indian element thereon be appointed in each province to enquire into and report upon—

(1) all cases of internment under the Defence of India Act;
(2) all cases of detentions under Bengal Regulation III of 1818 and cognate Regulations in Madras and Bombay; and
(3) all cases of persons who may hereafter be dealt with under the aforesaid Act and Regulations; the Committee being empowered to make recommendations with regard to the health, allowance, place of detention and other matters relating to the prisoners referred to above.'

Before the motion came on for debate, I had the opportunity of discussing it with the Home Member, Sir William Vincent. This was helpful to me, and I think it was useful to the Government. We could ascertain the points of agreement and the points of difference; and then, if necessary, fly at each other's throats. The reply of the Home Member was, of course, a defence of the Government, but it was also conceived in a vein of sympathy. In substance he accepted my Resolution and agreed to the appointment of an Advisory Committee. The concession was welcomed by the Indian Press, which was steadily developing Extremist leanings. Mr. Justice Beachcroft and the late Sir Narayan Chandravarkar were appointed members of the Committee; and in Bengal, I understood, six out of one hundred *détenus* were recommended for release by the Committee. The appointment of the Committee and its labours had a mollifying effect on public opinion. It did not indeed reconcile public opinion to the internments but it made them rather less unacceptable than before.

Here it may not be out of place to refer to the debate that took place in the Imperial Legislative Council, in connexion with the Rowlatt Act. It was a coercive measure that was a departure from the ordinary criminal law of the land, and evoked wide-spread opposition, which found its echo in the Council Chamber. Mr. Srinivasa Shastri, Dr. Tej Bahadur Sapru and myself were invited to an informal conference to discuss the matter with the Home Member, Sir William Vincent. We were all opposed to the Bill. Sir William agreed to make it temporary, but still we could not see our way to supporting it. In the Council I strongly opposed the Bill and warned the Government of the serious step it was about to take and of the intense agitation which it was bound to provoke. But our protest was of no avail. The Bill was passed into law; but it remained a dead letter, its provisions never being given effect. Our prophecy, however, was literally fulfilled. The Rowlatt Act was the parent of the Non-Co-operation movement.

The despatch of August 25, 1911, was a memorable one. It was a landmark in our annals. It recommended the modification of the Partition of Bengal, but it did something more. It promised the boon of provincial autonomy; and in all our subsequent Provincial Conferences special emphasis was laid on this pledge, and its speedy fulfilment was urged. In the Legislative Council I raised this point. The discussion was about the budget, and I pressed for the financial independence of the provinces as a part of the scheme of provincial autonomy. The view was challenged by Sir William Meyer, the Finance Minister, who said that I was 'an impatient idealist'. I retorted by replying that I certainly was an idealist, but not of the impatient or of the unpractical order, and that many of my ideals had been fulfilled, or were on the high road to consummation. In a conversation with Lord Hardinge, who was then Viceroy and was the author of the despatch, he said, 'Mr. Banerjea, you will have provincial autonomy in ten years' time.' We had indeed the beginnings of it much earlier.

In the elections of 1916, I lost my seat in the Imperial Legislative Council. Mr. Bhupendra Nath Basu and Mr. Sitanath Roy were the successful candidates. I reverted once again to the normal public life, outside the Council, that had been mine for the last forty years. The war had broken out in 1914, and an appeal was made for recruitment to the people of Bengal. I went about from town to town urging my countrymen of the better classes to enlist as soldiers and fight for the Empire, which was in danger. I addressed more than thirty meetings in different parts of the province. The keynote of my address was that self-government, which was the goal of our political aspirations, connoted self-defence, and that, if we sought the privileges of Imperial citizenship, we must bear its burdens and responsibilities, and the foremost among them was to fight for the defence of the Empire. The appeal went home, and in not one of the numerous meetings that were held was there a single dissentient voice heard. Non-Co-operation had not yet reared its head; and there was not the faintest trace of those developments in the political situation that now attract so large a measure of public attention.

To me, these recruitment meetings were a novel experience. I found myself for the first time in my public life standing side by side, and on the same platform, with high Government officials, pleading for a common cause, and receiving from them the courtesy for which I was hardly prepared. We were able to raise something over six thousand recruits, mostly from among the respectable classes in Bengal. The quality of the recruits, it is said, did not always come up to the mark; but it has to be borne in mind that this was altogether a novel experiment, and that for a hundred and fifty years Bengal had been a stranger to the art and the practice of soldiering. It is within my personal knowledge that many of the young men showed great enthusiasm, and that in some cases they defied even the sanctity of parental authority in order to satisfy their soldierly aspirations. Bengal is after all not such an unpromising field for recruitment, if one goes about it the right way. It is therefore with a sense of keen regret and disappointment that one notices the poor response that Bengal has made to the call for enlistment in the Territorial Army. It was a movement in which the leaders of Indian public opinion, including those of Bengal, took a keen interest. I claim to have had a hand in expediting through the Legislative Council the Act creating the Indian Territorial Army. The failure in Bengal is largely due to the spirit that Non-Co-operation has evoked among the classes from whom the Territorial force is to be recruited. With the subsidence of Non-Co-operation I expect better days for the movement.

Indeed, within the last few months, a great change has taken place in the political situation. The cult of Non-Co-operation, which dominated the political horizon, to-day stands suspended. Its constituent features, with one exception, have been dropped. All the boycotts, save that of foreign cloth, have been withdrawn. The fact is an open proclamation of its failure on the part of the leaders of the movement. A victorious general rushing to an assured triumph, with the monuments of his success strewn around him, would never think of abandoning, suspending or modifying his programme. It is a confession of failure, which no plea, however plausible and however closely it may be linked with a great name, can obscure. By all impartial spectators its doom was indeed foreseen and was felt to be inevitable. As far as the great leaders were concerned, Non-Co-operation had its roots in an intense and consuming love of country, coupled with hatred of the British Government, and all associated with it in the administration of the country. But as regards the non-co-operating masses, hatred of the British Government, its officials, and Englishmen in general, was the inspiring impulse. And when a sentiment is firmly rooted in the public mind it grows and expands. And from a hatred of the Government to that of political and religious opponents and of other castes and creeds, the transition was rapid and irresistible. Mr. Gandhi is my authority for it. He said that 'it was apparent that Non-Co-operation could not, in the present state of things, be presented by the nation as a national programme', for, said he, 'they were non-co-operating among themselves by carrying on a programme of hatred and violence amongst themselves.' It is this sentiment of hatred fostered amongst the masses, directed in the first instance against the British Government, that came, by a natural process of growth, to be extended to all others who worshipped in a different temple, culminating in those communal and caste feuds that have darkened our recent history. I cannot help thinking that these leaders were playing with fire, and they have intensified a feeling already latent, that in its development has been attended with disastrous results. Of course, we all admire the supreme solicitude and the earnest efforts of Mr. Gandhi to secure Hindu-Moslem unity. But, in judging of the communal strifes, which we all deplore, let us not, for the sake of historic justice, forget the part the Non-Co-operation movement had in fostering and promoting it.

30

The Reforms and the Growth of Extremism

Grant of responsible government, 1917 – Mr. Montagu in India – the Montagu-Chelmsford Report – cleavage between Moderates and Extremists – speech in the Imperial Council on the Reforms – interview with the Viceroy – what the Moderate party stands for – the Franchise Committee – unveiling of the Dadabhaï Naoroji portrait.

THE MOST STIRRING EVENT IN 1917 was the announcement made by Mr. Montagu in the House of Commons promising the grant of responsible government, to be realized by progressive stages. The announcement roused mixed feelings – hope in those who had not altogether lost faith in British pledges and promises; doubts and misgivings among the wavering; and incredulity among the sceptical. It was followed by a declaration, dramatic in its character, and bewildering in its novelty. Mr. Montagu announced that he would visit India, accompanied by a deputation, to consult Indian leaders and ascertain Indian public opinion. There could now be no suspicion as to his earnestness, or his personal sincerity. It was a memorable departure from the old official ways, and even the sceptics began to feel that here was a Secretary of State who had other qualifications than mere speech-making, and that some real work was intended. The pages of Anglo-Indian history were strewn with the fragments of broken promises (*disjecta membra*), but perhaps a new chapter was now to be opened.

Mr. Montagu came out to India with his Deputation in November, and began a thorough investigation of the problems involved. He visited many parts of the country and examined witnesses, Indian as well as European. The witnesses were examined in batches of two or three, and were subjected to severe cross-examination. Mr. Montagu was a past master in the art. I had to go through the ordeal along with Mr. R. N. Mudholkar of the Central Provinces, who was my companion in the examination. Later on, I had a further conversation with Mr. Montagu, when the idea of a diarchy had been developed. Mr. Lionel Curtis was, I believe, the originator of this idea. He came out to India about this time and held several conferences. I attended some of them, including one at Darjeeling at which some Extremist leaders, including Mr. C. R. Das, were present. Non-Co-operation had not then come into existence, and the atmosphere was serene. So far as I can remember, no serious objection was raised to diarchy or the placing of some of the departments under popular ministers responsible to the Legislative Council. Mr. Curtis was a firm believer in diarchy as a halfway house to full responsible government. He spoke with the fervid faith of an apostle. Of him, it could be truly said that he came and saw and conquered. He had conferences with the representatives of the European community, who at the outset had grave misgivings with regard to the whole scheme. Their idea was – and it found expression in the newspapers at the time – that the Government should begin by perfecting the system of Local Self-Government, and should then tackle the wider question of responsible government. In the course of the discussions that they held with Mr. Curtis and others (Lord Sinha being one) they modified their views; and, when they did so, let it be said to their credit, they never wavered or faltered and stuck to them with the tenacity characteristic of Englishmen. And now among the best friends of the Reforms are the non-official European community, who recognize the destiny that awaits India, namely, that she must through progressive stages become an equal partner of the British Commonwealth. In the Bengal Legislative Council, the European members usually acted with the Moderates, and their relations with the representatives of the Moderate party were friendly and even cordial. I remember that only in one matter was there a serious difference between them and their Hindu colleagues, and that was in regard to the question of communal representation in the Calcutta Corporation. They were in favour of such representation for the European community. They naturally looked at the matter from their own point of view. The European community had a separate electorate for themselves, to ensure proper and adequate representation of their interests, and they necessarily thought that what was good for them was equally good for the Mohamedan community, overlooking the fact that their case stood apart from that of the Mohamedans; that the Hindus and Mohamedans were bound to form, sooner or later, a united nationality, and that the communal system was a hindrance to the development of Indian nationhood.

In the meantime a storm was brewing that was destined to cause a serious split in the ranks of Indian politicians. On July 8, 1918, the Montagu-Chelmsford Report was published. It was the signal of war. There was an angry outcry from the Extremist organs. Even Mrs. Besant, who now takes the view of the Moderate party in regard to the Scheme, denounced it in her own eloquent and emphatic style. 'The scheme is unworthy to be offered by England or to be accepted by India' – so thundered forth Mrs. Besant in her organ, *New India*, on the very day the Scheme was published. Curiously enough, on the selfsame day a manifesto issued by fifteen gentlemen of Madras condemned the Scheme in terms equally emphatic. 'It is so radically wrong', said they, 'alike in principle and in detail that it is impossible to modify or improve it.' The late Mr. Tilak said the same thing in his simple and straightforward fashion. 'The Montagu Scheme' observed Mr. Tilak, 'is entirely unacceptable.'

In the midst of all this excitement and ferment, a special session of the Congress was called to consider the Report, and we who did not profess the same extreme views had to decide what we should do. Should we attend the Congress or not? We decided to abstain. We felt that these hasty and extreme views would dominate the deliberations of the Congress, and that we should not lend them the weight of our support by our presence. We accordingly held a conference of the Moderate party in Bombay on November 1, 1918. I was elected President. It was the first of the Moderate Conferences, which are now held from year to year. Some of our friends, the Rt. Hon. Mr. Shastri and the Hon. Sir Narasingha Sarma among others, continued to attend the Congress, in the hope of making their influence felt. But it was a vain hope. The Congress has become more Extremist than ever, and they have since discontinued their attendance. We have parted company – it is difficult to say for how long.

The schism indeed did not take place without a strenuous attempt on our part to arrive at a compromise. Our divisions have been the fruitful source of our weakness, and we tried to prevent a fresh one. Fully three weeks before the meeting of the Congress I wired to the Joint Secretary and to Mrs. Besant, asking them to postpone the Special Session of the Congress for a short time, for an interchange of views which might help to bring about an understanding. The request was not complied with, and at the last moment, just twenty-four hours before the sitting of the Congress, when a final effort was made, it was far too late – the psychological moment had passed by.

Our decision to abstain from the Congress was, as events have shown, a wise one, and I claim that we of the Moderate party saved the scheme. The combination against it was formidable. The European Associations in India, now so earnest for the success of the Reforms, were severe in their criticisms; Lord Sydenham condemned it in the Press and from his place in the House of Lords, strangely enough quoting Mr. Tilak in support of his views. The *Manchester Guardian* complained that the Indian Extremists were playing into the hands of Lord Sydenham and his party. In the midst of this formidable body of opposition, the only real and consistent support came from the Moderate party in India. If they had remained within the Congress fold, they would have been overwhelmed, their voice would have been that of a minority of little or no account. The British democracy would have said, in view of the practically unanimous opposition offered to the Scheme: 'Well, if you don't want it, let us drop it altogether.' And, there being no other scheme to take its place, the prospects of responsible government would thus have been indefinitely postponed. Our difficulties were aggravated by the non-committal attitude of the British Government, whose Indian policy would necessarily be largely inspired by Lord Curzon, who was then a member of the Cabinet. Our anxieties were deepened by the proposal to appoint a Joint Committee of both Houses to deal with the recommendations of the Bill before its introduction. At such a time and amid these accumulating difficulties a decisive policy in support of the scheme was called for, if it was to be saved from wreckage; and the Moderate party resolved upon such a policy, even though separation from the Congress would be necessary. It was a heavy price to pay, but it had to be paid if the prospect of the speedy inauguration of the beginnings of responsible government were to be realized. We counted the cost and we made up our minds to incur it. To many of us, and to me in a special sense, separation from the Congress was a painful wrench. We had contributed to build up the great National Institution with our life-blood. We had raised it up from infancy to adolescence, from adolescence to maturity, and now, in full view of the crowning reward of our lifelong labours, we found the sacred temple of national unity swayed by divided counsels, resounding with the voice of conflict and controversy, and divorced from the healing accents of moderation and prudence. We could not but secede; for the difference between those who had captured the machinery of the Congress and ourselves was fundamental, and that upon a matter equally fundamental, namely, the question of self-government for India. The Congress, however great an organization, was after all a means to an end. That end was self-government. We decided to sacrifice the means for the end. That was the *raison d'être* of the Moderate or Liberal party as a separate entity in the public life of India.

This was the parting of the ways, Extremists and Moderates following their line of work, with something of the bitter reminiscences familiar to the members of a Hindu joint family broken up under the pressure of internecine strife. The Extremists were the loudest in their denunciations of the Moderates, who in this as in other matters did not forget the cardinal principle of their creed – moderation in all things. The Moderates were classed by their political opponents as allies of the bureaucracy, and bracketed with them in their denunciations; nor were their meetings safe from invasion. Noisy demonstrations and rowdyism were often the features of meetings called by them, to discuss public questions in which there were differences of opinion between them and the Extremists. At these demonstrations non-violent Non-Co-operation often developed into pugilistic encounters, in which the rattle of sticks harmonized musically with the shouts that were raised and the blows that were dealt. Never in the whole course of my public life, now extending over nearly half a century, have I in our public meetings witnessed scenes so disgraceful as those which have met my eyes in the course of the last four or five years. The words 'traitor' and 'shame' have become familiar terms in the vocabulary of the Swarajist wing of Non-Co-operation, which seeks to secure its triumph by soul-force. There was more of brute-force than soul-force in all these exhibitions; and what is most regrettable is that the young are dragged into these questionable proceedings with all their attendant demoralization. The ancient spirit of tolerance that has been the heritage of our people has disappeared, and practices have been encouraged that are disastrous to the best interests of the youth of the province.

However that may be, let us not forget that Extremism is of recent origin in Bengal. Our fathers, the firstfruits of English education, were violently pro-British. They could see no flaw in the civilization or the culture of the West. They were charmed by its novelty and its strangeness. The enfranchisement of the individual, the substitution of the right of private judgment in place of traditional authority, the exaltation of duty over custom, all came with the force and suddenness of a revelation to an Oriental people who knew no more binding obligation than the mandate of immemorial usage and of venerable tradition. The story is told in a biography, the authority of which has not been challenged, of one of the most brilliant representatives of early English culture in Bengal, the late Rev. Krishna Mohan Banerjee, throwing the refuse of a meal of forbidden food, on which he had fed himself, into the house of a neighbouring Brahmin. Everything English was good – even the drinking of brandy was a virtue; everything not English was to be viewed with suspicion. It was obvious that this was a passing phase of the youthful mind of Bengal; and that this temperament had concealed in it the seeds of its own decay and eventual extinction. In due time came the reaction, and with a sudden rush. And from the adoration of all things Western, we are now in the whirlpool of a movement that would recall us back to our ancient civilization, and our time-honoured ways and customs, untempered by the impact of the ages that have rolled by and the forces of modern life, now so supremely operative in shaping the destinies of mankind. Will this movement succeed? I have grave doubts; for such a movement is against the eternal verities of things and that divine law of progress which the Unseen Hand of an Invisible Power has inscribed on every page of human history. But, whether the movement succeeds or not, the reaction against pro-British tendencies was partly the creation of the British Government itself, for no British Government can be wholly un-British in its traditions. In India, it has given pledges and promises, generous and beneficent, and has founded institutions with great potentialities of self-rule. In 1833, the Charter Act removed all disqualifications as regards the eligibility of Indians to high office. But the Charter Act remained practically a dead letter. In 1858, the Queen's Proclamation made merit the sole test of qualification. Here again the pledges and promises made remained substantially unredeemed. Local Self-government was conceded in 1882; but the restrictions imposed, about which Lord Morley as Secretary of State complained, largely nullified the boon. Then came Lord Curzon and his unpopular measures, the Official Secrets Act, the Universities Act, and, last but not least, the Partition of Bengal. All these created a strong revulsion of feeling. The methods of government followed in the new province intensified the growing sentiment and the culminating point was reached by the dispersal of the Barisal Conference in 1906. If I were asked to point to a single occasion as marking the genesis of modern Extremism in Bengal with its further developments, I should say it was the chapter of events that took place at Barisal in 1906, in connexion with the break-up of the Bengal Provincial Conference. There was then an upheaval among the leading men of Bengal assembled at Barisal, the like of which I have not witnessed. Even a man like Mr. Bhupendra Nath Basu, lately a member of the Executive Council, a public man so sedate and calculating, used language which neither he nor I would care to repeat. It was a time of intense excitement; and our faith in the efficacy of constitutional agitation was shaken. If that was the temper of tried politicians, the attitude of the younger generation, who mustered strong at Barisal, may be imagined. This was in 1906. The Alipore Conspiracy Case was discovered in 1908. I returned home from Barisal full of indignation, with my unshakable optimism sensibly impaired; and one of the first things that I did was to sever what remained of my connexion with the Government. For the moment, I became a Non-Co-operator, one of the earliest apostles of that cult, and resigned my office as Presidency Magistrate of Calcutta and Honorary Magistrate of Barrackpore. The resignations were a protest against the action of the Barisal authorities, and did not represent my acceptance of a definite policy or principle. I did the same thing when in 1899 I resigned my office as a Municipal Commissioner of Calcutta along with twenty-seven members of the Corporation. There are occasions when we must 'non-co-operate' and follow it up as a protest. But I altogether repudiate a persistent policy of non-co-operation, especially at a time when the Government is prepared to move along progressive lines, though the pace may not be as rapid as we should like it to be.

It was in an atmosphere of extreme views that the Reforms came under discussion. I gave notice of a resolution to be moved by me in the Imperial Legislative Council, where Moderate opinion would have fair play and would strengthen the cause of the Reforms. I was not disappointed. It was a full-dress debate with the Viceroy in the chair. The case for the Reforms was argued from every possible point of view. The support accorded to the Resolution was gratifying. The whole House with two exceptions voted in favour of it. Let me here set forth the terms of the Resolution:

(1) This Council thanks His Excellency the Viceroy and the Secretary of State for India for the Reform Proposals, and recognizes them as a genuine effort and a definite advance towards the progressive realization of responsible government in India.

(2) 'This Council recommends to the Governor-General in Council that a Committee consisting of all the non-official Members of this Council be appointed to consider the Reforms Report and make recommendations to the Government of India.'

The Resolution was, as will be seen, divided into two parts and was separately put. In regard to both parts, there were only two dissentients. Mr. Patel, now a prominent member of the Non-Co-operation party, was one of the two members who voted against the first part. He did not think that the Reform proposals represented a definite advance towards the progressive realization of responsible government. In regard to the second part, two European members, namely, Mr. Hogg of the Bombay Chamber of Commerce and Mr. Ironside of the Bengal Chamber of Commerce, recorded their votes against it, though they were present at our Committee meetings and helped us with their advice. Their attitude was due to the absence of any instruction from the Chambers they represented. The European Chambers, as I have stated, are now in full sympathy with the Reforms, and in the Councils their representatives actively co-operate for its success. In connexion with this Resolution I should like here to quote a passage from my speech, which explains my attitude and that of the Moderate party in regard to the Reforms:

'Taking the Report as a whole, I think it must be conceded that it affords a striking illustration of a change in the angle of vision on the part of our rulers, and I venture to assert that it ought to be accompanied by a similar transformation in our attitude in regard to the Government of the country. If an advance, a substantial advance, towards peace, conciliation and popular contentment is made by our rulers, I submit that the clearest considerations of common sense and patriotism demand that it should be followed by a similar movement on our side. Adaptability is the law of life, individual and collective. Adaptability is life, the lack of it is death. Adaptability has been the saving principle of our race throughout its long and chequered history, and we should, in pursuance of that eternal law and time-honoured principle, adapt ourselves to our new-born conditions. And, my Lord, if I am permitted to interpose a personal remark, I will say this, that opposition to Government has been the watchword of my public life now extending over a period of forty-five years. I claim this – no matter whether it be a merit or demerit – I claim this, that no living Indian politician has been more strenuous, more persistent, in his resistance to the policy and the measures of the Government than I have been. But my Lord, a change – a welcome change – has come over the spirit of the dreams of our rulers, and they have now stretched out to us the hand of fellowship and friendship, and I invite my countrymen to grasp it with alacrity and enthusiasm, and in co-operation with British statesmanship to march forward to the accomplishment of those high destinies which, under the providence of God, are reserved for our people.

'My Lord, we live in a psychological moment in the history of our country. We are at the parting of the ways. The future is committed to our care and keeping. We can make or mar it. I appeal to my countrymen to make it by the exhibition of those qualities of courage, prudence, sobriety and self-restraint, coupled with patriotic devotion, which constitute the crowning attributes of national life. I make this appeal and trust that it will not fall upon heedless ears.'

I can only say this, that the speech was well received by the House and was appreciated by the Viceroy. The same evening at about 5 p.m. I was asked by a telephonic message to see the Viceroy. I was asleep at the time. When I got up and was informed about the message, I started for Viceregal Lodge. I had a long interview with His Excellency. He was surprised to find that I had been asleep so late in the afternoon, and he added in very kindly tones, 'You must have felt tired after your great effort. It is surprising that you should be sleeping at such an hour.' I said in reply, 'I can sleep whenever I like, and that is one of the secrets of my good health.' He said, 'Mr. Banerjea, that is Napoleonic.' We discussed the day's debate in the Council, and His Excellency thought that I should be the Chairman of the Committee, as I had moved for its constitution.

One of the charges brought against the Moderate party, and especially against myself, by a section of the Press, is that in public life I am no longer what I used to be, and that I have changed my colours. To change one's opinions in the light of new conditions is neither a crime nor a sin. Consistency is not always a virtue. It may sometimes mean persistency in error; and a progressive mind must from time to time reconsider old ideas in the light of altered circumstances. In my case I claim that I have never changed in fundamentals; but that, as regards details, I have shifted my ground according to varying conditions. For me, the goal has always remained the same; the essential condition for reaching it has also remained unchanged, but there have been variations as regards minor points of detail. With me the goal has always been Self-government within the Empire; the method for its attainment has been constitutional agitation. In view of the announcement of the 20th of August 1917, I had to consider whether the path now to be pursued should be co-operation with the Government, or non-co-operation, opposing and fighting the Government. In the first years of my public life, it was all opposition – strenuous, persistent and unremitting. But when at last the Government showed signs of an advance to meet the popular demand, and took definite measures towards that end, my opposition gave place to a readiness for co-operation. Our ends being the same and our co-operation being invited for building up the fabric of responsible government, should not opposition, I asked, give place to co-operation, willing and active co-operation for the great end which we had in common? It is not we who have changed; there has been a fundamental change in the policy and the aims and aspirations of the Government. We welcomed it; we modified our attitude towards the Government, and we co-operated with it for the attainment of Self-government. To oppose where we should co-operate would be the height of unpatriotism; it would be something worse, it would be treason against the motherland. This is strong language, but it is the only language that rightly describes the situation. There were indeed those who regarded the Reforms as a sham and a delusion, who thought that they were a huge fraud sprung upon a credulous and unwary public. We quite concede that they were entitled to use every means they considered legitimate to oppose them, though they were not entitled to abuse us for holding a different view. Recognizing that the Reforms represented a definite advance towards responsible government, to have opposed them would have been a betrayal of our principles and a neglect of our duty to the country. We were, however, under no delusion. We accepted the Reforms for what they were worth. We knew their limitations. But in the existing circumstances it seemed to us that the best thing we could do was to work them, to qualify for more, and to press for more. Here was an opportunity for peaceful, orderly and progressive realization of responsible government. What alternative was there? None that we could think of. We had to accept this evolutionary movement, culminating, in due time, in full-fledged responsible government, or follow the dubious paths of a revolutionary programme, with its endless risks and uncertain triumphs. A revolutionary movement had indeed been tried in Bengal, backed by men whose selfless devotion to the country could not be called in question; and it failed; and the principal actors in that unhappy episode, recognizing their failure, have for the most part settled down as peaceful citizens, bowing to the inevitable. In modern times, revolutionary movements have only been successful with the aid of trained and organized armies. Where is the army to assist the Indian revolutionary? And even when revolutions have succeeded, they have left behind them a trail of blood, and the memories of ruin and devastation, which have taken generations to efface and to repair. Revolution, said the great Edmund Burke, is the last resort of the thinking and the good. Evolution has been the motto of the Congress since its birth; and the old leaders of the Congress advocated the progressive realization of Self-government, which is the outstanding principle of the message of August 20, 1917. So far back as the year 1902, speaking as President of the Ahmedabad Congress, I observed:

> 'We have no higher aspiration than that we should be admitted into the great confederacy of self-governing states of which England is the august mother'; and I added:
>
> 'We recognize that the journey towards the goal must necessarily be slow, and that the blessed consummation can be attained only after prolonged preparation and laborious apprenticeship. But a beginning has to be made.'

Mr. Gokhale, presiding at the Benares Congress in 1905, spoke in the same strain. 'For better or for worse' said he, 'our destinies are now linked with those of England, and what the Congress fully recognizes is that whatever advance we seek must be within the Empire itself. That advance, however, can only be gradual.'

The claim of the Moderate party, therefore, is that we are the legitimate successors of the founders and the early builders of the Congress, and that we uphold the ancient traditions of that great institution. It is those who have departed from these traditions that have really introduced a violent change, but we remain rooted to our ancient principles, which have brought us in sight of full responsible government and the fruition of the dreams of the early founders of the Congress.

The Committee appointed by the Legislative Council addressed themselves to their work with businesslike thoroughness. I was elected Chairman of the Committee and the Rt. Hon. Mr. Shastri its Secretary. In due time we submitted our report. Into its details I need not enter. The Scheme, although a genuine and a definite advance, did not come up to our expectations. Especially was this the case in regard to one point: no responsibility in the Central

Government was provided, and we urged it with unequivocal emphasis in our report, as we did in our evidence before the Joint Committee and in all our representations. The concession has not yet been made. There is no reason why it should be deferred. If diarchy is practicable and possible in the province, it should be tried in the Central Government with the exclusion of such departments as the Army and the Indian States.

The Montagu-Chelmsford Report recommended the appointment of two committees, subsequently known as the Franchise Committee and the Functions Committee. The Franchise Committee was to determine the franchise, the electorates, and the numerical strength of the Councils, the proportion of Hindu and Mohamedan representatives in them, and other cognate matters. The Functions Committee was to make recommendations regarding the departments that were to be ' reserved ' and those that were to be ' transferred '. I was appointed a member of the Franchise Committee. The Committee consisted of six members – three Europeans and three Indians, exclusive of the Chairman. The three Indian members were the Rt. Hon. Mr. Shastri, Mr. Aftab Mohamed, member of the India Council, and myself. The European members were Sir Frank Sly, Sir Malcolm Hailey and Sir Malcolm Hogg. The Committee was thus, within a small compass, representative of all interests, European and Indian, official and non-official. Its personnel, representing divergent and sometimes conflicting interests and points of view, would, one might expect, operate as a bar to the harmony of its proceedings and the unanimity of its decisions. But, as we set to work and proceeded with the business before us, our difficulties grew fewer and fewer until there was hardly a question which did not admit of a solution assented to by all. Here and there points of difference cropped up; but harmony and general unanimity were the predominant features of our deliberations. This result was largely due to Lord Southborough, and the general spirit of ' give and take ' that prevailed. Lord Southborough was an ideal chairman, broad-minded, sympathetic, and with an inborn courtesy that disarmed all opposition. I well remember the marvellous resourcefulness he displayed when, after a prolonged debate upon some knotty and controversial point, he would come forward with a form of words, reconciling the different views and solving the situation. I sometimes thought he would make an excellent Viceroy. But that was not to be. He did not keep good health in India, and at one of our meetings at Lahore he dropped senseless from his chair and had to be carried home. In my difficulties I would sometimes see him and obtain valuable help and advice. When I was in England, I met him occasionally, and he always spoke of India in terms of affection for our people and of sympathy for our aspirations.

Ours was a peripatetic committee. We visited the headquarters of the different provinces, examined witnesses, and consulted the local Governments. Everywhere we were received with open arms. There was no talk of boycotting us or refusing to give evidence or furnish information. Especially was the advice of the local Governments most helpful, and everywhere we had the opportunity of personal discussion with the heads of Governments and Councillors and Secretaries. The two Governments that we found the least sympathetic were those of Madras and the Punjab. The Madras Government was very unwilling to have a general electorate – it was to be communal throughout. The Punjab Government would have only a small number of members for the Legislative Council, and would not have the broad franchise recommended in the Montagu-Chelmsford Report. The Committee did not agree, and the Committee had their own way.

In taking leave of the Committee, I desire to say one word in regard to Sir Frank Sly, late Governor of the Central Provinces. He was our Vice-Chairman; and sometimes in the absence of Lord Southborough he presided at our meetings. His grasp of detail, his familiarity with the conduct and management of committees, and the effectiveness of his cross-examination of witnesses, hostile or unwilling, were all a valuable aid to the Committee. As I followed his cross-examination, it struck me at times that he had mistaken his vocation, and that his proper place was at the Bar and not in the Indian Civil Service. My friend Mr. Aftab Mohamed proved a stalwart champion of the Mohamedan community, and, though he never lost sight of the larger interests of the nation, he seemed to me as a member of the Committee to give preference to the particular views of his Mohamedan co-religionists. Mr. Shastri was generally fair, but he had a sort of suspicion that Bengal was having too much her own way, and at times he tried to put on the brake. The official members, in my opinion, tried to hold the balance evenly, and, on the whole, with fairness to all interests. Altogether we were a happy family, enjoying our work, delighting in the opportunity of meeting the representatives of so many interests and the rulers of so many provinces. To me this novel occupation, of sitting as a member of a Government Committee, charged with an important public duty, was an education, giving me an insight into the relations between governments and the people they controlled, which hours of newspaper reading could not have afforded. Living contact with men opens one's eyes to visions that are but dimly seen among the dusty records of the Secretariat, or even in the more animated effusions of the daily press. The man is before you. He is a ruler of men. You see him; you hear him; you look at his gestures – the whole man is there. The impression that he leaves on the mind of the beholder has the indelible mark of truth, unobscured by those artificial and adventitious darkenings which a transmitted message, whether through the pen or the voice, cannot fail to engender.

The Montagu-Chelmsford Report laid down certain definite principles, the details of which our Committee had to work out. The most important of these was undoubtedly the question of representation in the Legislative Councils. The Report condemned the communal principle as interfering with the civic spirit and the development of nationhood; but unfortunately that principle was recognized in the Morley-Minto Scheme and there was no going back upon it without the concurrence of the Mohamedan community; and, while conferring a boon, to withdraw one prized by the Mohamedan community would have been inconsistent and illogical. Communal representation being accepted, what we had to decide was the percentage of Hindu and Mohamedan members in the Legislative Councils; and here we had the Lucknow Convention of 1916 to guide us. Whether we should accept it as it was or modify it in any way, was the subject of anxious consideration by the Committee. We finally decided to proceed substantially upon the lines of the Lucknow Convention. The evidence that we received varied, as may well be imagined, in a most remarkable manner. There were Extremists on both sides – Hindus who would make little or no concession, Mohamedans who would go much further than the pact. We thought that the golden mean accepted at Lucknow was a fair solution, and consistent with the legitimate claims of both the communities. The question has been re-opened in Bengal by the Swarajists for party purposes. The proposals of the Swarajists, which will be discussed later on, have roused the indignation of the Hindu community, while they have been acclaimed with enthusiasm by the Mohamedan leaders. They constitute a veritable apple of discord.

There was another question, perhaps somewhat less controversial, which the Franchise Committee had to deal with namely, the special electorates for zemindars. I never favoured these special electorates, and in the Calcutta Municipal Bill, of which I was in charge as Minister, I cut them down as far as I could. They are undemocratic in principle. They favoured the formation of privileged classes, and they withdrew from the general body of electors seats that might have gone to them. I believe the Committee, as a whole, were averse to them. But higher authority had decided otherwise, and we were bound by its mandate. Indeed, while the democratic principle might be said to be the basis of the Montagu-Chelmsford Scheme, a new special electorate had to be created, again under orders, for the Sikh community. Their war services were highly distinguished; and a grateful Government had to yield to the insistent demand of a martial race friendly to British interests. Here we have an illustration of the truth that political principles cannot always be carried to their legitimate and logical conclusion, and that every principle has to be determined by the circumstances of its application.

There was again the question of residence. Should the franchise be confined to those actually residing in the constituency, or should it be extended to all residents of the province, whose names were borne on the electoral roll? Official opinion supported the former view. The English practice is different and is in conformity with educated Indian opinion. To restrict the qualification to actual residents would narrow the field of choice, and might in some cases operate to exclude the best men from the Legislative Council. Then again constituencies are notoriously fickle, and sometimes a good man might be thrown out, through the caprice of a not too stable electorate. In such a case a narrow residential qualification would exclude him. On the other hand it was contended that an unrestricted residential qualification would let in carpet-baggers and political adventurers, having no interest in the constituencies they represented, and perhaps little in the affairs of the province. However that might be, the local Governments, as a rule, were in favour of a residential qualification, and I remember the tussle I had with Lord Ronaldshay and the members of the Bengal Executive Council over this question. They were all opposed to me. Lord Southborough and the Indian members were of a different opinion, which in the end prevailed. In Bengal the electoral rules do not provide for residential qualification, which is confined to some of the other provinces.

In January, 1919, I visited Bombay as a member of the Southborough Committee. Some time before, while we were at Nagpore, my friend Mr. Dalvi had obtained from me the promise that I would unveil the portrait of Mr. Dadabhai Naoroji, which had been subscribed for by the students of the Elphinstone College. I had now to redeem this pledge. The function was performed at the University Convocation Hall, which had been lent for the purpose, before a large and distinguished gathering under the presidency of Principal Covernton. I delivered a fairly long speech, for which of course I can find no place in these reminiscences. But there is one matter which is perhaps of perennial interest to the Indian politician and has come to the forefront in connexion with the Non-Co-operation controversy. In all countries in the world, especially in India with its emotional people and its constitution still in the making, the struggle between the ideal and the real is an ever-present factor. The struggle has to be continued from generation to generation, until some reasonable approach to a fusion between the ideal and the real has been attained. To the young, the custodians of the future, the question is one of surpassing interest. Here was a great gathering of young men of Western India, and I spoke to them on this subject as follows:

'Gentlemen, Idealism is a good thing. I am an ardent idealist. We can never be content with the present. Discontent, when regulated and controlled, is divine. We are all yearning for a brighter, nobler, more glorious future. The first streaks of the dawn are almost visible, heralding the birth of a new day for India. We are all preparing ourselves to salute the new sun of liberty that will soon spread warmth and radiance over this ancient land, the land of the Vedic Rishis of old, who chanted on the banks of our sacred rivers those hymns which represent the first yearnings of infant humanity towards the divine ideal. Dadabhai and others, working under the inspiration of the noblest ideals, toiled for the advent of this great day. Let us not therefore minimize the value of ideals. They appeal to the imagination, stir the heart, stimulate the noblest springs of action; but the ideal and the practical must be blended into one harmonious whole. There must be no divorce between them. The ideal must be subordinated to the practical, governed by the environments of the situation, which must be slowly, steadily developed and improved towards the attainment of the ideal. In nature as well as in the moral world there is no such thing as a cataclysm. Evolution is the supreme law of life and of affairs. Our environments, such as they are, must be improved and developed, stage by stage, point by point, till the ideal of the present generation becomes the actual of the next. That again is a lesson which we derive from the life of Dadabhai Naoroji. Referring to the question of Self-government from the Congress platform in Calcutta, he spoke of a beginning which would develop itself into full legislatures of Self-government. There must be a beginning, there must be progressive stages, there must be the final culmination in the matter of Self-government.'

So thought the greatest political teacher of our generation; and these have been my ideals for a lifetime.' I formed them in my youth; I cherished them in my manhood; I firmly adhere to them in the evening of my days, as convictions deepened by long experience. I closely follow the lines of Tennyson's teachings – a majestic order, a gradual and regular development, without rest, but also without haste. 'Raw haste' he says, 'is but half-sister to delay.'

31

Deputation of the Moderate Party to England, 1919

Importance of the occasion – the Joint Committee – the Indian witnesses – necessity for responsibility in the Central Government – Diarchy – reflex action of Punjab Government – other activities in London.

IN DUE TIME the Report of the Franchise Committee was published; and we now applied ourselves to the task of organizing a deputation of the Moderate party to England. I had urged it a few months before, in my address as President of the first Moderate Conference. It was a supreme moment in the history of the Reforms. There were the enemies of Indian advancement like Lord Sydenham and others; there were the Indian Extremists playing into their hands; there were our own party, who were not satisfied with the Reforms and who wanted more. The whole atmosphere was charged with difference and discord. We felt it our clear duty to send a strong contingent to England, to support the Reforms so far as they were acceptable, and to press for their expansion where we thought necessary. I was the head of the Deputation; and among its members were Mr. Shastri, Mr. Samarth, Mr. Chintamani, Mr. Kamat, Mr. P. C. Roy, Mr. Chambers, Mr. Ram Chunder Rao, and Mr. K. C. Roy of the Associated Press. Sir Tej Bahadur Sapru joined us later. Mr. Samarth was the first to arrive in England. It is worthy of note that the Extremist party also had their Deputation. Mr. Patel was a member of the Congress Deputation. Mr. Tilak was in England in connexion with his case against Sir Valentine Chirol and he gave his evidence before the Joint Committee. Before he was examined as a witness, he had an interview with Mr. Montagu, and his extreme views with regard to the Reforms had already undergone a sensible modification in the light of his new surroundings. We had several Conferences with the Labour leaders, including Col. Wedgwood, lately a member of the Labour Government. They were all organized by Mrs. Besant, who was in close touch with them. She no longer held that the Reforms were 'unacceptable' or 'unworthy to be looked at'. Between her views and ours there was general agreement, and she was a tower of strength to us in London. There was an afternoon party at Lady

Lutyens' residence at which she and I and one or two others spoke on the Indian situation. It was a pleasant function, at which much sympathy was expressed for the Reforms. I saw Lord Southborough before I gave my evidence. We discussed the situation and the prospects of the Reforms; and they seemed to be hopeful. In the course of the conversation I suggested that our strongest witnesses should come last. Lord Southborough thought they should come first and create a favourable impression. I think his view was sound, and this was the course that was adopted. The official witnesses were first examined, Lord Meston being one of them. He had just vacated his office as Finance Minister to the Government of India, and represented its views.

The committee room where the Joint Committee sat, almost overlooking the Thames, used to be filled from day to day with an eager and expectant crowd of Indians, among whom there was to be seen a sprinkling of lady visitors. Such a display of colours and dresses, such a diversified array of representatives, all inspired by one idea and one hope, had perhaps never before been gathered together in that chamber. All India in miniature was there. It was not the pleasure of sightseeing that drew them. It was the intense interest in the theme, the momentous issues discussed, the underlying consciousness that here in that little room, businesslike and unpretentious, ideas were developing which would materialize in a policy that for generations would shape the destinies of India. Lord Sydenham might say what he liked about the unfitness of India for self-rule; Extremists might denounce the Reforms as worthless; but here was an object-lesson significant and convincing in the silent but eloquent testimony it bore to the passionate ardour of our people for self-rule, and their interest in the Reforms. Among them were lawyers who had sacrificed princely incomes, at least temporarily; there were orthodox Hindus, who, though swayed by social and religious ideas that interdicted sea-voyage, mustered from day to day in that committee room to hear the evidence and to note the temper of the Committee. All India was there, and from afar the proceedings were watched with breathless interest by the millions of an expectant people.

Lord Selborne, the Chairman, was of course the central figure, and occupied the place of honour. Calm, dignified, fair to every witness and to all interests, he conducted the proceedings with judicial impartiality. I confess I had a prejudice against him at the first start. He was Governor of South Africa, and South Africa stinks in the nostrils of every patriotic Indian for its anti-Indian policy. It is possible that the Governor, being the chief of a self-governing community, has little or nothing to do with the policy followed. But it is difficult to dissociate a policy from the head of the State. Public opinion is not always nice in its discriminations, but it carries everything before it, by its massiveness and weight. I further remembered that the suggestion of a Joint Parliamentary Committee emanated from him; and we all condemned it. I think we were premature in forming this adverse opinion. The Joint Committee was indeed helpful to Indian interests and the cause of the Reforms.

Next to the Chairman, the most striking figure on that Committee was Mr. Montagu. The Committee was his own; and at its open meetings he had a masterful hand in shaping its proceedings. His cross-examination was searching and effective; hostile witnesses writhed under it. One witness, a lawyer and an ex-Indian judge, was reduced to pulp, and he had to admit that, being away in the country, he had not studied all the papers. Lord Sinha inspired confidence. His demeanour was quiet and dignified. His examination and cross-examination of the witnesses was that of the practised lawyer: no offence was given, but the witness was sometimes turned inside out. The general attitude of the members of the Committee was friendly, except that of Lord Sydenham, and Lord Midleton was disposed to follow him, though at a distance. I once thought of interviewing the latter, but I gave up the idea, as the members of the Committee were in one sense judges, called to decide upon evidence before them.

The number of witnesses examined was quite large, and after a time they were examined in batches of three or four. The usual procedure was for the witness to make an oral statement, and then be examined upon it by the members of the Committee, one after another. I was not examined upon my statement either by Mr. Montagu or Lord Sinha. I was somewhat shortly cross-examined by Mr. Ben Spoor, a Labour member. He evidently had been primed by some members of the Congress Deputation. I was asked whether I had not moved a Resolution in the Congress fixing a time-limit within which responsible government was to be established. The object apparently was to convict me of contradiction, as my evidence before the Committee did not support the idea of a time-limit. I said in reply, 'Assuming that it was so, was I not at liberty to revise my opinion in the light of new conditions?' The point was not further pursued. Lord Sydenham was not present on the day that I was examined, so I missed his cross-examination. Mr. Tilak's examination lasted for a very short time. He made his statement, but was not cross-examined at all. This was quite unusual; and I think it was disappointing to Mr. Tilak himself. For, whatever might have been our differences, we all felt that Mr. Tilak was quite capable of supporting his views with judgment and ability. I am afraid Mr. Tilak was not *persona grata* with the British public, and his failure in his case added to whatever prejudice there was against him. Sir Tej Bahadur Sapru arrived late. His examination was necessarily short; he rendered yeoman service in securing the recognition of University Education among the Transferred Subjects. On the whole, I think that the witnesses of our Deputation acquitted themselves very creditably in their examination. A member of the Joint Committee told me a few days after we had been examined, 'You created an excellent impression but subsequently there was a set-back.' He mentioned names of those whose evidence had produced a bad impression, but I need not repeat them.

There was no point about which Indian witnesses of all shades of opinion were more emphatic and insistent than the introduction of responsibility into the Central Government; and, now that we have had the experience of the working of the Provincial Councils with some measure of responsibility, and of the Legislative Assembly without any, the soundness of this view is enforced with added weight. Responsibility has always a sobering effect upon a legislative body, even in respect of departments not under its immediate control, by creating a general atmosphere of sobriety. There must of course be 'die-hards' in every Council, but even they cannot but be infected with the prevailing temper of their colleagues, unless indeed a regular campaign has been organized for obstruction, or for wrecking, of which unfortunately we have had recent experience in Bengal and in the Central Provinces.

My own impression is that some of the difficulties that are now being experienced by the Central Government in dealing with the Legislative Assembly would have altogether disappeared or have been considerably minimized, if the view urged by the Indian witnesses had been accepted. The concession will have to be made sooner or later. *Bis dat qui cito dat;* and it would have been true wisdom to have acted upon this principle from the first. The truth embodied in the legend of the Sibylline books finds daily illustration in the timidity of governments willing to move, but over-cautious about the pace. If courage is a fine quality in the individual, it is the sovereign attitude of governments when tempered with prudence. There is hardly a more remarkable illustration of it in the records of British statesmanship than in Lord Durham's proposals for the reconstitution of the Canadian Government; and the Montagu-Chelmsford Scheme is on the whole a courageous advance in the same direction.

There is one point upon which considerable stress was laid in the examination of the witnesses. It was suggested in the Despatch of the Government of India that there should be a separate purse for the transferred departments. The point was urged with emphasis by Lord Meston in his evidence. The Indian witnesses were all opposed to it. Many of us felt that it would stereotype a distinction that was only transitional, and delay the transformation of the reserved into transferred departments, which we all desired and which the Reforms aimed at. The idea was not accepted by the Joint Committee and finds no place in the Reform Scheme. I cannot however help remarking that there is a growing body of feeling in favour of it, due largely to the financial difficulties of the reformed Governments and the belief that a separate purse would be a more effective protection of the financial interests of the transferred departments than what is provided under the existing conditions.

In Bengal, a large percentage of the revenues of the province is absorbed in expenditure on the reserved departments, leaving only about 34 to 35 per cent to be spent on what have aptly been called the nation-building departments. It is a legacy from the past, but it has seriously interfered with the growth and development of the province in many useful directions. Sanitation, primary education, agriculture and the industries, all suffer for the sake of departments which, however useful and even essential, contribute but indirectly towards the national well-being. The maintenance of law and order is indeed the first condition of stable progress; but the Indian patriot may well complain that, in laying the foundations, the national resources are exhausted for the adequate upbuilding of the superstructure. So strong is the feeling on the subject that on one occasion nearly the whole of the police grant was disallowed by the Bengal Legislative Council, and was restored only on further reconsideration and after discussion with the Governor.

The Montagu-Chelmsford Report had recommended that a Parliamentary Commission should come out to India five years after the scheme had been in operation, with a view to reporting upon its working and recommending its revision, if necessary. The period was extended by the parliamentary statute to ten years. From the Indian point of view, this seemed to be too long, and the restoration of the original period was urged. This was not accepted by the Joint Committee. I think it would have been wiser, even from the official point of view, to have adhered to the original proposal; for it would probably have averted the agitation for the immediate grant of full provincial autonomy which now finds favour with a large section of the Indian community. A quinquennium is not too short a period, even at the rate at which things are now progressing in India, and public opinion would have been content to wait without clamour when the prospect of a change was in sight and within so short a time. It was a mistake to have departed from a recommendation that held out the hope of an early advance. Diarchy was a novel experiment, and to many it seemed risky, and the prospect of an early limitation of its scope with its speedy disappearance in the near future would have had a soothing effect upon public opinion. However, that was not to be, and the original proposal was modified, despite the protests of the Indian witnesses.

It was indeed evident that diarchy did not commend itself to every member of the Joint Committee, nor did it seem to be quite acceptable to British public opinion. I had the opportunity of discussing the question with an important member of the British Press, who was by no means unfriendly to Indian aspirations, and had certainly no desire to embarrass the Government. I think I was able to convince him that, whatever might be the defects of the system from the critical standpoint, there was no escape from it in view of the Declaration of August 20, 1917. Responsible government was to be the end and aim of British rule in India, and in the terms of the message it was to be attained by progressive stages. The full measure of it was not to be granted at once: the evolution must take place step by step, until the final stage was reached. There was to be an experimental period, during which certain departments were to be transferred to ministers responsible to the Legislature and to a popular electorate, as preparatory to the grant of a full measure of responsible government. It was to be responsible government in part, or no responsible government at all. Mr. Montagu had, in the name of the British Government, promised the former at the first start; and to depart from it on the ground that it was impracticable, without having tried it, would be, in the words of Lord Ronaldshay and his Government, a breach of faith.

It was this argument which I think proved the decisive factor in determining the decision of the Committee and of the waverers among the British public. A pledge had been given in the name of the British democracy, and there could be no going back upon it. It has to be borne in mind that the Indian bureaucracy, with exceptions here and there, were opposed to diarchy. Five of the local Governments had recorded despatches against it, as an undesirable and impracticable system. Bengal and Behar were the only two Governments that supported it, and the Moderate party did so in their evidence before the Joint Committee; not that they were enamoured of it, or would not have gone further in their endeavour to liberalize the Government, but they felt that without their support the boon that had been promised would be lost, and the prospects of responsible government indefinitely postponed.

But while the Joint Committee were carrying on their work, in that peaceful and quiet chamber overlooking the Thames, the educated community in India were convulsed by one of those agitations that follow in the track of misgovernment. It was the fruit of the disastrous policy pursued by Sir Michael O'Dwyer in the Punjab. The deportation of Dr. Kitchlew and Mr. Satya Pal, the popular upheaval at Amritsar, followed by serious breaches of the peace, the martial law proceedings and the horrors of the Jallianwallabagh, kindled a conflagration throughout India which it will take many years to allay. It penetrated north, south, east and west, and for a time stirred the hearts of all, and invested the Reforms with a sinister hue. Lord Chelmsford wanted a calm atmosphere for their discussion. The proceedings of the Punjab Government created an atmosphere, not only in the Punjab, but throughout India, surcharged with the spirit of bitterness and resentment; and the feeling reacted, with more or less intensity, upon the deputations now in England. A public meeting was held, at which some of the members of the Labour party were present. Mr. Montagu was approached, and the Moderate party had more than one conference with him. It was we who urged an open enquiry and suggested the names of the Indian commissioners. We realized the gravity of the situation in India, and we counselled according to our lights.

Here there was no difference between Moderates and Extremists, except perhaps in regard to details. The sense of indignation at the proceedings of the Punjab Government was universal throughout India, and was shared by our countrymen residing in England. It is a matter of regret that the Despatch of the Secretary of State was not more thorough in its sense of disapproval, and more emphatic in its tone of condemnation; and the situation was aggravated by the subsequent debate in the House of Lords. Time is a great mollifier; but the sore has not yet healed; and the poison still lurks in the subterranean depths of the public consciousness in the Punjab, with its sympathetic reaction upon other provinces. It comes to the surface when contributory circumstances wake old memories. It is a grave warning to the rulers of men, of the incalculable mischief of wrongdoing in all high matters of State. Injustice truly revenges itself with compound interest. That is the writing on the wall for statesman to read and profit by.

There were other activities, outside the immediate sphere of the Deputation, in which I had to take part. The Secretary of State appointed me a member of a committee to enquire into and report upon the institutions of Local Self-government in England as regards their applicability to Indian conditions. My colleagues were all members of the Indian Civil Service who were on leave in England. I got on very well with them. They were kind, courteous and sympathetic to the only non-official member of the Committee and tried to help me. Among them were Mr. Lindsay, late Magistrate of the 24-Parganas, Mr. Clarke, Commissioner in the Central Provinces, and Mr. Allen of the Assam Commission. My duties, as a member of the Deputation, prevented my giving as much time to work of the Committee as I should have liked. But I attended several of its meetings and the conferences held in connexion with its work. I visited Birmingham and saw the wonderful sewerage outfall of the town, which I was told cost two millions sterling. We went all over the works and did not perceive the faintest trace of a bad smell in the place. I discussed with the engineer in charge the question of effluents discharged into the Hugli from the septic tanks in the mill areas. He was of opinion that, however much they might be sterilized, they must contribute to the pollution of the river water. He condemned it as a bad system.

In due time, the Committee submitted its Report. I signed it, subject to a supplementary note in which I strongly urged the formation of a Local Government Board in each province in India.

20

The note was circulated among the different Governments. With the exception of the Governments of Assam and of the Central Provinces, they were all against the proposal.

There is only one other matter to which I should like to make a passing allusion, as indicating the many-sided activities of our Deputation in London. We waited in deputation on Mr. Montagu in connexion with the question of the status and treatment of Indians in the Colonies. Mr. Polak, that indefatigable friend of the Indians in the Overseas Dominions, organized the Deputation. I was the nominal spokesman; he read the statement, which was drawn up by him; and among our European friends present were Sir John Rees and Sir William Meyer. I need hardly add that Mr. Montagu returned a sympathetic reply.

While in England I was asked to preside over a meeting of the Mohamedan residents in connexion with the Khilafat question, for I entirely sympathized with the demand of the Indian Mohamedans for its settlement, on lines in conformity with the declaration of the Prime Minister (Mr. Lloyd George). This has now, to a great extent, been achieved, thanks to the insistence of the Government of India backed by public opinion in India and reinforced by the military triumphs of Kemal Pasha.

In 1919 I had often to be at the India Office in connexion with my work. I found the atmosphere of the India Office very different now from what it was in my early days, say in 1874 or 1897. Within the precincts of that temple of bureaucracy, quite a new spirit seemed to move, charged with the invigorating breath of democracy. I felt, though certainly in a less degree than I did in Writers' Buildings when I was a Minister, that somehow or other the place seemed to be our own. It had been Indianized in spirit, if not in personnel. Everybody seemed willing to serve and to oblige. Dark skin was not a disqualification, but a passport. The stiffness of the bureaucratic mien was not there. Mr. Bhupendra Nath Basu was probably the central force in bringing about this transformation, aided by the masterful personality of Mr. Montagu and the new spirit which the Reforms had generated. Mr. Basu's room was the rendezvous of the Indians, their *baitakkhana* (an untranslatable word). An Indian having any business at Whitehall or in the neighbourhood would tumble into his room, stay for a few minutes, and relieve the strain of London life by a quiet chat with its occupant, who was all things to all men in the best sense – ready to advise and to assist. My relations with him were closer than those of many others, but he was the protector of the Indian community in general, and of the Bengalees in particular. His aid was often sought and readily given.

One of the most frequent of these visitors was perhaps Mr. Kedarnath Das-Gupta, a native of the district of Chittagong in Bengal, but now settled in London, organizing plays and amusements; and familiarizing the British public with the characteristic incidents in the life of ancient India. In the colossal life of Imperial London, his individuality and power of organization are lost. He is a walking chart of London. Tell him the street and the number of the house you want to go to, and he will take you there, perhaps more quickly and cheaply than even the omniscient London cab-driver. Sleepless in his activities and in his desire to serve others, Kedarnath Das-Gupta is a familiar figure to the Bengalees in London, and is loved and esteemed by all who know him. He was my guide, philosopher and friend, amid the bewildering facilities of communication that London presents to the newcomer. And you are a newcomer, although you may have been in London half a dozen times in your life, so rapid are the transformations in its topography, thanks to the swift-moving machinery of its system of local government.

These lines were written when Mr. Bhupendra Nath Basu was still in our midst. He died on September 16, 1924, mourned by all who knew him, leaving a gap in the ranks of our public life that it would be difficult to fill. For strength of conviction, for clearness of vision, for tact and judgment in handling affairs, he stood pre-eminent among the public men of his generation. He took to politics early in life, and enrolled himself as a volunteer in the first Calcutta Congress of 1886. A volunteer is not a delegate, though under recent Swarajist tactics he is sometimes elevated to that dignity as at Seraigunge, to swell the number of *Swarajist* votes. But the young volunteer, the newest recruit in the service of the Congress, had the Field-Marshall's baton concealed in his knapsack, and in 1914 became the President of the Indian National Congress. Once thrown into the whirlpool of political life, he was drawn into its deepest currents, and was closely identified, as a leading personality, with our all great public movements. He was one of the central figures in the anti-Partition and the *Swadeshi* movements of 1905. In 1906, when I was arrested at Barisal, he was placed in charge of the Conference proceedings. In 1909, when I was in England, he presided over the boycott celebration of August 7 of that year, despite high official pressure. In 1916 he was elected a member of the Imperial Legislative Council, and in the following year he was selected by Lord Chelmsford to fill a vacancy in the India Council. He came out to India with Mr. Montagu's Deputation in connexion with the Reform Scheme, and rendered valuable service as a member of that Deputation. He was again in India as a member of the Lee Commission, and was, a few months before his death, appointed a member of the Executive Council of the Governor of Bengal.

Throughout his life, he was a moderate in politics and consistently opposed the cult and creed of Non-Co-operation, which he regarded, with many others, as fraught with peril to the best interests of his country. I hope the day is not distant when Bengal will raise a pantheon dedicated to her great men. Such an institution will be an honour to the dead, and an incentive to the living. In that temple of peace and reconciliation, where all feuds will be forgotten, and where will commingle the spirits of the great dead, Bhupendra Nath Basu will find a high and honoured place.

32

My Return to India and Ministerial Appointment

Return to India, September, 1919 – Non-Co-operation – the Rotary Club – appointed Minister of Local Self-government – my colleagues – relations with Lord Ronaldshay.

I RETURNED TO INDIA IN SEPTEMBER, 1919, after an absence of over four months, during which time I claim to have spared no effort to serve the interests with which I was entrusted. It was a crowded season of strenuous work, in which all of us did our best. Now and then we had to face disappointments, the most notable of which was when one of our members went out of his way to plead for a second chamber in the new constitution, without the authority of the party. It was a surprise, and there was a feeling that there should be a public disavowal of this view from our party. This idea, however, was subsequently dropped, and no harm was done by our inaction. We have a second chamber in the Council of State, in connexion with the Central Government; and, in view of developments that are taking place, it may perhaps be worth while considering the question as to whether the restraining, and sometimes perhaps the compelling, influence of an upper House may not be needed in the machinery of the Provincial Governments. The question may have to be considered by the Parliamentary Committee which will be sent out to report upon the Government of India Act.

The welcome that I received on my return home in 1919 was sensibly less in warmth than those which had greeted me on former occasions of a similar nature. The work was perhaps more important than any I had done before in England. It was in one sense a partial consummation of our previous efforts; and yet it did not produce anything like the impression of old. The reason was not far to seek. Non-Co-operation had done its work by creating a profound sense of mistrust in British promises and pledges among a certain section of our people, despite evidence of earnest effort to redeem them. It was in such an atmosphere that the Reform Scheme had to be launched into operation. It was in such an atmosphere and amid surroundings so unpropitious that the first General Elections under the new Act were held. There were the forces of Non-Co-operation appealing to the electors not to vote and to the candidates not to stand. The name of religion was invoked, and Muslim electors and candidates were solemnly told by the doctors of their religion that it would be wicked and contrary to the injunctions of their sacred books to participate in any shape or form in the approaching elections. No wonder that some of their best men hesitated; and I was approached by a Mohamedan leader, who recently held a high position in the Government, with the request that I should appeal to Lord Ronaldshay to extend the time for the nominations of Mohamedan candidates. I made the request. It was granted; and thus it was possible for some of the Mohamedan leaders, who otherwise would have been left out, to join the Council. At that time, Non-Co-operation stuck to the formula of the triple boycott, including that of the Council, which was shunned as an unclean thing. So far, however, as the Hindus were concerned, the feeling against Council entry was confined to the professed Non-Co-operators and did not affect the bulk of the men of light and leading. The last Council was thus fairly representative of that element.

The question of entering the Councils on the part of Non-Co-operators was a subsequent development. It was due mainly to the failure of the cult. When it was quite apparent, even to the avowed advocates of Non-Co-operation, that they had achieved nothing on the constructive side, and that their career had been marked by unrest and rowdyism, sometimes accompanied by bloodshed – drawing tears of penitence from their leaders – a departure was initiated, in the name of Non-Co-operation. It was diplomatic in its conception. The pill was gilded. But the old label was retained. It was still Non-Co-operation, but of a type which in the opinion of a powerful wing of the party cut at the root of the cult. Council entry was resolved upon, but for the ends of obstruction and the wrecking of the Councils. It was to be co-operation at the start, non-co-operation in its operative part; and the wrecking of the Reforms as the sequel.

These methods were soon in full swing with varying success in the different provinces. It failed everywhere except in the Central Provinces and Bengal. In the Central Provinces it was completely successful; and in Bengal only partially so. What the ultimate result will be, it is difficult to anticipate. The future is on the knees of the gods. But we well know – it is a matter of common experience – that those who come to curse often remain to bless; and the last chapter in the evolution of Non-Co-operation may eclipse, in its kaleidoscopic transformation, the amazing developments of the past. The most persistent Non-Co-operator may yet be the most ardent of co-operators. Orthodox non-co-operation may develop into responsive co-operation.

Before I pass on to my active work in connexion with the Reforms, let me interrupt the narrative by reference to my association with a movement which is helping to draw Europeans and Indians together – I mean the Rotary Club.

Whatever may be the opinion about the merits of the Reforms – and here I frankly admit that there is considerable room for differences – it must be admitted by all that they have been largely instrumental in establishing better relations between Europeans and Indians than existed before. With the advent of the Reforms there came the recognition on the part of the European community of the equal status of Indians with them as fellow-subjects of the Empire. This is apparent from the writings of the European Press and the utterances of prominent European leaders. The same wholesome change is observable in our social relations, where a sense of ease and equality is the dominant note. On the Indian side the sober section of our people are beginning to realize that for good or for evil – for good as I believe – Europeans and Indians have to live together, and that we should make the best of the situation. With this conviction on both sides, our relations are bound to improve, to our mutual advantage.

A feature of the present situation has for me a personal aspect to which I must refer. In the pre-reform days, I was perhaps the one Indian who, above all others, excited feelings the reverse of friendly in the mind of the European community. I had no quarrel; the feeling was perfectly natural. I was the most persistent and the most outspoken among living Indian agitators, denouncing the Government for its shortcomings, and the European community for its narrowness of vision and its attachment to its special privileges. Further, we did not know one another sufficiently well, and ignorance is the mother of all that makes for hatred and resentment. Things have changed since then. Our angle of vision has changed with closer contact and with better knowledge. In public work and in helping the Reforms, we have become colleagues, and the feeling between European and Indian leaders is being gradually transformed into one of mutual esteem and respect.

While these momentous changes were silently shaping themselves in the bosom of society, European and Indian, and were struggling for outward expression, I received an invitation from the Rotary Club to be their guest at one of their lunch parties, and to speak.

The Rotary Club is a world-wide organization and has an important centre in Calcutta. It was an honour that I greatly appreciated, and the reception that was accorded to me was as hearty as any that I had received from an Indian gathering. The atmosphere was inspiring. I saw many new faces, but they were beaming with friendliness, and when I rose to address the gathering, which was large and enthusiastic, I felt that I was not merely an Indian but a Rotarian, with a cosmopolitan outlook and surrounded by friends who would overlook my faults. Let me quote a passage from my speech:

> 'The Empire is yours, but it is also ours. It is yours by creation; ours by adoption. You are the natural heirs; we are the adopted children of the Empire. Your status and our status are the same; and here let me make a frank confession of faith on my behalf as well as the great party to which I belong. We of the Moderate party believe that the connexion of England with India is a divine dispensation ordained for the holiest and highest of ends. Therefore do I appeal to you, representatives of the European community, members of the Empire, friends of human freedom, to stand by us, to co-operate with us in ensuring the success of the great experiment upon which the honour of England is staked, and the future of India so largely depends. I am sure I do not appeal in vain. I am strengthened in this hope by the cordiality of your reception and the kind and sympathetic hearing which you have accorded to me, and for which I am truly grateful.'

The Club marked its appreciation of my speech by making me an honorary member, a position that I still hold; and, though my preoccupations do not afford me the opportunity of frequent attendance at its sittings, I deem it an honour to be associated with a club with a world-wide organization and holding a high status. The Club serves a useful purpose in strengthening those bonds between Europeans and Indians so necessary for the good of India and of the Empire.

Let me now resume the thread of my narrative. I stood as a candidate for election to the Bengal Legislative Council from the municipalities in the Barrackpore Sub-division. I was returned unopposed. In an interview with the Governor, Lord Ronaldshay, soon after my election, I was offered the post of a Minister, and the choice of any portfolio that I preferred. The offer was not unexpected, though perhaps I did not anticipate that it would be made at that interview. It was in the air, and was the subject of common conversation. I accepted the offer and suggested that, as regards my subjects, I should like to have Education and Local Self-government. Lord Ronaldshay pointed out that such a combination was impossible in view of the arrangement of the work in the Secretariat. He sent for Mr. Gourlay, his Private Secretary, and obtained from him a printed list of the division of the portfolios, and showed it to me, adding that he would send me a copy later. I said that provisionally I would accept Local Self-government, with which was linked up the Medical Department, but I requested that His Excellency would give me time for further consideration and final decision. This was readily complied with, and Lord Ronaldshay thanked me for taking up Local Self-government, in which he was greatly interested and which he largely controlled.

In the course of the conversation His Excellency raised the question as to who should be my Hindu colleague, for he had already made up his mind that there should be three ministers, two Hindus and one Mohamedan. I had no hesitation in suggesting the name of Mr. P. C. Mitter. The only doubt that Lord Ronaldshay felt about the matter was that Mr. Mitter was not an educationist. I explained to him that every graduate of the Calcutta University was more or less familiar with our educational problems, and that Mr. Mitter had been for a number of years Secretary of the South Suburban School, one of the largest educational institutions in Calcutta, teaching at the time up to the Matriculation standard. The impression left on my mind was that he would prefer an educational expert, and was thinking of one outside the elected members of the Council. I pointed out that that would be contrary to the intentions of the Statute, and he seemed to agree.

He said nothing about the Mohamedan member. In a conversation I had with him a few days before, he had spoken to me about Dr. Abdulla Surhawardy as a highly cultured and intellectual Mohamedan. Dr. Surhawardy had been appointed by the Bengal Government a co-opted member on the Franchise Committee, Mr. P. C. Mitter holding a similar position on the Functions Committee. But in the meantime, while other Mohamedan leaders, swayed by the torrential gusts of the Khilafat movement, were wavering between co-operation and non-co-operation, Nawab

Newab Ali Chowdhury had published a striking pamphlet over his name, in which he marshalled with convincing force and the skill of a practised controversialist the arguments against Non-Co-operation. Coming from a Mohamedan leader of his position and at such a time, it was bound to make a great impression. Lord Ronaldshay wanted a representative from East Bengal among his Ministers; and here was a Mohamedan gentleman, of high social position, from that part of the country, who had definitely made up his mind – and made no secret of it – to co-operate with the Government and work for the Reforms. Courage is a valuable quality in politics, and the Nawab Sahib had shown it. I was therefore not surprised when I read in the newspapers the announcement that Nawab Newab Ali Chowdhury had been appointed Minister.

Between him and ourselves, his Hindu colleagues, the personal relations were friendly and even cordial; and, on the whole, in the business of Government, there was a general agreement. We often acted together and we tried to help one another. We entered into no binding agreement, no solemn league and covenant as in a neighbouring province; but here our personal relations were so satisfactory, that anything like a pact became unnecessary, and mutual trust and confidence became the cement of our union in the performance of our public duties. In our union, spontaneous and cordial, in the high functions of Government, is afforded evidence of the powerlessness of the disruptive influence of communal forces, when dominated and controlled by mutual goodwill and confidence.

Only in one matter was there any marked difference and despite the practical lesson afforded by our joint action as Ministers. That was in connexion with the question of communal representation. The Nawab Sahib and Sir Abdur Rahim, member of the Executive Council, were both its active and thoroughgoing supporters; and we, the Hindu Ministers, were as whole-heartedly opposed to it. Our Mohamedan colleagues would make no compromise. We, on the other hand, with the traditional tolerance of our race, exhibited a spirit of compromise even in regard to so vital a matter, provided the goal, which was the ultimate disappearance of communal representation, was brought nearer. Nawab Newab Ali Chowdhury and myself were not long before arrayed in hostile camps. I was one of the leaders of the anti-Partition agitation; he was warm in his support of the Partition. For years we fought against one another; but we carried no traces of our struggle into our ministerial work. We were both content to forget and forgive, and to unite in the common work that lay before us, which, in its ultimate results, would benefit Hindus and Mohamedans alike.

It is, however, useless to disguise the fact that the Nawab Sahib's appointment as Minister caused dissatisfaction in certain quarters. Some Mohamedan leaders felt aggrieved that one, perhaps not their equal in respect of literary qualifications, should, in preference to them, have been the recipient of so exalted a trust. The feeling was natural, but perhaps not reasonable. High literary qualifications, Eastern or Western, or both combined, do not necessarily connote the possession of administrative capacity. Statesmanship is a peculiar gift, sometimes natural, but oftener the product of common sense, tempered by prudence, broadened by a wide general outlook, and dominated by the recognition of the paramount claims of justice. Of Frederick the Great it was said that he would never employ a schoolmaster in any administrative post; and the story is told, and I heard it from the great Vidyasagar, that one of the early Lieutenant-Governors of Bengal would not appoint a schoolmaster as a Deputy Magistrate, but was persuaded on the insistence of the Pundit to make his one solitary departure from this policy.

Nor in this connexion should the fact be forgotten that some of Asia's greatest men were illiterate. Mohamed and Akbar, Sivaji and Hyder Ali, Ranjit Singh and Jung Bahadur compose a galaxy of brilliant men, the like of whom the world has not witnessed among the most illustrious group of literates. Let us not deprecate culture, but let us not exalt it beyond its merits. It is not for me, however, to make a pronouncement on the administration of a colleague; but the highest authority, no less than the Governor of the province himself, has recorded an emphatic eulogy. A similar pronouncement has been made by the same high authority in regard to my Hindu colleague, Mr. (now Sir) Provash Chunder Mitter. But his ability or fitness and even his culture was never questioned, though there was one member of Council who felt aggrieved that Mr. Mitter had been preferred to him, and laid the blame on me. I bore it without the slightest perturbation of mind, and listened to the indictment with a good-humoured laugh.

Before I proceed further, let me pause for a moment to trace the genesis of my relations with Lord Ronaldshay. They began, if I may so put it, in strife and contention, which, by a happy transformation, developed, so far as I am concerned, into warm personal regard and esteem for the late Governor of Bengal. The controversy was thrust upon us through no fault of ours. *Scriptum manet* – what is written endures and is remembered. Lord Ronaldshay had written a book on his Eastern travels, in which he referred in disparaging terms to the ethical code of Eastern nations. These reflections were very much on the lines of Lord Curzon's pronouncement on the character of Oriental nations that gave such offence to our people and was the subject of a Town Hall demonstration under the presidency of the late Sir Rash Behari Ghose. To have in Bengal, at the head of our province, a statesman belonging to the same school was viewed with lively apprehension. The Press and the public bodies were alarmed. The matter was taken up by the Indian Association, and on its behalf I wired to Mr. Austen Chamberlain, who was then Secretary of State, asking him to cancel the appointment. It was a unique proposal made for the first time by any public body in India. But feeling ran high, and we viewed with concern the prospect of a renewal of the Curzon regime in our domestic and provincial concerns. I likewise wired and wrote to Sir William Wedderburn, the Nestor of Indian politicians, who was the guiding spirit of the British Committee of the Indian National Congress in London. Sir William placed himself in communication with the Secretary of State, and, if I remember rightly, with Lord Ronaldshay himself, and obtained from him a reassuring message which, I believe, was repeated in an address delivered by him at a meeting of the East Indian Association. The controversy should have ended here, but there are die-hards in every camp, and when feelings have been roused it is not always so easy to control or to restrain them. It was even suggested that we should hold a public demonstration. The idea was given up on my insistence, and the wisdom of this course was abundantly justified by subsequent events. The whole lesson of my public life has been that extremism, however captivating, does not pay in the long run; and that in politics, as Edmund Burke has observed, prudence is a sovereign virtue.

On March 31, 1917, Lord Carmichael's term of office expired and in the following month Lord Ronaldshay became Governor of Bengal. The message of August 20, 1917, had not yet come. But the signs and portents seemed to point to the near advent of a coming change. Coming events cast their shadows before, and, in replying to an address presented on December 23, 1916, by a deputation of the Indian Association, of which I was the spokesman, Lord Chelmsford, who was then Viceroy, said: 'I hope some day to see India hold a position of equality among the sister nations of which the British Empire is composed. In this respect I earnestly invite your co-operation.' Here was a forecast of the message that was to follow and was to be delivered from the floor of the House of Commons in August, 1917. The temper of the administration was changing; and we were on the threshold of great happenings.

It was at such a time that Lord Ronaldshay became Governor of Bengal. He succeeded a ruler of great popularity, whose extension of office the people of Bengal would have welcomed. Indeed, there was a talk of presenting a petition to that effect. There was certainly a considerable body of feeling behind it. Lord Carmichael was a Radical of an advanced type, with genuine sympathy for Indian aspirations, of which he gave clear proof in his evidence before the Joint Parliamentary Committee. He was prepared, he said, to go beyond the Montagu-Chelmsford Report if the Viceroy and the Secretary of State approved. He was not remarkable for administrative vigour, and even while presiding at meetings of the Legislative Council, his periods of somnolence were not infrequent, though it must be admitted that Council speeches, in those days, and even now, delivered as they are for the most part from typed manuscripts, have a profoundly soporific effect upon the audience.

Soon after Lord Carmichael's arrival in Bengal in April, 1912, I remember to have discussed with him at Darjeeling the affairs of the Calcutta Municipality, with a view to the amendment of the Act. Mr. Payne, so well known as Chairman of the Calcutta Corporation, was appointed on special duty, but nothing was done during Lord Carmichael's term of office. A Bill was introduced in 1917, but was withdrawn, and the Act was not amended till 1923. However that may have been, Lord Carmichael's personality had a profoundly soothing effect on Bengal politics, at a time when they were more or less disturbed. He was the personal friend of almost every man of note in Bengal, and they were charmed with his courage, and candour, and his sympathy with Indian aspirations. He combined the shrewdness of the Scotchman with his love of freedom. I remember his telling somebody, 'I am not sure I would not be doing what some of these Extremists are up to if I were a Bengalee.' Frank talk like this on the part of the Governor of a province disarmed opposition, won the hearts of his visitors and inspired confidence. It was the charm of his personality and the influence which it broadcasted that constituted perhaps the most valuable asset of the Government.

To be popular after such a ruler was a task of some difficulty. But Lord Ronaldshay proved himself equal to it. To my surprise, soon after his arrival in Calcutta, I received a letter from Mr. Gourlay, Private Secretary, inviting me to meet Lord Ronaldshay at Government House. The usual procedure was not followed in this case. Anyone seeking an interview with the Governor has to write to the Private Secretary. In my case the interview was fixed by Mr. Gourlay on his own initiative or that of His Excellency. The message was a command, and I appeared at Government House on the day and hour fixed. I was received with kindness and courtesy, and during the whole of the interview not the slightest reference was made to my messages to the Secretary of State or Sir William Wedderburn. The conversation proceeded upon lines of general interest, affecting the present situation, and I parted, with my estimate of Lord Ronaldshay materially modified. It was the first of many interviews, and they were all as pleasant as this one.

33

My work as Minister

European colleagues – the Medical Department – atmosphere of the Secretariat – hostility of the Non Co-operators – Local Self-government.

WE WERE INSTALLED in office on January 4, 1921, amid some show of pomp and circumstance. The Executive Councillors and the Ministers, headed by His Excellency, went in procession to the throne room, where we took the oath of office. This being over, we sat as a Cabinet, round a table, at the head of which was the Governor. We signed a book and left the throne room again in procession. We then dispersed to our offices, and our work began in right earnest; and it was, work of no small difficulty and, for us, of no little anxiety. We were new to the work, to the office and its surroundings. The atmosphere was one we had never breathed before. It was strange and novel, though we found in it much to encourage us.

My Secretary was an Irishman with all the warm susceptibilities of his Celtic race. He showed every disposition to help, and sometimes to guide me, in the slippery, and to me, the untrodden, paths of official procedure. He tried, if I may so express myself, to get into my skin. He had known me by repute, as most Englishmen in India know me, but his official training and familiarity with detail had warned him that superficial knowledge did not always mean a real grasp of the inwardness of men or things. The flaming revolutionary would often, on closer inspection, turn out to be a good-natured gentleman, quite open to the influences of reason and common sense. So Mr. O'Malley, as he once told me, and as I often saw him in the act, took to reading my published speeches amid the dreary debates which sent so many of us to sleep in the Council Chamber. Thus he came to know me more closely than I was aware of, and I came to know him through the loyal help I received from him, and we got on wonderfully well. It was therefore with real regret that I parted from him in October, 1921, when he went away on long leave.

But the whole department was inspired by the same spirit. Dr. Bentley was the head of the Sanitary Department, my right-hand man in matters of public health. He saw me immediately after my appointment, and assured me of his co-operation. I could always count upon it with absolute reliance. An enthusiast, combining knowledge with almost apostolic fervour, he had less of red-tapism in him than almost any British official I have seen. Sometimes he got into trouble from a lack of this quality, but that was his own affair. On the whole, I thought it was a distinct gain to the public service. I fear that between him and the Indian Medical Service there was not much love lost. The feeling was reciprocal, and the troubles caused thereby had sometimes to be set right by the tactfulness of superior authority. Under Dr. Bentley's inspiration the whole department was instinct with a new spirit, and its work was carried on with vigour and enthusiasm. And yet every now and then resolutions were moved in the Legislative Council recommending the reduction of establishment, curtailment of propaganda work, and, on one occasion, the abolition of Dr. Bentley's post. I had no difficulty in securing their withdrawal or defeat. All this showed the sense of irresponsibility of some of those who had chosen to come to the Council as the representatives of the people and the guardians of their interests.

With equal spontaneity did I receive the support of Mr. D. B. Williams, the Chief Engineer in charge of Sanitary Works. There was on his part willing co-operation and readiness to support my schemes wherever practicable. Of this I had a signal illustration in connexion with the scheme of riparian water-supply which his department took up at my instance. It was an idea that had been started several years ago, and long before the Reforms, but had been dropped for reasons to which it is unnecessary to refer. I lived in the riparian area and was personally cognizant of the boon to public health which a supply of pure water ensured; and, what was still more important, public opinion was beginning to feel the want of it and the need for shouldering the financial burden that it must entail. It was the fortunate development of an advancing public opinion, and I felt that in my position, with my power and responsibilities, I should take the fullest advantage of it. One of the first things that I did was to appoint a committee for considering schemes of water-supply for the riparian municipalities on the left bank of the Hugli. The Committee with Mr. Williams as their head recommended tube-wells for these municipalities; and, but for financial stringency, which hampered us in all directions, the system would by this time have been installed in some of our municipal areas.

Coming now to the Medical Department, which is a transferred subject, I confess I had a more difficult task. My relations with the head of the department and the prominent members of the Indian Medical Service were friendly, and with some of them cordial. As for the personnel I had nothing to complain of and much to be thankful for. But it was my policy that was my difficulty, and it was a policy to which I had been wedded through life. I could not abandon or even modify it, without sacrificing my principles and proving false to the convictions of a lifetime. I wanted to Indianize the department, so far as I could, without of course impairing its efficiency, and without detriment to the cause of medical education and the proper administration of our hospitals. I believed this to be quite feasible; and I gratefully acknowledge the support I received from both Lord Ronaldshay and Lord Lytton. They were in full sympathy with it and helped me with their powerful support. It is only fair to add that the Surgeons-General with whom I was associated in the administration of the department all realized the soundness of my policy. They felt – so far as I could judge – that the time had come when a definite and distinct advance towards the Indianization of the Indian Medical Service and the association of independent medical practitioners in hospital work, should be made. Our differences arose in regard to details. It was the pace of the advance, the progressive stages towards the realization of the goal, that formed the subject-matter of discussion. There was no disposition on either side to magnifv the differences. We co-operated where we could; we differed where we had to, and with the courtesy and candour of gentlemen, all inspired by one motive, the good of India, exalting it above the minor interests of class and service. My relations with the Medical Department may be judged from the following letter, which I received from the Surgeon-General of Bengal, Major-General Deare, on vacating my office as Minister:

245, Lower Circular Road,
January 6, 1924

'My Dear Sir Surendra,

I feel I cannot let your vacation of the Minister's post pass without expressing the great regret I feel in severing a connexion with one who has always extended such courteous patience and sympathy to me as Surgeon-General. We may not on all points have seen eye to eye, but I have always felt we could discuss questions frankly and generally arrive at some common point of contact. I have valued the official relationship with a statesman of your ripe judgment, breadth of view, and constructive genius. Wishing you many years of service for the country we both love,

I am
yours sincerely,
BEN. H. DEARE.'

It is worthy of notice that during the three years I was Minister there was no Surgeon-General with whom I had so many fights. I think you really get to the heart of an Englishman if you give him one or two hard knocks, and he pays you back in kind. You become good friends after such a tussle. My experience tells me that this is the royal road to his heart. It engenders mutual esteem and confidence.

However that may be, it was not all plain sailing with me in the administration of a great department, where I was endeavouring to instil the breath of a new spirit, fostered by my lifelong association with popular ideas. I remember that, on one occasion at least, there was a passing breeze between myself and an acting Surgeon-General. It was in connexion with the transfer of a Civil Surgeon. There was a difference of opinion between him and the Magistrate of the district, and I had to decide the point; I supported the Magistrate's point of view for administrative reasons, which seemed to me to be sufficient. The Surgeon-General was unyielding. We discussed the matter, but he was unwilling to give way. I then said to him, 'If you are unable to persuade yourself to see eye to eye with me, will you please take it as an order from me ?' He readily assented with the discipline of the great Service to which he belonged. But this was only a passing incident, and left no unpleasant memories behind. Our relations continued to be as friendly as before.

What I tried to create was an atmosphere of trust and confidence. We were new to the office and the office staff. They were tried veterans in their work. I was a stranger to it. They had an advantage over me. I had none over them, except that I was in the position of their Chief, and had behind me a more or less well-known record of public work. The office was well disposed; their good will, however, had to be cemented. There was an air of confidence all around; but it had to be consolidated and deepened. I remembered a well-known passage in one of Herbert Spencer's books in which he says, 'If you want to win over people, you must seem to love them; and the best way to seem to love them is really to love them.' I tried to make every subordinate of mine in a responsible position who came in contact with me feel that I trusted him, and my confidence was well repaid.

I further felt that I stood face to face with the traditions of a great office, with rules and methods of procedure built up by generations of experienced administrators, which I was bound to respect, and which could only slowly be modified. Our critics and even our friends expected that we should, on our assumption of office, do great things and inaugurate vast changes. They forgot that we had not a *tabula rasa* upon which we might inscribe anything we pleased, and that no one could assume charge of the duties of a great department of the State with his bundle of first principles, if he had any, and straightway give effect to them in the practical work of administration. That work, in its most difficult and controversial aspects, resolved itself into a series of compromises, where the application of principles has to be determined by the circumstances of each case. The result is not always satisfactory to the Minister or the Member in charge, and even less so to the public. Disappointment follows; criticism is inevitable, while the unfortunate author of progressive measures, which but imperfectly come up to his own ideals or expectations, is prevented by the vow of silence and the obligations of his office from revealing the secrets of his prison-house. In countries where Parliamentary institutions have long been established all this is understood, and where there are party organizations and party organs the encouraging approval of a section of the public is readily obtained; and the Minister has not to continue from week's end to week's end his wearisome journey through the chill and suffocating atmosphere of hostile criticism, unrelieved by any sort of approbation, except that of his own conscience. That indeed is a cold comfort, but that is the only sort of comfort, the only form of solace, that we have had in the dreary journey, which for me is now at an end, and which I am not prepared to renew, except in circumstances very different from those that now prevail.

I have referred at some length to the atmosphere inside the Secretariat. Even under the new regime it is bound to be an important factor. The Minister formulates the policy of his department; but it is the permanent officials who have to carry it out and work out the details; and it is these details that in many cases impart shape and colour to the policy. An ideal policy without reference to details is no policy at all. But while there was all this goodwill, this spirit of co-operation in the Secretariat, the counterpart of it was more or less wanting outside the official circle. The Press of Bengal, with exceptions here and there, was saturated with the spirit of Non-Co-operation, and was Extremist in its views and utterances. The reception accorded to us was cold and even hostile. The Reforms were mere moonshine. They meant nothing. We were described as officials and bureaucrats, associated with a machinery that was designed to perpetuate a fraud and to whitewash a delusion. In vain did we protest that we were not 'officials', or point to the clear wording of the Government of India Act. In vain did our actions belie this view. Unlike officials, we continued to hold political offices and to address public meetings. I remained President of the Indian Association and for some time Chairman of the North Barrackpore Municipality. Only the other day I condemned the decision of the British Cabinet in connexion with the Kenya question, and warned the Government of India of its unwisdom. But ours was a voice crying in the wilderness, and to the last we continued to be the 'brown bureaucrats' of the Extremist Press. Facts and arguments would not appeal to those who, having eyes and ears, would neither see nor hear.

It was in an atmosphere of this kind that we started work. Burke has told us that conciliation is the sovereign remedy for public distempers. I tried to please and conciliate, but cannot say that I was very successful. When a fixed policy for a particular end is pursued by a party, they are usually deaf to arguments and entreaties. But these are the only weapons in the armoury of the public man. I employed them and I made a new departure. I appealed to the Press to help me in my work for the promotion of public health. I invited a conference of the members of the Press at the Town Hall in July, 1921. In opening its proceedings I said:

'This is the first time that a conference of this kind has been convened by the Government, to which the representatives of the Press have been invited to discuss the vital question of the sanitation of the province' and I added:

'It is an index of the democratic spirit which inspires the Government, of its solicitude to consult public opinion and approach its behests with attention and respect. It is your high mission, in the new conditions which have dawned in the land, to create, to regulate, and to lead and guide public opinion into useful and fructifying channels. I have invited you here to-day to fulfil this high mission of your vocation.'

A discussion followed my speech. There were comments in the newspapers. But the Extremist organs showed little or no signs of co-operation.

In the same spirit and with the same object in view, namely, the co-operation of public opinion, I had convened earlier in the year (in March, 1921), only two months after I had assumed office, a conference of leading representatives to discuss some of the more important provisions of a Bill to amend the Calcutta Municipal Act. An amendment of the Calcutta Municipal Act had long been overdue. The idea had been present to the mind of the Government ever since Lord Carmichael's time; a Bill was actually introduced into the Council in 1917, but was withdrawn. I decided to take the matter up and place the municipal system of Calcutta, and, if the opportunity occurred, that of the whole province, on a line with the newly inaugurated Reforms. In pursuance of this policy, after I had amended the Calcutta Municipal Act and had placed it on the statute book, I started framing a Bill to amend the Bengal municipal system, which was as old as the year 1884, and had been allowed to remain for forty years without any substantial amendment; and here again I followed the practice, which I had inaugurated, of convening a conference of some of the leading representatives of the mofussil municipalities, and I consulted them with regard to the important features of the proposed amendment. This is a procedure, I may add, that I uniformly followed during my tenure of office in connexion with all legislative projects.

Throughout I felt that in the new order of things popular co-operation was essential. I tried to secure it, so far as lay in my power; and, but for the unhappy atmosphere that had been created and to which I have referred, a more satisfactory measure of success would probably have attended my efforts. In pursuance of this policy I visited several towns in East, West and North Bengal, and held conferences with members of District Boards and with other leading inhabitants, and discussed with them their sanitary problems. In some places the Non-Co-operators tried to create difficulties, but the local officials were able to overcome them. Mr. Emerson, Commissioner of the Dacca Division, came all the way from Dacca to Barisal to prevent any trouble, and there was none in that stronghold of Non-Co-operation. It was the youthful section of the community that was most affected by its teachings and demonstrative in its condemnation of the Government.

It was at Barisal only fifteen years previously that we had had the historic Barisal Conference. It was here on that occasion that one of the most notable demonstrations against the Partition of Bengal had been held. I was the central figure and the hero of that demonstration. I was acclaimed by a populace who rent the air with their cries and whose overflowing gratitude would have softened the hearts of the sternest. Fifteen years had come and gone; and in the meantime Non-Co-operation had done its work, creating a bitter feeling against the Government and all associated with it. The Reforms and the spirit of the Reforms were not able to allay this. I had come to Barisal on a work of beneficence in which politics had no part or share. I had come to promote sanitation, equipped with all the resources and the organization of the Government. But even such a boon, so vital to the people, was unacceptable when offered by the Government, even in the person of one who not long before was hailed as a public benefactor. I was reminded of the words of Aeneas in Virgil: *timeo Danaos et dona ferentes* – I fear the Greeks even when they come with gifts in their hands. The feeling was not universal; perhaps it was not even general. But it was there, a living factor in the local public sentiment, blatant and demonstrative. I remember Mr. Montagu's remark when I said to him in London in 1919 that our people would remain grateful to him for the Reforms: ' Don't you be quite so sure of that; for there is no such thing as gratitude in politics. ' I did not then know that I was soon to realize this truth in my own case.

But this was not the only notable feature in connexion with my visit to Barisal. The irony of fate had ordained strange things. In 1906, when the Barisal Conference was held, Mr. Emerson was the Magistrate. It was under his orders that I was arrested and fined and the Conference was dispersed; and now, as Commissioner of the Division, he rendered me every possible help. *Quantum mutatus ab illo* – how changed from his former self!

A warm-hearted Irishman, a close contact with him has inspired in me feelings of respect and esteem for his personality. In India, it is often difficult to judge of a Government servant by his official conduct. He has sometimes to perform duties, under orders of superior authority, which would give a misleading idea of the man and his character. From Barisal I parted from Mr. Emerson in 1906, under an impression that had to be revised in the light of subsequent knowledge. We were brought into closer touch as members of the Imperial Legislative Council. He had under his supervision and control some of the *détenus*. As Magistrate he had to look after them, and, I am afraid, with a stern official eye. That was Mr. Emerson, the unbending Government servant. But behind the cold, rough exterior, there was beating a kindly heart, which had a soft corner for the sufferers and a clear vision of their patriotic purposes, however misguided. I remember his telling me, with undisguised respect, the story of the honesty and disinterestedness of one of the internees under his charge; and if I rightly recollect, he repeated it publicly in a speech in the Council Chamber.

I once had to refer to him, in the course of a speech in the Imperial Legislative Council in connexion with the Rowlatt Bill: it was a little bit of banter in which I indulged and which both of us enjoyed. I was moving an amendment, urging that the accused should be allowed the right of appeal, which had not been provided under the Bill; and I emphasized my point by reference to the Barisal incident in which Mr. Emerson was the Magistrate and I was the accused. I said, 'I was fined Rs. 400 in that case by the Magistrate who now sits in this Chamber not very far from where I am speaking (casting a glance at Mr. Emerson, who was seated almost next to me); the order was set aside by the High Court; but, if there had been no appeal, if I had not that right, a wrong would have been perpetrated without remedy, or redress.' There was a gentle titter among members who understood the reference; and when the meeting was over, I went up to Mr. Emerson and said, 'I hope I have not offended you.' 'Far from it' was the courteous reply; 'I felt proud of it' he added.

Ever since then our relations have been friendly; and, when I visited Dacca after my appointment as Minister, I heard golden accounts of the Commissioner from all sides. When, therefore, after Mr. Bompas's retirement, the office of Chairman of the Improvement Trust, one of the highest in my gift, became vacant, and his name was mentioned as that of a suitable candidate, I at once accepted the suggestion and appointed him to the office. It was an appointment involving hard work, and heavy responsibility, and I think Mr. Emerson fully justified my choice. The splendid work begun by Mr. Bompas, which has harmonized important sections of our great city, has been continued with unabated vigour and undiminished efficiency; and, when at a Conference of representatives it was proposed to form an Improvement Trust for Howrah on the other side of the river, it was decided that the Chairman of the Calcutta Improvement Trust should also be the Chairman of the new Trust.

Wherever I went on tour the idea of a *hartal* was started by the local Non-Co-operators. It never came to much anywhere. At Faridpore, it was not seriously thought of by anybody; for there was still living, though prostrated on the bed of sickness, that outstanding personality, Babu Ambika Churn Majumder, the Grand Old Man of East Bengal, the apostle of steady and orderly progress. At Dinajpore, in North Bengal, they attempted to keep people away from the meeting; but in vain. It was not that these people did not want sanitation, but they would not apparently have it from the Government. They had, however, no hesitation in frequenting the Government law courts, where in the pursuit of their profession they made money, or in availing themselves of the Government railways, and postal and telegraph services. It was a convenient kind of Non-Co-operation, ministering to one's wants and needs, but manifesting itself in fervid demonstrations of rowdyism at public meetings daring to proclaim views unacceptable to the leaders. Their friends in the Legislative Council had a notion that we drew handsome allowances from the public funds in making these tours, and a question was asked, and an answer was given, that showed we drew nothing of the kind and that railway accommodation alone was provided for us. As a matter of fact, these tours involved out-of-pocket expenses, and were a source of considerable personal trouble and inconvenience. At Dinajpore, which is badly infected with malarial fever, I slept in the Circuit House in a room covered with net-work as a precaution against mosquitoes. The net-work did not, however, protect me. I had an attack of fever and it took me months before I could shake it off.

The object of these tours was to create an atmosphere that would stimulate the discussion of local sanitary problems and their ultimate solution. The aim was popular co-operation, and I claim that my efforts contributed to awaken popular interest in problems that seemed to be too dry and uninteresting to appeal to the popular imagination. In defending myself against the charge of inaction in the work of my Department, I used language which will bear repetition. I said:

'Sir, passing from the consideration of our legislative programme to the work of our department, what do we find? I claim, Sir – not as an individual but as a member of the Reformed Government, – I claim that we have awakened a new spirit in the local bodies in regard to sanitary matters. We have created a new atmosphere, instinct with a new life. I attach far greater importance to the creation of an atmosphere than even to the actual work performed. An atmosphere is an ever-present and an ever-brooding influence, impregnating all who come within its sphere, guiding, stirring, and stimulating them in the paths of progressive work. I claim that we have created such an atmosphere in the mofussil, and what are the evidences in favour of this view? Why, Sir, we have received within the last few months schemes – I will not say numerous – a fairly large number of schemes, of water-supply and anti-malarial operations. That shows that our countrymen in the mofussil are beginning to think about the vital problems of sanitation. Further, Sir, what do we find in connexion with the Gangasagar Mela? The year before last, when the Gangasagar Mela was attended by thousands and hundreds of thousands of people, there were about twenty deaths from cholera. This year there was only one. The District Board of the 24-Parganas, under the guidance and inspiration of the influences which we have created, were able to avert the outbreak of an epidemic of any kind. Let us now pass on to the flood-stricken area. What do we find there? My friend here, the Chairman of the District Board of Rajshahi, and other local bodies, under the inspiration of our officers, were able to prevent the outbreak of disease; and, Sir, the same tale comes from all parts of the country. We averted an epidemic in Bajitpur, in Mymensingh and in other places. Our propaganda work, done by the local bodies assisted by the Health Department, has had the effect of diminishing the mortality from cholera in this province. I will give you the figures. In 1921, the deaths from cholera in this province amounted to 80,000; last year it was 50,000. Look at the atmosphere that we have created. Even the Non-Co-operators are seeking our help and assistance in the matter of health propaganda. Dr. Bentley told me this morning that he had received an invitation to a conference that was going to be held at Kanchrapara under the auspices of the Khilafat party. They want the advice of our experts – the Khilafat people and the Non-Co-operators are seeking our assistance, namely, that of the Health Department. What greater triumph could there be for the Department over which I have the honour to preside?'

To secure popular co-operation for the work of my Department was one of the main objects of my policy. I said in the Legislative Council, and I repeated it at public meetings, that malaria could be eradicated or its scope minimized only by the joint co-operation of the people and the Government; the Government must undertake the major works of flooding and flushing, and the minor works of village conservancy and sanitation, including local water-supply, could be left to local bodies, aided by voluntary organizations. This was a policy that I steadily pursued, and for the first time in the history of our Department a substantial money grant was made to the Anti-Malarial Co-operative Society and the Kala-azar Association. So far back as July, 1921, I commended the former society, the latter having not then come into existence, to the favourable notice of the Press Conference which I had invited, and I urged that the Union, the Local, and the District Boards should co-operate with these voluntary organizations. To me it is a matter of gratification to be able to feel that I have initiated a policy that in its development is bound to be fruitful of good results to village sanitation. The Anti-Malarial Co-operative Societies are spreading; and they have provided a field of beneficent activity to our village population, which will not only improve their health, but strengthen their public spirit and stimulate their civic life.

The institutions of Local Self-government are the great agencies for the promotion of public health. As Minister of Local Self-government, I sought to liberalize them and to add to their powers. Lord Morley complained in one of his Despatches that one of the reasons for the want of success of our local bodies was that they had little power and less responsibility. I myself had urged this view in the Press and from the platform; and now that I was in power I sought to remedy a state of things which I had condemned. One of the first things that I did was to de-officialize the Local Boards and to order that their Chairmen should be non-officials to be elected by the Boards. A step in the same direction was to allow the few remaining District Boards which did not yet enjoy the privilege to elect their own Chairmen. The same right was extended to several municipalities that did not possess it. Thus a definite and forward step was taken towards liberalizing the local bodies. This was done by executive order. But I went further. I initiated two projects of law one after another, only one of which I was able to place on the statute book, popularizing our municipal institutions – one of them concerning Calcutta and the other the rest of the province. I claim that both were progressive measures, a necessary corollary to the Reform Scheme. When introducing the Calcutta Municipal Bill in 1921, I said:

'We are on the threshold of a great task, and the Calcutta Municipal Bill will be the first of a series of similar projects of law whose aim and object will be to liberalize our local bodies and to place them in conformity with the spirit and essence of the Reforms.' I added:

'It is the intention of Government to follow up this Bill by the amendment of the Bengal Municipal Act and the Bengal Local Self-government Act. It is unnecessary for me to say that if the Reforms are to succeed our local institutions must be strengthened at the base.'

I was able during my term of office to amend the Calcutta Municipal Act, to introduce a Bill to amend the Bengal Municipal Act and a short Bill to amend the Local Self-government Act in regard to one or two important matters. Before proceeding further I may perhaps refer to the amendment of the Bengal Municipal Act as involving a notable departure from the present law. Under the law now in force one-third of the commissioners of every municipality except that of Calcutta are appointed by the Government; and under executive orders, one-third of the members of every District Board are appointed by the Commissioner of the Division, subject to the administrative control of the Local Government. In practice the control of the Local Government was, before my time, more or less nominal. I felt, however, that it must be real, as the Minister representing the Local Government Department was responsible to the Legislative Council, and the responsibility could only be properly exercised by his personal control of these appointments. In the exercise of this responsibility, which was altogether new and created by the Reforms, I had sometimes to override the decision of the local officers. Usually they took it in good part, but on occasions there were differences and the semblance of friction; my authority, however, upon which my responsibility rested, was always upheld by His Excellency the Governor. In one case I had to use strong language and to say that local officers must realize the new order of things and adapt themselves to it. The general disposition was in favour of such adaptation. And here it is only right that I should say that the attitude of both Lord Ronaldshay and Lord Lytton in relation to their Ministers was that of a constitutional sovereign, upholding, encouraging and assisting them in their work. I do not remember a single instance in which there was any serious difference of opinion leading to a dissent. I felt that I was supreme in my department, having behind me the authority and support of the Governor, and subject only to the restraint, at times somewhat irritating, of the Finance Department. On one occasion I had to urge that it was not at all the business of the Finance Department to enquire whether a particular department under me was overstaffed. That was a matter for us to decide and they must accept our decision. They had only the financial aspect of our proposals to deal with. I may add that I heard the same complaint from Madras and elsewhere.

As Minister-in-charge of Local Self-government, it was a part of my duty to deal with the election of chairmen by the District Boards, which, under the law, had to be confirmed by the Local Government. I had a serious difficulty in connexion with the case of Mr. B. N. Sasmal, who had been elected Chairman of the District Board of Midnapore. Mr. Sasmal was a prominent Non-Co-operator and was mainly instrumental in bringing about the abolition of the Union Boards in the Midnapore District; and the Union Boards form the basal units of the system of Local Self-government. As Minister in charge of Local Self-government responsible for its steady growth and development, was I to confirm his election, as the head of the most important organization of Local Self-government in the district? The law gave me the discretion to confirm or to veto it. All eyes were turned towards me, watching to see what I should do.

The position was one of difficulty and even of some delicacy. It was a serious matter to set aside the decision of a statutory body electing their chief. But the authority being there, vested in the Local Government, there must be occasions when it should be exercised. Was the present one of them? That was the issue I had to decide. I cut out for myself a *via media* which, I thought, would enable me to protect the interests of Local Self-government, and at the same time give effect to the decision of the District Board. I sent for Mr. B. N. Sasmal. He came and saw me along with Lieutenant Bejoy Prosad Sinha Roy, a member of the Legislative Council, and gave me the assurance that as Chairman he would loyally carry out the principles and provisions of the Local Self-government Act and of local institutions established in furtherance of that Act; and he added that after the coming Council elections he would help in the establishment of the Union Boards. With this declaration of his policy, I felt that I was at liberty, with due regard to the interests of Local Self-government, to confirm the election and appoint him Chairman of the District Board of Midnapore.

34
Municipal Legislation

The Calcutta Municipal Act: my part in it – the Swarajist party – Mr. C. R. Das and the Calcutta Corporation – Bengal Municipal Bill.

THE MOST IMPORTANT MEASURE of municipal legislation during my ministry was the Calcutta Municipal Act. Elsewhere I have given its history, and have shown that it was long overdue. What I claim is that I thoroughly revised the constitutional part of the old Act, and placed the new law in conformity with the spirit of the Reforms. In truth it vests the control of the municipal affairs of the city in the hands of the representatives of the rate-payers, elected for the most part upon a broad franchise. What is worthy of notice is that these constitutional changes were in entire accord with the public demand. There are some striking features of the new Act which, in happier times and in an atmosphere free from passion and prejudice, would have evoked public recognition. We hear a great deal about *Swaraj* in these days. I may say that I have been a Swarajist when many of those now most clamant about it were in their cradles. I was the first amongst Indian public men to urge the demand for dominion status. But here, in the control of the municipal affairs of Calcutta, as constituted under the new Act, we have a veritable *Swaraj* in the government of the second city in the Empire. Be it remembered that the revenues of municipal Calcutta are nearly one-fifth of the revenues of Bengal, and will under the new law be controlled by the representatives of the people. The Corporation, with four-fifths of the members elected by the rate-payers, will have supreme authority. Their Chief Executive Officer will be elected by them, subject to confirmation by the Government. The Mayor, who will be the Speaker of the House, will also owe his office to popular election. The constitution of the Corporation has been democratized by the broadening of the franchise, the abolition of plural voting and the admission of women into the electorate.

All these represent a notable advance. But not one word of recognition did they elicit from the Extremist Press, which fastened its criticism upon the introduction of the communal system. With a superb disregard of facts, it ignored the fact that the communal system had no place in the original Bill as introduced by me (though it was recognized in Lord Sinha's Bill of 1917, which I had deliberately omitted), that I fought tooth and nail against it, and that I agreed to admit it as temporary provision in order to avoid giving it a permanent place in the municipal law. Strangely enough, as Nemesis would have it, the Swarajist party in their Hindu-Moslem Pact proposed to extend this very system to all the municipalities in Bengal, which are one hundred and sixteen in number. They want Hindu-Moslem unity, and they propose to accomplish it by dividing the municipalities into water-tight compartments, thus effectually preventing them from acting together in the exercise of their electoral rights. They have started by making appointments in the Corporation based on the communal principle, which all Indian nationalists condemn as fatal to the development of Indian nationhood.

However that may be, the Calcutta Municipal Act represents the realization of one of the dreams of my life. When I introduced it in November, 1921, I said:

'These were my last words on September 27, 1899. Twenty-two years have come and gone. I expressed the hope and I ventured to indulge in the prediction that the inestimable boon of Local Self-government would within a measurable distance of time be restored to the city of my birth. The time has come. The day has arrived. I have lived to see it. I thank God on my knees. I will not cry *Nunc dimittis*, for I feel that my work in life is not yet over. But I claim that the faith that was in me (and which still glows with an inextinguishable flame) has been justified by the proceedings of to-day. May that faith penetrate among the millions of my countrymen and inspire them with the patience and the passion to work on constitutional lines, without disturbance, without dislocation of the existing social and political machinery, for the attainment of that freedom which has been guaranteed to us by our Sovereign and the Parliament of the United Kingdom, and which under the Providence of God is our destined inheritance in the evolution of the human race.'

And let me in this place quote the concluding words of my speech when I moved that the Bill be passed:

'To me, Sir, the Bill affords a matter for personal solace and gratification. To me, it means the fulfilment of one of the dreams of my life. Ever since 1899, I have lived in the hope of witnessing the re-birth of my native city, robed in the mantle of freedom. I thank God that it has been vouchsafed to me to have had some share in achieving this consummation. I have endeavoured to embody in this Bill the principles which I preached and for which I lived and worked, and now an unspeakable sense of gladness fills my soul – the truest antidote to the calumny and vituperation to which I am so often exposed. In the course of the debate many hard things have been said, many hard knocks have been received. I hope they will not be remembered. Let us emerge from this Council Chamber rejoicing at the work that we have done, forgetting and forgiving, with tolerance and charity for all who have criticized us. (Hear, hear.) I appeal to the citizens of Calcutta to co-operate for its success, which, when achieved, will be the proudest monument of their civic spirit and the strongest justification for that full measure of responsible government to which we all aspire, and which will be the crowning reward of the labours of this and of successive Legislative Councils. (Applause.) Let no party spirit mar the fruition of this great object.'

One important feature of the Bill was the further expansion of Calcutta by the inclusion of a large suburban area, a part of which lay in my own constituency. I obtained for it an important concession, which, again, was a departure from the precedent established in a similar case. The rate-payers of the added area were not likely for some time to enjoy the conveniences and amenities of Calcutta; and it was therefore only right and proper that they should not bear the same incidence of municipal taxation. The Government recognized the soundness of the proposal and accepted it; and the Legislative Council acquiesced in it. In the first year the rate-payers of the suburban area were to pay no enhanced rates, and in the next four years there was to be a differentiating rate in their favour, to be fixed by the Corporation at its discretion.

I followed a definite principle in including a suburban area within the limits of Calcutta. In the original Bill, with the exception of a small tract, there was no such proposal; for I adopted the democratic principle that there was to be no extension of boundaries, if it went wholly and decisively against the wishes of the people concerned. They were not to be treated as so many dumb, driven cattle in the vital matter of their local administration. I further knew from my experience in connexion with the Partition of Bengal the passions which a change of boundaries is apt to evoke when carried out in the teeth of popular opposition. But the demand for the inclusion of some of these areas was insistent, and it was based on considerations of the public health of Calcutta as well as of the areas concerned. I at last decided to appoint a Boundary Commission, with the Advocate-General as its President, and two other members, one a European, whose independence and impartiality could not be questioned. The personnel of the Commission and their Report commanded public approval. I accepted it and so did the Legislative Council, which added an area that the Commission did not recommend. Public opinion and local feeling on the whole supported the inclusion of the added area. In regard to this question of the expansion of boundaries, I explained my policy to the Legislative Council, and I hoped that in the years to come it would be followed by my successors in office and the Government of the day. I said:

'My idea is that as the years roll on the municipal limits of Calcutta will grow and expand until it includes even Barrackpore within its boundaries; that on both sides of the Grand Trunk Road, one of the finest roads in India, there will grow up little municipalities, self-governing institutions managed by local bodies under the guidance and control of the greater body dealing with the larger questions of drainage, sanitation, and water-supply. That is my conception of the future of Calcutta, and I trust that some one, filling the position I have the honour to hold at the present moment, will have the satisfaction of seeing this dream realized. To-day we meet in this Council Chamber to lay the foundation-stone of that fabric, which is destined to grow in the years to come; but the growth must be gradual and steady.'

Before I leave the Calcutta Municipal Bill, it is perhaps necessary to point out that it is now the law of the land and governs the municipal affairs of Calcutta. It is useless to disguise the fact that the operation of the Act has been received with mixed feelings. It has created a sense of anxiety and even alarm among a section of the community who have a considerable stake in the city and have largely contributed to its prosperity. Calcutta is one of the great centres of trade in Asia, in which representatives of many races and countries have a large interest. Calcutta is also the home of a great Hindu population, whose fears have been roused by the acceptance for the first time of the communal principle in the disposal of appointments in the Corporation. Municipal affairs should not form the battle-ground of political warfare. When the civic affairs of a great city are used for political or party purposes, they are exposed to grave menace. Party aggrandizement and not the public good becomes the objective of civic efforts. The public feeling is that the spirit of the new Act is being sacrificed, and its beneficent provisions abused to serve the ends of party interests.

The Swarajist party have captured the majority of the seats in the Corporation, and it is felt that they are utilizing their predominance for party purposes. Such a policy is natural, there are illustrations of it all over the world, but it is not equitable, and it is right and justice that prevail in the government of human affairs; and any departure therefrom is fatal to the public interests, and in the end recoils upon the party itself. Power is given to the righteous; and is held by the righteous so long as they do not deviate from the golden track of right dealing. That is the lesson of all history. It is the writing on the wall, which those in authority may not in the intoxication of power care to read. But it is there, as inexorable in its operation as the great and fundamental physical laws.

The first crowning blunder of the new regime has been the appointment of Mr. C. R. Das as Mayor. For Mr. Das's ability, tact and judgment I have great respect; and therefore it seems to me all the more inexplicable that he should have been led to commit this mistake. To the unbiassed spectator it would point to the deleterious effects of the intoxication of power. The Mayor is an officer of some responsibility and of great dignity. The office is usually held by venerable citizens who have grown grey in the service of the Corporation. It was never bestowed on a Gladstone, on a Palmerston or a Disraeli, but is the tribute to fame and distinction for civic service. Mr. C. R. Das has not during the whole of his public career been within miles of a municipal office. But all at once, because his party is in power and he is their leader, he is installed in the position of Mayor without a trace of municipal experience. Could any selection have been more unsuitable, more unfair to the numerous citizens of Calcutta far worthier of this office than Mr. Das? Is justice or partisan spirit to be the determining factor for high appointments in an institution from which, as Mr. Das has declared, politics should be divorced?

There is no principle to which the general public and the framers of the Bill attached greater importance than the total separation of what I may call the legislative and executive functions in the administration of the Corporation. But it was left to Mr. Das and the Swarajist majority to revert to a system that had been deliberately abandoned. Under the Municipal Act the office of the President of the Corporation had been separated from that of the Chief Executive Officer, but Mr. Das in actual practice combines both. By his office, he is the Speaker of the House, but he is also, to all intents and purposes, the real head of the executive. And the practice that he inaugurated was during his absence followed by the Deputy

Mayor, who directed the burial of a fakir within the precincts of the great municipal market of Calcutta, a proceeding that gave a shock to public sentiment. Who has ever heard of the Speaker of the House of Commons usurping the functions of the Prime Minister? One more illustration and I take leave of these considerations, which have been forced upon me by recent and somewhat unexpected developments.

The Municipal Act provides for the appointment of five aldermen, to be elected by the appointed and elected commissioners at their first meeting. The object of the new institution, which follows English precedent, was to provide seats in the Corporation for a few elderly men who would not care to face the risks of an election, but whose advice would be useful and whose presence would add to the dignity of the Corporation. The Corporation had recommended in their Report on the Bill, that the selection of aldermen should be confined to those who have been municipal commissioners. It was at my instance that the scope of the selection was broadened and the Corporation was allowed to elect anyone as an alderman. In the course of the discussion I pointed out that the restricted scope proposed by the Corporation would keep out such men as Sir Jagadish Bose, Dr. Rabindranath Tagore and others like them. The view was accepted by my colleagues. In introducing the Bill, I said:

> 'There must always be in a community men who by their temperament and the habits of a lifetime would be unwilling to face the trouble and the risks of a popular election, but whose presence in the Corporation would enhance its dignity, and whose counsels would add to its deliberative strength. I could almost name persons in our community who would answer this description, but personal references are unnecessary to add to the weight of this argument, which stands confirmed by the most obvious considerations. Such men should find a place in the Corporation, and a system of co-option by a limited and select constituency, such as the elected and nominated members of the Corporation, would secure this end.'

I am well aware that discussions in the Legislative Council cannot be used for the interpretation of any provision of the law. But at least they are a guide to the intentions of the framers of the law. At any rate, the practice in all countries is to follow the principle to which I have referred. It was, however, set at nought by the Swarajist party. Young men who might easily have contested seats were elected aldermen for no other reason apparently than that they were Swarajists. Better men might have been found, and the interests of the rate-payers and the intentions of the Legislature would have been more faithfully served. I do not, however, despair. One swallow does not make a summer. Democratized Calcutta is a novel institution; and the environments which conduce to the success of democracies have to be gradually created. They are in the making. They will grow, and the abuses of a temporary autocracy, equipped, it may be, with the most modern devices, and masquerading as democracy, are bound to be swept away before the irresistible forces, generated by the popular consciousness, which no shams or shows or shibboleths can check or destroy. Democracy has been firmly established in the government of Calcutta. It will weather many a storm. It will survive them all. The struggles of its infantile days, beset with the lingering spirit of an expiring autocracy, will strengthen its fibre, and qualify it for its future achievement, which will be the establishment of a civic government in Calcutta, not for the enthronement of a party or a clique, but for the benefit of the people, and worked through the people.

The Calcutta Municipal Bill was passed by the Legislative Council on March 7, 1923. But before its final stages had been reached I had prepared a Bill to amend the Bengal Municipal Act. I introduced it in the Legislative Council on August 16, 1923. In its constitutional features, it was very much in advance of the existing law; and its administrative provisions conferred large powers on the municipalities, subject to the control of the local Government. Indeed, so far as the controlling sections are concerned, they are less drastic than the powers vested in the Local Government Board under the English Act. The Bill, as I stated in the Legislative Council, is a progressive but not a revolutionary measure. We build upon the old foundations, but we broaden and still further liberalize them. The percentage of elected members is raised from two-thirds, which is the present law, to three-fourths, and in some cases to four-fifths, of the entire body of municipal commissioners. The system of nominated chairmen or of wholly nominated commissioners is done away with, except in the case of municipalities in the industrial centres, and, even as regards them, where there is a population, in any fringe area, unconnected with the industries, they would have a constituency of their own to elect their own representatives.

The whole policy of the Bill is to invest the municipal commissioners with real power and responsibility, to relax all internal control and to exercise it from without. That was the underlying principle of Lord Ripon's Resolution of May, 1882, and of Lord Morley's Despatch of 1908. But, progressive as the measure is, I have seen it described as reactionary, because the Government keeps for itself a reserve of control, to be enforced when required in the public interests. There are often difficult and even delicate questions between local factions in municipal areas, which need the intervention of superior authority, capable of looking at them from a detached point of view. These critics seem to forget that in England, where the population is more homogeneous, and local controversies are less complicated, even greater power is reserved to the Local Government Board.

Again, there is criticism of another kind with which the Bill has been assailed. A Mohamedan member of the Legislative Council objected to it, and opposed its introduction, on the ground, as he said, that 'the principle of communal representation has not been accepted in the Bill'. I plead guilty to the charge. It was reserved for the Swarajist party to support and extend this principle by the adoption of a Hindu-Moslem Pact, which proposes to apply the communal system to all the municipalities in Bengal. In the meantime I remain unconvinced and prefer to tread the old path of obstinate opposition to the communal system in the constitution of our local bodies.

In taking leave of these Municipal Bills I feel that I must refer to the good service rendered in this connexion by my Secretary, Mr. Goode. Of municipal affairs he had wide and varied experience. He was for several years Deputy Chairman of the Calcutta Corporation, and for some time its Chairman. As Magistrate of the 24-Parganas and Deputy Commissioner of Darjeeling, he had an intimate knowledge of the working of mofussil municipalities, and his mastery of legal technicalities and municipal details was of great assistance in the preparation of our Municipal Bills.

35

My Work as Minister - *(Continued)*

Indianization of departments – Mr. Surendranath Mullick – relations with the Medical Department – Medical schools – a familiar method of attacking Ministers – the 1922 floods in Bengal.

THE POLICY THAT I FOLLOWED as Minister of Local Self-government was the steady and progressive Indianization of the departments under my charge. I placed efficiency in the forefront of my administrative ideals. Other things being equal, the Indian was to be preferred. I could do little in this respect; but the policy was there, definitely recognized and steadily followed whenever there was an opportunity. At times there were difficulties, and even opposition, but, with the support of the Governor, I was able to overcome them. The most striking case of the kind was the appointment of Mr. S. N. Mullick as Chairman of the Corporation. In 1921, on Mr. Payne, the permanent Chairman of the Corporation, taking leave, I appointed Mr. J. N. Gupta to officiate for him. Mr. Gupta was at the time Commissioner of the Burdwan Division, and in that capacity had done excellent service. The point to be noted is that this was the first time an Indian member of the Civil Service was appointed to this high office.

But a still more notable departure was made when, Mr. Gupta having taken leave for reasons of health, I had to find his successor. I left the ordinary groove and offered the appointment to Mr. Surendranath Mullick, who was a non-official and an elected member of the Corporation, as also of the Legislative Council. There was opposition offered from two different standpoints. Mr. Surendranath Mullick had from his place in the Legislative Council often opposed the Government. Would not the offer made to him be taken as a bribe? To that my reply was, 'Don't they do such things in England, which furnishes us with the models of conduct in these matters? Of course they do.' The answer was quite enough for me, but perhaps not for my objector. But that did not trouble me.

The next objection raised was that Mr. Surendranath Mullick, distinguished as he was as a lawyer and a debater, was unfamiliar with the details of municipal administration and the inner workings of the municipal machinery. To this I said, 'What did Mr. Lloyd George know about the English financial system when he became

Chancellor of the Exchequer? There are the permanent officials of the Corporation, who will furnish Mr. Mullick with all the details that he need know.' What is wanted in the head of a great department like the Corporation is a broad outlook, the capacity to formulate policies and to master details, so as to guide and instruct the permanent officials. These views commended themselves to His Excellency the Governor, whose entire approval I had in making this appointment.

At first the appointment was an officiating one, and the sanction of the Government of India was all that was needed. But after a few months Mr. Payne, the permanent incumbent of the office, definitely resigned, and his successor had to be appointed. And here it was not all plain sailing. The Chairmanship of the Corporation was one of the appointments reserved for the Indian Civil Service, and I had to move the Government of India and the Secretary of State to obtain their sanction to its being withdrawn from the reserved list. I had no difficulty in obtaining it. As a matter of fact, the appointment had in any case to be removed from the reserved list, as under the new Municipal Act it has been broken up into two separate appointments, both elected by the Corporation.

Mr. Mullick's conspicuous success as Chairman undoubtedly facilitated his confirmation in his office. The Chairmanship of the Corporation is one of the most important administrative offices in the province, and Mr. Mullick has vindicated the capacity of our people for the higher executive responsibilities. I received the thanks of the General Committee of the Corporation, and, indeed, the appointment evoked general approbation, and, in a more or less subdued form, of even the Extremist Press. They recognized my courage and were willing to admit that it was a departure. But it was only a temporary aberration from their settled attitude of uniform disapproval. Soon the fit was over, and they relapsed into their old ways, seeing nothing good in me or my administration, or in the Government.

Mr. Mullick was the subject of universal idolization. Parties and entertainments were got up in his honour – here, there and everywhere. All of a sudden the discovery was made by an apparently somnolent public that there was living among them, almost unknown to them and in obscurity, a highly meritorious citizen whose worth they had not appreciated, or to whom they had not rendered sufficient homage. A prophet is not honoured in his own country; but even this time-honoured saying, sanctified by immemorial experience, was falsified by a popular demonstration held within a mile of his residence in the South Suburban School. But how changed is all this now! And how rapid and sudden has been the transformation! It seems as if a whirlwind has swept over the prevailing temper of local public opinion, dissipating its old colourings and transforming it beyond recognition. The idol of yesterday is the demon of to-day, ruthlessly trodden in the dust. His great merits and eminent services – his vindication of the capacity of our people in an untrodden path of administrative work – are all forgotten and effaced from the public memory; and, in an electoral contest with a Swarajist candidate for his seat in the Bengal Legislative Council, he was defeated, apparently for no other reason than that he had recently accepted a Ministerial portfolio in the newly constituted Government of Bengal.

To work the Reforms and to be a member of the Government is, in the estimation of the Swarajists, an unforgivable sin. Logically, therefore, to be a member of the Legislative Council must be sinful, though perhaps the degree of criminality may be a shade less; for the Legislative Council is a part of the machinery of Government, and the member is a limb of that machinery. But neither logic nor common sense, not even the ordinary considerations of patriotic expediency, dominate the counsels of Swarajism. They are out to destroy the Reforms, and they must hound the ministers out of office. Without ministers the transferred subjects could not be administered, there would be a deadlock, and the Reforms would be wrecked. But that does not mean that there would be no Government. It may mean a reversion to the old bureaucratic system, untempered by even a partially popular Government. The Swarajists, however, believe that it would mean the immediate grant of full responsible government under the overwhelming pressure of an irresistible compulsion. A recent debate in the House of Lords and the whole trend of British public opinion should suffice to dispel this delusion.

Mr. Surendranath Mullick having resigned in order to accept a ministerial office, I had to appoint his successor, as I was still Minister in charge of Local Self-government. It was a matter of some difficulty, as the appointment was for only a few months. There were the claims of Mr. C. C. Chatterjee, Deputy Chairman, a tried and experienced officer, quite familiar with all the details of municipal administration. As the appointment was really a temporary one, I should, if I followed the office precedent, have given him the officiating post. But I had inaugurated a new departure, and I was not prepared to go back upon it. The exigencies of my policy demanded that I should follow it up. I accordingly appointed, with the approval of the Governor, an elected commissioner (Rai Haridhan Dutt Bahadur) who had over twenty years' experience of municipal work, as Mr. Mullick's successor. There was some little opposition, but my view prevailed.

It is worthy of mention, that as a member of the Legislative Council, Rai Haridhan Dutt Bahadur was often opposed to the Government. This was true, perhaps even in a more emphatic sense, of Mr. Surendranath Mullick. But I never allowed opposition, if honest, to stand in the way of Government's choice to high office, if the person selected was otherwise qualified by character and ability. Such selections were evidence of the solicitude of Government to utilize the services of the ablest and the most qualified. They were bound to have a healthy moral effect even upon those critics of Government who saw nothing good in the Reforms.

I made no secret of my policy to Indianize the departments under my control, but with absolute fairness to vested interests and without any detriment to the public service. I applied it to the Corporation, with the full concurrence of the Government as a whole, and the same policy was extended to the Medical Department, where its application was not altogether free from difficulties. At the time when I took charge of the Medical Department, there was an outstanding question of some importance. The Secretary of State (Mr. Montagu) wanted to know the Minister's views with regard to the numerical strength of the cadre of the Indian Medical Service on the Bengal establishment. I wired to say that there should be no expansion of the number employed or of the reserved posts in Bengal, and that I would examine the matter and submit a detailed statement of my views later on. I consulted the Surgeon-General, the late Major-General Robinson and one or two friends, and drew up a scheme, which I laid before my Standing Committee for consideration and an expression of their opinion.

The Standing Committee are an advisory body who, according to the convention that has grown up, are consulted by members of the Government in matters within their scope and jurisdiction. The Member or Minister is not bound by their views, though undoubtedly, being his constitutional advisers, he must treat such advice with deference. His obligation in this respect is moral rather than legal. The Standing Committees play a useful part in the Reform

Scheme. They serve to liberalize the administrative measures of the Ministers and infuse into them the colouring and the weight of popular opinion. The Standing Committee discussed the scheme that I had drawn up – and for which the responsibility was entirely mine – and they accepted it. The scheme was from the Indian point of view a cautious but definite advance; and the Secretary of State sanctioned it with a small reservation.

The sanction came nearly a couple of years after I had submitted my note, but it would be scarcely fair to raise a complaint on this score, in view of the important and complicated interests concerned, and the various departments through which it had to pass, not to speak of the objections raised. The gist of my recommendations was the reduction of appointments reserved for the Indian Medical Service from forty to twenty-four, including the withdrawal of certain appointments in the Medical College from the reserved list. The proposals elicited a strong protest from the head of the Medical Department, and a rejoinder from me, in the course of which I still further elaborated my policy. I said:

> 'I am quite as anxious as the Surgeon-General to make the Calcutta Medical College a model institution; but I venture to think that it can only retain its high position by making a departure in conformity with the spirit of the times, and the demands of public opinion, which require that its professoriat should be partially thrown open to the independent medical profession, whose influence and position in the Indian community are daily growing, and who are rapidly monopolizing medical practice in Calcutta. Thus officials and non-officials, the representatives of the Government and of the people, will combine to maintain the ancient reputation of the Medical College and make it the greatest medical institution in India.'

While admitting the great debt that the Government and the public owe to the Indian Medical Service for their splendid work, I disputed the position taken up that ' Service conditions are the best guarantee of administrative success'. I observed:

> 'They are on the contrary, apt – if I may say so without offence – to engender a spirit of narrowness and even cliquism, fatal to a broad outlook and a generous sympathy, which are the cardinal factors in successful administration.'

As a part of this policy I appointed Sir Koylas Chunder Bose as Honorary Physician, and Major Hussain Surahwardy as Honorary Surgeon, of the Medical College Hospital. Another departure in a similar direction had been made a few months earlier by the appointment of Dr. U. N. Brahmachari and Dr. K. K. Chatterjee as additional physician and surgeon, respectively, to the Medical College Hospitals. This was the first time in the history of the Medical College that Indian medical officers in the grade of Assistant Surgeons were appointed to these posts. In referring to these facts, a leading English newspaper observed at the time:

> 'In any case, it is evident that Sir Surendranath Banerjea means to do his utmost to give effect to the ideal of India for the Indians.'

That must be the ideal of every true citizen of the Empire. The Imperial civic spirit must have its roots in local patriotism. The hearth and the home, the province and the country, are the centres of those patriotic affections which radiate forth and include in their comprehensive sweep the larger and wider interests of the Empire. And what is the Empire, but the Commonwealth of a congeries of self-governing nations, each protecting and safeguarding its special interests, with justice to all, and with an eye to the solidarity of the Imperial system? That is the creed of the party to which I belong. It ensures domestic freedom and local autonomy, combined with Imperial unity, the surest guarantee for peace at home and of prosperity abroad.

Before I leave this subject, I desire to call attention to an important constitutional question which I raised in connexion with the appointment of Indian Medical Service officers in Bengal. Hitherto these appointments, though paid for by the Government of Bengal, used to be made by the Government of India. I pointed out that the procedure involved an infraction of my constitutional position. I was responsible to the Legislative Council for the administration of the transferred departments under my charge, and the personnel of those departments was an important factor in their administration, for which I could not be held responsible unless mine was the determining voice. I claimed that these appointments should be made by me, subject to the advice of the Government of India, information being given to that Government in every case. The claim has been practically admitted, and the justice of my contention upheld.

As Minister, I claim to have given an impetus to the establishment of medical schools in Bengal. Of Arts colleges for higher education, we have enough and perhaps more than enough. I myself have helped this movement by the establishment of the Ripon College. But there is a woeful lack of effort for the expansion of medical education in the province. Medical education is certainly more expensive, needing more outlay, initial and recurring; but the urgent need for it cannot be gainsaid. We have in Bengal one qualified medical practitioner for over forty thousand of our people; while in England they have one for eighteen hundred of the population.

In India, public benefactions do not flow so readily towards the expansion of medical relief as in other civilized countries; and yet it would be grossly unfair to charge our people with callousness to human suffering or the lack of charity for public purposes. Look at the princely benefactions, the gift of past generations, from the proceeds of which the poor are fed, the learned are supported, and the ministrations of religion nobly upheld. Public opinion has to be guided and led into this channel; and the Government should honour the distinguished men whose benefactions have helped to widen the area of medical education. I am afraid this has not always been done in recent times; and the lack of encouragement has stifled the flow of charity in this useful channel.

During my time, and in spite of financial stringency, the foundation-stone was laid of a medical school at Mymensingh; and the Government stands definitely pledged to establish similar schools, one after another, at Chittagong, Berhampore and Jalpaiguri. The impulse has been created, but it needs to be stimulated. I repeat that it is not done to the extent that it should be. Government honours, despite Non-Co-operation, are still appreciated; and the Raja is still somebody in the mofussil; and the Rai Bahadur too, only in a lesser degree. These distinctions afford a stimulus to the beneficence of the wealthy, and they have the further effect of ranging them definitely on the side of the Government. It is no use telling them that the Government is pleased. Government should afford practical proof of its approbation. Not words, but deeds, are wanted.

One of the familiar ways of attacking the Ministers was to charge them with inaction, or to father upon them measures for which they were in no way responsible. I have already referred to the Town Hall meeting where the Ministers were attacked for supporting the deportations. As a matter of fact, they knew nothing at all about them. The orders were issued by the Executive Government on their own responsibility, in the exercise of powers with which they were fully invested. Let us take another instance. A grave situation was developed at Chandpur, an important railway station in East Bengal, owing to an influx of coolies from Assam, who had struck work and were returning to their homes. I was asked by some of my friends to run up to Chandpur, although the matter was one that did not concern my department, and the Government was already dealing with it. I went and saw Sir Henry Wheeler, since Governor of Behar, who was then in charge of the department. As he himself was going down to Chandpur, he did not think it necessary that I should do so. Sir Henry Wheeler went down to Chandpur. He stayed there for days together and made an elaborate report. But our critics were not satisfied, and the matter was discussed at a meeting of the Legislative Council. Mr. Kissory Mohan Chowdhury, a member of Council representing the Rajshahi Division in North Bengal, charged us with doing nothing. He said:

'Though there was public agitation our popular Ministers did not think it necessary to do anything, though we expected much from them. We expected that they would personally go there to see things for themselves, but that was not done. No contribution was made by them, though from the Hon. Sir Henry Wheeler's report it would be seen that the coolies were suffering very much. But nothing was done by our popular Ministers.'

As soon as the hon. member sat down, I got up and challenged his statement. I said:

'I challenge the statement which has been made by the hon'ble member, and which he has been repeating again and again – that the Ministers have done nothing. He ought to have known that, as soon as I heard from the Chairman of the Chandpur Municipality that there was a chance of the outbreak of cholera, I sent out Rs. 6,000 and nine doctors to look after the coolies; and yet my hon'ble friend says that we did nothing, as if by repetition he could convert falsehood into truth.'

My friend climbed down by saying 'I did not know it.'

One other incident in this connexion, and I close this chapter of my reminiscences.

In October 1922, a disastrous flood overwhelmed North Bengal, causing havoc and loss of life over an extensive area. The Government was then at Darjeeling, and I was there as a member of the Government, having fixed Darjeeling as the place for the meetings of the Select Committee on the Calcutta Municipal Bill. Some friends who had come up to Darjeeling had seen, as they passed up the railway line, the terrible havoc that had been caused, and they pressed me to visit the affected area. Here again I was confronted with the same difficulty as at Chandpur, the department dealing with the matter not being within my jurisdiction. I felt the strongest inclination to visit the affected area and see if I could do anything. The medical needs, so far as I could ascertain, had already been supplied, but I felt that my presence would encourage our men and perhaps give me useful information. Having made up my mind I waited upon His Excellency, in order to obtain his permission, which was readily granted.

I went down on the following day, accompanied by some friends, three of whom were members of the Legislative Council. We trollied twenty miles under a burning sun, the land on both sides of the railway line being submerged, with carcases of dead animals floating here and there on the water. The area was infected, and it was a dismal and painful sight. The Magistrate, Mr. Reid, was good enough to accompany me and give me such information as I wanted.

I returned on the following day to Darjeeling, and immediately hurried to attend a meeting of the Select Committee on the Calcutta Municipal Bill. The strain was too much for me. I had an attack of fever followed by broncho-pneumonia, which at one time caused grave apprehension to my medical friends, whose kindness and care I can never forget. Sir Nilratan Sircar, foremost among our Indian medical practitioners, hurried up from Calcutta to Darjeeling. Col. Wilson, then acting as Surgeon-General, Major Hussain Surahwardy and Major K. K. Chatterjee were among those who were untiring in their care and attention of me.

Here let me say a word about Sir Nilratan Sircar, whose many-sided activities bear testimony to the ardour of his public spirit. He is not merely a doctor. An educationist, a public man, a social reformer, a pioneer in the domain of the industries, the range of his work extends far beyond the limits of the great profession of which he is an ornament. And his life, too, is an object-lesson to his countrymen. From the Campbell Medical School he passed on to the Calcutta Medical College, and it would be no exaggeration to say that he is one of the most brilliant products of his 'Alma Mater'. My case was a bad one but fortunately I recovered, my sound constitution helping the doctors, for broncho-pneumonia is a serious matter at the age of seventy-four. But there was a section of the Press that saw nothing good in an act of sacrifice on the part of a Minister, even though it might have brought him near to death's door. In reply to them my friends who went down with me to North Bengal addressed the following letter to the Press:

TO THE EDITOR OF THE 'STATESMAN'

Sir,—We have been painfully surprised by a perusal of the leading article in your issue of last Wednesday. It constitutes an attack on the Ministry of Local Self-government, which is the more surprising in view of the fact that the *Statesman* has always been forward in expressing its appreciation of the work Sir Surendranath Banerjea has been doing ever since he became Minister. The administration of relief in the flooded area appertains to the Reserved Branch of the Administration, and not to the Ministry of Local Self-government, and it is the ignoring of this cardinal fact which vitiates the outlook of the writer of the article in question, and leads him into erroneous, and we may add ungenerous, suppositions regarding the attitude of Government as a whole towards the problem of relieving distress, and of the reserved half of the Government of Bengal towards its transferred counterpart.

Leaving aside the above matters, however, we deem it our imperative duty to enlighten your readers regarding the fine work done by Sir Surendranath himself for relieving the distress in the affected districts. Although having little concern with the matter as Minister, he was deeply moved by the tales of woe pouring into him from the various sources, and, as soon as he got a reliable account of the ruin and devastation worked by the floods, from the Chairman of the Calcutta Corporation, who had come up to attend the meetings of the Select Committee on the Calcutta Municipal Bill, he summoned a few friends, including the Hon. Mr. P. C. Mitter, Mr. S. R. Das and Mr. Mullick, and started a fund there and then, to which both the Ministers contributed a thousand rupees each; and decided to proceed to Santahar by the next day's down mail, which, it is now public knowledge, he did. We who had the honour of accompanying him with Mr. Krishna Kumar Mitter, who had in the meantime arrived in response to an urgent telegram from Sir Surendranath, wish most distinctly to testify to the untiring zeal and devotion to duty which characterized his movements and acts during the whole time that he stayed at Santahar. He met Dr. Bentley on arrival in the morning, and had the gratification of learning that fourteen officers of the Health Department had been on the spot from the outset, working strenuously in their respective spheres; and Sir Surendranath personally saw them carrying on the work of burying or burning (as circumstances required) the floating carcases and dead human bodies, as he trollied down the railway line towards Bogra, along with Mr. Krishna Kumar Mitter and others, including the Sub-divisional Officer of Bogra. He had interviews with the representatives of the different relief parties on the spot; and was taken after breakfast by Mr. Reid, the Collector, Mr. Himayetuddin, the Chairman of the District Board of Rajshahi, and the Kumar of Natore, in the direction of Natore. The splendid and infectious enthusiasm of these public servants and relief workers filled Sir Surendranath with pride, and sustained him throughout the day's arduous activities, including trolly trips of close upon twenty miles in different directions in the boiling sun. He left for Darjeeling in the evening, after satisfying himself that the needed work had been taken well in hand, and that the official and non-official elements were in co-operation, and after deputing Mr. Krishna Kumar Mitter – another of Bengal's gifted sons – to take charge of the relief work in the parts of Naogong subdivision, where workers were still wanted. No one in his seventy-fourth year could do more, and we venture to think that Sir Surrendranath has set an example of public duty than which no finer is available in the India of to-day.

He had, however, gone down to Santahar with a cold, which got none the better for his going about the whole day in the sun, and he was down, on arrival back, with a touch of bronchitis and fever, which is now fortunately on the wane. We think, sir, you will admit that the above constitutes a record worthy of Bengal's Grand Old Man, as we all love to call him.—Yours, etc.,

SURENDRANATH MULLICK.
D. C. GHOSE,
Member, Bengal Legislative Council.
FANINDRALAL DE,
Member, Bengal Legislative Council.
B. C. CHATTERJEE,
Barrister-at-Law.

October 18, 1922.

36

Diarchy

Diarchy the essence of the Reforms – a tentative experiment – has diarchy failed ? – dependence upon the personal element – Ministerial salaries.

I HAVE REFERRED perhaps at some length to my work as a Minister, not so much for personal reasons as for the vindication of the Reforms. The cry has been raised, and this time within the precincts of the Council Chambers, that the Reforms are moonshine and that diarchy has been a dead failure. It is in one sense the renewal of an old attack. When the Reform Scheme was first published, and indeed on the eve of its publication, it was fiercely assailed by Extremist politicians. It was in an atmosphere critical and even hostile that the Reforms were launched into operation. The Meston award seriously handicapped their working; and financial stringency stood in the way of the inauguration and expansion of beneficent schemes of education, sanitation and industrial development. The attack has been renewed after the first term of the Legislative Councils with the added cry that diarchy has failed. Diarchy is the essence of the new system, and, if it is once conceded that it has not been successful, the Reforms must go, at least in their present form; and one of two things must happen, either the concession of complete autonomous government or a reversal to the old bureaucratic system. Whether it should be the one or the other must depend upon the judgment of Parliament.

What the final decision of Parliament is to be, we cannot anticipate. But Parliament and the British democracy have clearly indicated their views upon the grave issue of responsible government for India. Of course, they may change. I hope they will, in favour of a fresh advance. But, from all that we know of the English people, it may be safely assumed that they will not change in a hurry. And, when they do change, they stick to the old traditions and put on the old garb, as in the great Revolution of 1688. The preamble to the Government of India Act of 1919 (which is a parliamentary statute) provides that responsible government is the end and aim of British rule and that it is to be attained by progressive stages. The Act also provides that after 1929 a Parliamentary Commission is to make an enquiry and report upon what further changes in the constitution may be necessary. All these preliminaries are laid down with a view to giving effect to the message of August 20, 1917.

It will thus be seen that the British Parliament and democracy are definitely pledged to the introduction and progressive expansion of responsible government, the full measure of which will be conceded only after a trial of ten years. The immediate grant of full-fledged responsible government therefore goes beyond the declared policy of Parliament. Are they likely to be hustled into a change of this policy under the pressure of obstructionist tactics? That has never been the traditional attitude of a British Parliament; and the great organs of English opinion have strongly condemned the obstructionist methods that are being followed in some of the Legislatures, declaring that they are calculated to prolong rather than shorten the period of probation. If these obstructionist tactics inside the Councils are a prelude to revolutionary methods outside, by inflaming the minds of the masses, they are intelligible and perhaps logical; otherwise they are futile and meaningless. They will not wreck the Government, but may deprive it of its popular element, and a return to the old bureaucratic system may be the outcome of presistence in this policy. The obstructionists may temporarily pose as heroes who have defied an autocratic Government, but they will leave behind them for their countrymen the bitter harvest of their sinister activities. That has already been the result in Bengal and the Central Provinces. In this connexion, it may not be out of place to quote a few lines from the letter of a revolutionary produced in the Cawnpore cases, reports of which have appeared in the newspapers. The letter says:

> 'Without a party with a revolutionary outlook, the tactics of breaking the Councils can hardly be carried on successfully.'

Thus Revolution and the breaking up of the Councils go together in the opinion of this revolutionary writer.

In this onslaught upon diarchy, the fundamental conditions, subject to which diarchy found a place in the Reform Scheme, seem to have been ignored. Nobody, not even its supporters, were enamoured of diarchy, many were frankly doubtful of its success. At best it was a tentative beginning, the first starting-point of a great experiment. I said in my evidence before the Joint Parliamentary Committee: 'We (and here I was speaking on behalf of the National Liberal Federation) support diarchy, not because it is

23

an ideal system, but because it seems to be the only feasible system for giving effect to the message of August 20, 1917. It provides for Responsible Government at the first start, and it brings Responsible Government within sight by providing progressive stages, and therefore we support it.'

I recognize that in the attack now made upon diarchy several ex-Ministers and prominent leaders of the Liberal or Moderate party have joined. One may differ from them, but no one can call their motives in question. They supported diarchy at the first start. They have now turned against it. Their assault, however, stands upon a different footing from that of the Swarajists, who are out to wreck the Reforms, and are not scrupulous as to the means that they employ. The late Secretary of State, Lord Olivier, despite the restraints of his official position, felt constrained to charge their leaders with intrigue, bribery and corruption. However much we may admire the organization of the Swarajists, we must wholeheartedly condemn their tactics, and scan with scrupulous care their political shibboleths and their resonant war-cries. In August, 1923, when the question of Ministerial salaries came on for discussion before the Bengal Legislative Council, a member who was to have recorded his vote in favour of the Ministers was besieged in his house by a Swarajist crowd, and by a sheer demonstration of force prevented from attending the meeting. The newspapers publish particulars of definite sums given for abstention from the recording of votes. The dominance of the Swarajists has demoralized the public life of Bengal. The purity of the past is gone. Force and fraud have become determining factors in deciding public issues.

Has diarchy then so hopelessly failed, beyond the possibility of correction or improvement within the period still left to it for trial, that it must forthwith be given up? Or has it been so completely successful that further trial in the progressive stages is no longer necessary? The last point has not been raised. It is attacked because it is said to have been a failure, a hopeless failure due to radical defects in the system. The point needs examination. I cannot say that diarchy has failed in Bengal. It would have been more successful if we did not suffer from financial stringency, and if we were not encumbered by the stepmotherly attentions of the Finance Department. It is the Meston award and the Finance Department that between them checked some of the beneficent activities of the department of which I was in charge.

This is not the place in which to enter into a discussion of the financial considerations involved, but the Meston award perpetrated a grave injustice by depriving Bengal of one half of the proceeds of the income-tax, which it formerly had, and by diverting the whole of the yield of the jute tax, which is peculiar to Bengal, to the coffers of the Imperial Government. In Bengal it would be difficult to raise the cry of the failure of the Reforms if we had more money and could liberally distribute it among the nation-building departments, such as Sanitation, Education and the Industries. I know as a matter of fact that several schemes of water-supply for the riparian municipalities were ready, but could not be started, because there was no money, and the new taxes imposed did not yield the surplus that was expected, and upon the basis of which we could have raised a loan for water-supply and anti-malarial operations. Funds were not forthcoming and our activities were crippled.

Where we could get on without money, we were not hampered by a diarchical form of Government. In the matter of legislation and of public appointments my department made a notable advance. The number of municipalities vested with the right of electing their Chairmen was increased. A bill was introduced into the Bengal Legislative Council liberalizing the constitution of the mofussil municipalities. The constitution of the Local Boards, which deal with the institutions of Local Self-government in the rural areas of a sub-division, was broadened, and they now have the right of electing their own non-official chairmen. When I assumed office there were five District Boards which did not enjoy the right of electing their Chairmen. This privilege was conceded to them. But the most advanced piece of municipal legislation during my tenure of office was the enactment of the Calcutta Municipal Law. It democratized the constitution of the Corporation of Calcutta, the second city in the Empire. In other departments too there has been an advance as circumstances have permitted. A tree is judged by its fruits. How is it possible, in the face of these facts, to say, with anything like regard for truth, that diarchy has been a failure in the departments I controlled?

The success of a diarchy seems to me to depend largely upon the atmosphere created in the Secretariat in which it has to work. It depends upon the goodwill and the hearty co-operation of the Governor, the members of the Executive Council in charge of the reserved side, and of the permanent officials of the various departments. It is the Governor who gives the cue, the first and ruling impulse; the members of the Executive Council must sympathetically respond; and the permanent officials must follow their lead. It was this condition of things, this atmosphere, that was established in Bengal from the start of the Reforms. Both Lord Ronaldshay and Lord Lytton were statesmanlike in their attitude of sympathy and help, and stood by the Ministers with their generous support. They acted as constitutional sovereigns and made no distinction between Members and Ministers. Possibly their experience of English public life helped them, and members of the Executive Council, in their turn, made no distinction between themselves and their ministerial colleagues. Goodwill was the predominating note; it was coupled with the practical recognition of an equal status.

The Government thus formed on the whole a happy family, despite differences of opinion inseparable from the discussion of public affairs. Of heated conflict and collision we had little or none; and in our discussions we had not much of the taste of the alleged evils of diarchy. A sweet reasonableness, dominated by the spirit of compromise, was the prevailing feature of our deliberations. During Lord Lytton's time the Government, as a whole, would often meet to discuss questions on the reserved side. Here we had no responsibility; we could only give our opinion, and our colleagues on the reserved side were under no obligation to follow our advice, and sometimes they did not even consult us. But our position was rendered difficult by our being held responsible for what have been called the repressive measures. The Joint Parliamentary Committee absolved us from all responsibility in regard to them. All the same, our critics would fasten responsibility upon us, for it afforded them an opportunity for attacking us. Our lips were sealed, we could not reply: chivalry had no place in these attacks. Our silence was interpreted as acquiescence, and the campaign of vilification went on apace.

I remember the Ministers being attacked at a Town Hall meeting for an act of the Executive Government in regard to which they were not consulted and the Government was not bound to consult them. The irresponsibility of some of the speakers – and they were supposed to be men of light and leading – went so far that they demanded our resignation, forgetting that the law provided a machinery for compelling us to resign, through a vote of censure of the Legislative Council, when we were guilty of any serious dereliction of duty in regard to any matter for which we were responsible. The extraordinary feature of the meeting was that, not the members of the Executive Council who passed the order, but the Ministers who did not, were summoned to retire. Such was the even-handed justice done to Ministers in India charged with great affairs of State.

The instance affords illustration of the mentality of some of those who have so glibly condemned diarchy in Bengal, and of the atmosphere in which it was condemned. To me it seems that it is the old cry in a new garb raised by some of the Extremists, 'Down with the Reforms!' The old cry would now have fallen flat. It was necessary in the interests of the game to refurbish and rehabilitate it. The resignation of some Ministers in different parts of India and their evidence added to its weight. Let me not be misunderstood. I do not for one moment mean to assert that diarchy is an ideal system, or that it is anything but a temporary expedient. I do not know sufficient of the condition of things in the other provinces, but I claim for Bengal that diarchy has done useful work and would probably have done more if we had not suffered from financial stringency.

I would refer to the Calcutta Municipal Act, which has democratized the municipal constitution of Calcutta. Apart from its merits, even from the Swarajist point of view it must be a good Act, for they have largely availed themselves of it, not indeed with a view to destroying, but to working it. Their acceptance of office under it is evidence of their approval of the measure. I wonder with what consistency or even show of fairness they can condemn diarchy, the system that gave them this Act. The very men who are loud in their professions of dislike and hatred for the Government have occupied positions which are departments of that Government and subject to that Government's control. I hold that it would not be consistent with the facts of the case to say that diarchy has failed in Bengal as far as its own legitimate business is concerned.

Let us probe the matter a little further. What about the various administrative measures, for the Indianization of the Services in Bengal, that have been inaugurated under a diarchical Government? What about the reduction of Indian Medical Service appointments in Bengal from forty-two to twenty-four? What about the impetus to the establishment of medical schools in the mofussil, and to the study of Ayurvedic medicine? What about the advance in Local Self-government in every department under the diarchy? Lastly, what about the transformation of the atmosphere in the various departments of the transferred subjects, in Sanitation, Local Self-government, Medical relief, and other branches?

The real difficulty about diarchy is that it depends upon the uncertainties of the personal element, which may vary in the different provinces, and in the same province from time to time, and against which no rules and no hard and fast convention can afford adequate protection. Further, it may often set up two divergent and even conflicting interests (the reserved and transferred), which must interfere with that homogeneity and solidarity which is the truest guarantee of efficiency, and which in the long run secures public approbation. Lastly, so far as one can judge, educated public opinion condemns it; and no popular institution can in these days thrive without the support of public opinion. I would therefore support the recommendation in the Montagu-Chelmsford Report that after five years a Parlimentary Commission should be sent out to report on the whole situation.

Diarchy should go as quickly as possible, not because it has been a failure everywhere, but because public opinion does not want it. But in any case full provincial autonomy cannot be given without the necessary safeguards. We must have liberty, but not licence. Licence is the mother of revolutions. The freest institutions must be subject to the necessary checks, provided by statute, or by rules, or by conventions. The English constitution is thus safeguarded against the risks incidental to all human institutions, and England is the mother of parliaments, furnishing the model to all parliamentary institutions. I recognize that there is a possible risk of the loss of efficiency; but we must face it, for good government is no substitute for self-government.

The real danger is the domination of the Swarajist party. They have been tried in constructive statesmanship and administration, and they have failed. Their methods are selfish and unscrupulous. They have in the administration of the Corporation subordinated the general weal to party interests. In the large concerns of the province there is no guarantee that the same principles and the same objectives will not guide them. In their case power, instead of exercising a sobering influence, has generated a dangerous intoxication. But a party that does not make righteousness the guiding impulse of its policy cannot long remain in power. Therein lies the hope of the future of self-government. The divine gift of self-government has in it the seeds of its own self-preservation and self-correction.

Almost from the very moment that the Bengal Legislative Council was constituted the Extremist Press raised the cry for a reduction of the salaries of the Ministers. It was taken up with greedy avidity by disappointed ministerial office-seekers. There were 140 members, and among them only three were to be Ministers. The more ambitious among the remainder were dissatisfied. One of these gentlemen told me, almost immediately after the formation of the Council, that he would have the Ministers dismissed or their salaries reduced in three months' time. Many three months passed within the specified time of three years – the life-time of the Council. But the Ministers were not dismissed nor their salaries reduced. The Council was dissolved. My friend retired to his constituency for their suffrages. They were not particularly charmed with his shibboleth. They would not have him. He withdrew into private life, a dissatisfied man, and went back to the contentious wranglings of his great profession.

In connexion with this controversy, a curious fact comes to light, which so far has not been explained, and which without sufficient explanation would afford an unfortunate commentary upon the consistency and soundness of certain phases of Indian public opinion. On the eve of the enactment of the Reforms Act, in 1919, Indian opinion of every shade and complexion was unanimous in demanding that the status and emoluments of the popular Minister should be the same as those of Members of the Executive Council; but, as soon as the Act was passed and the Councils were constituted with popular Ministers in charge of the transferred departments, a demand was put forth in every Council for a reduction of their salaries, while keeping intact the salaries of the Members of the Executive Councils, which were not subject to the vote of the Legislative Council. The movement was universal and persistent; and was engineered by the Extremist Press. It had its roots partly in personal feeling and partly in the triumph of the Moderate party, which had successfully secured the passage of the Reforms through Parliament in the face of strenuous Extremist opposition. In the Bengal Legislative Council there were five motions made during its brief tenure of life. Every one of them was defeated. But the opposition continued its work, in defiance of the unanimous sentiment of the country uttered only twelve months before. Let me for a moment call attention to the solid body of the opinion of united India, untempered by a single dissentient voice.

At the special session of the Congress held in Bombay in September, 1918, under the presidency of Mr. Hassan Imam, the following Resolution was passed on the motion of Pundit Madan Mohan Malavya: 'The status and salary of the Ministers shall be the same as those of the members of the Executive Council.' The motion was supported by Mr. Nehru and Mr. Tilak, among others.

At the first conference of the Moderate party held in Bombay in November, 1918, the following resolution was passed on the motion of the Rt. Hon. Mr. Srinivasa Shastri:

> 'That the status and emoluments of the Ministers should be identical with those of the Executive Councillors.'

Again, at the special session of the All-India Moslem League, also held in Bombay in September, 1918, under the presidency of the Hon. the Raja of Mahmudabad, on the motion of the Hon. Moulvi Fazlul Huq, the following resolution was passed: 'The status and salary of the Ministers shall be the same as that of the the members of the Executive Council'.

The report of the Committee of the non-official members of the Imperial Legislative Council recommended 'that the Ministers be placed as regards pay and emoluments on a footing of equality with the members of the Executive Councils'.

The non-official members of the Bengal Legislative Council in their report on the Reforms Scheme observed that 'the status, privileges and emoluments of Ministers should be the same as those of the members of the Provincial Executive Council'. But the most authoritative body of opinion on the subject was that of prominent leaders who gave evidence before the Joint Parliamentary Committee in London; and here again we note the same solid unanimity without a single dissentient note. When Non-Co-operators like Mr. Patel and co-operators like Mr. Shastri stand on the same platform, we are entitled to hold that the plea for the reduction of Ministers' salaries stood on the flimsiest ground. Mr. Madhava Rao and Mr. Patel, members of the Congress Deputation, deposed in their evidence before the Joint Committee, 'Ministers are to be on equality in pay and status with the members of the Executive Council'. It was a charge brought against me by the Extremist Press that, in voting against the reduction of ministerial salary, I had gone back on the principles of my past life, for I have always pleaded for retrenchment in public expenditure and the curtailment of high salaries. But they conveniently overlooked the fact that, in regard to this one matter, I made an exception. Let me quote my evidence before the Joint Parliamentary Committee on this point. Here are the question and answer:

Q. 'If you consider a dual form of Government acceptable in principle, are there any points of detail, the modification of which you regard as necessary? If so, what are those points and what modifications would you suggest?

A. I consider it essential that (1) there should be a common purse, accompanied by joint deliberation of both parts of Government, before the Budget is framed; (2) the Budget resolutions of the Legislature, whether on reserved or transferred subjects, should be binding on the Executive, subject to the power of certification provided for in the Joint Report; (3) the Executive Council should consist of two members only, one of whom should be an Indian; (4) the Ministers should occupy the same position as to salary, status, etc., as members of the Executive Council; (5) there should be standing Committees both as to reserved and transferred departments, and Under-Secretaries, as suggested in the Joint Report; and (6) that "taxation for provincial purposes" should be a transferred subject, and no proposals for taxation should be brought forward before the Legislature without the approval of the Ministers.'

What was at the back of the mind of all India was equality of status, based upon equal emoluments as between Ministers and members of the Executive Council. I deliberately expressed this opinion, and never wavered from it. It would have been disastrous to the usefulness and the authority, the invisible power that the man in authority, apart from his official position, exercises over his fellows, if it went forth that a difference had been made between the popular Minister and the Executive Councillor who were both members of the same Government, wielding similar powers. Financial considerations are valuable; but in this case there was yet another factor more important, affecting the fate of a great and novel experiment. Nor was the slightest shade of an argument adduced to show why the opinion of united India in 1918 and 1919 should be brushed aside in 1921. It was all party spirit, reinforced by personal feeling and the lurking desire to wreck the Reforms. The sacred name of retrenchment was invoked as a mask to cover a movement that had a far less righteous purpose to serve.

I think I may fittingly close this chapter by referring for a moment to my justification for accepting the office of Minister. The cry was raised, by a section of the Extremist Press, that I should not have accepted ministerial office; and it was employed by Mr. C. R. Das in his electioneering campaign against me. The head and front of my offence was that I was a member of the Government. To that I have a reply as conclusive as any that can be found in the armoury of controversy. For self-government, step by step, stage by stage, I have worked through life. I worked for it when really nobody in India dreamt of it, when the country was content to work in the old ways and was satisfied with the old institutions. I worked for it when the Government treated it as a fantastic dream. In the Imperial Legislative Council, only ten years ago, I was described as an impatient idealist, in this very connexion, by my lamented friend, Sir William Meyer, who was then Finance Minister. Our efforts, persistent and strenuous, have changed all this and even the view-point of the Government. The message of August 20 is a tribute to our success. We were now invited to co-operate and to join hands with the Government, in order to ensure the success of the very thing for which we had been fighting for nearly half a century, to raise in our midst the temple of self-government, which would efface all distinctions and all inequalities and be for all time to come the symbol of our equal status with the free nations of the earth. Should we have rejected this offer, which we believed to be genuine and sincere? I have no hesitation in saying that it would have been unwise, unpatriotic, almost treacherous to do so. Therefore, in all sincerity and singleness of heart, which even the voice of slander will not be able to cloud, did I join the Government in a ministerial position. The familiar trick is to urge that we have changed. It is not *we* who have changed, but the Government, which, according to its lights, is adapting itself to the rapidly progressive tendencies of modern India. The point of difference between us and the Government is that it is not moving fast enough to meet the progressive requirements of the country or the growing aspirations of the people.

37
Conclusion

The secret of long life – my views on Hindu social problems – the conservatism of the Hindu – a moral and a message to my countrymen.

MANY OF MY FRIENDS have asked me to record a note as to what I consider to be the secret of health and longevity. I am now on the wrong side of seventy-five, but I enjoy fairly good health, and my mental agility remains unimpaired. They say that my experience would prove useful.

I have endeavoured in life to carry out the principle that the preservation of health is our first and foremost duty; everything else depends upon it. The machine must be kept fit and in a high degree of efficiency before it can do its work properly. Our best men, with a few exceptions, have nearly all died early, Ram Mohun Roy, Keshub Chunder Sen, Kristo Das Pal, Ram Gopal Ghose, and others died in the prime of life. They exemplified the old Latin proverb: 'Those whom the gods love die young.' What a gain it would have been, if they had been spared longer to guide and lead their countrymen with their ripe judgment and experience.

The first and essential condition of good health, to my mind, is regular exercise at stated times. It should be moderate and given up as soon as one feels a sense of hilarity. Excess is to be avoided and is bound to do harm. The physical system accustoms itself to respond to the muscular rhythm that nature feels as the result of regular exercise. Throughout life, and even now, I take half-an-hour's exercise in the morning upon an empty stomach, and forty minutes' in the afternoon after tea. The latter I have sometimes to give up on account of public engagements, but I must have this exercise before dinner. Walking, in my opinion, is the best form of exercise. I used to add to it dumb-bells and Indian clubs in my early days. To take exercise early in the morning before a meal is the Indian practice, and I find that Miss Harriet Martineau recommends it. Almost equally essential is the habit of orderly and regular living. I am sorry to have to say that our countrymen do not always realize its importance. Their hours of meal and sleep are not always fixed, and they hardly recognize that the body is a machine, working with orderly precision, whose wants must be carefully attended to. One of my mottoes through life has been to avoid evening functions and dinners as far as possible. ' Early to bed and early to rise ' is a wise precept, which I read in Todd's *Students' Guide* while yet a boy, and I have consistently tried to practise it. Even when, as a member of the Government, I had to attend State functions, I tried to run away as early as I could. On one occasion, when Lord Strathcona gave a dinner to the Press representatives in London, of whom I was one, I quietly slipped away as soon as the dinner was over and the toasts began. Fortunately for me, there was a door left open to admit fresh air close to where I had my seat. I had marked it before dinner, and as soon as that was over, I quickly and quietly made my exit. I do not know if anybody noticed me, but I was comfortably in bed by eleven o'clock.

On another occasion, when at a meeting of the Imperial Legislative Council we were discussing the Rowlatt Bill, Lord Chelmsford readjourned the Council at dinner time and asked members to reassemble in an hour and a half. I got up as soon as the announcement was made, and said, 'My Lord, I go to bed at nine o'clock'. 'You are excused, Mr. Banerjea,' said Lord Chelmsford, with that winsome goodwill which never failed him. On the following morning when we reassembled, I learnt that some of those who had attended the night sitting had to be roused from sleep to give their votes. I will give another instance to illustrate my incorrigible habit of going to bed early. This was in 1897, when Mr. Gokhale and myself were in London as witnesses for the Welby Commission. He wanted me to see Sir Henry Irving play the part of Napoleon at Drury Lane Theatre, which was close to the Hotel Victoria, where we were both staying. I said, ' If you really want me, you must drag me out of bed and let me return home by eleven o'clock'. He said, 'All right, I will do that'. I was in bed, and at nine o'clock I heard a knock at my door. On the stroke of the hour, Gokhale was there. Now there was no escape for me. I had to get up and be ready. Gokhale escorted me to the theatre, where he sat by me, watching me with keen interest. For me it was more or less a novel experience. To him also it was novel in another sense: watching a stiff-necked Puritan like myself, who avoided theatres, succumb to the charms of the greatest living actor among Englishmen. I enjoyed the acting thoroughly. For Gokhale it was a personal triumph; I shared it in the joy of the spectacle I witnessed. I never could understand, and to me it is still an enigma, how Sir Henry Irving, who was, I think, above six feet, could adapt himself to the stature of Napoleon, who was not more than five feet four inches in height. However that may be, Gokhale, splendid fellow that he was, brought me back to my room by about eleven o'clock.

Early to bed has been the invariable practice of my life, and to it I largely ascribe the good health I enjoy. I am not so sure about the early rising. I have always been a late riser. I usually sleep about eight hours out of the twenty-four, and sometimes I extend it to nine or even ten hours. Sleep has been my greatest enjoyment, and I find that it is more or less a family gift. When I retire for sleep I close the chambers of my mind against all worry and anxiety, and that is the secret of sound sleep. At the start, perhaps, it requires a little will-power, but with practice it becomes a matter of habit. I do not think excessive brain work is a real menace to health, provided it is congenial and does not interfere with sleep. On the contrary, when congenial, it acts as a tonic, and the fatigue of it is all merged in the delight which it generates and the stimulus it imparts to the nerves.

I have said nothing about food or drink. Abstention from smoking and intoxicating drinks has always been recommended for good health. I have been a total abstainer from both, and cannot say that my enjoyment of life has been less hearty than that of those who smoke or drink. They may perhaps help to add to our social amenities, but they are neither indispensable nor free from risks to health, even though they may not be indulged in immoderately. As for food, it varies according to climatic conditions and racial predilections. Every community has a rough sort of idea of the food upon which it can best thrive, and the idea is generally an ancestral bequest, subject to limitations that time or changes in local conditions may impose. The European is a meat-eater. The Indian is a vegetarian. The Bengalee is a fish-eater, and fish is a light, healthy, and nourishing food. There is a marked similarity in the matter of food between the Japanese and the Bengalees. Both are rice and fish-eaters, though the Japanese is more generous in his patronage of a meat diet. One thing is clear – at least that is my experience – that food should vary with age. One should follow the intimations of nature, which, with the advance of years, creates a steadily growing disinclination for animal food.

After all is said and done, the crowning aspiration of the Latin poet holds as good to-day as it did in his own time. The highest of earthly blessings is a sound mind in a sound body – *mens sana in corpore sano*. The sound body, *corpus sanum,* is the foundation, and *mens sana,* the sound mind, is the superstructure. A clear conscience, freedom from worry and from hatred and malice, and peace and goodwill to all, are the stable foundations upon which the physical system must rest. They are moral rather than material in their essence. After all the mind and body must act and react upon one another, and strengthen one another. The mind dominating the body, the physical co-operating with the moral, must form a homogeneous whole, checking and restraining whatever is evil in human nature, improving and elevating whatever is good in us, thus qualifying the individual man to do his duty to himself and to society, and to rise to the full measure of his stature.

My reminiscences disclose my views and my mental attitude with regard to the political situation in India and the side-issues that they raise. Concerning the social side, however, I have said little or nothing, except incidentally, when they have formed a part of political problems or of quasi-political discussions. For instance, I have referred once or twice to the question of enforced widowhood prevailing in Hindu society. The problem occupies a large place in Hindu thought. It is daily growing in importance. Its discussion is welcomed even by those who are not in favour of any reform or change. The other social problems, indeed, stand upon a more or less different plane. There is not about them, perhaps, the same popular interest, the same history linked with one of the greatest names in modern India, nor the same growing sense of a wrong done to the weaker sex, which the latter are beginning to realize. But all the same, it is useless to disguise the fact that the social problem in India is weighted with issues of unusual difficulty and complexity. You cannot think of a social question affecting the Hindu community that is not bound up with religious considerations; and when divine sanction, in whatever form, is invoked in aid of a social institution, it sits enthroned in the popular heart with added firmness and fixity, having its roots in sentiment rather than in reason.

Thus the social reformer in India has to fight against forces believed to be semi-divine in their character, and more or less invulnerable against the commonplace and mundane weapons of expediency and common sense. This feeling transmitted through generations has assumed the complexion of a deep-seated instinct. It is against a social edifice, resting upon traditional instinct and reinforced by religious conviction, that the Indian social reformer has had to fight; and that he has been able at times to make an appreciable impression, as in the case of Chaitanya, not only bears testimony to his forceful and commanding personality, but also to the attitude of the Indian masses, always responsive to real greatness, and to the necromancy of high endeavours, when inspired by lofty motives, though these may be pitted against injunctions professedly sacred. The glamour of divine origin, claimed for the social custom that is assailed, is eclipsed by the actual presence of the semi-divine person who claims to communicate his message amid a flood of heavenly effulgence, which overpowers the faithful and inspires them with an enthusiasm that carries everything before it. The people feel the advent of an avatar with a message repealing the old and communicating the new. He is bound by no convention; he is above and beyond all formula. He has in him the inspiration of a revelation, proclaiming the truth that is in him, and he proclaims it in a form that touches the heart and appeals to the imagination.

Such an avatar was Chaitanya, the greatest reformer that Bengal has produced. He, like Buddha, was an iconoclast, waging war against caste and denouncing enforced widowhood. One divine message is thus arrayed against another, through the mouth of an elect of the Almighty. But the old lingers, the struggle between the old and the new still continues; and the friends of humanity turn to the progressive forces of the world for their ultimate triumph. Nevertheless, a definite stage towards progress is reached. Thought is let loose, winged with a new inspiration, and there is nothing more potent than the influence of new ideas, which, like a streamlet, flow down the mountain-side of established custom, eat into its substance and broaden and deepen into an ever-extending channel.

The course of social progress has thus been slow; for great men are not as plentiful as blackberries. The religious feeling introduces an element of complexity; and, further, the forward movement of a huge society is necessarily slow. Nevertheless, the movement is there, and a little leaven leaveneth the mass.

Our surroundings being what they are, and what they have been for generations, every Hindu has in him a strong conservative bias. The great Napoleon used to say, 'Scratch a Russian and you will find a tartar.' Scratch a Hindu and you will find him a conservative. Of course, there are notable exceptions. All honour to the men, such, for instance, as the members of the Brahmo Samaj, who in obedience to the call of duty have adopted and practised in their lives more advanced ideas in regard to social observances. They represent a standing protest against our more conservative community. I have, however, never been able to make up my mind to follow the advanced principles of the Brahmo Samaj. They are the goal to be reached, and, to my mind, they should be reached by progressive stages. There is no such thing as a principle in public affairs, but every principle has to be determined by the circumstances of its application. This is a maxim which Edmund Burke is never tired of repeating, and in India its most illustrious advocate was Raja Ram Mohun Roy, the founder of the Brahmo Samaj. He was the inaugurator of the new faith, but he kept up his touch with the old, by his persistence in wearing the Brahminical thread to the end. Maharshi Debendranath Tagore followed him in this respect, and the Adi Brahmo Samaj have taken their lead from the saintly Maharshi.

I feel that, if we have to advance in social matters, we must, so far as practicable, take the community with us, by a process of steady and gradual uplift, so that there may be no sudden disturbance or dislocation, the new being adapted to the old, and the old assimilated to the new. That has been the normal path of progress in Hindu society through the long centuries. It would be idle to contend that Hindu society is to-day where it was two hundred years ago. It moves slowly, perhaps more slowly than many would wish, but in the words of Galileo 'it does move', more or less according to the lines of adaptation that I have indicated. The question of sea-voyage, or child-marriage, or even enforced widowhood, is not to-day where it was in the latter part of the last century. Fifty years ago I was an outcaste (being an England-returned Brahmin) in the village where I live. To-day I am an honoured member of the community. My public services have, perhaps, partly contributed to the result. But they would have been impotent, as in the case of Raja Ram Mohun Roy for many long years after his death, if they were not backed by the slow, the silent, the majestic forces of progress, working noiselessly but irresistibly in the bosom of society, helping on the fruition of those ideas which have been sown in the public mind. Remarkable indeed have been, in many respects, the relaxations and the removal of restrictions of caste. Dining with non-Hindus, which was an abomination not many years ago, is now connived at, if not openly countenanced. A still more forward step towards loosening the bonds of caste has been taken within the last few years. The barriers of marriage between some sub-castes have been relaxed, and marriages between hitherto prohibited sub-castes of Brahmins and Kayasthas are not infrequent, and I have had some personal share in this reform. Beneficent are the activities of the Brahmo Samaj, but behind them is the slower but larger movement of the general community, all making towards progress.

I have now closed my reminiscences. They are the product of mature thought and prolonged deliberation, and of the conviction that a public life so eventful as mine, so full of changes, from the prison to the council chamber, from dismissal from public service to elevation to Ministerial office, may prove useful to my countrymen. There is yet a long journey ahead of us before we reach the promised land. The desert has not yet been crossed. We are scarcely over the first stage. A long, long period of toil and travail awaits us; and perhaps in this wearisome journey the counsel and example of a fellow-traveller, who has some experience of it in its early stages, and has tasted its toils and its triumphs, may be welcomed by those who, foot-sore with travel and oppressed with the burdensomeness of their task, may look around for inspiration, if not guidance. I claim to have had a high patriotic purpose in writing these reminiscences. I want to do justice to the memories of honoured colleagues, many of whom are now dead. I want to indicate the beginnings, the growth, and the early development of national life, so that they may afford a guide for the future. Above all, I want to guard against the perils and temptations that beset us in the onward march to our goal. I began these reminiscences on May 31, 1915, in my quiet little villa in the suburbs of Ranchi, now in the province of Behar, and I continued them steadily till they were interrupted by my appointment as Minister of Local Self-government. I resumed the work in January, 1924; and it has been to me a labour of love; for it has enabled me to live over again the days of my youth and manhood in the companionship of honoured colleagues whom death has removed from our ranks. No pleasure is comparable to that which one feels amid surroundings which have passed away, but the memory of which still lives. Indeed, it takes one away from the living present to the dead past – a past, however, no longer inanimate or inert, but revived into life by the touch of the memories of strenuous work and high aspirations.

Now what is the moral to which these reminiscences point, and the lesson which they seek to enforce? Let me here quote Mr. Romesh Chunder Dutt – and he was no dreamer, not even an enthusiast. He was a man of affairs, and one of the most level-headed amongst them. He had, indeed, the gift of an historic imagination, as evidenced by his fine novels, but it was an imagination chastened by his grasp of the inwardness of things. Writing to me from Baroda, where he was Prime Minister at the time, he said – and the letter appears in his life by Mr. J. N. Gupta of the Indian Civil Service –: 'What a wonderful revolution we have seen within the lifetime of a generation. What a change – what a noble part you have played in leading that change.' 'We have witnessed in our times' said Romesh Chunder Dutt 'a wonderful change.' It assumes the form and complexion of a bloodless revolution.

This is no exaggeration of language, but the bare truth; and contemporary history bears it out. Looking at the political side, what do we find? In 1875, when I began my public life, our local bodies were devoid of the popular element. With the exception of four municipalities in Bengal – their number now is 116 – the members were all nominated by the Government, and so was the chairman, their executive head. The Legislative Councils were in the same position. The members were all nominees of the Government. On the executive Government, which determined the policy and the measures of the administration, there were no Indian representatives, nominated or elected. There was only a handful of Indians in the Indian Civil Service which is the *corps d'élite* governing the country. Indian opinion was weak, hardly vocal. The pulsations of national life were not felt. The great Indian continent consisted of innumerable units, disintegrated, without coherence or consistency, without unity of purpose or aim; speaking with different voices, wrangling, quarrelling, contending, with their energies dissipated amid a conflict of views and a Babel of tongues.

Now contrast this picture with what we see before us. In Bengal, as in other provinces, the local bodies are constituted on a popular basis; the constitution of the Calcutta Corporation, the greatest in the Indian Empire, is democratic. The Legislative Councils are all organized on popular lines, with a predominance of the popular element. On the Executive Councils there is a fair representation of the Indian element which has a potential voice in the government of the country; and, lastly, the beginnings of Parliamentary institutions have been introduced in the provinces with the definite pledge that full responsible government is in sight. The Indianization of the services is proceeding apace. There may be, and indeed there are, complaints as to the pace, but the idea that India is for the

Indians is definitely recognized as a cardinal principle of the Government.

The potency of Indian public opinion has been fully established by the modification of the Partition of Bengal, which had been repeatedly declared by high authority to be a settled fact, but which Indian opinion declined to accept as such, and Indian opinion triumphed. The Press to-day is free, vocal, all but omnipotent. Our organizations – social, political, and industrial – cover the land from end to end. Thus a stupendous revolution has been achieved in less than fifty years' time. It is bloodless except for occasional and transient outbursts of anarchical violence. The more ardent spirits may not be, and perhaps are not, satisfied with what has been achieved. They urge a more rapid pace, perhaps even a shorter cut to the goal. But that there has been a vast transformation none can gainsay. The world-forces may have helped the movement. But we too did our bit. Self-government was the end and aim of our political efforts; constitutional methods the means for its attainment. The Indian National Congress was our great outstanding organization, and it recognized no method except by, and through, the constitution for the achievement of self-government within the Empire. For more than thirty years it worked upon these constitutional lines with undeviating singleness of purpose; and marvellous has been its achievement.

And here let me raise a warning note. There is a feeling amongst some that, if necessary, we should travel beyond the constitution and the limits of the British Empire to achieve the full measure of our freedom and our status in the civilized world. To that my reply is that the necessity has not yet arisen; nor does it seem to me, from all that one knows of British history, that it will arise within a measurable distance of time of which we need take any note. It is a mistake in politics to take too long views of things. We may then be apt to drift into ideals the realization of which may hamper our present activities and our immediate growth and progress. 'Sufficient unto the day is the evil thereof' is a scriptural text which the man of affairs should never lose sight of. If we proclaim that we aspire to be independent of the British connexion, that we want self-government, pure and simple, without being hampered by the obligations of our position as members of the British Commonwealth, no one can oppose an aspiration which in the abstract is so just and patriotic. But it is circumstances that impart to every political principle its colour and its discriminating effect. Now what will happen if we accept this ideal and seek to enforce it in our everyday political activities? We shall get the whole of the British Empire, with its immense power, against us and the fulfilment of our ideal. Whereas, if we limit our aspiration to the dominion status, we get the whole of this influence on our side. We are not only not handicapped, but we enlist on our behalf the sympathies, and it may be the active help, of the British democracy, and even in some cases of the self-governing dominions. Severance they will object to, and perhaps strenuously oppose. Union and incorporation they will welcome, and even help.

After we have attained dominion status we may leave to our successors to decide what should be done towards the accomplishment of further progress, if deemed necessary and desirable. They will be the best judges; they will decide according to the conditions then prèvalent. And in the meantime we go on with our work of securing dominion status with the full support of the British Empire, and perhaps of civilized mankind. Is it possible to withstand the force of these considerations?

But is dominion status to be obtained by a process of orderly evolution, or by methods that are frankly revolutionary, or are at least ancillary to them, and must be regarded as a part of them? My long public life and my chequered public career enable me to speak with some authority. I was in England in 1909 when Dhingra committed the anarchical crime to which I have already referred, namely, the murder of Sir William Curzon-Wyllie and Dr. Lalkaka. What happened? I was fearfully handicapped; my public work came to a standstill. The Indian students in the English universities were in a serious plight. I did my best to undo the mischief; but a remnant of the atmosphere, then created, still lingers. I would appeal to my countrymen and I would say to them: 'Talk not of revolutions, or of tactics, such as obstruction, which are allied to revolutionary methods. You would then stand upon a dangerous precipice and might be hurried, despite yourselves, into the abysmal depths of a real revolutionary movement, with all the terrible consequences, the bloodshed and the reaction that follow in its train. Pray do not play with fire. When a movement has been set on foot, forces gather round it of which perhaps you had not the faintest conception, and impart to it a volume and a momentum beyond the ideas of its originators, who are now powerless to control it.'

We Hindus abhor revolution and even the semblance of it.

Evolution is our motto, and here we follow the intimations of nature. The infant grows to boyhood, and the boy to manhood. So, too, there is no cataclysm in the moral universe. It follows the orderings of the material world-development stage by stage, generated by forces that have their roots in the bosom of society, and are fostered and stimulated by the beneficent activities of patriotic workers and the generous help and patronage of progressive Governments.

Non-Co-operation may help us to stand on our own legs by making us wholly dependent upon our own resources and activities. But at the same time, it cuts us off from the perennial and ever-sustaining sap afforded by the culture and civilization of the world, and the wide outlook which is a stimulus to progress. We cannot stand alone, isolated and detached from the rest of mankind, but must be in close association with them, giving to them what we have to give, receiving from them what we have to receive, swelling the common fund of human knowledge and experience. We thus broaden and elevate our own culture and civilization by the touch of the world-forces, and in our turn impart to them the spirituality that has been the heritage of our race. We have to make our contribution to humanity; and humanity repays us with compound interest, in the rich treasure of wisdom and inspiration that it places at our disposal.

We must indeed take our stand upon the old foundations. We broaden and liberalize them; and we build thereon. National life flows on in one continuous stream, the past running into the present, the present rolling on, in one majestic sweep, into the invisible and ever-expanding future, broadening at each stage, and scattering its fertilizing and beneficent influences all around. Our moorings must indeed be fixed in the past, in instincts and traditions that have built up our history, and will largely shape and mould the future.

But we cannot remain wedded to the past. We cannot remain where we are. There is no standing still in this world of God's Providence. Move on we must, with eyes reverentially fixed on the past, with a loving concern for the present and with deep solicitude for the future. We must, in this onward journey, assimilate from all sides into our character, our culture, and our civilization, whatever is suited to our genius and is calculated to strengthen and invigorate it, and weave it into the texture of our national life. Thus co-operation, and not non-co-operation, association and not isolation, must be a living and a growing factor in the evolution of our people. Any other policy would be suicidal and fraught with peril to our best interests. That is my message to my countrymen, delivered not in haste or in impatience, but as the mature result of my deliberations, and of my lifelong labours in the service of the motherland.

Appendix A

MR. HUME'S ARTICLE IN *India*, 1893 (*see p. 30*).

'The election of Babu Surendra Nath Banerjea by the Calcutta Corporation, to a seat on the Bengal Legislative Council, completes happily the first act of a drama of real life which at one time threatened to evolve in a painful tragedy.

'Mr. Surendra Nath, the greatest of our Indian orators, was many years ago recognized by his tutors in England, which he visited to compete for the Indian Civil Service, as one of the most talented and at the same time amiable and lovable young men with whom they had ever had to deal. He passed the examination with great credit and in due course returned to India as a member of the Covenanted Civil Service. All for a time went well. Then, certain charges of rendering untrue returns of the state of his files, with a view to concealing a certain laziness which was alleged to be his leading foible, were considered by the local Government to be of sufficient importance to require investigation by a special official Commission. The special Commission, thus appointed, found that certain irregularities were proved against him, and the Government then and there dismissed him from the service.

'Now in the first place, many then in India, ourselves among the number, who had the opportunity of seeing all the papers, while not dissenting as regards most of the facts that the Commission found to be established, differed altogether as to the interpretation to be placed upon them, and held, and still hold, that Babu Surendra Nath was guilty of nothing more than a certain carelessness and laziness, that might well have been passed over, in a quite young officer, with a mild rebuke, and an exhortation to be more zealous in future. But putting this aside, the judges themselves – and one of these repeated this to us only last week – considered that even for the faults that they held to have been established, suspension from promotion for a year would have been an adequate punishment, and no one, not even Suredra Nath himself, was more astonished than were these judges when the terrible sentence of expulsion from the service was pronounced against him by the Government.

'To English readers it is necessary to explain that Mr. Surendra Nath was one of the pioneers of the Indians into the Covenanted Civil Service. Almost throughout the bureaucracy, the admission of Indians within their sacred pale was viewed with the utmost jealousy and disapproval, and this summary expulsion of one of the most distinguished of the invaders was utilized as the basis for paeans glorifying the British officials and their foresight in opposing the introduction of Indian colleagues. Virtually, what all the Anglo-Indians said was this, "Oh yes, clever enough, but just as we told you, a d—d set of rogues, utterly unfit for the Civil Service, the noblest, most upright, and most essentially gentlemanly service in the world.

Here is the crack man of the Indians, and Government has to expel him before he has been three years in the service !"

'How far this widespread feeling had any share in bringing about the monstrous sentence passed upon poor Surendra we cannot say, but certainly it did prevent any fair hearing for his appeals for justice and mercy. He protested and appealed, as did thousands of his countrymen for him, but all in vain.'

And then Mr. Hume proceeds to contrast my treatment with that of a European Civilian who had been guilty of a much graver offence:

'What to those of us who were impartial in the matter seemed to cast a very lurid light on the transaction was this. Not long after the events above referred to, an English Covenanted Civilian was found guilty, by the officers appointed to investigate *his* case, of offences far more grave – involving pecuniary vagaries unparalleled in the modern history of the Service – than any that even his judges thought to be established against Mr. Surendra Nath. Was this officer dismissed the Service ? No, he was compelled to refund a sum of money belonging to Government that had somehow found its way into his private accounts, and he was suspended for a period of twelve or fifteen months, thereby suffering a considerable loss of salary for the time, but almost immediately on the expiration of the period of suspension, he, being a relative of the Lieutenant-Governor of Bengal, was jobbed into the favourite, and one of the highest paid, appointments in the province, an appointment to which, even had there been nothing against him, he would not have been entitled either by standing in the Service or ability.

'The establishment of the British Committèe of the Indian National Congress has rendered the unpunished perpetration of any similarly atrocious job at the present time almost impossible, but it illustrates the very different modes in which Indians and Europeans have been systematically dealt with by the Indian officials ; and the fates of these two officials are thoroughly characteristic examples of the spirit which has for the last quarter of a century pervaded the majority of the bureaucracy.'

Mr. Hume thus concludes his article:

'In the meantime how fared it with Surendra Nath ? Crushed, utterly disgraced, and almost a pauper (for nearly all his means had been expended on his visit to England and his education there) had he committed suicide in despair, who could have marvelled ? But, like the brave man and dear good fellow that he is, he set himself to the nobler task of fighting out the battle to the last, and living down the injustice that thus clouded his early years, and disproving by his life the mistaken estimate that had been formed of his character.

'Few in England can realize the almost hopeless character of the struggle, in India's official-ridden land, of one under the official ban seeking once more to recover a decent position in public life. For years Mr. Surendra Nath fought on like Grant, determined to fight along this line until death or victory crowned his efforts. He founded a school and taught in it; he started a paper and both edited and managed it; he spoke at every popular meeting and established his reputation for those oratorical powers which, *inter alia*, so endear him to his countrymen. But for long he made little or no progress, though he bravely still kept his head above the waters and swam on in dogged earnestness.

'Truly is it said that all comes to him who knows how to wait. Suddenly for Surendra Nath appeared the *Deux ex machina* – to cut the knots of the cords of neglect and disgrace in which he was bound – appeared in the shape of the Calcutta High Court, a bench of which clapped him into prison on a charge of contempt of court, in consequence of certain editorial comments of his on their proceedings. Then the tide turned; backed up by a majority of his fellow-citizens, his school widened into the largest independent college in India; his paper, the *Bengalee*, became gradually acknowledged as one of the very best and most just and moderate papers in the country. Elected to the Calcutta Corporation, his industry, his integrity and uncompromising independence extorted first the admiration and finally won the confidence of even the official Chairman of the Corporation; and now his long years of resolute labour have been fitly crowned by his election by that Corporation as their first representative to the Legislature – a representation to which his magnificent oratory has not a little contributed, though indirectly, to extort from an unwilling and retrograde Government.

'Surely this story is a noble one, instinct with noble lessons; but best of all is the fact to which all of us privileged to call him friend can testify; that never amidst all his labours, trials, and sufferings has he ever varied in his love for, and loyalty to, Great Britain; never has he spoken bitterly or unreasonably even of those who condemned him. He has ever accepted his troubles as the decree of Fate, an evil fate that it behoved him to fight against – a fate he has fought against and defeated.

'Long may his triumph last! long may he live to enjoy the fruit of his great courage and his manly perseverance! it will not be many years, we hope, before he sits upon the Viceregal Council; and as time runs on a younger generation shall hail him in the British Parliament, where we may hope that his magnificent gift of oratory may avail to awaken the House to some sense of India's wrongs; some fixed and honourable resolution to see justice at last fairly meted out to India's people.

Appendix B

A NOTE ON MY COLLEAGUES ON THE WELBY COMMISSION (*see p. 150*).

The names of my colleagues, who were witnesses before the Commission, will pass into the history of their times. Gopal Krishna Gokhale was one of the greatest political leaders of his generation, a true-born statesman in the front rank of Indian public men. A leader of the Moderate party, his premature death was a heavy loss to the country. Mr. G. Subramanya Iyer was one of the makers of modern Madras. He too died early, mourned by his province and by his countrymen in other parts of India. In 1914, I had the melancholy satisfaction of unveiling his portrait, which was subscribed by the people of Madras as a token of their affection and gratitude. Of Sir Dinshaw Wacha, who is happily still amongst us, no one can speak without admiration for his personal worth and public character. His long life has been dedicated to the service of the motherland, and in the evening of his career, he draws to himself in an unstinted measure, the love and esteem of all who know him. He was one of the founders of the Congress, attended its first meeting in Bombay in 1885, and throughout served it with unsurpassed devotion and fidelity. He has since seceded from the Congress, with the rest of the Moderate party, but his services to that body will be cherished by his grateful countrymen, when the heat and the dust of the present controversies shall have been allayed.